Zapata Lives!

Zapata Lives!

Histories and Cultural Politics in Southern Mexico

Lynn Stephen

UNIVERSITY OF CALIFORNIA PRESS
Berkeley · Los Angeles · London

University of California Press
Berkeley and Los Angeles, California

University of California Press, Ltd.
London, England

Library of Congress Cataloging-in-Publication Data

Stephen, Lynn.
  Zapata lives! : histories and cultural politics in
southern Mexico / Lynn Stephen.
     p.   cm.
  Includes bibliographical references and index.
  ISBN 0-520-22237-7 (cloth : alk. paper).—
ISBN 0-520-23052-3 (pbk. : alk. paper)
     1. Chiapas (Mexico)—History—Peasant Upris-
ing, 1994–2.   2. Ejército Zapatista de Liberación
Nacional (Mexico).   3. Social movements—Mex-
ico—History—20th century.   4. Mexico—Social
conditions.   I. Title.

F1256.S84   2002
972'.740836—dc21   00-054497

Manufactured in the United States of America
10   09   08   07   06   05   04   03   02   01
10   9   8   7   6   5   4   3   2   1

This book is dedicated to the memory of Martin Diskin, a pioneer in the anthropology of human rights and in activist research.

Contents

Maps, Illustrations, and Tables

MAPS

ILLUSTRATIONS

TABLES

Acknowledgments

Zapata lives in southern Mexico through local histories that claim the demands of Emiliano Zapata as their own and that, like all histories, interpret the past through the present. These histories were given a particular interpretation in *ejido* communities in Oaxaca and Chiapas during the 1990s. The period during which this book was researched and written, 1993–2001, was an important transitional era in Mexican history. Marked by the beginning of the North American Free Trade Agreement, the Zapatista rebellion, and the fall of the Institutional Revolutionary Party from power after seventy-one years of presidential rule, these years spun out tumultuous currents in Mexican politics, culture, and society. Indigenous Mexicans organized at a national level to claim their rights and autonomy; militarization and monitoring of Mexican civil society increased; social movements in many sectors took to the streets; new billionaires emerged; the ranks of those living on less than U.S. $2 per day increased; political parties splintered and forged new coalitions. Change was certainly in the air.

I have learned a tremendous amount by sharing this period of Mexican history with a wide range of people. The first hint of what this book was to be came in 1989 when I was a postdoctoral visiting research fellow at the Center for U.S.–Mexican Studies at the University of California, San Diego. There, during a discussion with several top-level politicians from the PRI, it was suggested that part of President Salinas de Gortari's program would include ending agrarian reform and revising

Article 27 of the Mexican Constitution. At the time, several of us argued that this would "undo" the Mexican Revolution. Three years later, in preparation for NAFTA, Article 27 was changed, ending the government's obligation to redistribute land to the landless and encouraging privatization of ejido land.

There are many kinds of support to be acknowledged on completing a long-term project. While it is traditional to first acknowledge sources of financial support, I would like to first acknowledge the men and women in Mexico critical to this project. First and foremost are those in the communities in Oaxaca and Chiapas where I was privileged to visit and work from 1993 to 2001. To protect their identities, I have given them all pseudonyms, as requested. In Oaxaca, ejido authorities in Santa María del Tule and in Unión Zapata invited me to discuss my work with the ejido assemblies and, after assembly approval, facilitated my work over many years. The men, women, and children who took time to talk with me again and again in these two ejidos have been wonderful to work with. At the time this book goes to print, it appears that the community of Santa María del Tule may begin its own community history project, using some of my work as a resource for developing a local history and possible museum; I hope this idea comes to fruition.

For several years, the staff of the Procuraduría Agraria in Oaxaca, led by Carlos Moreno Derbez, were very forthcoming with time, information, and, most important, interest in developing a collaborative relationship with myself and several graduate students. María de la Luz Acevedo, María de la Paz Padilla Sória, and María Edith Baños were particularly generous with their time. Carlos Moreno Derbez continued to support my work, in his later role as the Oaxacan state delegate for the Secretary of Agrarian Reform. José Armando Guzmán Alcantara, head of the Registro Agrario Nacional (RAN) in Oaxaca, was always very helpful in providing updated statistics and access to agrarian historical records. Indigenous activists Adelfo Regino Montes and Carlos Béas Tórres took time on several occasions to share their thoughts about movements for indigenous autonomy.

In Oaxaca, Alejandro de Avila provided endless support for this project over the years in more ways than he can know, as have others at the Jardín Etnobotanico. A warm circle of friends, including Teresa Pardo, Paola Sesia, Margarita Dalton, Julia Barco, Paco González, Petra Bautista, Irais Saynes, Cecilio Blas, Silvia Salas Morales, Leo Schibli, and Chepa Aranda, were a source of good times, comfortable conversations, shared family joy, and relaxing hours. My dear friend Guadalupe

Musalem M.—who was to pass away in 1995—offered friendship, food, and "hammock-time" for me and this project. Some of the most important and enthusiastic moments in the project's beginning stages happened in her home, where I often stayed in Oaxaca.

In Chiapas, my visits were facilitated by the men and women of Guadalupe Tepeyac, La Realidad, Ejido Morelia, and Acteal. When I was traveling and working in Zapatista territory, my activity was supported and facilitated by many I could never directly acknowledge. I thank all of them, and all in the EZLN who took the time to talk with me and exchange ideas. Connecting with people in many communities I visited and worked in was facilitated by non-governmental organizations in Chiapas. From 1993 through 1997, personal friendships and exchanges with individuals such as Gerardo González and Abraham Castañeda, who worked with CONPAZ (Coordinación de Organismos No Gubernamentales por la Paz), were critical to my understanding of the ever-changing situation in Chiapas and to my ability to work in particular areas. The nuns at the San Carlos Clinic in Altamirano, and Marta Figueroa, were invaluable in helping me to understand the gendered dynamics of the impact of the Zapatista rebellion, as was the writing of Guiomar Rovira. Staff at the Centro de Derechos Humanos, "Fray Bartolomé de las Casas," were extremely helpful in providing updates, information, publications, and analysis; I particularly thank Marina Patricia Jiménez Ramírez. Gustavo Castro and Onecimo Hidálgo at the Centro de Investigaciones Económicas y Políticas de Acción Comunitaria (CIEPAC) provided, on several occasions, invaluable information and analysis. Ernesto Leresma of Global Exchange in Chiapas provided important organizational help and connections on a recent trip there. I applaud all of these individuals for their ongoing work, activism, and dedication to peace in Chiapas.

While I was visiting Chiapas and attending the peace dialogues, EZLN forums, and other events, particularly from 1994 through 1996, Luis Hernández Navarro was an invaluable friend, and our conversations, not only then but since, have been key in helping me to interpret ongoing events there. Other friends, living in San Cristóbal and working at the Centro de Investigaciones y Estudios Superiores en Antropología Social (CIESAS) at the time—including Rosalva Aída Hernández Castillo, Ron Nigh, Gabriela Várgas Cetina, and Stefan Igor Ayora Díaz—provided important intellectual support, parties, housing, music, and good company. While not a permanent resident of San Cristóbal, June Nash might have been; many of my visits to the city were accompanied by pleasant

lunches, conversations, and exchanges with her, and we shared many forums for presenting our work. George Collier and Jane Collier were also
often in San Cristóbal, and I thank them for sharing insights with me
there and at intellectual forums in the United States. A panel that I co-
organized with George Collier for the American Anthropological Association was particularly helpful in bringing together a range of scholars
and generating comparative conclusions about the impact of the Zapatista rebellion. Jan Rus, another part-time resident of San Cristóbal, provided intellectual support, suggestions, and encouragement for this project at various stages; I particularly thank him for his role in facilitating
in-person and online discussions on issues of research in Chiapas and for
his detailed comments on this book.

In the office of the Procuraduría Agraria in Tuxtla Gutiérrez, Chiapas, Jorge Portillo was extremely helpful on many occasions, freely sharing information and helping to arrange contacts. José Becerra, state delegate for the Secretaría de Reforma Agraria (SRA) in Chiapas, was also
generous with time and information. The staff of the Registro Agrario
Nacional in Tuxtla Gutiérrez were most helpful in locating and copying
agrarian records from several communities in the Lacandon; I thank
them for their help and interest in the project.

Numerous organizations and individuals in the United States were instrumental in helping me to travel and make connections in Chiapas.
Cecilia Rodríguez, who in 1994 worked for what became the National
Commission for Democracy in Mexico, facilitated an invitation to the
National Democratic Convention in Guadalupe Tepeyac in 1994 and
organized one of the first U.S. delegations to Chiapas in which I participated. I took several trips with Pastors for Peace facilitated by Tom Han-
sen and Robin Hayes, and one with Wes Rayberg as part of a delegation
to Acteal for SPAN (Strategic Pastoral Action). My most recent trip to
Chiapas was as a pre-electoral observer with a Global Exchange delegation, for which Ted Lewis and Rebecca Charnas were key organizers.
I thank all these persons for their ongoing solidarity work with Mexico
and for their flexibility in working with an activist researcher.

In Boston, my friends and colleagues in the group Tonantzín: Boston
Committee to Support the Indigenous Peoples of Chiapas were impor-
tant intellectual and activist collaborators while I was writing this book.
They include Anna Utech, Bob Warren, Kevin Batt, Kristen Harper,
Juan González, Rosalba Solís, and David Amdur.

A number of grants I received through the Center for U.S.–Mexican
Studies, as well as my participation in the Ejido Reform Research Proj-

ect and in the Transformation of Rural Mexico Project from 1993 to 1997, were instrumental in providing financial and intellectual support for the research that went into this book. The Ejido Reform Project included more than forty senior-level scholars and more than fifty graduate students from Mexican, U.S., and Canadian universities, who conducted research on the impact of the changes to Article 27 and participated in four conferences. I wish to thank Wayne Cornelius and David Mhyre for their vision in putting this project together and for including me in it. I received two field research grants from the Ejido Reform Project and the Transformation of Rural Mexico Project, which were helpful to my understanding of events.

Through my participation in the Ejido Reform Research Project I came to know an impressive group of scholars. I would like to particularly thank Kirsten Appendini, Helga Baitenmann, Luin Goldring, Neil Harvey, Pilar López Sierra, Julio Moguel, Gerardo Otero, David Runsten, Lois Stanford, Peter Ward, Scott Whiteford, Carol Zabin, and Sergio Zendejas for their feedback and for our intellectual exchanges. I also thank my students Rosaria Pisa and Veronica Wilson, with whom I worked closely during this period.

In the fall of 1994, I was invited to a key conference at the Colegio de Michoacán, organized by Sergio Zendejas and Gail Mummert. Titled "The Dispute for Rural Mexico," this event brought together scholars in a three-day forum that provided pivotal analytical elements for interpreting my increasing corpus of field data. Conversations with John Gledhill, William Roseberry, Antonio García de León, Robert Smith, Alan Knight, Roger Rouse, Gail Mummert, Gavin Smith, Guillermo de la Peña, Daniel Nugent, Sergio Zendejas, and Adriana López Monjardin were especially helpful and marked the beginning of ongoing exchanges and friendships.

In the spring of 1995, I participated in a conference at Columbia University, "The Reform of the Agrarian Reform," coordinated by Laura Randall. I thank her for organizing this interesting gathering, and also acknowledge Armando Bartra, Carlota Botey, Linda Green, and Matt Wexler for stimulating presentations and for our discussions of our work; these helped me to move forward.

A second phase of the Ejido Project, "The Transformation of Rural Mexico Research Project," jointly sponsored by the Center for U.S.–Mexican Studies at the University of California, San Diego, and Centro de Investigaciones y Estudios Superiores en Antropología Social del Occidente (CIESAS), Guadalajara, was coordinated by Richard Snyder from 1995 to 1997. I wish to thank him for feedback on my work, and to acknowledge the useful input from Neil Harvey and Gabriel Torres throughout this second phase of the project.

In 1995, I enjoyed a second stint as a post-doctoral visiting research fellow at the Center for U.S.–Mexican Studies. It was there that I had the first solid block of writing time to work on what would become this book. There, David Myhre, Helga Baitenman, and Jane Hindley were cherished colleagues, critics, and friends. During this period, Kevin Middlebrook was director. He created a friendly, stimulating environment, and took personal care that all the fellows were happy and inspired; I thank him for his concern for me and others. The Center provided an outstanding setting for intellectual exchange, research, and writing.

During the period 1993–1995, my research was also supported by NSF grant SBR-9312042, which permitted me to conduct field research during the summer and fall of 1994 as well as the next summer. Two grants (no. 5746 in 1994 and no. 6168 in 1997) from the Wenner-Gren Foundation for Anthropological Research also permitted me to continue fieldwork in the summers of 1994 and 1995, as well as in 1997 and 1998; the Wenner-Gren Foundation provided support for research in Chiapas as well as in Oaxaca. Kristen Harper, supported in part by the second Wenner-Gren grant, was an invaluable historical research assistant during the summer of 1997, and I deeply appreciate her high-quality archival work in Oaxaca and Chiapas.

A National Endowment for Humanities Fellowship for University Teachers (FA-34700), awarded for March 1999 through December 1999, gave me the luxury of a nine-month chunk of time to complete this book. The anthropology department and the international studies program of the University of Oregon facilitated this writing time and provided additional funds to allow me to finish. Time for making revisions and putting the finishing touches on the book was provided through the Oregon Humanities Center at the University of Oregon during the spring term of 2000.

In the United States, a group of close friends and colleagues have been instrumental in providing feedback during this project. I want to thank Jennie Purnell, Jeffrey Rubin, Jonathan Fox, Neil Harvey, Shannan Mattiace, Jean Jackson, and Martin Diskin for their long-standing support and intellectual friendship during the years I worked on this project, and for their direct and indirect suggestions for its improvement. Martin Diskin passed away in the middle of this project; he had, as always, provided an important vision of the key role that anthropologists can and should play in human rights work.

Matthew Gutmann and Kay Warren reviewed the manuscript for the University of California Press and provided many valuable suggestions to improve the final product. My editor, Naomi Schneider, showed continued enthusiasm and support for the project, shepherding it through the publication process with good humor and style.

In 1998, my family underwent a major change and we moved to Eugene, Oregon, after almost eighteen years in Boston. At the University of Oregon, colleagues in the anthropology department were particularly supportive of my work, and I thank Terry O'Nell, Karen Kelsky, Diane Baxter, Carol Silverman, and Ken George for valuable feedback through our writers' group, where we read and discussed works-in-progress. I also thank Bill Ayres for his support of my research and writing when I was a newly arrived colleague. Graduate students David Lewis, Tami Hill, Marcy Miranda Janes, and Kristina Tiedje have provided intellectual support and delightful conversations that helped move this book forward.

In Boston, an old circle of friends, including Kate Raisz, Lynn Tibbets, Kate Dobroth, and Ellen Lapowsky, provided ongoing friendship and good times. Colleagues and friends at Northeastern University, where I worked until 1998, were also very supportive of me and of this project. They include Christine Gailey, Felix Matos-Rodríguez, Amilcar Baretto, Laura Frader, Debra Kaufman, Janet Randall, Luis Falcón, Neil Larsen, and Daniel Faber.

New friends in Eugene, including Sandy Morgen, Gerry Berk, Karen Giese, Dan and Hannah Goldrich, Cristina Cowger, Scott Miksch, and others, have made me and my family feel welcome and helped us adjust to a new life that included finishing this book.

My family—now spread out across the country—including my mother, Suzanne Brown, my brother, Bruce Stephen, nephews Ben, Jordan, and Daniel, and my father, Jim Stephen, have provided support up-close and long-distance. Alice de Avila, Alejandro de Avila Sr., Marco de Avila, Brian Bennett, Adrian, and Michael have all been sources of love, good vacations, and shared joy. Rebecca Herman, Bill Mack, Sarah, and Hannah have been additional sources of joy and good times. Alejandro de Avila has provided ongoing friendship and support, and has been there at some crucial times during the past seven years.

Ellen Herman and Gabriel Stephen-Herman have seen me through this project day by day. Without their ongoing love, care, encouragement, and daily presence, I surely would never have completed this book. It is the day-to-day things in life that count and nourish us. Ellen and Gabriel have given me that daily nourishment and love, and I can never thank them enough. As a partner, Ellen has provided an enormous amount of support that contributed not only to the book but to the fieldwork, thinking, writing, and daily living behind it. As my oldest son, Gabi gave me love, fun, and his own brand of sympathy.

As I completed the final draft, we added a new member to our family, José Angel Stephen. His wonderful smile and presence have helped me to make it through the final push of manuscript completion and to appreciate the little pleasures and achievements of each day.

Several parts of this work have been published elsewhere. Parts of the concluding section of chapter 3 are drawn from "The Cultural and Political Dynamics of Agrarian Reform in Oaxaca and Chiapas" in *The Future Role of the Ejido in Rural Mexico,* published by the Center for U.S.–Mexican Studies, University of California, San Diego. Most of chapter 11 first appeared as "Pro-Zapatista and Pro-PRI: Resolving the Contradictions of Zaptismo in Rural Oaxaca," *Latin American Research Review* 32, 2: 41–70 (1997). The first section of chapter 11 is drawn from "Interpreting Agrarian Reform in Two Oaxacan Ejidos: Differentiation, History, and Identities" in *The Transformation of Rural Mexico: Reforming the Ejido Sector,* published by the Center for U.S.–Mexican Studies. Several pages of chapter 12 appeared as "Introduction" to a special issue on "Indigenous Rights and Self-Determination" in *Cultural Survival Quarterly* 23, 1 (Spring 1999): 23–26. These pages are reprinted courtesy of *Cultural Survival.* The section in chapter 12 on the Movement for Indigenous Rights and Autonomy draws in part on material first published as "The Zapatista Opening: The Movement for Indigenous Autonomy and State Discourses on Indigenous Rights in Mexico, 1970–1996," *Journal of Latin American Anthropology* 2, 2 (1997): 2–41, and "Redefined Nationalism in Building a Movement for Indigenous Autonomy in Southern Mexico," *Journal of Latin American Anthropology* 3, 1 (1997): 72–101.

Acronyms and Abbreviations

ACIEZ	Alianza Campesina Independiente "Emiliano Zapata"/Independent Peasant Alliance "Emiliano Zapata"
ANCIEZ	Alianza Nacional Campesina Independiente "Emiliano Zapata"/Independent National Peasant Alliance "Emiliano Zapata"
ARIC	Asociación Rural de Interés Colectivo/Rural Collective Interest Association
ARIC–UU	ARIC–Unión de Uniones (two regional organizations combined)
CCM	Confederación Campesina Mexicana/Mexican Peasant Confederation
CCRI	Comité Clandestino Revolucionario Indígena/Clandestine Revolutionary Indigenous Committee
CCRI–CG	Comité Clandestino Revolucionario Indígena–Comandancia General/Clandestine Revolutionary Indigenous Committee–General Command (governing body of the EZLN)

CEOIC   Consejo Estatal de Organizaciones Indígenas y Cam-
             pesinas / State Council of Indigenous and Peasant
             Organizations

CIOAC   Central Independiente de Obreros Agrícolas y Cam-
             pesinos / Independent Federation of Agricultural
             Workers and Peasants

CNC   Confederación Nacional Campesina / National
             Peasants' Confederation

CNI   Congreso Nacional Indígena / National Indigenous
             Congress

CNOC   Coordinadora Nacional de Organizaciones Cafeta-
             leras / National Coordinating Committee for Coffee
             Producers' Organizations

CNPA   Coordinadora Nacional "Plan de Ayala" / National
             Coordinator "Ayala Plan"

CNPI   Consejo Nacional de Pueblos Indios / National
             Council of Indian Peoples

COC/COCO   Confederación Oaxaqueño de Campesinos / Oaxa-
             can Peasants' Confederation

COCEI   Coalición de Obreros, Campesinos y Estudiantes del
             Istmo / Coalition of Workers, Peasants, and Students
             of the Isthmus

COCOPA   Comisión de Concordia y Pacificación / National
             Commission of Concord and Pacification

CONAI   Comisión Nacional de Intermediación / National
             Intermediation Commission

CRIACH   Consejo de Representantes Indígenas de Los Altos
             de Chiapas / Council of Indigenous Representatives
             From the Highlands of Chiapas

DAAC   Departamento de Asuntos Agrarios y Colonización /
             Department of Agrarian Issues and Settlement

EIM   Ejército Insurgente Mexicano / Mexican Insurgent
             Army

EZLN	Ejército Zapatista de Liberación Nacional / Zapatista Army of National Liberation
FIOB	Frente Indígena Oaxaqueño Binacional / Oaxacan Binational Indigenous Front
FLN	Fuerzas de Liberación Nacional / Forces of National Liberation
FNDP	Frente Nacional Democrático Popular / National Democratic Popular Front
FOSCH	Frente de Organizaciones Sociales de Chiapas / Front of Social Organizations of Chiapas
INEGI	Instituto Nacional de Estadística, Geografía e Informática / National Institute of Statistics, Geography, and Informatics
INI	Instituto Nacional Indigenista / National Indigenous Institute
INMECAFÉ	Instituto Mexicano de Café / Mexican Coffee Institute
LP	Linea Proletaria / Proletarian Line
NAFTA	North American Free Trade Agreement
OCEZ	Organización Campesina Emiliano Zapata / Emiliano Zapata Peasant Organization
PA	Procuraduría Agraria / Office of the Agrarian Attorney General
PAN	Partido Acción Nacional / National Action Party
PEMEX	Petróleos Mexicanos / Mexican Petroleum Corporation
PNR	Partido Nacional Revolucionario / National Revolutionary Party
PRD	Partido de la Revolución Democrática / Party of the Democratic Revolution
PRI	Partido Revolucionario Institucional / Institutional Revolutionary Party

PROCAMPO	Programa de Apoyo Directo al Campo / Direct Rural Support Program
PROCEDE	Programa de Certificación de Derechos Ejidales y Titulación de Solares Urbanos / Program for the Certification of Ejido Land Rights and the Titling of Urban House Plots
PRODH	Centro de Derechos Humanos Miguel Augustín Pro Júarez, A.C. / Miguel Augustín Pro Júarez Human Rights Center
PROGRESA	Programa de Educación, Salud y Alimentación / Program for Education, Health, and Nutrition
PSUM	Partido Socialista Unificado de México / Unified Socialist Party of Mexico
RAN	Registro Agrario Nacional / National Agrarian Registry
SARH	Secretaría de Agricultura y Recursos Hidráulicos / Ministry of Agriculture and Water Resources
SEP	Secretaría de Educación Pública / Ministry of Public Education
SER	Servicios del Pueblo Mixe / Services of the Mixe People
SRA	Secretaría de la Reforma Agraria / Ministry of Agrarian Reform
UCIZONI	Unión de Comunidades Indígenas de la Zona Norte del Istmo / Union of Indigenous Communities of the Northern Zone of the Isthmus
UE de la Selva	Unión de Ejidos de la Selva / Ejido Union of the Jungle
UELC	Unión de Ejidos "Lucha Campesina" / Ejido Union "Peasant Struggle"
UEQTL	Unión de Ejidos "Quiptic ta Lecubtesel" / Ejido Union "United in Our Strength"
UETL	Unión de Ejidos "Tierra y Libertad" / Ejido Union "Land and Liberty"

UNAM	Universidad Nacional Autónoma de México / National Autonomous University of Mexico
UNCAFESUR	Unión de Productores de Café de la Frontera Sur / Union of Coffee Producers of the Southern Border
UNORCA	Unión Nacional de Organizaciones Regionales Campesinas Autónomas / National Network of Autonomous Regional Peasant Organizations
UP	Unión del Pueblo / The People's Union
UU	Unión de Uniones y Grupos Campesinos Solidarios de Chiapas / Ejido of Unions and Solidarity Peasant Organizations of Chiapas

Preface

As the year 1993 drew to a close, high-ranking members of Mexico's government prepared to celebrate the initiation of the North American Free Trade Agreement (NAFTA) on 1 January 1994. Approval of this agreement by the U.S. Congress in fall 1993 closed years of preparation and bargaining between the two countries. For those in the upper echelons of Mexico's government, those in the elite tiers of the financial service and banking center, and the twenty-four new billionaires who had prospered during the term of Mexican President Carlos Salinas de Gortari, NAFTA appeared to offer a new beginning, new hope, and a new national image for Mexico as a player in the global economy. The buzzwords of NAFTA—privatization, investment, individual opportunity, economic growth, international markets, global capital, and increased production—could be the basis for a new nationalism that would unify all Mexicans as they assumed their rightful place at the table with "first world" countries. For them, NAFTA would help Mexico to be recognized as a modern nation.

Far away from Mexico City, in the last days of 1993, another group was also preparing for 1 January. Throughout the highlands and in the Lacandon jungle of eastern Chiapas, thousands of indigenous soldiers, militia members, and community base members of the Zapatista Army of National Liberation (EZLN) were assembling and preparing to carry out coordinated attacks on five municipal seats in the state of Chiapas (see map 3). These people were not getting ready to celebrate NAFTA.

They were using the legacy of Emiliano Zapata and the Mexican Revolution to stake a claim against NAFTA and the kind of Mexico associated with the political and economic elite supporting NAFTA. They were getting ready to let the world know that there was another Mexico—an impoverished rural and indigenous Mexico where most people had nothing. "We have nothing, absolutely nothing, not even a decent roof over our heads, no land, no work, no healthcare, no food, or education; without the right to freely and democratically elect our authorities, without independence from foreigners, without peace or justice for ourselves and our children. But TODAY WE SAY, ENOUGH! We are the heirs of those who truly forged our nationality" (Womack 1999, 248, translating Ejército Zapatista de Liberación Nacional 1994, 33).

These words, from the "First Declaration of the Lacandon Jungle," did not take Mexicans by surprise. Many knew that there was extreme economic stratification in their country—that going from the coffee cafes of Coyoacán to the thatch-roofed huts of indigenous farmers in Chiapas was akin to traveling to a separate world. What did surprise many, however, was that organized indigenous peoples were willing to go to war and die to ensure that the words from this declaration were heard and understood in Mexico and around the world. In representing themselves as "the heirs who truly forged our nationality," these peoples staked a loud and clear claim to a different vision of the Mexican nation than that imagined by the initiators of NAFTA. In the days following the Zapatista uprising, the imagery of the Zapatistas' nation views was disseminated throughout Mexico. The Zapatistas had clearly demonstrated their willingness to project their visions. And they had passed the crucial test of nationalists—they were willing to die for their imaginings.

While the words and ideas of indigenous Zapotecs from places like Santa María del Tule in Oaxaca may not be as dramatic or as well publicized as the words of the EZLN, like the EZLN, such persons have a distinct view of the nation and of their rightful place in it (see maps 1 and 2). In 1993, people from El Tule openly questioned the intentions of NAFTA and its accompanying agrarian restructuring. They are members of an *ejido*, a communal form of land tenure, in which members have use rights, usually in the form of an individual plot of land.

Ejidos were created after the Mexican Revolution to satisfy the demands of landless peasants who had seen their communal village lands eaten up by large agricultural estates and/or who served as laborers on those estates. The term *ejido* refers to a specific area of land as well. For many communities, their ejido land refers to territory, actual land tied

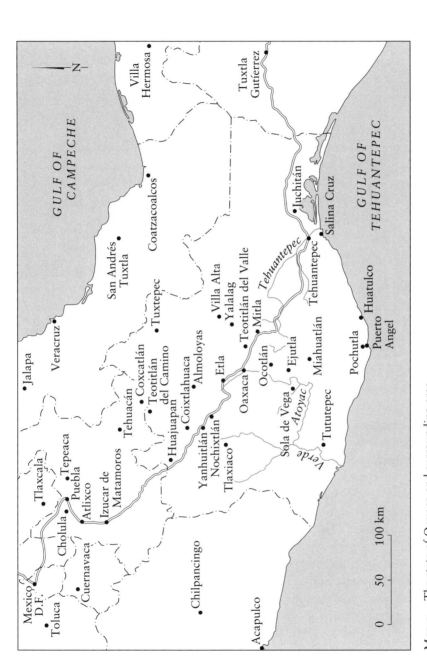

Map 1. The state of Oaxaca and surrounding area

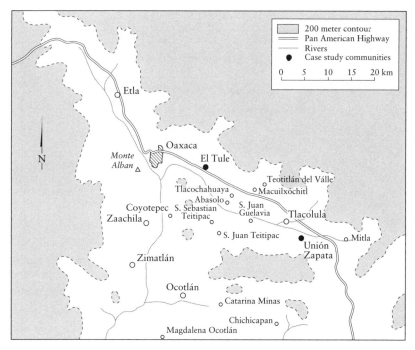

Map 2.   Santa María del Tule and Unión Zapata.

to the community. Specific areas of land granted as ejidos often, but not always, have long-standing historical meaning—particularly if they were occupied precolonially and then usurped during the colonial period. In Oaxaca, this is the case with much ejido land. In the Lacandon jungle of eastern Chiapas, where the Zapatista rebellion took place, landless communities were eventually granted pieces of land in new areas to which they migrated; they have thus no long historical tie to the particular land that is their ejido today.

The formation of ejidos since the Mexican Revolution has involved the transference of over 70 million hectares from large estates to slightly more than three million peasant beneficiaries. The term *ejidatarios* refers to those people who have land rights in the ejido—the right to work ejido lands. This right is either granted through petitioning the government as a part of a group of people in order to receive access to land or through the inheritance of such rights.

The ejido of Santa María del Tule had been visited in 1993 by officials from the Agrarian Attorney's Office, who were encouraging them to join

Map 3.   Area of the Zapatista rebellion and the location of Chiapas in Mexico

a new program to measure, map, and provide certificates convertible to private titles for their ejido plots. The following edited transcript is from a 1993 ejido assembly attended by both men and women where the merits of NAFTA and the land-measuring and certification program were discussed in conjunction with a proposal from the Mexican Petroleum Corporation (PEMEX) to annex a perimeter of 500 meters of ejido land on all sides of their plant to prevent ground-leaking of oil onto ejido plots. PEMEX has a major depository located on former ejido lands of El Tule.

EJIDO COMMISSIONER: PEMEX is saying that we have to leave 500 meters of room as a buffer zone between the depository and the ejido. They say it is to prevent polluted ejido plots and crops. . . . We don't have to agree with it, either. We just have to discuss it and decide whether

	or not we are going to have this kind of agreement with PEMEX. What do you think about this?
EJIDATARIO:	They probably just want to expropriate our land for some business venture. That is why they are talking about pollution. . . .
ANOTHER EJIDATARIO:	We have to take care of our ejido land because the strategy of President Salinas is clear. We have to be ready to defend our land. The free trade agreement and the certification program mean that a lot of private contractors are going to be interested in our land because it is close to Oaxaca and in an urbanized area.
EJIDO COMMISSIONER:	That's right. What the compañero says is right. When you get your titles, please don't sell the land. We need to keep the ejido together.

While PEMEX's proposal was advanced on ecological grounds, it was interpreted by ejidatarios as a threat to expropriate their ejido land and undermine local control of the future of the ejido. At that meeting, ejidatarios rejected the PEMEX proposal and did not cede them the land they requested at the depository's perimeter. They also decided to continue their participation in the government's new land certification program, but with caution.

Before the assembly, José Martínez (quoted at length in chapter 1), told me: "The United States has a lot of people and it needs more land. They are going to come here from the United States and buy our land. And who isn't going to sell to them? If they pay a high enough price, then people will sell." In 1999, his words of caution were still discussed in his ejido, where more than fifteen ejidatarios have sold their land, some to outsiders, and people are worried about whether the remaining ejidatarios will keep their land so that the ejido can continue to function.

José's view of himself and his community was deeply tied to the local struggle that El Tule waged against both neighboring Zapotecs and hacendados to acquire land, to the roles of Emiliano Zapata and Lázaro Cárdenas (Mexico's president from 1934 to 1940) in facilitating that claim, and to the positive role of government agrarian officials in helping the community to receive all of their land.

José was familiar with the language of struggle and poverty in 1993, as he discussed the possible outcome of NAFTA. Like those who committed to the EZLN, José saw the Mexican nation from the historical standpoint of a local struggle for land, the rights of rural Mexicans to their land and resources, and the legitimation of those rights through the

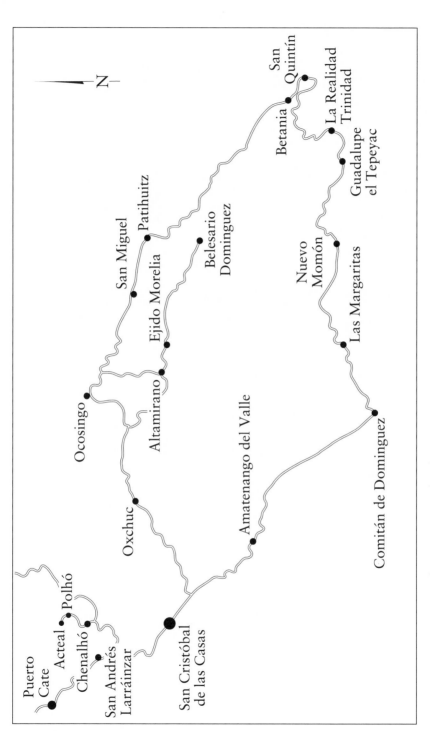

Map 4.   Towns in eastern Chiapas mentioned in the text.

Figure 1.   Image of Emiliano Zapata from a protest in Tuxtla
Guttiérez, Chiapas in 1996. Photo by Lynn Stephen.

legacy of Emiliano Zapata. While his personal views and experiences
with officials representing the government were more positive than those
of most ejidatarios in Zapatista ejidos like Guadalupe Tepeyac in Chiapas, his vision of the Mexican nation in the 1990s was clearly different
from that projected by the architects of NAFTA. In the case of José and
other ejidatarios from El Tule and Unión Zapata, as well as of those
from Guadalupe Tepeyac and La Realidad who joined the EZLN, their
local nation views incorporated past symbolism of the Mexican Revo-

lution long claimed by the government, but by reclaiming these symbols (Zapata and the right to ejido land) as their own, the ejidatarios and EZLN militants changed them and converted them into tools for maintaining an autonomous view of the nation, a view that in the 1990s was clearly at odds with the new nationalism—or, more accurately, the antinationalist globalism—being built around NAFTA (see maps 2 and 4). The strategy of NAFTA did not seek to distinguish Mexico from other nations, but to make it a primary part of the global economy.

WHOSE ZAPATA? WHOSE REVOLUTION?

Known for his role in the Mexican Revolution as the chief of a guerrilla army of the South, Emiliano Zapata fought alongside the peasants of Morelos to gain control over the land they worked. The original Zapatistas also fashioned a land redistribution plan, known as the Plan de Ayala, which was more an ideological think-piece than an actual policy, that became partially incorporated into the Mexican Constitution of 1917. Zapata was assassinated by government emissaries in 1919, but his name has continued to inspire peasant militancy in Mexico and to serve as a symbol for the institutionalization and nationalization of the Mexican Revolution, primarily under the tutelage of the Institutional Revolutionary Party, or PRI, which remained in power in Mexico for seventy-one years until its defeat in the July 2000 presidential elections by the National Action Party (PAN) candidate, Vicente Fox Quesada.

The figure of Emiliano Zapata is a shared icon throughout Mexico. In the chapters that follow, we shall see Zapata deployed by ejidatarios in Oaxaca as they discuss community histories. We shall also see indigenous Tojolabal, Tzeltal, Ch'ol, and Tzotzil men and women rallying around Zapata as they oppose the government, state and government military forces, and paramilitary groups in their demands for work, land, housing, food, health care, education, independence, freedom, democracy, justice, and peace. They have done this as members and sympathizers of the contemporary Zapatista Army of National Liberation (EZLN) in Chiapas. We shall see government employees of the Agrarian Attorney General's Office under the Salinas de Gortari and Ernesto Zedillo administrations using Zapata and the Mexican Revolution as a framework for demonstrating their continued commitment to Mexico's rural population, while simultaneously dismantling land reform and some of the services that supported the rural population.

How did Emiliano Zapata and the Mexican Revolution come to

mean so many different things to so many different people? What are the
sources of inspiration for these different positions on Zapata and the Revolution? Are there common threads among the ejidatarios of Oaxaca,
the much newer ejidatarios of the Lacandon jungle, leaders of indigenous movements, urban and rural intellectuals who mentored peasant
and indigenous movements, and government agrarian officials? What
paths have the images of Emiliano Zapata and the Mexican Revolution
traveled as they made their way into the minds of many different Mexican people? Through examining the trajectory of the figure of Emiliano
Zapata and the popularization of the Mexican revolution in rural education, in the creation of agrarian communities, or ejidos, in the formation of the National Peasants' Confederation (CNC) as part of the consolidation of the National Revolutionary Party (PNR, precursor to the
PRI), in the formation of independent peasant organizations, and in interactions between government agrarian officials and rural communities,
I hope to show the paths of imagination, storytelling, memory, and codi-
fication that allow such different takes on Zapata and the Mexican Revolution to coexist in contemporary Mexico. Multiple deployments of
Zapata and the Mexican Revolution alert us to the existence of the many
Mexicos manifest in the twenty-first century as major shifts take place at
the top of the formal political system, accompanied both by high levels
of militarization in some parts of Mexico and by a wide range of grassroots movements that operate outside of the formal political system yet
strongly influence politics.

NATION VIEWS AND THE SHAPING OF THE NATION

The story told here demonstrates the ways that different views of a nation—what have been called multiple "nation views,"—are informed
by local identities and histories, and in turn actually redefine and constitute the nation (Duara 1996, 161). Prasenjit Duara suggests this perspective both in his analysis of the relationship between nationalism and
history in China (Duara 1995) and more broadly: "In the place of a
monologic voice of the Nation, we find a polyphony of voices, overlapping and criss-crossing; contradictory and ambiguous, opposing, affirming, and negotiating their views of the nation" (Duara 1996, 162). By
showing how it was possible for two rural communities in Oaxaca in the
mid 1990s to come to a pro-government and pro-Zapatista (pro-EZLN)
stance through relatively positive historical relations with the government, and comparing this to the antigovernment and pro-Zapatista

stance of two ejidos in Chiapas that have had decidedly negative relations with the government, we can begin to unravel the complexities of
the differential resonance of nationalism. By 2000, the political stance
of one of the communities in Oaxaca had shifted to rejecting the PRI
in presidential elections. While all four communities may share specific
symbolic images and metaphors with the government—specifically, Emiliano Zapata and the Mexican Revolution—the contextual meaning of
these symbols varies with each place and forms a key part of reactions
to contemporary state policy such as the end of agrarian reform, efforts
to promote privatization of communally held land, and NAFTA. If nationalism is constructed in regionally and locally distinct manners from
below, then ideas about how one belongs to the nation are also variably
understood.

In the case of the contested meanings of the Mexican nation highlighted here, the primary focus is on specific cultural symbols mobilized
in the name of nationalism: particular heroes such as Emiliano Zapata
and the *agrarista,* or agrarian activist, "the Mexican Revolution," the
flag, and specific articles of the Constitution. The discursive production
of these symbols is examined in a variety of contexts: in texts (government publications, newspapers, letters, pamphlets, school texts, communiqués), in speech (presidential and other speeches, individual and
group conversation, public statements), and in public performances (celebration of patriotic holidays, the granting of land certificates, meetings
and assemblies, rituals).

Since different nation views, and thus the shaping and reshaping of
the nation itself, are largely produced through discursive views, such
views are also subject to change through time. The claims to the Mexican Revolution staked by the government of Lázaro Cárdenas and subsequent PRI governments have built on each other's legacy, but have
ultimately shifted the meaning of the Revolution. The most extreme
change is probably President Salinas de Gortari's use of Emiliano Zapata
to market the end of agrarian reform—a message distinctly different
from that of President Cárdenas, who used the same symbol to actively
promote land redistribution, the formation of ejidos, and the building of
a government-sponsored national peasant organization.

Just as elite constructions of the nation change through time, so do
local positionings of the nation and national symbols in local history.
The meaning of Emiliano Zapata in the 1930s in the ejido of El Tule in
Oaxaca was different from that in the mid 1990s and 2000, when I did
my fieldwork and talked with people about the meaning of Zapata and

contemporary Zapatismo. These changes through time, as well as the influence of local experience and history captured in differential nation views, are the basis for competing dissenting narratives of the nation that may themselves become dominant discourses. The fashioning of local Zapatismo through the process (described in chapter 5) of building the Zapatista Army of National Liberation in distinct regions of Chiapas in the 1980s, and then the projection of that Zapatismo to the Mexican nation and to other parts of the world (described in chapter 6), is such an example.

UNSTABLE HEGEMONIES AND SELECTIVE TRADITIONS

The fashioning of multiple nation views, and the process by which an oppositional view of the nation becomes a part of mainstream national discourse, can also be understood through an examination of the concepts of unstable hegemony and the invention of tradition. The multiple discourses concerning land, government, reform, and Zapata in Mexico discussed in the chapters that follow can be seen as competing components in an unstable hegemony. Raymond Williams reminds us that hegemony is "a lived system of meanings and values—constitutive and constituting—which as they are experienced as practices appear as reciprocally confirming" (Williams 1994, 596). If we accept the notion that the government is granted a certain degree of power in establishing dominant discourses that influence, and are in turn shaped by, civil society, then we can easily agree that the PRI, as a government political party in power for seventy-one years had been able to make strong efforts from the 1930s to the present to establish official versions of the Mexican Revolution (as seen in the chapters that follow). And to do so, it put major figures of the Revolution, such as Zapata, at its disposition at various times.

Hegemony is not absolute, however, and as a lived process, it is profoundly changed by competing discourses that emerge in response (Williams 1994, 598). Thus attempts made at establishing dominant meanings are always subject to competing interpretations, including previous hegemonies, which may counteract the current ones. These competing interpretations can, in turn, serve as the basis for periodically contesting the state and its various actors, who are also often divided and in disagreement. The reality of hegemony is that "while by definition it is always dominant, it is never either total or exclusive. At any time, forms of alternative or directly oppositional politics and culture exist as significant elements in the society" (Williams 1994, 599).

All of the discourses examined here (government, Unión Zapata and El Tule, and contemporary Zapatismo, both in general and in two specific communities in Chiapas) on Zapata and the Mexican Revolution make use of what Williams calls selective tradition, "an intentionally selective version of a shaping past and pre-shaped present, which is then powerfully operative in the process of social and cultural definition and identification" (1994, 601). Each discourse seeks to capture the past and to connect it to a specific version of the present. These discourses, which mobilize national symbols and integrate them with local history, use a strategy of selective tradition to generate what Florencia Mallon has called community hegemonies. Mallon has outlined how a particular group of local intellectuals—political officials, teachers, elders, healers— can provide mediation with the larger world and supervise "communal hegemonic processes, organizing and molding the different levels of the communal dialogue and conflict into a credible consensus" (Mallon 1995, 12). In the four communities analyzed here, local intellectuals include both elderly community members, who act as local historians, and younger activists, who have interacted with people ranging from priests to leftist urban students, Maoist organizers, state officials, and members of armed movements.

Les Field has also written about the conditions under which local intellectuals have "defended, defined, avoided, and transformed local social and cultural identities" (Field 1999a, 9). Like myself in exploring the case of Mexico here, Field is concerned with how local intellectuals respond to and can help transform dominant ideas about national identity.[1] The revolution that Field analyzes did not produce local intellectuals who operated in line with dominant ideas about how revolutionary classes are formed and operate. Nevertheless, the presence of Sandinista and independent discourses about class consciousness and gender were part of the material that local artisans/intellectuals worked with in attempting to fashion an autonomous place for themselves in a redefined Nicaraguan nation. In Mexico, state-claimed symbols and discourses are also redefined by local intellectuals in communities and in movements. Some of these local intellectuals are currently participating in a national indigenous movement that is challenging the Mexican state to support a multi-ethnic nation recognizing indigenous self-determination. In the stories told here, local intellectuals are key in the process of creating lo-

cal hegemonies (such as the new Zapatismo in Chiapas) and in projecting these back to the center.

GEOGRAPHIES OF IDENTITIES

In their analysis from seven different sites of what they call the "decentered nation" of Ecuador, Sarah Radcliffe and Sallie Westwood develop
the concept of "geographies of identities" to explain how individuals
and communities develop senses of belonging and subjectivities which
"are constituted in (and which in turn act to constitute) different spaces
and social sites" (Radcliffe and Westwood 1996, 27). While stating that
geographies of identity are embodied at a personal level deriving from individual biography, their primary focus is on *shared* geographies of identities, what they call "the local codes of reception" grounding collective
identities. While geographies of identity are "lived geographies" in the
sense of daily life interactions and material reality tied to one or more
physical sites of existence, they are also spaces of representation and
imagination. In the construction of the different nation views developed
(in the chapters that follow) through examining the perspectives of ejidatarios from Oaxaca and Chiapas, the geography of identity is linked
both to physical place and to the representational space that place comes
to occupy through local histories.

Local histories are the representational spaces that link local identities to the larger nation. This process involves the deliberate reclaiming of
nation-building symbols generated by the state, and their incorporation
into local histories. In the two ejidos explored in Oaxaca, this reclama-
tion happens through incorporating the personal visits of Lázaro Cárdenas into local histories, and through interpreting personal connections
to Cárdenas as direct links to Emiliano Zapata. (Cárdenas is portrayed
as an agent of Zapata carrying through his ideas on land reform.) Direct
links to Zapata are also claimed through the fact that the struggle of all
ejidos to obtain their land is a direct legacy of the historical struggle of
Zapata for all landless men and women.

In eastern Chiapas, the claim to Zapata follows a different route.
There, the creation by Subcommandante Marcos and perhaps others of
a hybrid symbol, Votán Zapata, joined what was said to be indigenous
cosmology with the cult figure of Zapata as imported by various strains
of the Mexican left working to build regional peasant organizations as
well as an armed movement. Both the invented Votán Zapata and the
figure of Zapata have become key icons in Zapatista communiqués. The

local Zapatismo of the Lacandon jungle is therefore a hybrid, a mixture of local and national elements, of ideas brought by a range of people and cooked in the particular stew of eastern Chiapas at a particular time. By 1994, the figure of Zapata had become a significant part of the local histories of Zapatista communities such as those of Guadalupe Tepeyac and La Realidad through his ongoing integration into local art, music, and public discourse. As in Oaxaca, the representational space linking local geographical identities to the nation was local history.

Ana Alonso writes about the importance of the *local* in describing the way that Namiquipans in Chihuahua construct their past and use the product of memory to bring together past, present, and future. "The Namiquipans' construction of the past and vision of frontier society is rooted in concrete historical experience. At the same time, it is a fiction, an idealization, a symbolic elaboration of lived history" (Alonso 1995, 235). Like the ejidatarios in Oaxaca and Chiapas, Namiquipans mobilize concrete, local lived experience in the construction of history and memory. The way that lived experience becomes infused with meaning through time is a process which, as Alonso notes, involves considerable slippage between "myth" and " history" (ibid., 234). What remains important and distinctive is the way that the local remains key in the construction of representational space constructing the nation from below.

For Alonso, the way that Namiquipans reconstructed the past and used it in the present is also gendered. The local community is represented through the idea of the *patria chica,* or *motherland,* according to Alonso, which is ideally sovereign and definitely female. This female gendering of local historical and geographic space is contrasted with the male gendering of the state as father. The state is a good father when it is beneficent, open, and respectful of the "sovereignty of the patria chica and the honor of her 'sons'" (Alonso 1995, 231); the state is a bad father when it encroaches on local sovereignty. While I did not find such a clearly dichotomous view of a good and a bad state in my work with ejidatarios in Oaxaca and Chiapas, the notion of the sovereignty of the local patria chica certainly rings true. Ejidatarios in Santa María del Tule and Unión Zapata ultimately found a contradictory state (good and bad father), while those ejidatarios in Guadalupe Tepeyac and La Realidad who joined the EZLN ultimately came to identify the state with the bad, or "el mal gobierno" (the bad government). In constructions of the nation in Unión Zapata and Santa Maria del Tule in Oaxaca, and in Guadalupe Tepeyac and La Realidad in Chiapas, local sovereignty was extremely important. But the view of the larger nation constructed from a position of local sovereignty is also tied to land and physical geography.

There are physical and material aspects to the geographies of identity in the case-study communities that are important to emphasize (see maps 1, 2, 3, and 4). The very different nation views held by rural men and women in the four communities examined in Oaxaca and Chiapas are concretely tied to regional and historical differences in long-term relationships among communities, individuals in those communities, and agents of the state. This reality is consistent with the findings of others who have conducted regional histories of Mexico and found tremendous variation in the ability of the postrevolutionary Mexican state to incorporate disparate regions of the country into a centralized model of government in which the official party controls all (Nugent 1993; Alonso 1995; Rubin 1997; Purnell 1999).

In the two communities profiled in the Central Valleys of Oaxaca, proximity to the state capital translated into a relatively high level of contact between state officials and rural community members. Even in the 1930s, it was possible to go to Oaxaca in one day and return late that night from Santa María del Tule and—although with a longer journey—from Unión Zapata. In the ejidos of Guadalupe Tepeyac and La Realidad, founded in the Lacandon jungle in eastern Chiapas in the 1950s, it was a very long way to the capital of the state. There were no roads, no services, and little contact for quite some time. The locational differences of these communities influenced their political relations. And in each, the particular local, historical experiences that people accumulated in relation to the government became part of the representational and physical geographies from which they viewed the nation; their sense of literal and representational place informed their nation views. These views, and the ways that they have challenged the vision of Mexico projected by the new order of the North American Free Trade Agreement, are at the heart of this book.

FLEXIBLE CITIZENSHIP WITHIN THE NATION

One final task of this book is to put the views of ejidatarios from the four communities in Oaxaca and Chiapas into the wider context of contemporary Mexico, particularly in relation to what many perceive as a fundamental change wrought when the 2000 elections toppled the PRI from power. While change at the top of the formal political system is important, there are many arenas of action outside that system that are key to understanding rural and indigenous Mexico's future. The book closes by looking, in the context of electoral change and of ongoing militarization and surveillance of indigenous parts of southern Mexico, at one of Mexico's strongest grassroots movements, which offers a vision for refashioning Mexico into a multi-ethnic nation. This movement for indigenous rights and autonomy has been strengthened by the political opening of the EZLN, as well as by indigenous organizing that has been going on at local and regional levels for decades. Exploring this movement allows us to take some specific historical, political, and cultural insights from the four case-study communities and look at how they may be mobilized from below to change the notion of what it means to be an indigenous citizen of Mexico.

Recent anthropology of transnational capital and populations can be turned on its head to suggest some useful ways to think about this concept. In her analysis of transnational Chinese businessmen, Aiwa Ong has coined the term "flexible citizenship" to refer to "the cultural logics of capitalist accumulation, travel, and displacement that induce subjects to respond fluidly and opportunistically to the changing political-economic conditions" (Ong 1999, 6). While she uses this concept primarily to explain how investors favor flexibility and mobility, and reposition themselves in relation to markets and governments, she also suggests the continued importance of the state in setting parameters for how people relate to sovereignty, and for governability. The state cannot be left out of theorizing about citizenship. What she suggests about her physically transnational subjects is that they develop multiple allegiances and cross through different zones of sovereignty that subject them to different regimes of rights and obligations (ibid., 7). This way of conceptualizing citizenship can also be useful in considering relations among individuals, communities, regions, and nations. The movement for indigenous autonomy provides an alternative vision of who citizens are, what kinds of rights they have, and how individuals, communities, and regions should relate to the nation and be integrated into the political, social, and economic concentration of power administered by the state. As such, it is an appropriate subject to consider as some source of hope for a more equitable and inclusive Mexico.

THE ORGANIZATION OF THIS BOOK

Part 1 of this book begins by offering readers political and historical context for understanding historical and current Zapatismo. Chapter 1 introduces the reader to relevant background information and locates the author in relation to the international political economy. The chapter further discusses the moral and ethical responsibilities anthropologists have and makes an argument for a flexible understanding of anthropology that can incorporate the functions of witness and observer, particularly in relation to human rights work and the human experience of social suffering. The chapter also discusses the longer anthropological tradition of ethnography carried out during times of conflict and violence, suggests responsible ways of conducting such research, and how to follow the lead of indigenous organizations in Latin America doing work on violence and human rights.

Chapter 2 begins by outlining the problem of creating a coherent national identity beginning with the Mexican Revolution and focuses on how the Mexican state attempted to consolidate national identity and institutions in the 1930s and again in the 1990s, particularly in relation to education and agrarian reform. The chapter looks closely at the ways in which the educational system, particularly beginning in the 1930s, has been used as a way to disseminate the state's claim to Emiliano Zapata and the Mexican Revolution as a tool for forging nationalist ideology. The role of the Secretary of Agrarian Reform, the National Peasant Confederation, and other government agencies that interact with the rural population is also discussed. The chapter ends by discussing how the figure of Emiliano Zapata and the Mexican Revolution were deployed by the PRI governments of Carlos Salinas de Gortari (1988–94) and Ernesto Zedillo (1994–2000) in the nationalistic marketing of a recent policy in the 1990s linked to NAFTA that ended the state's obligation to redistribute land, attempted to measure and title all existing landholdings, and encourage privatization. This chapter sets the scene for the two comparative parts of the book, which focus first on eastern Chiapas and then on central Oaxaca.

Chapter 3 provides a historical orientation and explanation of the ethnic and racial categories that appear in the case-study chapters in the parts of the book that follow on Chiapas and Oaxaca. Indians, Mestizos, Ladinos, *mestizaje, indigenismo,* self-defined ethnicity, and indigenous autonomy are among the subjects discussed

Part 2 moves to the state of Chiapas and develops a historical discussion of land and indigenous struggle in eastern Chiapas, focusing on the ejidos of Guadalupe Tepeyac and La Realidad, which became centers of contemporary Zapatismo. Chapter 4 looks historically at the loss of land indigenous peoples suffered, the systems of indebted servitude that emerged in many communities in eastern Chiapas, and at a previous indigenous rebellion as a way of understanding how land struggles, religious currents, independent peasant organizations, and a historical narrative of "the times of slavery" were important factors in how Zapatismo came together in some communities in the Lacandon jungle. The Tojolabal population is the focal point of the discussion, with a comparative discussion of some highland Tzotzil events and examples.

Chapter 5 uses the community of Guadalupe Tepeyac as a lens for understanding the process by which some indigenous activists and ejido members ultimately became members of the EZLN after a long series of interactions with agrarian officials in Chiapas in efforts to obtain land and to improve the conditions of production, marketing, and distribution through participation in independent peasant organizations in the 1980s. The chapter relies on archival documents concerning interactions with the government in the ejido of Guadalupe Tepeyac, published and video interviews, participant observation, and interviews.

Chapter 6 examines the origins of Zapatismo in eastern Chiapas through the encounter between northern activists who came to form a guerrilla army in Chiapas and indigenous leaders and activists who had a twenty year history in a nonviolent struggle to improve their lives. This unique mix resulted in a local Zapatismo, which was then translated and redeployed nationally as the EZLN worked to gain the support of larger Mexican society. The chapter discusses the process of transvaluation by which the local particulars of Chiapas Zapatismo were then adopted by a wide range of sectors and causes within Mexico and resulted in unity across different sectors in the name of Zapatismo, but also increased polarity as the threat of widespread Zapatismo and its sympathizers suggested the possibility of disrupting the political system. The chapter also discusses the limits to the local Zapatismo forged in the Lacandon jungle of Chiapas.

Chapter 7 highlights interviews with Zapatista insurgents, comandantes, and base members as a way of profiling the distinct origins, goals, and visions of Zapatista struggle. It critically assesses the role of women in the EZLN and the struggle to maintain the Zapatista vision in the middle of an army occupation and low-intensity war.

Part 3 of the book moves to the state of Oaxaca, where Zapatismo has a very different origin than in Chiapas. In the case-study ejidos in Oaxaca, contemporary understandings of Zapatismo are read through positive past interactions with government officials, beginning in the 1920s, as well as current links to government through a program to facilitate measurement and privatization of ejido land. Chapter 8 documents the origins of land conflicts, rebellions, and cooperation between local communities with state authorities during the colonial and independence periods. It attempts to show the diversity in relations between indigenous communities and the colonial government and independent state of Mexico. While Zapotecs of the Isthmus and the Mixtecs have historically maintained a position of political independence and autonomy, the Zapotec populations of the central valleys have often collaborated with state authorities.

Chapter 9 offers the first of two ejido stories to counter those of Guadalupe Tepeyac and La Realidad in Chiapas. Santa María del Tule was one of the first ejidos formed in Oaxaca in 1917. In the story of its formation, locals recognize the positive role played by government agrarian officials in helping them gain access to land they were granted from a local hacienda. In their struggle to occupy their ejido land, they also had to battle with their Zapotec neighbors. The positive role of government officials in this process is also linked in the minds of ejidatarios to the historical struggle that Zapata waged on behalf of poor peasants and the role that President Lázaro Cárdenas played in carrying out the vision of Zapata. Zapata and Cárdenas are part of local history in Santa María del Tule. Cárdenas personally visited the community twice.

Like the ejido of Santa María del Tule discussed in the previous chapter, the local history of Unión Zapata, outlined in Chapter 10, is strongly tied to the figure of Lázaro Cárdenas. Unlike Santa María del Tule, Unión Zapata barely existed as a population site prior to the formation of the ejido. In fact, it was cobbled together in the early 1930s in order to facilitate the formation of an ejido. This chapter documents the formation of Unión Zapata, its relationship with Cárdenas, and current memories and understandings of local history in relation to Zapata and Cárdenas. Both this and the previous chapter also serve as background to chapter 11, which contrasts the rejection of state land regularization policy in Chiapas with its relative acceptance in two ejidos in Oaxaca. Chapter 11 also explains how Zapotec and mestizo ejidatarios could both seemingly embrace the dominant political party (the Institutional Revolutionary Party, PRI) in the mid 1990s, yet also support the anti-government Zapatistas in Chiapas. The chapter also provides an analysis of electoral participation by ejidatarios in 1994 and 2000 and outlines how the contradictory position of ejidatarios of 1994 provides evidence of tenuous support for the government, which was further undermined by 2000. In the 2000 elections, the PAN won a majority vote for the first time in Santa María del Tule, defeating the "Pro-PRI" tradition.

The book's Conclusion emphasizes how new ejidatarios in Oaxaca and Chiapas have fashioned their own responses to the neoliberal economic policy that ended land reform, encouraged privatization, and has resulted in increasing socioeconomic stratification in Mexico. The Conclusion takes the insights offered by the Oaxacan and Chiapan case-study communities concerning the role of local histories and identities in producing responses to government policy and places these responses in the larger context of contemporary Mexico after the 2000 elections. I suggest that while ending the PRI's 71-year reign in Mexico is a very significant event, there are other aspects of Mexican society that are important to recognize in understanding further political and social change, especially for rural and indigenous populations. The Conclusion highlights the continued existence of high levels of militarization in indigenous areas of the country in combination with a strong national movement for indigenous rights as a way to emphasize ongoing contradictions in Mexico. It ends by asking what the most effective strategies and levels are for moving toward a more equitable and inclusive Mexico, as well as suggesting the role that U.S. anthropologists might have in that process.

Unless otherwise indicated, all translations are my own.

PART I

The Political and Historical Contexts of Zapatismo

CHAPTER I

Introduction

The "Fields" of Anthropology, Human Rights, and Contemporary Zapatismo

The purpose of this chapter is twofold: to introduce relevant background information, and, more important, to locate myself within the context of my research in terms of my position in the international political economy, my relationship to those I work with, and my ethical responsibilities as an anthropologist—in other words, what is my role in the stories told in this book, and how and why did I take on the research questions I did? In addition, I argue in this chapter for a flexible understanding of anthropology, one that includes using the tools of anthropology to function as a witness and human rights observer, and communicating what we see as anthropologists in a variety of forums. I make this argument in dialogue with many others who have examined these questions.

NAFTA AND ERASING ZAPATA'S LEGACY

Without a doubt, the most enduring legacy of the Mexican Revolution was the agrarian reform constituted under Article 27 of the Constitution that allowed for the formation of ejidos as collective entities with legal stature, specific territorial limits, and representative bodies of governance. Rights to ejido land most often went to men who petitioned or who inherited such rights; they then became ejidatarios, with voting rights in the ejido governance body.

Women's access to land rights was limited in Mexican agrarian law, primarily through their exclusion from being "heads of households" unless they were widows or single mothers. Helga Baitenmann has written (1997; 2000) the most detailed analysis of gender and agrarian rights in twentieth-century Mexico. As she documents, women and men did not become equal under the law until 1971 with regard to their ability to qualify for ejidal rights. The 1971 Federal Law of Agrarian Reform, Article 200, states that to receive land rights, people must simply be "Mexican by birth, male or female, older than sixteen or of any age if they are supporting a family" (Botey Estapé 1991, iii); under this law, women were no longer required to be mothers or widows maintaining a family to qualify for land rights. The law also allowed women to hold any position of authority (*cargo*) within ejidos, and called for the creation of Agro-Industrial Units for Women (UAIMS). These units allowed groups of women collectively to hold use rights to ejido parcels equivalent to those of one ejidatario.

But, a decade after women were finally granted equality with men under the law to receive land rights, the government began a process that ultimately resulted in the dismantling of the right to petition for land, and that aimed to promote privatization of land and of many other resources.

A series of 1980s measures aimed at privatization of government enterprises, a loosening of federal regulations to permit and encourage foreign investment and ownership, and the individualization of property and social relations between the state and its citizens found their logical conclusions in the 1990s reforms to Article 27 of the Mexican Constitution and in the North American Free Trade Agreement (NAFTA). As viewed from Mexico, the purpose of NAFTA was to facilitate the entrance of U.S. capital into the Mexican economy. This was achieved through the privatization of national industry—airlines, telephones, mining, railroads, banks—and the lowering of trade barriers to allow U.S. companies into all economic sectors. Further, to allow U.S. products to compete in the Mexican market, Mexico eliminated price supports and subsidies to basic food items; this resulted in a decrease in the value of real wages, as people had to pay more for basic goods while their wages remained unchanged. Overall, NAFTA led to the acceleration of corporate-led economic integration between Mexico and the United States, benefiting a few but not most.

What were the results of NAFTA in Mexico? After the first few years, it became evident that public policy in Mexico focused much more on the needs of foreign capital and foreign markets than on domestic producers and consumers. During the first two years of NAFTA, it is estimated, more than two million jobs were lost as the country's productive apparatus more or less collapsed (Heredia 1996, 34). Small and medium-size businesses could not compete with foreign corporations, and local and regional businesses were being replaced by large U.S. firms such as Wal-Mart. Domestic consumer debt increased dramatically. The big winners after NAFTA were the owners of newly privatized companies. Privatization of national businesses led to massive profits for a small number of people. In 1995, "the combined wealth of Mexico's fifteen richest individuals was 25.6 billion dollars" (ibid., 35). Most of Mexico's population had to survive with very low wages and no social services. Two-thirds of the economically active population (25 million of 36 million workers) in 1996 survived on informal activities without access to social security, medical care, or insurance (ibid.). While some predicted that, with NAFTA, wages in the United States and Mexico would grow closer, this has not proven true; the minimum wage in most parts of the United States is twelve times higher than in Mexico. In late 1996, the U.S. minimum wage was at least $4.75 per hour, versus $0.41 in Mexico. In the Mexican countryside, wages were even less, often about $3.00 per day—the legal rural minimum wage, but in Chiapas and elsewhere only about half of the rural workforce receive the minimum wage. The rest get between $1.50 and $3.00 a day. Between 1994 and 1999, the minimum wage in Mexico lost between 22 percent and 24 percent of its purchasing power (González 1999).

Social polarization has become a trademark of contemporary Mexico. By mid 1998, although the average per capita monthly income was $75.00, in rural communities, it barely reached $37.00; in more marginal and indigenous areas, it was $18.00 (Cevallos 1998). In 1998, more than half of Mexico—50 million people—still lived in poverty, with incomes of about U.S.$3.00 per day. The 24 million people residing in rural Mexico in 1998 represented about 25 percent of the population, but two-thirds of those in extreme poverty (Gunson 1998). Those living in extreme poverty were often surviving on the equivalent of $2 per day or less.

NAFTA had a major impact on Mexico's rural population. It opened Mexico's grain market to U.S. exports in exchange for opening U.S. fruit and vegetable markets to Mexican exports. People in the United States can now buy more Mexican avocados at lower prices, while cheap U.S. corn is available to Mexican consumers. To facilitate competition from Mexican crops, the Mexican government eliminated price supports on most grains. This action had a strong impact on small farmers who sold corn on the domestic market and benefited from guaranteed prices more

than double the international market price. As support prices were eliminated, farmers dropped out of the market and tried to find other ways
to make a living.

One key aspect of preparing for NAFTA was announced by the Mexican government in late 1991 and implemented in 1992. At that time, reforms made to Article 27 of the Mexican Constitution eliminated the
government's obligation to redistribute land, and made it possible for
collectively held land to be privatized. For those still hoping to solicit the
government for ejido land, it was too late; the door had shut. For those
interested in gaining access to some of the most productive pieces of collectively held land in prime agricultural, urban, and tourist locations,
the door was opened. The piece of real estate at stake was equal to about
50 percent of Mexico's national territory.

A new bureaucracy was set up to carry out the reforms, the Agrarian
Attorney General's Office, or Procuraduría Agraria. An army of new
employees set out to Mexico's ejidos to offer information and—if ejidos
agreed—to help them join a program to measure and map boundaries
between communities and between individual plots. After all disputes
were resolved (if they were resolved, often a major question), people in
ejidos received certificates designating their rights to the land and outlining the precise location and measurements of their plots. The certificates
could serve as a basis for conversion to a land title, if the individual so
desired and if a majority of ejido members voted in favor of the individual receiving a title so as to sell his or her land. The process served to
measure and codify as many plots of land as possible in relation to the
individuals who worked them, in preparation for privatization. It also
mapped those other lands held as collective resources, such as forests,
pastures, and watersheds.

While many who watched this process pronounced it the final nail
in the coffin of the Mexican Revolution of 1910, what I came to understand was that the process revealed new revolutions burning in the hearts
and minds of rural Mexicans and, probably, many others; numerous responses to the end of agrarian reform and to the increasing social and
economic stratification associated with NAFTA were bubbling beneath
the surface of Mexican society. These revolutions had long and complex
histories; many were silent and unseen. Silence that had been interpreted
as agreement or indifference masked a different reality.

These other revolutions—perhaps ultimately to be seen as the revolutions of the twenty-first century—are tied to the 1910 revolution and
its use as a framework for promoting nationalism in Mexico during the

twentieth century. They are also, however, regionally based in their deployment of local histories to make the Mexican Revolution and nation belong to everyone, although in different ways in different communities.

During the summer of 1993, I worked in Oaxaca, my eighteen-month-old son in tow. I spent much time going to meetings called by the Agrarian Attorney General's Office, in which well-meaning staff explained to ejidatarios how the new program to measure land and provide certificates of land rights would benefit them by guaranteeing the security of their land. What unfolded in these initial meetings revealed in great detail the historical visions, divisions, and claims that ejidatarios had about their communities, themselves, and their relation to Mexican history, particularly to the Mexican Revolution. After attending more than a dozen such meetings, and settling into three communities where I followed the interactions between ejidatario men and women and agrarian officials from the Agrarian Attorney General's Office, I soon sensed that the process unfolding concerned much more than bureaucratic details. The act of mapping and measuring land brought up every kind of historical land dispute, pushed people to examine their historical relationship with the government, and highlighted the contradictions of government agrarian policies through time.

THE "FIELDS" OF U.S.–MEXICAN POLITICAL RELATIONS

During this initial fieldwork, an elderly friend named José Martínez, an original ejidatario of Santa María del Tule, provided me with a historical map for understanding the end of agrarian reform. He also clarified beyond a doubt that he, and many like him, understood what was happening in the neoliberal restructuring of Mexico about to be formalized through the initiation of NAFTA that 1 January 1994. I spoke often with José that summer when I visited the ejido. Our mutual interest in the history of the ejido of Santa María del Tule brought us together, and he was extremely supportive of my efforts to conduct oral histories and talk with people about their feelings concerning the agrarian reform and other topics.

In addition, his responses to my questions reconstituted our relationship and "the field" of our interaction. While anthropologists often assume that "being in the field" refers to taking themselves somewhere else, José had a different idea. By first positioning himself locally and then bringing in his view of the Mexican government, the U.S. government, people in the United States, and the imperialism of U.S. territorial

expansion, he bound us into one set of historical, political, and economic relationships; I was in his "field," he in my "field." Being "in the
field" thus was an ongoing, constant process and place, from which I
could not remove myself or come and go at will. Both of us were always "in the field." Whether talking together in Oaxaca or occupying
the separate places we called "home" (Boston for me at the time, Oaxaca for him), we were appropriately constructed by him as part of the
same larger system and set of relationships. His lesson to me was that I
could not come and go from his community and consider that I had left
the "field." Because of who I am, where I come from, and the nature of
my inquiry, I would always be "in the field." Consider his responses to
my questions about changes to agrarian reform laws.

LYNN: What do you think will happen with the new agrarian reform law?
          Will it change things? What will happen?

JOSÉ: All the land that is now part of the ejido used to be private property.
          Before, people in El Tule were really poor. All they could do was to
          sell their labor. They also sold their land if they had any. If someone
          was sick and they died, where were the poor people going to go to get
          money to bury them? They would go to the rich and borrow money
          from them. Then the rich would buy their land. In [the neighboring
          town of] Lachigolo, they lost all of their land. Here, too. Then they
          passed a law to take away all of the land from the hacienda [large
          landed estate or sizeable property of privately titled land]. We got our
          ejido. Now they still want to take it away. Even after we got the land,
          the hacendados [owners of large, landed private estates] still tried to
          take it away. We would find them with their oxen working on our
          ejido land. We had to run them off the land. We suffered a lot get-
          ting rid of these people. The people from the hacienda had the federal
          forces on their side. Zapata was the one who helped the poor. He had
          to force the hacendados out. All of the poor were on the side of Za-
          pata. The hacendados were with the rich. They killed a lot of poor
          people to hang onto their land. . . .
             Now [in 1993] the government of the United States is probably speak-
          ing with the Mexican government. That's what they say. . . . The gov-
          ernment of the United States wants to expand its territory. The United
          States has a lot of people and it needs more land. They are going to
          come here from the United States to buy our land. And who isn't go-
          ing to sell to them? If they pay a high enough price, then people will
          sell. Little by little, they will buy up the ejido, just like the hacendados
          did before. That is what is going to happen.

By the end of his response, José has wrapped us both in the larger political economy of the United States and Mexico. His reframing of the
discussion was the beginning of a five-year journey that made me con-

clude that "the field" is unbounded and I/we are always in it (see Gupta and Ferguson 1997). Anthropologists do not go to work in an objectively bounded place. Rather, we construct research "fields" that fit with our personal agendas and ideologies. We are the creators of "fields" as well as of what we call "field" work. Such creations are built on the assumption that anthropologists are powerful, determining actors, who can impose boundaries around peoples and places, and that we can pop ourselves in and out of those imposed boundaries at will. We usually become conscious of the bounded "fields" we have created when we engage in certain acts of thinking, analyzing, and writing. If, however, we imagine ourselves in permanent, ongoing relationships with those people we study and work with, "the field" disappears and becomes a part of larger global relations that we do not create but simply live in, like everyone else.

REWRITING OUR HANDBOOKS TO FIELDWORK

My prior experience living and working in a nearby Zapotec community, Teotitlán del Valle (Stephen 1991), as well as my ability to still speak some Zapotec, was of interest to many elderly ejidatarios in Santa María del Tule. After I presented myself to the ejido authorities, provided them with a copy of my first book about Teotitlán, and gave them letters of presentation from a research institute and university in Oaxaca, as well as a Spanish translation of my proposal, they told me that *they* could not decide whether I could conduct my project on the history of the ejido and on reactions to the reforms to Article 27. The *comisariado ejidal* (ejidal commissioner) stated: "Here, we decide things in our assembly. The ejidatarios have to all hear your proposal and then vote on it. Come this Sunday afternoon and we will listen to your proposal and give you an answer."

That Sunday, I returned and found people beginning to mill around outside the Casa Ejidal (the meeting hall and office of the ejido authorities). I noticed that many were elderly and that there was a strong contingent of women. I began to talk with a group of women, alternating between Zapotec and Spanish. It was at this meeting that I met José. He introduced me to several other original ejidatarios.

The meeting was long, with fascinating details. Much time was spent discussing the new program for measuring land, the PROCEDE (Program for the Certification of Ejido Land Rights and the Titling of Urban House Plots, which I discuss in the next chapter). Many voiced concern about whether or not people would sell land. Opinions were expressed about the impending beginning of NAFTA as well. Toward the end, I was invited to present my project. I spoke about my experience in Teotitlán, about how I would go about writing a history and talking with people. I emphasized the importance of respect, of only talking with those who were interested, and my willingness to write a document, in Spanish, for the community that would take into consideration whatever items the community might want to include. After I presented my proposal, there was a discussion period in which people engaged in small conversations with those around them. Then a more formal exchange ensued. People raised their hands and asked questions. "Who pays you?" asked an elderly woman. "Where did you get the money to come to Oaxaca?" asked a man in his forties, knitting his brow together. "How much does it cost to fly to Boston?" asked another. "What will happen to the history you collect?" inquired an elderly man, a member of the ejido vigilance committee. "Will you make copies for people here?" I answered these questions as best I could. "I received a grant from a research center at the University of California in San Diego that is looking at whether or not changes to the agrarian reform law and PROCEDE program will help or hurt people in Mexico." "It costs about six hundred American dollars to fly round-trip from Boston." "The history I collect will first be turned over to the community, the ejido committee, and then be used in a book. I will bring a copy of that book here and do my very best to have it published in Spanish. I will also provide a Spanish version of ejido history to anyone interested. That will be my first priority."

After this, the comisariado asked for a vote of those in favor of permitting me to work in the ejido. I held my breath and sighed in relief when most raised their hands. I was delighted that the ejidatarios of Santa María had agreed to work with me. I was equally delighted to see a political process where strong debate and discussion was encouraged and where community members carefully considered who could come to conduct research; the ejidatarios were thinking about what the community would risk and gain from the presence of a researcher.

The process that took place in Santa María del Tule was more or less repeated in the other communities I worked in. Approval required I present myself in the ejido assemblies and, if I wanted to work with a subgroup of the ejido, such as a women's group, I also met with them and discussed their interests as well as my ideas.

My experience in Santa María del Tule and elsewhere led me to reflect on my anthropological training for fieldwork, which had emphasized:

- writing a proposal with a hypothesis for which one will seek funding and then "prove" in the field
- making initial contacts in a community
- gaining formal approval from community authorities
- cultivating key informants
- taking care to be neutral and objective, trying to avoid participation in community divisions
- keeping a safe distance between one's emotional life and life in "the field"
- conceiving "the field" as something one goes "into" and "out" of, a clearly defined space detached from one's person
- engaging in participant observation
- doing interviews
- surveying
- taking detailed daily fieldnotes

I found myself wishing that the ejidatarios of Santa María del Tule could provide a new field guide for anthropologists to prepare them with an entirely new set of priorities. Key parts would include:

- writing a proposal in the local language and being prepared to change it substantially in response to the needs of those one works with
- presenting oneself and one's proposal to the community, answering questions, and being prepared to submit to collective opinion the issues of whether and how one may proceed
- holding conversations with only those people willing and interested in one's research and only when convenient for them
- understanding that observing is a participatory and political act, and being prepared to justify how and why information collected is used and who has rights to it
- understanding that neutrality is not possible and that every person, including an outsider, who participates in community life is a political actor
- knowing one cannot expect others to share life histories, thoughts, hopes, opinions, and observations without being ready to do the same
- understanding that personal priorities and interpretations will neces-

sarily influence the words and ideas of anthropologists as well as of
those whom anthropologists have traditionally labeled "informants"
- being prepared to have one's first research product be that which the
  people one works with request

Such suggestions are not new. Indigenous peoples of the Americas have
been challenging North American and European anthropologists about
the politics of their research for quite some time now. Emblematic of this
critique are four ethical failures pointed out by Luis Enrique Sam Colop,
a Mayan intellectual, in a 1990 newsletter. They include "foreign scholars who do not consult with the community where they are going to
work about their project" and who "rarely present a final report of the
study to the community"; large bodies of knowledge compiled by foreigners not made available to Mayan communities, leaving them "igno-
rant of what foreign scholars have said about their language, culture, or
community"; foreigners who hide "religious or proselytizing agendas
behind their academic status" and may interfere in community decision-
making; researchers whose chief concern is with fulfilling academic aspirations and who "take the service of the community for granted" (Sam
Colop 1990, as cited in Warren 1998, 82). The publication of such a critique and ongoing exchanges between indigenous and North American
researchers are part of a move to create engaged anthropology.
    This exchange between indigenous activists and scholars and nonin-
digenous academics often involves a tension between the essentialist
constructions of ethnicity used to build movements and tribal legitimacy,
and the constructivist perspectives on ethnicity predominant in contemporary cultural anthropology. Kay Warren describes the tensions of this
dialogue with Mayan intellectuals (1998, 69–85), as does Les Field in
his collaborations with "unacknowledged tribes" of California (Field
1999b). In his frank discussion of the need to sometimes strategically deploy essentialism, as well as in his search to bridge the work of activist
anthropologists and indigenous intellectuals, Field brings forward important issues that are not easily resolved. An example is the tension
between deconstructivist anthropologists and indigenous intellectuals
deploying essentialist constructions of identity for political purposes.
Anthropologists working in Latin America with indigenous intellectuals
and activists have dealt with an ongoing questioning of the anthropological model (see Jackson 1989, 1991; Rappaport 1998; Ramos 1998,
1999–2000). Thus I see my work as part of ongoing collaborative ef-

forts that are reshaping the nature of anthropology through research that seeks to serve the communities it studies.

DECENTERING THE FIELD: THE FORCED
DECONSTRUCTION OF BOUNDARIES

On 1 January 1994, just a little more than four months after I finished my summer fieldwork in Oaxaca, the Zapatista rebellion exploded in Chiapas. I was not surprised at the appearance of the Zapatistas; all summer long in Oaxaca, we had heard rumors about a possible guerrilla movement in the south. The national magazine *Proceso* had reported on a confrontation on 23–24 May 1993 between the Mexican Army and an armed group in the Lacandon jungle. Friends in the city of Oaxaca were discussing the article and other rumors. Some commented that there were guerrillas in Oaxaca and other places as well. José Martínez may not have been surprised by the Zapatista rebellion. I did not get a chance to talk to him about it before he died in the spring of 1994; I greatly missed him when I returned to continue work in Santa María del Tule in 1994.

Shortly after the Zapatistas made the international press by occupying five county seats in the state of Chiapas (see map 3) and gained immediate notoriety through Subcomandante Marcos's interviews and the first of many communiqués from the Clandestine Revolutionary Indigenous Committee, I began to receive calls—from the press, from friends, from students, from political connections. They all wanted to know, "What is going on in Chiapas?" "What is happening with the Indians of Mexico?" For the first time in my life, being an anthropologist who wrote about indigenous people in the south of Mexico made me interesting to a wide range of people. It turned out that in New England, there were not many people writing about Indians in Mexico. In February of 1994, I was asked to be part of a panel at Harvard University, a panel that subsequently traveled to the Council on Foreign Relations in New York—a high-powered forum and think tank for mainstream policy makers, financial brokers, politicians, and academics. The panel was titled "The Chiapas Rebellion and the Future of Mexico." My conversations with José Martínez flashed through my mind—first, because he understood the stakes of the Agrarian Reform and NAFTA, and, second, because his reconstruction of our interaction into one integrated field of Mexican–U.S. political relations was staring me right in the face.

As I sat in a cab zooming through downtown Manhattan to the posh building housing the Council on Foreign Relations, I realized that who I was, what I know, whom I learned it from, whom I tell it to, and how I tell it is profoundly political. I was about to address, along with several others, some of the elite policy makers and power brokers who would actually influence U.S. policy toward Mexico—financial, military, and otherwise. José and I indeed were both in the same "field."

On the panel, in front of bankers, development officers, and foreign investors, we talked about Chiapas from our varied viewpoints. In the sherry hour following the discussion, several people sought me out as an anthropologist and wanted to know "What do those Indians down there really want?" "Are they unhappy?" "What do they think about NAFTA?" "Could this rebellion really destabilize Mexico?" These questions were similar to those I had received from press persons who wanted to know not only about Chiapas but also about what was going on with other Indians—for instance, in neighboring Oaxaca.

For the first time in my professional career, being an anthropologist was suddenly a credential of interest to bankers. This gave me pause. In answering the questions of people at the Council on Foreign Relations, or those of journalists, I often repeated the words of José Martínez, stating that most indigenous people I knew in Mexico had clear and strong opinions about NAFTA, about U.S. foreign policy, and about their government's economic policies. Many were concerned about losing their land and about whether all the economic changes would benefit them, and were suspicious of promises made by the Mexican government. They also had their own ideas for how to modify government policies; they were not mystified. The people at the sherry hour were polite, seemed quite interested, but remained puzzled about what the Indians might really want.

For me, an ethical corner in this research project had been turned. I realized, as during the Salvadoran civil war, that most people with real decision-making power have no solid information about the perspectives of those affected by U.S. policies and, even if they are given it, do not have the ability to assimilate it. If I had information and analysis about the situation in Mexico, offered by people usually far removed from the halls of economic and political power, I had a moral responsibility and commitment to impart that information and analysis to as broad an audience as possible with as much respect for those who offered the information as possible. Since the U.S.–Mexican political economy is integrated, then, as a U.S. citizen who is an anthropologist I am most definitely a participant, a native in those relations. My invitation to the Council on Foreign Relations clearly demonstrated that. Thus, another important process had broadened "the field" where I was operating as an anthropologist.

In response to conversations in early 1994 with an old friend in Mexico City, a warrior in the human rights movement, six of us—both Mexican and American—formed an organization in Boston called Tonantzin: The Boston Committee in Support of Native Peoples of Mexico. We put together information packets and were able to draw large gatherings, mostly of representatives of the Latino media and a wide range of Latino social movements and grassroots organizations, to informational meetings and a press conference. Of particular note was the interest of Native American groups. Mexicans in the group were concerned also to reach out to the small Mexican community in Boston. We had the first of many meetings with the staff of the Mexican Consulate and became a regular presence in Boston, putting on educational events, organizing humanitarian aid campaigns, participating in human rights delegations, and connecting the situation in Mexico to U.S. foreign policy and local concerns. (The group was still going strong in 1999, after I had moved to Oregon.)

It is this work over time that lent me credibility in Chiapas and provided entrée to certain communities: Guadalupe Tepeyac in 1994, La Realidad in 1995, 1996, and 1997, Ejido Morelia in 1995, San Andrés Larráinzar and Oventic in 1996 and 1997, Acteal in 1998 and 2000, and Ocosingo, Chenalhó, and Polhó in 2000. Old friendships from the 1980s, when I lived in Mexico and knew a range of people working in peasant and indigenous organizations and in the beginnings of the human rights movement, were also key in providing a perspective and in helping me gain access to participate in forums and meetings organized by the EZLN. I brought the skills of anthropology to human rights and humanitarian aid work, and used my experiences while engaged in such work to write anthropologically.

WHEN REBELLION TURNS TO LOW-INTENSITY WAR

During the summer of 1994, I spent two months in Oaxaca with the specific intention of monitoring receptions to the government's land-measuring and certification program (PROCEDE), observing national presidential elections and responses to them, and seeing what people thought about the Zapatista rebellion—if anything. I was particularly interested in assessing whether the presence of the Zapatista movement had influenced opinions about the government and its agrarian reform and farm-subsidy programs in Oaxaca. I thought that observing participation during national elections would provide a good context for evaluating whether people continued to exhibit dissatisfaction with the government and suspicion of its programs. What emerged from this period of fieldwork was intriguing. Many men and women I interviewed supported and often even identified with the Zapatistas and their demands, yet many voted for the PRI (Institutional Revolutionary Party) at the time. The oppositional part of this identity (pro-Zapatista) would eventually cause some to vote against the PRI (in the 2000 elections—see chapter 11). In 1994, however, many were both pro-Zapatista and pro-PRI. I found this fascinating, in light of my understanding, from a distance, of the Zapatistas' antigovernment stance. What I had yet to comprehend was how the progovernment Zapatista sympathizers of Oaxaca were connected to the antigovernment Zapatistas of Chiapas. What were the common threads, if any, that connected the two, and how did they construct distinct views of the Mexican nation, the government, and its policies in the past and present?

In addition, I felt that if I was going to be a participant in conversations about the Zapatista rebellion and its meaning, then I had to go to Chiapas and see for myself what was going on. What I learned during the next six years, on eight trips to what became known as "the zone of conflict," was much more than I bargained for. I did not simply learn about new interpretations of Emiliano Zapata and his meaning to the indigenous peasants of Chiapas. I learned that this new vision of Zapatismo was so threatening that it required a massive effort to first contain it and then to attempt (so far unsuccessfully) to snuff it out. This process mobilized not only older patterns of human rights abuses in Mexico, documented in the 1980s and before, but a massive militarization of large parts of Chiapas and other indigenous regions of Mexico (Oaxaca, Guerrero, Hidalgo), the displacement of populations, the integration of the army and several police forces, the training and maintenance of paramilitary groups, sophisticated strategies of intimidation and psychological warfare, and efforts to divide local populations. What emerged as most ironic is that this process was occurring in Chiapas and selective other parts of Mexico such as Oaxaca and Guerrero simultaneously with a political opening in the more formal arena of electoral politics at the center.

From 1993 through 2000, while gathering material for this book, I would often shuttle back and forth between working with two ejidos in the central valleys of Oaxaca and working in Chiapas. While in Oaxaca, I could, with each return trip, more or less pick up where I had left off. In Chiapas, that was never possible. Each time I went there, the situation was radically different. In a location where I might have been able to travel and talk with people on my previous trip, this would not be possible on the next. My first two trips to the ejidos of Guadalupe Tepeyac and La Realidad in the municipality of Las Margaritas, for example, were a study in contrast. In August 1994, my visit to Guadalupe Tepeyac was framed by the National Democratic Convention organized by the EZLN that month (see Stephen 1995). This historic meeting allowed the EZLN to consult with more than six thousand delegates and observers on issues including a transition to democracy in the Mexican political system, a constitutional congress, and a new constitution. With thousands of others, I traveled by bus to the site of the convention, carved out of a hillside on the outskirts of the ejido of Guadalupe Tepeyac.

The road into Guadalupe Tepeyac was winding, rutted, and full of mud. In 1994, travel from Las Margaritas, where the paved road ended, could take from five to ten hours or longer, depending on the vehicle and the rains. That August, the center of Guadalupe Tepeyac was dominated by a large hospital, dedicated by President Salinas de Gortari only a few months before the uprising. The town's population was scattered along a few dirt streets, and most lived in outlying areas, in wooden houses—often with thatched roofs though some had roofs of corrugated iron. Most homes had some chickens and a few pigs, and occasionally there was a horse. Zapatista slogans were painted in places, and during the National Democratic Convention the town was full of visitors from surrounding areas. Local mom-and-pop stores were stocked with cases of Boing—a Kool-Aid equivalent—and mountains of Sabritas, a Mexican brand of chips, in many flavors. Government trucks from various agencies had been commandeered for the convention, and most of the huge number of cars and buses present during the convention belonged to outside visitors. Normally, there were few vehicles in the community. Local transportation consisted primarily of a second-class school bus that made the trip to Las Margaritas once or twice a day.

The Zapatistas controlled the territory in and around Guadalupe Tepeyac, with checkpoints every mile or so. The area surrounding Guadalupe Tepeyac was lined with groves of coffee trees and with corn and bean patches. Banana trees were also visible. Just outside the town, a cold river rushed by, serving as a local bathing place; there was a women's bathing section and a men's bathing section. Locals ensured that each area remained segregated.

Uniformed Zapatistas were all over, eager and interested to talk. People were happy to discuss what seemed a triumphal time, full of hope for change. The National Democratic Convention was one of the most amazing events I have participated in. I shall always remember the hope, optimism, and possibility in that scene—thousands of Mexicans from all walks of life in dialogue and celebration with hundreds of indigenous Zapatistas, including men, women, and children. Zapatista territory was very open and accessible both before and after the convention, until February 1995. It was a hopeful time.

I returned to Chiapas in March and April 1995 to find a very different situation. In February 1995, the Mexican Army had carried out a major offensive to capture the leadership of the EZLN and to retake military control of EZLN-occupied territory. The leadership was not captured, but more than twenty thousand EZLN sympathizers fled from their homes and communities, which were ransacked, often destroyed, and then occupied by the army. The "low-intensity" war had begun, and provided me with some of the in-your-face categories necessary to convey the urgency of the situation: militarization, community and family divisions, paramilitarization, displaced populations, death and near-death, hunger, and exposure. Below are edited sections from my field diary from that trip of March and April 1995.

> In addition to spending time in San Cristóbal de las Casas and interviewing a range of people in NGOS, I spent seven days with a humanitarian aid delegation documenting the human rights situation in Chiapas after a major incursion by the Mexican military which displaced thousands of people from their communities. In visiting interior areas outside of Las Margaritas and Altamirano, we found a tense and difficult situation. Despite government claims that the military has withdrawn, the army maintains a strong presence in and around many communities. Some of the civilian population has been displaced for nearly six weeks and has suffered repression and destruction of property and homes. While humanitarian aid has begun to reach many areas and some people are now returning home, the situation remains critical.
>
> The greatest danger is not only the army, but the strong divisions that have been created in many communities by the presence of the military. Many communities are now strongly polarized and even if people return home, the possibility of local confrontations remains high.

I. Military Situation

The Mexican Army has withdrawn from blockades established on main roads leading into San Cristóbal, Comitán, Ocosingo, Altamirano, and Las Margaritas. Trenches, sandbags, and garbage line the roads where military encampments were. The army is still clearly established inside of Altamirano, with wooden trailers and buildings. In many places we saw empty boxes of U.S. army rations, such as "instant corn beef hash."

Heavy earth-moving equipment accompanies the army camps. The army has graded the road to Guadalupe Tepeyac and improved it considerably to accommodate heavy trucks. Road improvements are also visible in the area around Altamirano.

The army has not withdrawn, but has hidden itself. Along the way to Guadalupe Tepeyac and beyond, soldiers are dug into foxholes. We came across two humvees on patrol in the vicinity of San Juan del Río, one hour before Guadalupe Tepeyac. We saw several soldiers in foxholes right off the road with their machine guns pointed out.

In five communities we visited, the army had occupied the communities for hours, days, or sometimes weeks. In some cases they appear to have moved permanently into the communities, occupying ejido land and community buildings.

The most visible activity of the EZLN is the huge numbers of trees that were chopped down with axes and are blocking the roads. There are hundreds of felled trees across the road beginning at Nuevo Momón and continuing past Guadalupe Tepeyac. The army has sawed through them with chain saws, clearing the road.

The technology of the two armies is clearly visible in the trees where the EZLN used axes and machetes to chop them down and the army used chain saws to clear them away.

The EZLN has a very subtle, but clear, presence. We met several times with people who were not uniformed, did not identify themselves directly as Zapatistas, but let us know their position through comments and the positions they took in conversation. They passed along a communiqué in one instance and also engaged in political analysis of the situation. They were most keen for any information about the peace process. . . .

II. Displaced Communities

Morelia   The area after Ejido Morelia and up the road for 1 1/2 hours has been occupied by the military. Every town had people in it that were detained and, in two cases (in Venustiano Carranza and in La Grandeza), soldiers had shot one person after questioning them and chasing them. They also destroyed people's belongings. Parts of these communities were still in the mountains along with about half of the population of Ejido Morelia.

We met with a group of women and children and men, primarily from Ejido Morelia, but from elsewhere as well, who were deep in the jungle. Most have been living in the open for at least six weeks. We were told that there was nothing to eat for about 20 days. Most of the adults did not eat and gave food to children and to pregnant women. Everyone was covered with insect bites, with chiggers, some with skin fungus that was on their scalps as well. None had shoes, clothing was very tattered. We were not permitted to take pictures or to tape record for fear of the army getting hold of the information and photographs.

I had a long conversation with one of the local political leaders and several other people. I will never forget when they all told me, "we are prepared to die for our struggle—we are dying anyway of preventable diseases. Better to die for a just cause. We mean it. We will not give up."

After our arrival, we were asked to transport a woman, Juana, who had been in labor, to the San Carlos hospital. She was lowered on two boards from an area far above where we were. Juana was completely dehydrated, had a low temperature, and was extremely catatonic. We opened her eyes to see if there was any response. She had been in labor for two days and her baby had died inside of her. She was about to go into shock. She had four other children with her. We had brought medical supplies and fortunately one of our party turned out to be a doctor. We gave her rehydration fluid, electrolytes, and antibiotics. We then drove her and her family and several other people in the middle of the night back to the San Carlos hospital in Altamirano through areas with strong paramilitary presence. There was danger that, if the bumping motion of the truck on the rough dirt road started her contractions again, Juana could begin to bleed and have an internal hemorrhage. Four people and the doctor held her in the back of the truck for more than two hours. About 15 kilometers before Altamirano, several people jumped out and said they couldn't go into town because they had been fichados or marked for repression. The sick woman's husband had been in jail in January 1994 and was liberated by the EZLN about 10 days after the war began. The truck driver asked me to run to the hospital, get the nuns to open the door so he could quickly back the truck in. He didn't want to be seen or have any of the people in the truck seen. They would all be marked, he explained.

As soon as we arrived, the woman was given Pitocin and the baby was delivered stillborn in 40 minutes. Her condition began to improve. She would be in the hospital for 5 days. If we hadn't arrived, she would have died of shock within 24 hours, according to the doctor who attended her. The doctor also believed that the complications in the labor were due to dehydration and her weak health. She had four previous deliveries that were normal. If a midwife had been present, then the baby could have been delivered. The woman normally lives in Ejido Morelia about ½ hour from the hospital. If she had been in her home, the child would probably not have died and she would not have been in grave danger.

The stakes of the low-intensity war in Chiapas were quickly shoved into focus on that trip. Back in San Cristóbal de las Casas, friends talked about the tightening of the situation, the increasing pressure on indigenous communities with Zapatista sympathizers, and the unfortunate turn created by the state's decision to deal with the Zapatista rebellion through military means and not through dialogue. By this time, the Zapatistas had ignited much of Mexico in debate, and the opening they provided was taken by a wide range of organizations that had been consolidating for up to two decades: regional indigenous movements that began to communicate with one another at a national level; a growing debtors' movement that joined together farmers unable to get credit and middle-class housewives who could not pay credit card bills; students; environmentalists; human rights organizations; labor; and others. After that trip, I understood that something very important was going on in Mexico. It could be measured both by the intensity of the government's response to the Zapatista rebellion and by the rest of the country's engagement with the basic demands of the EZLN's 1 January declaration from the Lacandon jungle: work, land, housing, food, health, education, independence, liberty, democracy, justice, and peace. At the same time, the legitimacy of the ruling PRI party was called into question, and a series of political assassinations in 1994, including the killing of the PRI presidential candidate Luis Colosio in Tijuana, Baja California, provided further evidence that the PRI was losing its grip on power. The revolutions that had been hidden were bubbling to the surface. And, as these revolutions surfaced, so did counterrevolutions such as the paramilitary groups in Chiapas that targeted Zapatista sympathizers and were responsible for the massacre of forty-five Tzotzil women, children, and men in Acteal Chiapas in 1997.

After my experiences in Chiapas, I felt I could add another section to my handbook for fieldworkers, which would include the following points:

- "The field" is all-inclusive. Anthropologists are a part of the field, responsible for their place in the moral economy and political economy of the broader relations encompassing them and those they work with.

- Models of fieldwork must be flexible and able to accommodate to situations of war, refugees, and violence. Under such circumstances, shorter, unpredictable visits will be the norm.

- In situations such as low-intensity war, the idea of neutral "participant observation" is not credible. Researchers have to be prepared to participate more than observe and to take responsibility for using their access to the media and other resources to report on what they see and participate in.

· Researchers must be prepared to cope with circumstances where they will not be permitted to tape record, videotape, or often even take notes, because of fear of government or other reprisal should the anthropologist's materials be confiscated. Other ways of documenting and remembering will have to be found.

· In some cases, the only legitimate access anthropologists will gain to communities in the midst of a low-intensity war will be through participating in human rights and humanitarian aid efforts. In this capacity, anthropologists can bring the tools of anthropology to bear on this important work.

· Analysis done by anthropologists who have participated in human rights and humanitarian aid efforts is important. Its goals and purposes are distinct from those of traditional fieldwork, but analysis based on experiences gained through human rights observation and humanitarian aid distribution can make an important contribution to the discipline.

THE ANTHROPOLOGIST AS WITNESS

As an observer—and as, indeed, a participant, through my insertion, as a *person,* into the political, economic, and cultural relations bridging the U.S. and Mexico—I came to reevaluate my role as anthropologist. I did not see myself as being an "investigator" seeking to unearth all mysteries and answer all questions, but more as what Liisa Malkki calls a witness—"trying to be an attentive listener, recognizing the situatedness of one's intellectual work, and affirming one's own connections to the ideas, processes, and people one is studying" (Haraway 1991; Malkki 1997, 96, quotation 94–95). In describing her work in a refugee camp that housed some thirty-five thousand Hutu refugees, Malkki also describes the ways in which the presumed uniqueness of the circumstances of such locations as refugee camps or of particular events often construed as news (such as most episodes of the Zapatista rebellion) often implies a "diminished scholarly weight for the evidence" (Malkki 1997, 89). In other words, if anthropologists cover situations such as low-intensity war, and their coverage does not involve the virtues of traditional fieldwork methods (conducting long-term participatory research in a community or society, and observing people's ordinary, everyday routines and practices), then the research may be labeled as less than adequate, denigrating its integrity (ibid., 90).

If we are able to accept that one (not the only) role of anthropology can be as witness, then we must expand our notion of what is legitimate fieldwork. Situations such as the low-intensity war in Chiapas do not usually permit classical modes of fieldwork in communities that are displaced, divided, and militarized—particularly if the anthropologist has little or no history with the community or group studied. Governments that do not want anthropologists, or anyone else, to act as witnesses will certainly provide obstacles to long-term research on situations they want to hide. And long-term research may bring danger not only to the researcher but, more important, to the communities being studied, should the long-term presence of a foreigner mark a community as suspicious. What is important is to act as a witness and to use the tools and resources of an anthropologist to report on what we witness.

Carolyn Nordstrom, who has written a creative and moving book on war in Mozambique in the 1990s, states on the ethnography of war:

> [T]o be representative, ethnographic analyses should be conducted at the centers, and not just the sidelines, of conflict. For ultimately, the doctrines of the politico-military elite, the exposés of journalists, and the critical theories of scholars are wor[l]ds apart from the experiences of those living and dying in the center of war. To include research at the epicenters of violence involves a number of responsibilities above and beyond those associated with more traditional ethnography: responsibilities to the fieldworker's safety, to that of his or her informants, and to the theories that help forge attitudes towards the reality of violence both expressed and experienced. This research . . . has led me to delve into questions concerning a responsible and responsive ethnography of warfare and to explore the relationships of self, identity, sociocultural processes, and power as they are highlighted in the deconstructive environment of war. (Nordstrom 1997, 8–9)

Nordstrom, like Malkki, suggests a rethinking, not only of whom we do ethnography with, but also of how, and of what kinds of theories we use. Like me, Nordstrom concludes that exploring a responsible and responsive ethnography of warfare requires a reexamination of the relationships between self, those at the center of the research, and global relations of power. She also writes that "treating a person's experiences of violence with dignity is arguably the most important part of studying and writing about violence" (ibid., 9). In other words, doing a responsible ethnography of war involves analyzing not only the structural conditions of war—military strategies, techniques, and counteroffensives—but also what is the lived experience of war on a daily basis. Anthropologists working in Latin America have had ample opportunity to do this.

ANTHROPOLOGISTS IN WARTIME CENTRAL AMERICA

This book actually belongs to a longer anthropological tradition in Latin America of wartime ethnography arising from the cold war / post-cold-war history of the region. The dominant political position exercised by the United States there for most of the twentieth century has pushed many anthropologists to write self-consciously about their subject positions, the limits to what they can do in war situations, the need to witness, and the urgency of finding new and more accessible ways of presenting research results.[1] For some anthropologists, explicating one's political positioning in relation to the people one works with has, with regard to Latin America, become a basic part of fieldwork and writing.

American scholars working in Central America over the past decade have often made explicit reference to how their subject position, the terms of civil and ethnic conflict, and the foreign policy of the United States have strongly affected how they work. Charles Hale, in his book *Resistance and Contradiction: Miskitu Indians and the Nicaraguan State, 1894–1987,* carefully describes his position, as a "Miskitu-speaking white North American," as one providing the privilege of Miskitu "affinities with Anglo culture, which resulted from a history of Anglo-American hegemony on the Miskitu coast" (Hale 1994, 11). Hale finds that this perception of him by the Miskitu as a "Miriki" or American associated with "missionaries, company bosses and workers, participants in a University of Wisconsin health promotion program funded by U.S. AID, and other North American fieldworkers," had a counterpart among the Sandinistas, who at the time were still in charge of the Nicaraguan government. In Sandinista eyes, when he resumed an identity as an internationalist/*internationalista,* his anti-imperialist convictions were assumed, as was his support for the Nicaraguan Revolution. In his book, in which he offers insightful critiques of both the Miskitu leadership and Sandinista cadres, Hale demonstrates a method of activist research he describes as "aligned with movements of social change, yet capable of contributing to critique, even struggle, from within" (ibid., 220). Hale acknowledges that his commitment to illuminating ethnic conflict in revolutionary Nicaragua was strongly linked to the interventionist policy of the United States at the time. By working in support of the processes of conflict resolution under way on the Atlantic Coast, he demonstrated his opposition to U.S. policy—a stance that led him to reject an Inter-American Foundation fellowship after being told he would be awarded one provided he carried out his study in Bolivia (ibid., 13).

Other North American scholars of Central America, such as Leigh Binford, author of *The El Mozote Massacre: Anthropology and Human Rights,* have also clearly stated positions in opposition to U.S. foreign policy. Binford explicates his political position throughout his book, concluding with the suggestion that anthropologists follow the lead of liberation theologians and practice the "preferential option for the poor," which he interprets as

> struggling and working closely with grassroots organizations in the investigation of human rights abuses; it means scrutinizing the institutions and agencies that are at the forefront of the "New World Order"; it means anthropologists working actively in their own communities to oppose the growing assault on social programs such as welfare, public education, and public housing; it means dedicating more time to translation and dissemination of materials produced by people who have little or no access to a larger public in the decision-making imperial centers and sponsoring, as well, speaking tours in which witnesses testify directly to the chaos being wreaked upon them as well as their resistance to it. (Binford 1996, 202)

For Binford, to engage in wartime anthropology implies a complete reconfiguring of many basic assumptions of how anthropology is done and what the priorities of the anthropologist are. Anthropologists committed to human rights, he also states, need to look for new discursive strategies for presenting human rights problems, since the "universal valuation and other humanitarian ideals that underpin progress in human rights reporting are not necessarily shared by the target audience" (ibid., 7).

Both Hale and Binford offer concrete strategies for anthropologists working in wartime and engaged with issues of ethnic and human rights. These authors' sympathies are clearly with illuminating the causes and complications of war and ethnic conflict while taking a critical stance on national policies and U.S. foreign policies in part responsible for the conflicts being analyzed. Such an agenda could have been at the center of David Stoll's 1999 work in Guatemala; however, his political positioning in *Rigoberta Menchú and the Story of All Poor Guatemalans* is quite contrary to that found in Hale's and Binford's work. In fact, Stoll's book appears indirectly to support the agenda of the postwar military in Guatemala. While questioning the literal truth of the stories of Rigoberta Menchú's testimony, the intentions of the Guerrilla Army of the Poor, and the impact of the Guatemalan human rights movement are certainly controversial endeavors that can yield useful debates and exchanges, by not offering an equally harsh critique and analysis of the systematic and planned violence perpetrated by the armed forces and the Guatemalan government against the Mayan population and others, Stoll undermines his stated objectives. Because Stoll does not acknowledge the findings documented in the Report of the Historical Memory Project of the Human Rights Office, Archdiocese of Guatemala, presented on 24 April 1998 (and previously [Oficina de Derechos Humanos del Arzobispado de Guatemala 1998])—massacres, scorched-earth operations, forced disappearances, and executions—the points he attempts (such as questioning the strategy of guerrilla movements in terms of their actual results for rural indigenous people, dissecting the romanticism of revolutionary movements and their supporters, and discussing the nature of "truth" reflected in testimonial literature) are lost for this reader, and discredited.

Other anthropologists working in wartime Guatemala have taken clearer approaches in their documentation of national war, state repression, and the peace process. Robert Carmack's collection published in 1988 details the social impact of life under militarization and includes pieces by many anthropologists with distinguished research records in Guatemala. In a different book, Beatriz Manz (1988) documented the aftermath of counterinsurgency in indigenous communities and life under military patrol. The Guatemalan anthropologist-priest Ricardo Falla has also carefully researched and publicized the political turmoil in the Ixcan jungle and the horrifying massacres there in 1982; Falla was very clear about the importance and implications of his subject: "This fight can be tremendously dangerous: It unleashes social forces that demand that the crimes be investigated and that the material and intellectual authors of the crimes and their counterinsurgency theories and practices be brought out into the open" (Falla 1994, 3). These authors bring forward information, events, and questions missing from Stoll's 1999 book, and offer important examples of how anthropologists can operate in the context of sustained wartime.

The anthropologist Kay Warren integrates the civil war into her analysis of pan-Mayan activism through exploring how people's accounts of their own experiences of the violence were central to their attempts to cope with a world of insecurity and were also used to mobilize elements of traditionalist culture by local leaders (Warren 1998, 86–112). In her postscript to the testimonials of violence and self-transformation, Warren inserts a discussion of the contradictions and limitations of anthropology in studying situations where human rights are being violated: "Our contribution is to give voice to those who are muted by cultural difference and marginalization, and to explore the interconnectedness of U.S. and Latin American realities. We also maintain personal moral commitments to the people we work with" (ibid., 111).

Warren's larger interest is the ways in which Mayan activists "produce, circulate, read, and appropriate literature," reaching hundreds of communities through a variety of venues. In this analysis, the role of witnessing violence is seen as a key component of Mayan intellectuals' writing and cultural activism as they move from violence and displacement to cultural renewal. Warren's analysis brings forward the voices of Mayan intellectuals often overshadowed by the perspectives of testimonials such as Rigoberta Menchú's. The perspectives of the Mayan activists Victor Montejo, Luis Enrique Sam Colop, and others not only provide new models of how to document and disseminate the experience of war, but also question many basic premises of anthropological research and writing—such as interview-based research and the concept of academic monographs as products.

The recent work of Diane Nelson (1999) also provides an alternative model of how to integrate issues of war, violence, and human rights violations in a cultural analysis of nationalism and its fragments.

THE HUMAN EXPERIENCE OF SOCIAL SUFFERING

Recent writings on the anthropology of violence (Nordstrom and Robben 1995; Nordstrom 1997; Green 1995) and on social suffering (Kleinman, Das, and Lock 1997) have called attention to the need to give voice to "the puzzling contradictions of lives perturbed by violence"

(Robben and Nordstrom 1995, 10). I dedicate part of this book to this goal, through trying to bring out the feelings and stories of men and women who have suffered the violence of low-intensity war in Chiapas.

Such fieldwork requires that anthropologists not only provide cultural, political, and economic explanations of what they see, but also communicate both the human dimensions of daily fear, insecurity, horror, pain, and suffering and the periodic hope and optimism that are the everyday experiences of political violence (see Scheper-Hughes 1992 for such a perspective in a different context). In their volume on social suffering, Arthur Kleinman, Veena Das, and Margaret Lock propose that we collapse old dichotomies such as those that "separate individual from social levels of analysis, health from social problems, representation from experience, suffering from intervention" (1997, x). In their search for ways to connect social-structural violence with language and pain, with image and suffering, they suggest that we use a "language of dismay, disappointment, bereavement, and alarm" to get at the human experience of social suffering. The work in these pages is, I believe, in the spirit of the call issued by Kleinman, Das, and Lock.

WITNESSING AND THE ANTHROPOLOGY OF HUMAN RIGHTS

Taking on a commitment to witness and write about suffering and violence requires that we critically engage with the anthropology of human rights. The insights of anthropological analysis—particularly cultural and historical analysis—are key in clarifying the rationales often provided for treating some people differently than others and for constructing them as less-than-human.

> If torture is unimaginable in unmediated form, unpresentable for what it is, its representation must be fit into existing, acceptable discourses: patriotism, retaliation for real or imagined past injustices, separatism, terrorism, communism, subversion, anarchy, the need to preserve the state's territorial integrity, the need to protect the nation from subversion through ethnic cleansing, the fight against crime, the war on drugs. (Nagengast 1994, 120)

No state or its agencies will endorse decontextualized violence as an explicit policy tool. The cultural packaging of violence—of who are acceptable victims and why—is a key ingredient in how human rights abuses come to be committed and how they are justified by states. State use of justified physical and symbolic violence is a time-honored, cross-cultural tradition. Symbolic violence includes aggressive behavior, vehement conduct, infringement of property or dignity, use of physical force, and the threat or dramatic portrayal of any of these.[2] State-sponsored political violence may involve direct physical assault but may also include "actions taken or not by the state or its agents with the express intent of realizing certain social, ethnic, economic, and political goals in the realm of public affairs, especially affairs of the state or even of social life in general" (Nagengast 1994: 114).

Many discussions of human rights in anthropology have focused on whether it is appropriate for anthropologists to impose universal definitions of human rights on particular cultures and what the consequences are of accepting culturally relevant criteria as a basis for defining human rights (Thompson 1997; Renteln 1990; Howard 1992; Messer 1993, 1995; Wilson 1997). Richard Wilson notes that debate continues to focus on universalism versus relativism and on the relevance of culture (1997, 3). As Wilson suggests, universalism is necessary to any comparative standards for human treatment, while relativism allows focus on the importance of immediate contexts.

Anthropology can provide the tools for exploring how dominant representations of the dangerous, the worthless, the marginal, and the unimportant become linked to making particular groups of people susceptible to violent abuses and to allowing them to be treated with less than human respect and dignity (see Nagengast 1994: 122; Taussig 1984; Müller-Hill 1988; Binford 1996). In each situation of human rights abuse, the key to what actually happens lies less in a deliberate ignoring of universal human rights declarations than in some particular ideological interpretation that permits and justifies the use of violence for particular ends, often political. Thus the most important criterion for analyzing human rights from an anthropological perspective is that the analysis be grounded in a particular situation linked to the actions and intentions of specific actors within the context of institutionalized power.

Critiques of the notion of universal human rights center around a falsely constructed notion of "universal" rights that, rather than being true for all beings, can be traced to the mentality of the Enlightenment and specifically to the production of a particular document, at a particular time, tied to particular ideological interests: the Universal Declaration of Human Rights, written in 1948 in the aftermath of World War II and tied to a political philosophy seeking to unify Europe. Relativists argue that there is no universal concept of human nature—rather, human rights are based on Western notions of freedom, equality, and participation in a political system (see Jelin 1997).

As Sally Merry (1997, 28) points out, anthropologists have often been reluctant to associate themselves with engagement with human rights movements because "they feel that the concept of human rights is an artifact of Western cultural traditions raised to the status of global normativity." The stance of cultural relativism has been used by anthropologists to try to understand violence in its particular context and to avoid universal pronouncements of truth—essentially an effort to avoid ethnocentrism. I believe, with Merry, however, that this stance is no longer acceptable or even viable for anthropologists. Human rights legal discourses are no longer strictly bound to Western legal and political institutions.

Human rights discourses now exist in a globalized context and have been deployed and debated by a wide range of states and by indigenous communities and movements from a variety of perspectives. Some states have used the logic of cultural relativism to criticize universal notions of human rights and to defend political practices considered abhorrent by many—defending, for instance, the maintenance of unequal and repressive political systems as "traditional." The global human rights discourse has also been appropriated and refashioned by a great range of social movements to make claims on states. Indigenous movements in many contexts have circumvented governments and gone directly to international human rights bodies to try to pressure states to adhere to agreements already signed (see Keck and Sikkink 1998; Sikkink 1991; Brysk 2000). Thus the notions of human rights currently claimed and practiced by indigenous movements are perhaps based on Western liberal legal ideas but are "no longer exclusively owned by the West" (Merry 1997, 29). As Merry notes: "As various societies mobilize Western law in their demands for human rights, they reinterpret and transform Western law in accordance with their own local legal conceptions and with the resources provided by the global human rights system. They talk rights, reparations, and claims—the language of law—but construct a new law out of fragments of the old" (ibid., 29).

If we follow the lead of indigenous leaders and movements in Mexico that have used spaces such as the International Labor Organization of the United Nations and elsewhere to argue, not only for individual freedoms, but also for collective rights to territory, cultural recognition, and education, the universalist/relativist debate over concepts of human rights becomes moot. Groups that have experienced political violence and marginalization from national political systems such as that of Mexico have adapted what Merry calls "a multi-layered amalgam of United Nations resolutions, national law, and local categories and customs" (1997, 29). The human rights discourse is a political tool that marginalized communities and organizations are now using to make their voices heard and to gain access to political and social systems—and to nations—from which they have long been excluded. If we anthropologists possess skills, tools, resources, and access useful in carrying out human rights work, and are expected and requested to do so by the people we work work, then we must seriously consider the relation between such work and anthropological fieldwork. As stated by Linda Green (about working in Guatemala), "[W]hat is at issue for anthropologists is with whom to cast their lot" (1995, 107).

People in communities living under the circumstances of low-intensity war often request assistance in publicizing their situation and dare not wait for several years while an anthropologist collects, analyzes, and publishes data. They may ask anthropologists to take responsibility for their privileged access to the media, other intellectuals, government officials, and policy makers, and to disseminate information to as many people as soon as possible through public presentations, teaching, writing in popular forums, and, last, perhaps, in such traditional academic products as articles in refereed journals or books published by university presses. Such were the expectations in Chiapas when I conducted fieldwork in the 1990s.

This book is written in the spirit of joining more traditional anthropological fieldwork, such as that I carried out in two ejidos in Oaxaca, with the anthropology of witnessing—a more accurate description of part of my fieldwork in Chiapas. To tell the story of how and why Emiliano Zapata, the Mexican Revolution, and the Mexican nation mean different things to rural men and women in Chiapas and Oaxaca, I had to reach deep into the methodological toolkits of anthropology and history. In the process, I found that the "field" of my project was global, as was the set of relations binding me to those I worked with. Witnessing, telling, and conversing were primary modes of conveying information both "in the field" and on the page—and how and why we become engaged in the research projects we do is an important part of the stories we tell. Finally, I found that I was expected to follow the lead of those I was working with, and to use my skills, resources, and access to make a contribution to ongoing work in what have come to be called the human rights and indigenous rights movements.

CHAPTER 2

Government Construction and Reappropriation of Emiliano Zapata

This chapter looks primarily at one side of the interaction between the Mexican government and local communities, focusing on how the government mobilized Emiliano Zapata and the Mexican Revolution to consolidate a postrevolutionary state and promote a dominant nationalism, first in the 1920s and 1930s, then from 1990 through the end of agrarian reform as Mexico restructured economically to meet NAFTA guidelines. During the 1930s, the arenas of education, art, peasant organizing, and the granting of land to rural communities as *ejidos* were primary paths for the diffusion of government claims to Zapata and the Mexican Revolution. In the 1990s, the primary paths were through a government program to map, measure, and encourage privatization of land, the Programa de Certificación de Derechos Ejidales y Titulación de Solares Urbanos (Program for the Certification of Ejidal Land Rights and the Titling of Urban House Lots), or PROCEDE, and a crop-subsidy program, the Programa de Apoyo Directo al Campo (Direct Rural Support Program), or PROCAMPO. Just as rural school teachers promoting socialist education in rural communities in the 1930s were agents of nationalism, PROCEDE personnel who flocked to thousands of Mexico's ejidos in the 1990s were also peddling a new vision of the nation—one consistent with free trade and the positive value of individual property.

This chapter emphasizes what the government has put forward as national ideology linked to the revolution, and how programs to disseminate this ideology functioned in the states of Chiapas and Oaxaca in the

1930s and in the 1990s, while the following chapters focus on the absorption, reworking, reinterpretation, and redeployment of this ideology back to the center by rural communities. The present chapter thus documents and compares the dominant visions of nationalism disseminated by the government in the 1930s and 1990s that provided primary material for counterhegemonic and multiple views of the nation generated at the local level; the chapters that follow make clear that there are large gaps between elite visions of nationalism and their reception and reinterpretation in various population sectors and regions.

Another focus in this chapter is the special role of educational institutions and materials (both inside and outside formal efforts by the government's department of education). Schooling—both within formal educational institutions and through other efforts to inculcate knowledge into people, such as educational meetings in communities—is an important arena of elite attempts at cultural reproduction (see Bourdieu 1967, 1977; Anderson 1983; Vaughn 1997; Arnove 1993, 1999). Indeed, textbooks and other materials with wide dissemination are important sources of official histories to examine for clues to the origins of raw material for varied nation views.

ZAPATA AND THE FIRST POSTREVOLUTIONARY DECADES

One key problem of nation-states is how to transcend difference. States claim to transcend individual and local differences by molding citizens into a unitary identity, much as do religious systems such as Christianity (Herzfeld 1992, 6). As stated by Clifford Geertz in an important early essay on nationalism and postcolonialism:

> The first, formative stage of nationalism consisted essentially of confronting the dense assemblage of cultural, racial, local, and linguistic categories of self-identification and social loyalty that centuries of uninstructed history had produced with a simple, abstract, deliberately constructed, and almost painful self-conscious concept of political ethnicity—a proper "nationality" in the modern manner. . . . The men who raised this challenge, the nationalist intellectuals, were thus launching a revolution as much cultural, even epistemological, as it was political. (Geertz 1973, 239)

Key in this unification is the shaping of the individual as a citizen and the promotion of "equality" for all citizens under state power. To create citizens out of differing individuals, a sense of national identity must be created and successfully disseminated through ideological systems and symbols; the system of symbols disseminated by nationalist intellectuals through education and agrarian reform in the 1930s in Mexico, documented in this chapter, is an example of how nationalism is constructed.

While states clearly engage in campaigns to promote national unity and create national identity (i.e., Anderson 1983's sense of "imagined community"), local nationalisms (imagined communities in the plural) also produce different interpretations of "the nation." Prasenjit Duara (1996) has referred to such interpretations as "nation views" informed by local identities and histories. The process of nation-building involves dissemination by government institutions and employees of coordinated sets of ideas about what it means to be a citizen and a part of "the nation," but these disseminated ideas are also subject to local and regional interpretations that are redeployed back to the national level, where they in turn affect state policy and ideology. Key in the state's attempts to create systems that unify the nation are attempts at "legibility and simplification" through which officials take complex, unrecognizable local social practices, "such as land tenure customs or naming customs," to create "a standard grid" whereby they can be centrally recorded and monitored (Scott 1998, 2). The fact that twentieth-century state-building requires standardization and uniformity is a testimony to on-the-ground local variety of social, legal, cultural and economic practices.

Taking off from James Scott's notion of "seeing like a state" (1998), let us consider the problem of consolidating many different Mexicos into one nation following the Mexican Revolution. In 1910, Mexico had roughly 15 million inhabitants. About 11 million were rural, either attached to large ranches and plantations or struggling to survive on very small plots of land, plots continually eroded by pressure from liberal land laws that permitted measuring and privatization of "empty" lands. The urban worker population was only about 195,000, divided between an anticlerical anarchist-syndicalist tradition and the Catholic tradition of cooperativism and mutual aid societies modeled on those of Europe (Brachet-Márquez 1997, 1120). The upper classes were divided between factions associated with the Porfirian state (hacienda owners, foreign investors, the Catholic Church), a faction opposed to the Díaz regime (small industry owners), and others (ibid., 1118). Mexico also had considerable regional and ethnic diversity. At the end of the Porfiriato, the mestizo population was about 50 percent, indigenous Mexicans were 35 percent, and criollos of Spanish descent and foreigners made up the rest of the total Mexican population (Lewis 1997b, 839).

This diversity of ethnic, regional, class, and political interest groups allowed for neither a unified Mexican Revolution nor a unified population when it was over. Quite the contrary.

EMILIANO ZAPATA AND THE MEXICAN REVOLUTION

Emiliano Zapata came to represent the landless rural people of the south of Mexico after he helped organize a small guerrilla movement in 1911 in response to Francisco Madero's 1910 call to arms to remove Porfirio Díaz from power. Zapata was born in 1879 and raised in the village of Anenecuilco in the state of Morelos. He is described by John Womack as not a poor man. The Zapata family "lived in a solid adobe-and-stone house, not a hut. Neither he [Emiliano] nor his older brother, Eufemio, had ever worked as day laborers on the haciendas, and both had inherited a little land and some livestock when their parents died" (Womack 1968, 6). Womack states that Anenecuilcans recalled that as a child, Emiliano had seen his father cry in frustration when he saw a village orchard enclosed by a local hacienda. This local story recounts that Emiliano promised his father he would get the land back. This is supposed to have occurred when he was nine years old (ibid., 6).

As an adult, Emiliano worked his land, sharecropped a few more acres for a local hacienda, and trained horses. He occasionally bought and sold horses. When he was seventeen, he had to flee the state of Morelos to avoid arrest for a minor infraction at a fiesta (Brunk 1997, 1633). According to Womack, getting in trouble with the police was "almost a puberty rite" (Womack 1968, 5). In his twenties, Emiliano began to focus on defending local lands, and in 1906 he became involved in the defense, in the courts, of Anenecuilco's land (Brunk 1997, 1633). He also became involved in village defense and in organizing the campaign of an opposition candidate for governor. Womack points out that, although the political party Zapata worked for suffered a humiliating defeat— "voters intimidated, votes not counted, leaders arrested and deported to labor camps in Yucatán"—in the process of participating in the campaign, Emiliano met many opposition politicians and established personal connections with them (Womack 1968, 5). This was a useful resource during the revolution. In 1909, Emiliano Zapata was elected president of the Anenecuilco village council, and in 1910 he resolved a local land dispute by occupying the land in question with a group of eighty armed men (Brunk 1997, 1533).

Although at first a small guerrilla army, Zapata's forces quickly grew large enough to capture Cuautla, Morelos. In 1911, peace treaties allowed Porfirio Díaz to go into exile, an interim president was named, and elections were held. In June 1911, as he neared his thirty-second birthday, Emiliano Zapata married Josefa Espejo, the daughter of a modestly prosperous livestock dealer. Womack writes about the meaning of this marriage for Zapata, and relates it to the fact that he already had at least one child by another woman.

> In rural Mexico, marriage was not simply for siring offspring, or for love. Zapata already had at least one child (by another woman) and no doubt assumed—it was a common male assumption—he would have many more by many women he cared about. Marriage was a more solemn proceeding: a contract, a *contrato de matrimonio,* as people called it, entry into which gave a man a place in his community. Marriage was for the grave business of establishing a legitimate family, for creating recognized heirs and securing incontestably one more generation in the clan's name—which was what a man did to institute a private life among his neighbors. (Womack 1968, 107–8)

In the winter of 1911, Francisco I. Madero, who had been jailed while running for president against Porfirio Díaz in 1910, overthrew the Díaz government. Before his election to the presidency, Madero ordered all the revolutionary bands and armies to turn in their weapons. Zapata met with Madero in the summer of 1911 and told him that his troops would not lay down arms until there was agrarian reform. In August 1911, while Emiliano Zapata was still celebrating his wedding, troops were sent against him, under the command of General Victoriano Huerta. Zapata took up arms again, this time to fight against what was supposed to be a revolutionary regime. Over that summer and fall, Zapata's movement picked up steam in Morelos.

In November 1911, Zapata joined forces with a schoolmaster, Otilio Montaño, to compose the "Plan of Ayala." This document was intended to explain his cause to those outside the state of Morelos and articulated many of the Zapatistas' key demands. The Plan of Ayala demanded land and water rights for peasants and called not only for the return of property stolen by the haciendas but also for expropriation of additional lands from the haciendas to give to landless peasants. As noted by Samuel Brunk (1997, 1633), the Plan also called for complete confiscation of the property of those who opposed the Zapatistas. The Plan also insisted on people's right to choose their own representatives.

When Zapata signed the Plan of Ayala, he and his chiefs declared themselves in rebellion against the federal government of Madero. He and his movement held to the content of the Plan throughout the next decade.

Madero faced three armed rebellions in addition to that of the Zapatistas, before a coup orchestrated by Victoriano Huerta abruptly ended his term by assassination in 1913. While Huerta sought to make peace with the Zapatistas, Emiliano did not trust the new leader's promises and the war continued. Zapatismo grew, and peasants from Morelos, Mexico, Puebla, Guerrero, and even Oaxaca joined Zapata or his allies against the Huerta regime (Brunk 1997, 1633). The Zapatistas seized major centers of sugar production, commerce, communication, and government administration, running them on models of community self-government (Cockcroft 1998, 97). By 1914, Zapata had become one of the most prominent leaders of the revolution, controlled large parts of Morelos and neighboring states, and was a serious threat to Mexico City. That year, Huerta's dictatorial regime was defeated by the Constitutionalists, led by Venustiano Carranza.

By 1915, the Constitutionalists had driven a firm wedge between the allied forces of Zapata in Morelos and Pancho Villa north of Mexico City, and, by the end of 1915, the Zapatistas and Villistas were no longer a military threat to the Carrancistas. While the Villistas and Zapatistas continued to fight in 1916 and 1917—and even later—they could not maintain a strong opposition. In 1917, Carranza, "first chief of the Constitutionalist Army," was inaugurated president of Mexico.

Radical and moderate factions among the constitutionalists disrupted the Constitutional Convention of 1914 in Aguascalientes, and even after the 1917 constitution was written, setting forth a program of many social and labor reforms, the agrarian reform called for was not nearly as extensive as that advocated by the Zapatistas. The model of a strong central government written into the constitution would severely limit the political autonomy of local communities and, at least implicitly, condition those rights upon support for the government. This was particularly true for rural Mexicans, since the government bestowed property rights (ejido rights) on behalf of the nation. Zapata and his followers continued to militate for more radical agrarian reform and redistribution. In 1919, Carranza had Zapata assassinated, silencing an agrarian radical on his way to becoming a national saint.

CONSOLIDATION OF THE POSTREVOLUTIONARY GOVERNMENT

Presidents Alvaro Obregón (1920–24) and Plutarco Elías Calles (1924–28) both worked to consolidate the government after the revolution, in which nearly two million Mexicans, or 12 percent of the population, perished (Cockcroft 1998, 107). At the beginning of the 1920s, political power was regional, lodged with military governors. Central instruments of economic and monetary policy had to be created, and national censuses, as well as a new system of rural normal schools, cultural missions, and training seminaries were established. Elections also became more centrally controlled. Obregón used the bureaucracy of education and rural schools, as well as the National Agrarian Commission and the Partido Agrarista (Agrarianist Party), to extend control over the rural population. Obregón and successive presidents of Mexico became closely identified with land redistribution because, as a result of legislation passed in 1921 and 1922, only the president could grant definitive title to land, by presidential decree (Vaughn 1982, 129)—although states could provisionally distribute land with the approval of the National Agrarian Commission. The 1921–22 legislation fostered much correspondence between local ejido authorities and Mexican presidents in the struggle to secure land. The central government also attempted to gain control over the states through eliminating stubborn generals' holds on regional power, through professionalizing the army, and through providing investment opportunities. Calles strengthened his control over the military through a series of alliances with power holders at the state level.

The greatest challenge to centralized government power was posed by the Cristero Rebellion. Between 1926 and 1929, when Calles enforced the anticlerical clauses of the 1917 constitution, tens of thousands of peasants rebelled, primarily in central-west Mexico. They were protesting not only the anticlerical regime of Calles, but also the government's agrarian reform program and the removal of local religious and political authorities. For those in the Cristero Rebellion, anticlericalism was perceived as an attack on communities, local cultures, and local political autonomy (see Purnell 1997, 1999). The revolt was a major financial and political preoccupation of the government.

During his tenure, Calles had to limit social reform in order to increase capital investment in Mexico (see Vaughn 1982, 131–32). This meant serving the needs of both foreign and national capital. Banking and financial reforms were instituted in 1924 and 1925 to create an alliance between private capital and the government. Throughout his tenure, Calles progressively expropriated less and less land for redistribution as ejidos; in 1925 he decreed the expropriation of 956,852 hectares, in 1926 the expropriation of 502,700 hectares, and in 1927 the expropriation of 289,933 hectares (Vaughn 1982, 132). In 1927, Luis Léon, Calles's minister of agriculture, emphasized the right of owners to contest peasant land claims. In states such as Oaxaca, many petitions for land were denied by Calles. In 1928, the assassination of Alvaro Obregón, who was to succeed Calles, precipitated a political crisis, resolved by forming the Partido Nacional Revolucionario (PNR—National Revolutionary Party,), which brought the military and regional political power brokers into one structure. This event marked a turning point in the government's move to consolidate power over the disparate regions of Mexico.

The Mexican government made itself a central actor in education when, in 1921, President Alvaro Obregón created the Ministry of Public Education (Secretaría de Educación Pública, or SEP). The proposal for the creation of the SEP came from the philosopher and social critic José Vasconcelos, who equated Mexican national identity with the mestizo—"the final race, the cosmic race." His proposal for nationalism called for "mestizoizing" the nation. The cosmic race, according to Vasconcelos, would capture "the abyss of the Indian soul; the Negro's eagerness for sensual happiness; the Mongol, whose oblique eyes make him see everything in unexpected perspectives; the Judaic strains in the Spanish blood; the melancholy of the Arab; and the [rationality] of the white whose thought is as lucid as his skin" (1958, 923). As stated by Stephen E. Lewis, "state- and nation-builders after 1920 came to an ideological consensus concerning 'the Indian problem.' There would be no room for the defenders of indigenous languages and culture in the postrevolutionary Mexican state. 'Incorporation' became gospel" (Lewis 1997b, 839). The Ministry of Public Education and the establishment of a federal system of schools, particularly in rural areas, would be key to slowly but surely assimilating Mexico's indigenous population into the nation. The dominant theme of public education was "civilizing" rural, primarily indigenous, peasants.

In the 1920s, pedagogues such as Moisés Saenz and Rafael Ramírez "took on contemporary notions of child-centered, action education and fashioned them into a learning-by-doing curriculum oriented towards community development" (Vaughn 1997, 443). Rural schools were conceived as places where the indigenous population would be civilized— meaning they would be trained in rationality and modern market behavior. The educator's view of rural people came from the nineteenth-century liberal view of indigenous communities as closed and backward, comprised of individuals who needed an education for skills, behavior modification, and product diversification (Vaughn 1982, 145). The focus of SEP rural education in the 1920s was thus to integrate individuals into the market economy, communities into the nation. The educational philosophy of the SEP is an excellent example of what James Scott calls high-modernist ideology: a strong "version of the self-confidence about scientific and technical progress, the expansion of production, the growing satisfaction of human needs, the mastery of nature (including human nature), and, above all, the rational design of social order commensurate with the scientific understanding of natural laws" (Scott 1998, 4). The impact of rural schools in the 1920s, of course, varied from place to place.

The states of Oaxaca and Chiapas make an interesting comparison in evaluating the penetration of rural schools in the 1920s, although looking at each state as a whole underplays regional variation in each. The state of Oaxaca seems to have been much more aggressive in its primary school policy than was Chiapas. While Oaxaca had a 27 percent increase in state primary school enrollment from 1920 to 1928, Chiapas had a 55 percent decline in such enrollment during this period (Vaughn 1982, 156). In 1928, 35 percent of the school-age population in Oaxaca was in primary school, but only 10 percent in Chiapas. Nevertheless, by the end of Calles's reign, the vast majority of children in both states were not attending school.

Other cultural processes took place in the 1920s under the educational leadership of Vasconcelos, primarily in the urban spaces of Mexico. In 1920, Vasconcelos called together such artists as Davíd Alfaro Siquieros, José Clemento Orozco, and Diego Rivera to participate in a crusade for Mexican national culture as expressed through art. In 1923, the Syndicate of Revolutionary Painters was formed, including Rivera, Orozco, Siquieros, and others. These painters committed themselves to painting Mexican history and to depicting the Mexican Revolution through monumental art accessible to the public. Upsetting the prevailing notions of beauty tied to nostalgia, order, and lyricism, the muralists conceived of beauty that "would suggest struggle and arouse it" (Vaughn 1982, 261). Their initial murals, in the National Preparatory School, were not well received at first. The murals were roundly condemned by students, public intellectuals, and others. Rivera painted Emiliano Zapata and the Revolution in broad strokes, on buildings ranging from the

Ministry of Education to the National Palace. In the "Court of Fiestas," painted by Rivera in 1925–26 inside the Ministry of Public Education, Zapata appears as a martyred saint. In another Rivera mural in the SEP buildings, "Cantando el corrido" ("Singing the Ballad"), a Zapata-look-alike guitarist accompanies a singer from whose mouth come the words "Zapata, beloved here, everyone is united, there isn't anyone to fight with" (Secretaría de Educación Pública 1982, cover).

Rivera's images of Zapata and the Mexican Revolution were seen by few in the 1920s. It was not until the 1930s, when the left wing of the PNR came to power under Lázaro Cárdenas, that the mural movement achieved greater legitimacy and the images became more broadly diffused in Mexican society. Under Cárdenas, the work of the muralists was incorporated into school textbooks and other publications of the SEP. These 1930s publications became the official canon of Mexican history, particularly in their portrayal of Zapata and the Mexican Revolution, and since the 1930s, they have been part of the common educational experience of many Mexican children.

CONSOLIDATING THE HEROISM OF ZAPATA IN THE 1930S

During the period 1934–40, under President Lázaro Cárdenas, the growth of the SEP and the promotion of socialist education in rural schools, as well as the accelerated agrarian reform program and the subsequent organization of ejidatarios into the Confederación Nacional Campesina (National Peasants' Confederation), or CNC, originally formed as the Committee of Organizations of Peasant Unification in 1935, were key pieces in a government-run campaign to create a national popular culture around the Mexican Revolution signaling the Mexican government as its main inheritor (see Vaughn 1997). This period marks a time when thousands of rural schoolteachers, engineers, and other government personnel fanned over the Mexican countryside and attempted to connect its farthest corners with the central government. A parallel can be made with the sending of thousands of personnel in the 1990s from the Agrarian Attorney's Office to ejidos throughout Mexico to market and implement the end of agrarian reform and PROCEDE. In the 1930s, the sanitization of Emiliano Zapata and his re-creation as a popular national hero, the writing of songs about the Revolution, the promotion of civic rituals on the day of Zapata's death to reinforce his memory, the use of the Mexican Revolution, Plan de

Ayala, and Zapata's image to sell, celebrate, and codify agrarian reform and agricultural programs, the SEP-sponsored radio shows emphasizing the revolution—all of these events, texts, and interactions created a common set of national symbols received in widely varying segments of Mexican society. Anyone who attended school for any period of time from the 1930s onward received significant doses of state revolutionary culture and heroics. Those who may have interacted with agrarian officials since the 1930s—through petitioning for land, receiving small loans, participating in productive programs, receiving guaranteed prices, or taking part in the CNC—also were exposed to official discourses on Zapata and the inheritance of the Mexican Revolution, at CNC-sponsored rallies, particularly those held on the day of Zapata's death. A wide range of people—including elite urban pupils who later went into the government, leftist intellectuals who became organizers and mentors in regional peasant and production-oriented organizations, rural men and women who attended primary school or who lived in a town where a school held civic activities, and ejidatarios/as who petitioned for land and interacted with agrarian officials and may have been part of the CNC—were exposed to decades of nationalist culture built around images of the Mexican Revolution, solidified under the Cárdenas presidency.

A significant number of researchers have documented the efforts of the Mexican government to create and continue to promote its claim to the Mexican Revolution, efforts beginning in the 1920s, but developed in a concerted way in the 1930s under Lázaro Cárdenas (Vaughn 1997; Palacios 1998; Martin 1993; Knight 1994). While these works document the resources put into promoting national culture, particularly in the 1930s, all are circumspect about the results of the state's investment. Rather than subscribing to a version of state hegemony that results in the uniform absorption of national cultural icons, programs, and symbols, these authors find significant variation in local community and regional responses to nationalist education and propaganda since the 1930s. Such findings are significant to the story in the present volume, which also suggests that, while a wide range of the Mexican populace were repeatedly exposed to a uniform set of national symbols and elements from the 1930s to the present, its deployment in local contexts, and then from local contexts back to regional and national contexts, exhibits tremendous variation. What distinguishes this process in the 1990s from the past is that the current neo-Zapatista reinterpretation of Mex-

ican history broadcast from Chiapas has a national and global resonance owing to the presence of the media and the use of the Internet as
an organizing tool.

EMILIANO ZAPATA AND *AGRARISMO* IN THE 1930S

In the SEP construction of Zapata, his image was retooled to match the
needs of a nationalist campaign to build the political party of Cárdenas
and ensure values that inspired loyalty to the government. "When the
SEP constructed Zapata as a hero, they sanitized him: He did not drink,
womanize, or gamble, nor did he carry the banner of the Virgin of Guadalupe. The snappy horseman from Tlalitzapan, who enjoyed a match
of fighting cocks and had fathered many children in his short life, became a didactic articulator of SEP values" (Vaughn 1997, 42). Because
the formation of ejidos usually involved the designation of a plot of land
and the construction of a school, the agrarian rhetoric that circulated
through the process of petitioning for land often coincided with discussions of education. Ejidos usually solicited additional funds for building
a school while petitioning for ejido land, as Unión Zapata in Oaxaca did
in 1936. The government's discourse about the revolution circulated
through communities through a variety of official channels. Revolutionary rhetoric was also used by would-be ejidatarios to push higher level
officials to act on their petitions—bidding them to exercise their authority to "provide land for those who work it."

Where and how was Zapata canonized in education in the 1930s?
The primary arena was textbooks and, of course, the rural schoolteachers who used the texts. Books such as *Fermín,* one of the first readers to
focus on rural life published in 1933, consciously attempts to popularize the Mexican Revolution. In the preface, author Manuel Velásquez
Andrade informs readers that Fermín—the son of a peon who labored
on an hacienda—"is [one] of thousands of Mexican children whose
existence we don't know about or have ignored" (Velásquez Andrade
1933, 5). He adds that "Fermín symbolizes the past, the present, and a
future reality of the benefits that the Mexican Revolution has already
brought and those that it will bring in the future for peasant and workers." (ibid., 6). The intentions of the author in producing this book for
thousands of schoolchildren are clearly stated. Works of Diego Rivera
celebrating the Revolution were integrated into the text as illustrations.

The book begins in 1910, describing how Fermín and his family live
and work, highlighting an evil hacienda majordomo who "never is happy

with the work" and "sometimes gets so mad that he even beats the workers" (ibid.). Fermín's father joins the Revolution and, about midway through the book, encounters a "leader in the Revolution " who "grabbed the flag of the rural proletarian cause and began the struggle again" (ibid., 33–34). Next to the text is a picture of Emiliano Zapata bearing a flag reading "Land and Liberty."

Two pages later, in a discussion of the redistribution of land, another drawing by Rivera shows an armed group of Zapatistas speaking to a group of peasants. A bubble from one person's mouth reads: "The land belongs to everyone, like the air, the water, the light, and the heat of the sun. Those who work the land with their own hands have the right to it" (ibid., 37). The tale ends in 1917, with Fermín and his mother and father living in a modest adobe house, working their ejido land, and also renting land from a nearby hacienda. At the end of the book, Fermín is "dressed better than the majordomo," and he has two six-guns crossed above his bed to "protect his rights." The content of *Fermín* efficiently distills the SEP version of the revolution through words and Rivera's illustrations: the rural peasants overthrew the landlords, the foreign exploiters, and the rich. They won the right to ejido lands, which were redistributed by the government. They organized themselves and are ever-vigilant in continuing to defend the rights of the rural proletariat. And the revolutionary government backs them 100 percent.

In 1935, the SEP published *Simiente,* a set of four illustrated books for rural primary schools by Gabriel Lucio. These four books were disseminated widely to rural areas, and a close analysis of them reveals a consistent set of messages regarding the importance of agrarian and worker activism; the rights and obligations of peasants to have land, work hard on it, and farm it collectively; the problems with individualism; the importance of hygiene; the importance of community activities and organizing; the importance of schools and teachers and of national figures (most prominently Cuauhtémoc, Hidalgo, Juárez, and Zapata); and appropriate gender roles for rural boys and girls, men and women (Lucio 1935a, 1935b, 1935c, 1935d). In examining textbook orders placed by school officials in Oaxaca from 1935 to 1940 stored in the General Archives of the State of Oaxaca, I found the *Simiente* series to have been widely used (see, e.g., Pinacho 1938, an inventory report that documents the presence of *Simiente* books). A few lessons from the *Simiente* series may be outlined that deal with agrarian activism themes and Emiliano Zapata. I argue that these ideas were disseminated through textbooks, as well as through popular cultural events such as the annual mass meetings on 10 April to commemorate the death of Emiliano Zapata. Such dissemination efforts were consolidated under the presidency of Cárdenas and continued for decades.

The first book in the *Simiente* series saves the ideas of Zapata for the end of the school year. At the end of the book—after several lessons on how bees, spiders, ants, and children are all workers—the concluding entry is a poem entitled "I will be an *agrarista* [agrarian activist]." The illustration features a peasant in the countryside sporting a rifle, sandals, and flag. Assuming a male subject, the poem reads:

I will be an agrarista
when I am grown up
dear mother,
I will be an agrarista
like my father.
I will have my
well-built house,
a pair of oxen
and a cow;
a bunch of rabbits,
a lot of chickens;
my beehives
and my vegetables.
Near or far
from my house,
I will have my sown ground,
I will be an agrarista.
I will have my horse
I will have my gun
so that the fruit of my labor
can't be taken from me
and those audacious *latifundistas* [large estate owners]
won't even think of asking me for it.
For my class,
my suffering class,
when I work
I will be an agrarista.
Always fighting,
all of my life,
these words
will be my guide
ALL OF THE LAND, ALL, ALL OF IT
FOR THE PEOPLE WHO WORK IT
[LA TIERRA TODA,
TODA, TODITA,
PARA LOS HOMBRES

QUE LA CULTIVAN].
When I am grown up
my dear mother,
I will be an agrarista
like my father.

Manuel G. Mejia (Lucio 1935a, 89–91)

A classroom of twenty children reciting this poem together would verbally articulate some of the key elements the SEP used to reconstruct the Mexican Revolution and integrate it into education. The right of all peasants to land is implicit in the poem, as is the notion of the progress brought by the Revolution (as carried out by the Cárdenas government in the 1930s), represented by the well-built house, the animals being raised, and the vegetable garden. The notion of class—that is, a peasant class—is introduced vis-à-vis a "suffering class," and implied by the future agrarista's unwillingness to let "audacious landowners" even think of asking for his land. The security of the land is ensured through the presence of a horse and a gun. The identity of the future agrarista is thus coded as that of a rural peasant, with a reasonably comfortable material existence, who opposes latifundistas, identifies as part of a "suffering" class of people who work the land, and is prepared to defend his gains with arms, if necessary. The message is similar to that projected in *Fermín*. The figure of Zapata is behind this poem, by implication, in the words "All of the land, all, all of it for the people who work it."

The second textbook of *Simiente* formally introduces children to the figure of Zapata in a new entry and repeats themes found in the poem. Zapata is featured in a drawing showing him wearing his characteristic hat and posed in front of a large banner reading "Land and Liberty." The text begins: "If the peasants have achieved having their own lands to cultivate, they owe this to Emiliano Zapata. It was he who demanded with great courage that the revolution initiated in 1910 should defend the principle 'free land for everyone, land without overseers and landlords'" (Lucio 1935b, 94). This passage thus links the future agraristas clearly to the figure of Emiliano Zapata. The text continues:

Emiliano Zapata was the son of peasants who lived in the state of Morelos.
Ever since he was a boy he could see the sad life that the workers in the countryside had on the large haciendas.
They earned really low wages, just a few cents per day, which were then taken away by the hacienda owners in the *tiendas de raya* [company or hacienda stores], where basic goods were sold at very high prices.
The ignorance that existed because of the lack of schools and religious fanaticism kept them [the rural workers] in conditions of infamous slavery.

When Emiliano Zapata was only eight years old, he saw the land that was all of his father's property taken away by an hacienda owner. Indignant at the injustice he had just witnessed, the boy exclaimed:

—Father, when I am grown up, I am going to make them return our land! . . .

He grew up and when he learned about all of the abuses suffered by the peasants, the desire in his heart to free his brothers and sisters from their suffering grew stronger.

Because of this he began a revolution, which was followed by thousands of peasants who loved him and respected him.

He came to dominate a vast region of the country and distributed lands to the peasants.

He was a brave man who was feared by his enemies. They couldn't beat him in battle so they resorted to the villainy of deceit: a colonel of the enemy assassinated the leader of the south in a cowardly way after he motioned the Zapatista troops past him.

That is how Emiliano Zapata, defender of the peasants, died.

But his ideas of justice have extended through the entire nation and now reside in the soul of the Mexican people.

His desire that land be distributed to all of the people in the countryside is being realized. The peasants should honor the memory of this noble and generous Mexican, they should defend the rights they have won, working hard on their land so that they don't lose their existence as free men. (Lucio 1935b, 94–96)

If there was any doubt in the minds of children attending school in the 1930s that they should see their personal situation as linked to the legacy of Zapata, it would probably have been resolved in reading such a passage. Through seeing Zapata as a key national figure in the *Simiente* series of textbooks, young children learned that the government was part of Zapata's legacy and was the entity responsible for ensuring that Emiliano's desire "that land be distributed to all the people in the countryside" was realized. The sanitized version of Zapata's life served up in *Simiente* focuses solely on his role in struggling for land, his betrayal by an enemy, and the importance of his ideas for all Mexicans. He is the "defender" of the peasants. Because he died through treachery, lived to serve the rural poor, and "lives in the soul of the Mexican people," he is also set up for martyrdom in the national canon. He is clearly positioned as a national symbol with special resonance and meaning for rural children and families.

Another entry in the second *Simiente* textbook, preceding that on Zapata, makes Cárdenas's claim to Zapata explicit for any reader. Referring to the rights of all those living in the countryside to possess a piece of land, the text states, "[B]ecause of this, our Government is taking care of distributing land to peasants" (Lucio 1935b, 64). The accompanying illustration shows two engineers surveying land and shaking hands with a peasant in front of a thatched house and palm tree. The entry admonishes students that it is important to cultivate the land distributed with enthusiasm, to use new cultivation methods and fertilizers, and to form cooperatives. It concludes: "[I]ntelligent farming methods will bring wealth and well-being to our peasants and will help Mexico to become a strong and powerful country" (ibid., 65). This passage neatly links the state to Zapata, and the individual to the state and to Zapata, and suggests that hard work with the appropriate fertilizer and tools will benefit not only peasants but also the country. The passage is an attempt to craft individual citizens' links to the state and to a national ideology. At the same time, it legitimizes scientific and technical progress.

These messages are also reinforced in a history lesson, "Agrarianism in Mexico: The Current Distribution of Land," in the last book in the *Simiente* series, which states:

> In the present, thanks to legislation that we have, land is being distributed to peasants and to the communities that the ejidos belong to. . . .
> The workers of the countryside have understood that this . . . opens up for them the possibility of a prosperous life in the future. Now, through groups of peasants who unify themselves and make possible the convenient organization of work, the strengthening of their class consciousness has been achieved so that they can preserve the rights they have received and obtain their complete social and economic emancipation. (Lucio 1935d, 47)

Here, the government is directly credited with giving land to communities. Having land is supposed to facilitate a prosperous life and "social and economic emancipation." The text sets up a direct relationship between rural citizens and the government. The clear use of Marxist language—"class consciousness" and "workers of the countryside"—is also an attempt to define a specific sector of the population as "peasants" or "rural workers," coinciding with the formation of the CNC a bare two years later.

Language describing peasants as a class is also used to lead children to identify with national heroes, specifically with Emiliano Zapata—by 1935, well on his way to canonization by the SEP. While some elementary textbooks briefly mention "aboriginal peoples"—for instance, an entry in *Simiente*, "Un Niño de Raza Aborigen" (A Boy of the Aboriginal Race) (Lucio 1935c, 20–21)—most of the few references to Indians locate them in the past, as part of the story of the Conquest of Mexico or as a national hero such as Cuauhtémoc, "last emperor of the valiant Aztecs" (Lucio 1935b, 24). The illustrations in the textbooks convey explicitly "mestizo" images and appear to deliberately avoid use of indigenous cultural symbols, unless in reference to the past. The language and images of the "working class" clearly predominate.

A further example of how the *Simiente* texts connect Zapata to peasants and "the working class" is found in book 3, in an entry on "Defenders of Agrarianism":

> Peasant children: conserve in your hearts with true veneration the memory of Emiliano Zapata and the other brave champions who died defending agrarian rights; to them our parents owe the right to cultivate freely on their own lands; when we are grown up, we will always remain united, struggling for the betterment of the working class we belong to. (Lucio 1935c, 126)

As a package, the *Simiente* series thus distills many elements of agrarian nationalism that the Cárdenas government sought to instill in rural children and their families, as the government centralized and attempted to incorporate as many rural people into its structures as possible, primarily through schools and the organization of ejidos, and through the subsequent organization of ejidatarios into what became the CNC.[1]

While it is not difficult to demonstrate the canonizing of Zapata and promotion of the Mexican Revolution through the program of socialist education in the 1930s, the impact over time of SEP programs on indigenous communities in states like Chiapas and Oaxaca is a different and complex question. In the chapters that follow, it will become clear that the intent of the various SEP programs to promote a top-down, uniform nationalist ideology was clearly not realized. Regional differences within and between states, as well as the different paths that images and ideas about Zapata traveled to reach rural communities in Oaxaca and Chiapas, are important considerations. While formal educational programs were clearly not the path that Zapata traveled to the Lacandon region of Chiapas, they did have some impact in local appropriations and use of Zapata in the fashioning of community histories in central Oaxaca as revealed in oral histories conducted there. In eastern Chiapas, the incorporation of Zapata into local and regional culture came much later; it was not until the 1970s and 1980s, through the creation of regional peasant organizations carried out in conjunction with organizers from the urban Mexican left, that Zapata entered the language of agrarian struggle in Chiapas.

SCHOOLING IN OAXACA IN THE 1930S

If impact were measured through attendance, then the SEP could have initially declared success in integrating Oaxaca's children into the nation in the early 1930s. Between the years 1930 and 1935, the number of children in school in the state of Oaxaca nearly doubled, from 54,289 to 111,103 (Martínez Vásquez 1994, 113). This figure decreased in 1940 to 78,697, but still represented a substantial gain (ibid., 116). The numbers of teachers in the state increased from 1,631 in 1930 to 2,037 in 1940 (ibid., 115). The reason for this qualitative leap is linked to an intensive campaign, outlined by Lázaro Cárdenas in his six-year presidential plan, to substantially increase the number of schools in the country.

Cárdenas's presidency was personalized for many in Oaxaca through two visits he made to the state. The first was in April 1934, when he was the presidential candidate of the PNR. The second was in March 1937, midway through his presidency, as he sought to consolidate support for sectoral worker and peasant organizations, as well as for his program of socialist education. On both occasions, he spent several weeks in the state and met with thousands of individuals from a wide range of regional areas and social sectors. Following each visit, there was a flurry of activity to follow up on his plans. His strong presence in the central valleys on both visits helped inspire educators and others to promote his educational plans. He had less of this kind of contact in indigenous highland Chiapas.

In 1934, the third article of the Mexican constitution was modified to implement the government's call for socialist education. The vocabulary of a socialist discourse was part of mainstream educational pedagogy in Mexico, as illustrated by the *Simiente* textbook series. Under Cárdenas, the ideas of socialist education were supposed to reach to the farthest and most isolated corners of the nation. In a speech in Guadalajara, Cárdenas stated that socialist education should be available to all, so that "it can spiritually liberate the working and peasant classes so that they will not remain in the hands of hypocrites and deceivers who only want to keep them in the dark, so it [socialist education] can maintain the spirit of the masses like workers and peasants and especially the consciousness of women and the spirit of children living in ignorance" (Martínez Vásquez 1994, 131).

Efforts to promote socialist education in Oaxaca got under way in 1934 with the naming of a professor to study the problems of such education there. Several state-level committees, including the "Central Committee against Vice," "Committee for Peasant and Worker Homes," and "Committee for the Proletarian Child," were formed. These sought to foment similar committees at the local level (see Martínez Vásquez 1994, 133). Communities throughout the state were instructed to form committees such as the "Committee to Combat Fanaticism," which aimed at eliminating religious doctrine and disempowering local priests; the "Anti-Alcohol Committee"; the "League of Mothers of Families" and "League of Fathers of Families"; and the "Holiday Committee," which organized civic events, including homages to Emiliano Zapata, Benito Juárez, and other national figures. The education section of the General Archives of the State of Oaxaca contains reams of reports on the activities and finances from these groups, which were formed throughout the state but were most successful in the city of Oaxaca and in the central valleys, if the numbers of reports are accurate indicators.

The First Congress for Socialist Education was held in the city of Oaxaca on 25–28 February 1935. Its sponsors included the Confederation of Peasant Leagues and the Chamber of Labor of the State of Oaxaca. All school personnel were "invited" to the event, in a memo circulated by the general secretary of public education of the state of Oaxaca. The invitation was in fact notification of required attendance, as all teachers not at the opening ceremony and program would be reported to the state government (Ramírez Erastro 1935).

Efforts to promote socialist education seemed to take hold in some places outside the central valleys, as well, as evidenced by local publications submitted to the governor of the state and the general secretary of public education. In July 1935, Inocencio Félix Zárate, subinspector for schools in Putla, Oaxaca, sent the governor a copy of a local publication called *El Socialista*. According to Félix Zárate, the publication was motivated by teachers to "impart socialist education and combat fanaticism" (religious fanaticism) (Félix Zárate 1935). *El Socialista* featured articles on socialist education, a poem on the fraternity of workers and peasants united through the symbols of hammer and sickle, a piece on garden planting, discussions of how the modern school differs from the traditional, and other articles (*El Socialista* 1935). As previously noted, a review of the books ordered by schools in Oaxaca also indicates that books such as *Simiente* promoting the ideals of socialist education were widely used.

Following the visit of Lázaro Cárdenas to Oaxaca in 1937, the intensification of educational activities increased, as did teacher militancy. The governor of Oaxaca in 1937, Constantino Chapital, who had previously been a senator to the National Congress, considered himself part of the leftist congressional wing connected to President Cárdenas. Chapital had coordinated large parts of the president's visit, and earnestly tried to follow through on efforts initiated by Cárdenas at that time. During the summer of 1937, Chapital's efforts were frustrated by militant teachers.

During the 1930s, teachers in Oaxaca were organized primarily by the Sindicato Único de Trabajadores de la Enseñanza (Sole Union of Education Workers). Before 1937, the increasing number of teachers in the state had varied payment and labor arrangements. Some were contracted by municipal and local town governments, others by the state, and others by the federal government. Often community officials would be unable or unwilling to pay on time. To press their demands for timely pay and the federalization of schools, teachers across the state went on strike on 1 July 1937. The strike ended on 6 July, after Chapital agreed to meet some of the demands.

A few days before the strike, officials from the Oaxaca state government and federal government signed a federalization agreement that all schools, child-care centers, cultural centers, and, in general, educational systems of the state would be administered by the secretary of federal education. This change allowed more uniform national procedures and almost doubled the salaries of teachers in Oaxaca between 1935 and 1940 (Martínez Vásquez 1994, 127).

Their closer ties to the federal government also brought teachers in Oaxaca into even more intimate contact with a range of Cárdenas programs, including agrarian reform. Again, this level of contact does not appear to have happened in highland indigenous Chiapas, but to have been concentrated in the coastal plantation region. In 1937, state education officials from Oaxaca were invited to Mexico City to attend the First National Congress in Favor of Popular Education. The agenda of the congress was to set national program priorities to be carried out at the state level. The work outlined by this program called for teachers and others to be involved in improving school attendance, to help form revolutionary committees of youth and women, to eliminate illiteracy, to promote better standards of cleanliness in rural communities and among workers, and to help carry out Cárdenas's six-year educational plan (Primer Congreso Nacional Pro-Educación Popular 1937).

Teachers in Oaxaca were active in organizing local agrarian committees. Teachers and peasants held conferences in various regions of the state. In 1937, federal teachers organized the First Grand Regional Convention of Peasants of the Chinanteca, which drew two hundred delegates from twenty-two towns (Martínez Vásquez 1994, 135). In 1938, the First Regional Peasant Convention was celebrated in the Vanguard School of San Antonio de la Cal, close to Oaxaca. This convention was organized by the Department of Agricultural Learning and the Rural Normal School. There were seventy-two delegates from a range of valley communities, as well as other authorities, who discussed agrarian reform, the collectivization of work, irrigation, the role of women, and other themes (ibid., 134). Teachers also helped to found the Oaxacan Peasant Confederation.

In a nutshell, teachers worked simultaneously as agrarian activists, often playing key roles in initiating local agrarian committees and regional conferences and organizations. The figure of Zapata figured prominently in these discourses.

ZAPATA, AGRARIAN REFORM, AND THE
FORMATION OF EJIDOS IN OAXACA

While education was one way to market nationalism, another equally important arena in the Mexican countryside was the formation of hierarchical and horizontal linkages to national and state government officials through Cárdenas's massive land reform program and promotion of the CNC. Literature from the CNC was rife with references to the revolution and the agrarian radicalism of Zapata. For example, notices and letterhead from the National Peasant Confederation featured phrases such as "La tierra debe ser de quien trabaja" ("The land belongs to those who work it"), "La libertad de los trabajadores debe ser obra de los trabajadores mismos" ("The liberty of workers should be determined by workers themselves"), and "Tierra y Libertad" ("Land and Liberty," a slogan attributed to Emiliano Zapata) (see, e.g., Balleza Jr. 1933). The rhetoric of class struggle, proletarian rights, and exploitation of the land by large landholders and foreigners permeated agrarian petitions and correspondence.

In areas such as Oaxaca, where ejidos were formed and schools built in the 1930s, revolutionary rhetoric was common. In the two ejidos in Oaxaca that this volume focuses on, the resonance of Zapata can be found through residents' experience of creating ejidos when a national culture was being created to consolidate the National Revolutionary Party under Lázaro Cárdenas. To what degree this effort was successful, and how it varied in different parts of Mexico, is an important part of the story. In the Oaxacan ejidos of Santa María del Tule and Unión Zapata, through participation in rural schools, high levels of interaction with agrarian officials, and contentious relations with neighboring hacendados and indigenous Zapotec community members, ejidatarios experienced a frustrating but ultimately positive interaction with the government in securing their ejido land. As emerging national citizens organized as ejidatarios, men and women in these ejidos endorsed the "concepts of rebellion, struggle, and the right to social justice" that were "etched into the core of the Mexican cultural nation in the 1930s and afterward" (Vaughn 1997, 190). However, the view of Mexico as a nation found in these two ejidos in the mid to late 1990s was a significant departure from that promoted by the government. Indeed, interactions with government officials from the 1930s to the present would produce a divergent take on national and local history, refracted through local experience, the radical alternative nationalist discourse of the Zapatistas, and many other sources. The distillation of this process has produced a local nationalism that, if not against the government, is at least suspicious of it—very different from the intentions of the 1930s teachers and government officials promoting the formation of ejidos.

Many interactions of people in Santa María del Tule and Unión Zapata with the government were mediated through the Confederación Oaxaqueña de Campesinos, the Oaxacan branch of what became the CNC. For example, in a series of nine letters to presidents Abelardo Rodríguez and Lázaro Cárdenas from 1934 to 1938, ejidatarios from Unión Zapata continually deployed the rhetoric of the revolution in an effort not only to have their petition for land resolved quickly, but also to influence where the land came from. In writing to President Cárdenas, they also advocated for socialist education, land for those who work it, formation of cooperatives, and collective farming.

In 1935, three members of the Executive Agrarian Committee of Unión Zapata wrote a letter detailing the highlights of their organizational project. Isaias Ramírez, Lauro Aragón, and Guadalupe Bautista sent copies of their letter to the president of Mexico (Cárdenas), the director of federal education in Oaxaca, and the secretary of agrarian action of the PNR. The letter is addressed to the head of the Agrarian Department. It is a wonderful example of how the structure of federal schooling, agrarian reform, and the PNR converged in one community and fostered a direct relationship with state officials in the mid 1930s. It also suggests that the state's promotion of the revolution, peasants' rights, and socialist education was understood by these ejidatarios in cen-

tral Oaxaca, who used the rhetoric of the revolution to seek land for
their community:

> The signatories below continue to support and amplify our petitions, which
> were sent to the president of the Republic and which have arrived at this
> [Agrarian] Department in order to obtain the results of the movements that
> we have been making. In light of the fact that the peasants of this agrarian
> population are animated by the heat of class struggle that will bring about the
> transformation of our masses of peasants . . . we would like to solicit support
> for the following points of our project:
>
> I.   Support of the points of memo #88 of June 19 of this year in which
>   we solicited fifteen hectares of land for each ejidatario in order to sat-
>   isfy the material, cultural, economic, social, and physical necessities
>   of life.
> II.   Collectivize our agricultural production with a cooperative system
>   that could allow us integrally to enjoy the benefits of our social life.
> III.   Select seeds and begin to rotate our crops as was recommended by the
>   Ministry of Agriculture of this country.
> IV.   Help the campesinos, through a Cooperative Society to conceive and
>   select high quality cattle to efficiently develop the agricultural labor of
>   the same peasants. . . .
> VI.   To destroy . . . religious dogmas, superstitions, etc., that cause social
>   prejudices and to adopt as our only religion, work, which brings us
>   happiness, and to disregard at once all words of divine origin and any
>   books that rely on that model.
> VII.   To help other local and regional organizations in whatever they need
>   in order to help them in the social struggle.
> VIII. To form a traditional musical orchestra for theatrical events, which
>   can serve to orient, inspire, and provide recreation for the people in
>   this community.
> IX.   To obtain modern agricultural implements and pumps with gas mo-
>   tors for irrigation
> X.   To carry out with our best effort the plan of action of the Socialist Pri-
>   mary School promoted by the secretary of public education so that we
>   can change our situation to become more hygienic, persevering, and
>   more conscious of our responsibilities as campesinos. . . .
>
>   Unión Zapata (before, Loma Larga), Mitla, 11 October
>   1935 (Ramírez, Aragon, and Bautista 1935)

How locals conceived of ideas such as socialist education, class struggle,
cooperatives, and the religion of work is difficult to deduce from the letter. What is clear, in this letter and others in the series, is that local agraristas pushing to have their petitions for land formally resolved by the
president understood what kind of language they needed to deploy for
their cases to receive attention. For two years, a group of five local officials continued to write regularly to Cárdenas to pressure him to act on

their petition. They also used their channel to Cárdenas to pressure unresponsive agrarian authorities. Their letters (and those cited in subsequent chapters) provide examples of the savvy and intelligence of local intellectuals in packaging community needs in the language of dominant rhetoric to "get stuff" that was needed. The letters also suggest the role that local intellectuals have played historically in refashioning dominant hegemonies, creating new local hegemonies, and projecting these oppositional hegemonies into national spaces. This process will also be seen at work in Chiapas.

In a letter to Cárdenas dated 4 June 1936, Guadalupe Bautista, the president of the Ejido Committee of Unión Zapata, wrote of the community's frustration in waiting to receive resolution of its land petition while continuing in a precarious economic situation, again deploying the rhetoric of the revolution:

> We thus wait for you, fellow citizen, President of the Republic, begging once more that they pay attention to the just petitions [for land] of the disinherited and the needy who struggle to survive at great cost. I repeat to you, Mr. Citizen president, that the campesinos of this organization are waiting to see their petitions attended to so that they can finally get out of this horrible misery. . . .
> Land, Liberty, and Justice!
> Justice for the Organized Peasants!
>
> Unión Zapata (previously Loma Larga),
> Mitla, Oaxaca, 4 June 1936 (Bautista 1936)

Having taken the name of Zapata for the new ejido Unión Zapata, the community members of what had been Loma Larga laid claim to a key symbol of the Revolution. Their case is a clear illustration of how the rhetoric and symbols promoted by the Cárdenas government through the SEP, the Agrarian Department, and the CNC were appropriated by local communities and redeployed in their own interests. In indigenous parts of Chiapas, however, the education program of the SEP and the agrarian bureaucracy appear to have made many fewer connections than in central Oaxaca.

SCHOOLING IN INDIGENOUS CHIAPAS IN THE 1930S

This legacy in central Oaxaca of intense interaction and correspondence with agrarian officials at all levels and with the president of the country, as well as with the positive resolution of their petitions, gave some ejidatarios there relatively positive associations with agrarian rhetoric emphasizing their rights in relation to the Mexican Revolution. In eastern Chiapas, where some ejidos were formed in the 1930s, the influence of the revolutionary rhetoric of the 1930s was much less. The extent of ejido formation in that state is covered in more detail in chapter 4; here I shall discuss the limited influence of federal education programs in rural indigenous Chiapas during the 1930s and 1940s and of efforts to organize rural workers, as a contrast to what occurred in central Oaxaca. It should be noted that this contrast between Oaxaca and Chiapas was not complete. Some regions of Chiapas acted more like central Oaxaca. While there is clearly some influence in Chiapas of Mexican national icons such as Zapata through rural education during the 1930s, the success of federal teachers there in this period was minimal, limited primarily to mestizo workers and peasants, according to Stephen Lewis (1997a); the SEP's impact on indigenous populations in Chiapas during the 1930s was negligible. Beginning in the 1920s, most mestizo Chiapanecans in the zones of export agriculture supported the SEP rural schools, teachers, and radicalized curriculum. This may in part be due to the fact that in the plantation zone of the Soconusco, the agrarian reform process was very active in the 1920s and 1930s. Communities in this area of Chiapas may have seen teachers as useful allies to help fight local landowners. At the same time, indigenous responses to the national education project and to teachers remained unenthusiastic, particularly among the Tzotzil Maya of the highlands. There, teachers reported communities and local authorities actively opposing "slightly more than half (52%) of SEP's schools" (Lewis 1997a, 361). A school inspector reporting on the very negative reception to schools and teachers in the highlands wrote in 1936:

> [T]he education problem of the Chamulan is more complicated than that of any other indígena in the Republic. . . . [I]n no part of the Republic nor in this state are they more brutalized by alcohol, nor is the exploitation of the Indian—through which the greater part of the mestizo population lives—so well organized. . . . [N]owhere, I repeat, do so many factors conspire against the school as in this corner of the Chiapanecan mountains.
>
>   Inspector de la Zona Manuel Castellaños, dated from
>   Ciudad de las Casas, 11 May 1936 (Lewis 1997a, 360)

In the highlands, mestizos opposed SEP programs because the state's economic and political institutions depended on indebted indigenous highland labor on lowland plantations, and because state alcohol interests relied on indigenous consumption. By keeping education out of highland indigenous communities, mestizos could continue to maintain economic control, while such education might result in a disruption of established economic patterns.

Boarding schools for highland indigenous boys and girls fared no better. According to Stephen Lewis, all indigenous boarding schools in the 1930s and early 1940s were in miserable disrepair, had inadequate staff, and were barely functioning (Lewis 1997a, 402–9). Teachers determined to implement Cárdenas's radical pedagogy faced an opposition army of ranchers, planters, alcohol merchants, debt contractors, ladino municipal presidents, and, often, the state governor (ibid., 431). In the 1950s, after more than thirty years of federal education programs, only a small dent had been made in rural indigenous literacy rates. In Chamula and Huixtán, where both rural schools and indigenous boarding schools had been established, literacy rates were only 2 percent and 15 percent respectively (ibid.).

The failure of SEP programs to prosper in the indigenous highlands because of mestizo resistance is a telling reminder of the regional variation with which government policy was implemented in the 1930s. As noted by Jenny Purnell, the government that emerged after the Mexican Revolution was neither a democratic vehicle for the realization of popular aspirations nor a centralized force driven by the needs of capital or the logic of political centralization. Instead, "it [was] a product of historically contingent struggle between diverse elite and popular groups, entailing multiple arenas of contestation and negotiation" (Purnell 1999, 191). Authors such as Alicia Hernández Chávez (1979), Nora Hamilton (1982), and Jeffrey Rubin (1997) have shown how regional power blocs resisted the Cárdenas regime, in spite of Cárdenas's ability to transform the national institutional landscape of Mexico. In some parts of Chiapas, entrenched interests kept educational programs from indigenous communities until such programs could be a vehicle for creating a new economic and political elite loyal to the center. While in Oaxaca there were some areas where local interests kept education out of local communities, and some areas simply too isolated to reach, resistance to education programs there was much less. The fact that Cárdenas personally toured large areas of Oaxaca on two occasions, as well as touring Chiapas, suggests that the visits themselves were not enough to result in the acceptance of education. The local context was also key in each state.

Ultimately, the impact of SEP programs, including the socialist education promoted under Cárdenas, were much more influential in mestizo communities, particularly from 1934 to 1940, after teachers took an expanded social, political, and economic role in their communities. "Grass-

roots support for SEP teachers and schools was greatest where rural pro-
letarians came to regard federal teachers as their natural allies against
(often foreign) capitalists in the export sector. Throughout the 1930s,
teachers played important roles in organizing laborers, defending their
rights, and preparing agrarian reform requests" (Lewis 1997a, 428).

RURAL LABOR UNIONS AND THE PNR IN CHIAPAS

Rather than reaching the indigenous peoples of Chiapas through education, concentrated efforts were made to harness highland Tzotzils and
Tzeltals to the PNR through their organization into a statewide labor
and peasant coalition. Even these efforts, however, were limited. As documented by Jan Rus, in the 1930s the Tzotzils and Tzeltals represented
one-third of the Chiapas population, and they were also the bulk of the
migratory workforce that underwrote the state's export agriculture. In
1937, after a PNR candidate for governor won the elections, twenty-five
thousand Indian workers were enrolled in the Sindicato de Trabajadores Indígenas (Union of Indigenous Workers). Many were coffee pickers,
and it became illegal in Chiapas to hire coffee workers who were not
part of the union. To set the political scene for organizing the indigenous
workers, a widely publicized federal labor commission report was circulated by Cárdenas's supporters exposing "the virtual enslavement" of
Chiapas' Indian workers (Rus 1994, 274, 277, 273).

The architect of the Union of Indigenous Workers, Erastro Urbina,
carried out his own style of land reform, expropriating *fincas* on the spot.
For a two-and-a-half year period, Urbina simply seized the properties
and left it for someone else to sort out the niceties of legal procedure and
indemnification (Urbina 1944, 56–58, cited in Rus 1994, 276). While
the Union of Indigenous Workers may have improved some conditions, it
also became the primary supplier of labor to coffee planters (Rus 1994).
In the process of establishing this union, and in instituting a Wild West
style of land reform, quite possibly official rhetoric about the Mexican
Revolution was deployed but its overall influence was no doubt limited.

As a further means of harnessing indigenous voters to the PRN, Urbina sought out bilingual and literate men in *municipios* under his jurisdiction, then had them appointed scribes in their community's governments (Rus 1994, 275). Beginning in 1939, it was announced that
only bilingual municipal presidents would be allowed to interact with
the Department of Indigenous Protection—a key government agency

for obtaining resources. The agency was headed by Erastro Urbina. The net result of this process is summarized by Rus (1994, 278):

> [B]etween 1936 and 1940, the Tzotzils and Tzeltals suddenly found the very structures of those communities being commandeered by the state and party —outsiders—as part of what was proclaimed as their common struggle against exploitation. Moreover, the scribes who had facilitated this transformation had begun to acquire powers far beyond those of traditional native leaders. By 1940, they were no long simply *escribanos* [scribes/secretaries] subordinated to the traditional *ayuntamientos* [local governments] but had also become labor union officers, heads of their municipal agrarian committees, leaders of local branches of the official party (known after 1937 as the Partido Revolucionario Mexicano, PRM) and representatives to the regional committee of the Confederación Nacional Campesina.

Thus, in the Tzotzil and Tzeltal highlands of Chiapas, the rhetoric of the Mexican Revolution in the 1930s was delivered through concentration of political power in the hands of bilingual scribes who linked the communities to various national institutions, including the CNC. After Cárdenas's term ended in 1940, the pace of agrarian reform greatly slowed in Chiapas. Petitioning for land did not pick up again until the late 1950s and 1960s. However, the bilingual scribes remained in positions of power and "[B]y the time the PRM became the PRI in the mid-forties, the former self-defensive, closed communities of the Chiapas highlands had become integrated parts of the party's local machine," ensuring continued effective delivery of state rhetoric (Rus 1994, 281).

In the highlands of Chiapas, it was not until the 1950s that education emerged as another primary channel for the PRI's claim to the Mexican Revolution. After the National Indigenous Institute (INI) located its first regional development program, the Centro Coordinador Tzeltal-Tzotzil, in San Cristóbal de las Casas in 1951, INI hired and trained forty-six former scribes as bilingual teachers, installing each in a primary school in his home community. The former scribes thus continued to maintain their positions of power and roles as channels to the state and ruling party. Ultimately, their domination in highland communities not only endowed them with wide-ranging political powers and access to resources, but also created an economic elite.

Despite some limited impact made through educational channels, beginning in the 1950s, the importation of the symbols and rhetoric of Zapata and the Mexican Revolution in Chiapas did not reach a meaningful level until regional peasant organizations were formed, beginning in the late 1970s.

GOVERNMENT DEPLOYMENT OF THE
MEXICAN REVOLUTION IN THE 1990S

THE END OF AGRARIAN REFORM AND PROCEDE

The Mexican government's rural socialist education program, the organization of landless peasants into ejidos, and the creation and promotion of the CNC in the 1930s comprised a crucial period in postrevolutionary state formation in which the government redefined and claimed Zapata and the Mexican Revolution. During that period, thousands of teachers, engineers, and government officials blanketed the countryside in an attempt to unify the nation under a postrevolutionary nationalism that tried to link all Mexicans to the Revolution and the Revolution to the government. This effort to consolidate a dominant vision of Mexican nationalism had varied results. Nevertheless, as a government strategy attempting to move the entire nation forward with a centrally disseminated vision of "the nation," this 1930s effort was duplicated, in some ways, under the Salinas de Gortari (1988–94) and Zedillo (1994–2000) administrations, as these presidents worked to promote a new, international image of Mexico as a player in the global economy. A key part of that message focused on the positive merits of a Mexico that had an economy centered on privatization, investment, and individual opportunity.

In the 1990s, an army of government employees—primarily from the newly created Procuraduría Agraria (Agrarian Attorney General's Office)—blanketed the Mexican countryside to educate and organize rural men and women around the new, modern nationalism tied to NAFTA. This time, their message was not "petition for land," "form an ejido," and "organize and join the CNC." Indeed, it was quite different. Employees of the Procuraduría Agraria promoting PROCEDE urged ejidatarios to "defend your rights to your individual parcel," to "measure, map, and title your land," and to "guarantee your individual freedom." While the selling method involved cloaking PROCEDE in the mantle of the revolution and overt and covert references to Zapata—following the sixty-year tradition of postrevolutionary government bureaucracies associated with agrarian reform—another message of the government envoys was the *end* of agrarian reform. Instead of guaranteeing the right to land to those who worked it, the government wanted to guarantee the right of individual ejidatarios who already had land security for their individual parcels—primarily through measuring, mapping, certifying and "titling"—so that individual plots could now be held in private tenancy. If you were landless in the 1990s, you were out of luck.

Thus a cornerstone of Mexico's 1990s neoliberal policy encouraging privatization and foreign investment, found in changes to Article 27 of the Constitution, ended the government's constitutional obligation to redistribute land in response to landless peasants' petitions, and allowed the privatization of previously inalienable, communally held ejido land. Ejidos, it should be noted, belong to what is called the social sector of land tenancy. Nationally, Mexico has 27,410 ejidos, which occupy almost half of the country's agricultural land. Ejidos at least partially supported three million ejidatarios and millions more of their dependents in the 1980s and 1990s (Cockcroft 1998, 290–91; Cornelius and Myhre 1998a, 1). In 1990, Oaxaca had 732 ejidos, benefiting 88,299 families—about 485,644 people, or 16 percent, of the state's 1990 population (Secretaría de Reforma Agraria, CORETT 1996, *cuadro* 1).[2] In Chiapas in 1990, a total of 1,405,025 people out of 3,210,496, or 43.7 percent of the state's total population, lived on ejidos (Instituto Nacional de Estadística, Geografía e Informática 1995, 3). Chiapas has a total of between 1,873 and 2,015 ejidos (the exact figure depends on the method of counting) (ibid., 16).[3] Thus, in Chiapas, reforms to the ejidos affected a major part of the population.

In addition to ejidos, an important part of the rural land held in social tenancy lies in *comunidades agrarias* (agrarian communities). This land constitutes a significant part of the holdings of indigenous communities and is based on historical claims, usually dating to pre-Colombian or colonial times. In many cases, these lands are known as *comunales* (communal lands). So far, communal lands cannot be privatized, while ejido lands can; however, changes to Article 27 in 1992 do permit agrarian communities to change from designation as comunidades agrarias, with inalienable communal land, to ejidos; if an agrarian community should convert to an ejido, then its land could be individually parceled and privatized.

Comunidades agrarias is a term coined in the 1970s. While the Constitution of 1917 recognized the right of rural Mexicans to hold communal property, it was not until the 1940s that a series of changes to the agrarian code led to more explicit recognition of the distinction between ejido land and communal land. These changes also provided mechanisms to resolve conflicts between private property owners, ejidatarios, and those who claimed communal property. Nevertheless, the procedures for recognizing and titling communal lands were not fully spelled out until 1958. And it was only in 1971, through further modification to the agrarian code, that the government for the first time explicitly rec-

ognized the "agrarian community" as a corporate entity distinct from
the ejido and distinguished between the legal rights of *comuneros* (those
in agrarian communities holding rights to communal land) and ejidatarios.[4] Historically, it is impossible to distinguish agrarian communities
from ejidos until the 1970s or later. As discussed below, even in the
1990s, the two types of landholdings were often not disaggregrated in
official statistics.

Today, the state of Oaxaca has 674 comunidades agrarias, benefiting
264,866 families, or approximately 1,456,763 people (Secretaría de Reforma Agraria, CORETT 1996, *cuadro* 1). This is almost half the state's
population. By contrast, Chiapas has 101 comunidades agrarias (Instituto Nacional de Estadística, Geografía e Informática 1995, xvi). I
could not find an exact figure for the number of families or individuals
benefiting from comunidades agrarias in Chiapas. Some of the comunidades agrarias have huge extensions of land, benefiting 30,000 to 40,000
people, such as in the municipalities of Chamula, Zinacantan, and Chenalhó. Others benefit smaller numbers of people. The total number of
beneficiaries could be as high as 200,000 to 300,000. What is significant
for the future comparison of Oaxaca and Chiapas is that the change in
Article 27 and the end of land redistribution and possible privatization
affected many more people in Chiapas than in Oaxaca, since in Chiapas
many more people depended on ejidos. The desperation felt in Chiapas
when Article 27 was changed was not only anxiety about potential privatization but also disbelief on the part of those still waiting to receive
land that now they could not obtain any. Another key concern came
from those who occupied land still in dispute. At the time Article 27 was
changed, Chiapas had the greatest number of unresolved land conflicts
of any state in Mexico.

Modifications to Article 27 in 1992 grant ejidatarios the ability to
sell, buy, or rent land; to hire labor or to associate with other producers
and third parties; and to hold contracts with, or establish joint-venture
schemes with, domestic and foreign private investors. This opens up the
ejido sector to foreign direct investment, allowing foreign private investors to join with ejidatarios in capitalizing land, although such investors' participation in such associations is supposed to be limited to
49 percent of equity capital (Cornelius and Myhre 1998b, 4).

Most significantly, changes to Article 27 allow individual ejidatarios
who have had use rights to land to hold individual title to land. If ejidatarios have a title, then they can sell their plots of land either to persons
inside the ejido or to outsiders. Ejidatarios who have the boundaries of

their parcels certified must obtain a two-thirds majority vote in an ejido assembly to sell their lands to an outsider (with a quorum of 75 percent of the ejido members). To privatize land inside the ejido, a 50 percent quorum is necessary, and only a simple majority of ejidatarios need approve an internal privatization (Cornelius and Myhre 1998a, 3; and see also Harvey 1996, Cornelius and Myhre 1998b; Snyder and Torres 1998; Randall 1996).

To facilitate the proposed changes in landholdings in Mexico's 27,410 ejidos, the Procuraduría Agraria set up a massive outreach and education campaign. As soon as ejidatarios indicate interest in learning about PROCEDE, they receive an onslaught of information, official visits from lawyers and agronomists, advice, teams to measure community boundaries and individual plots, invitations to participate in programs to "help" peasants, and a pile of paper to document the entire process. If a community votes to join PROCEDE, this does not lead automatically to privatization or to the breakup of the ejido. Such a result can only happen, as already noted, at the end of the titling process, if a significant number of ejidatarios decide to privatize their land. Nevertheless, one aim of PROCEDE has been to facilitate and even encourage the privatization of previously inalienable, communally held ejido land (Cornelius and Myhre 1998a, 1).

For many communities, the period 1992–96 (which involved heavy promotion and implementation of PROCEDE) marked the most intense level of contact in decades with government officials. The bearers of PROCEDE also brought a new message on how to be a rural Mexican citizen: protect your individual rights to land. They brought the philosophy of NAFTA to the countryside.

In an era of downsizing, decentralization, and government spending cuts, the creation of the Procuraduría Agraria in Mexico was a striking occurrence. Created in early 1992 to carry out the national ejido certification program, by March 1993 the office had 3,161 employees and was growing (Warman 1993, 3). President Carlos Salinas de Gortari commented in March 1993 that there was not a single federal government entity in which the Procuraduría was not known (Salinas de Gortari 1993). The administration of Ernesto Zedillo, which followed, pledged to complete the titling process by the end of the year 2000 (Zedillo 1997, 13, cited in Cornelius and Myhre 1998a, 12).

The Procuraduría has a structure of regional offices (*delegaciones*) and local districts. Each local district is overseen by a *residente* who acts as coordinator and overseer. Below this person are *visitadores* (literally, "visitors"), young professionals who have completed an intensive three-week training session on the 1992 agrarian reform law. Below but working closely with them are *becarios campesinos / auxiliares,* auxiliary "peasant scholars." These are also young people, usually from rural backgrounds, who work with the visitadores in researching legal issues and organizing and training ejidatarios as they go through the certification process. Together the visitadores and auxiliares have been the foot soldiers of the government's project to measure, map, and provide certificates for all land held in nonprivate tenancy in Mexico. They have become the face of the government in local communities as they work to get ejidos to enroll and then to follow through on the long and detailed processes to obtain certificates.

While the Procuraduría is the primary government entity responsible for administering the new law, the bureau works in conjunction with five other agencies that have also sent out personnel to rural communities. Most important to the certification process is the Instituto de Estadística, Geografía, e Informática (Institute of Statistics, Geography, and Informatics), or INEGI, responsible for measuring the perimeters of ejido land, individual plots, and house lots, and for drawing up maps of these. In the certification program, INEGI personnel measure land in the presence of a specially created auxiliary commission, ejido authorities, and all parties whose land is involved. Beyond the Procuraduría, INEGI staff are the most active government participants in the first half of the certification process, and many ejidatarios got to know INEGI engineers in the process of participating in PROCEDE. The Registro Agrario Nacional (National Agrarian Registry), or RAN, issues individual and common use certificates and titles when requested. To resolve disputes, special agrarian tribunals (*tribunales agrarias*) have been installed, in many cases, next door to the office of the Procuraduría.

The Secretaría de Agricultura y Recursos Hidraulicos (i.e., Ministry of Agriculture and Water Resources), or SARH, is also involved. SARH personnel are supposed to promote observance of regulations and procedures regarding water resources and forests. In addition, they administer PROCAMPO (further discussed in chapter 11), which offers Mexican farmers of corn, beans, wheat, rice, soy beans, sorghum, and cotton a subsidy of about $U.S.100 per hectare over fifteen years. Guaranteed price supports for these crops were phased out in the autumn and winter seasons of 1994–95, pitting Mexican producers against cheaper U.S. imports and aligning Mexican crop prices with international prices. The announcement of this program by the government evidences a certain backpedaling in the structural adjustments being carried out to facilitate NAFTA. PROCAMPO may slightly soften being eased out of the rural sector for the three million ejidatarios (and their families) whom the Mexican government is predicting will benefit from PROCAMPO (Moguel 1993, 8). However, the subsidies offered do not come close to covering farmers' planting and harvesting costs, and President Vicente Fox has suggested that he may prepay all future PROCAMPO subsidies and may get out of subsidizing small agriculture once and for all.

Beginning in 1992, a systematic effort was made by the Mexican government to incorporate as many ejidos as possible into PROCEDE. As the army of Procuraduría employees, along with INEGI personnel, SARH agronomists, and others entered communities—and returned for regular visits over a one- to two-year period—an intensification of community-government relations occurred. Apart from the populace's reactions to this attempt by the government to (1) end land redistribution, and (2) engage them in efforts to map, measure, certify, and, if desired by the ejidatario, title individual ejido plots, one of the most interesting parts of the whole process was the ideological and symbolic packaging that the government used to sell PROCEDE to rural Mexicans. (Reactions to the program are discussed later in this chapter and in the chapters that follow.)

USING THE REVOLUTION TO MARKET PROCEDE

The "Defense of the Mexican Ejido" was the rallying cry of PROCEDE, and, in its textual, rhetorical, and visual representations of the reforms to Article 27, the government invoked the inheritance of the Mexican Revolution and of Emiliano Zapata. At the end of 1991, when Salinas de Gortari initiated the legislative process to change Article 27, he used the theme "Liberty and Justice for the Countryside," because ending the government's obligation to redistribute land made the slogan "Tierra y Libertad" obsolete. "Libertad" was redefined by state publications to mean the freedom of ejidatarios to make their own decisions and to have individual control over land. A PROCEDE brochure passed out to ejidatarios in 1993 stated that the reforms were designed to "strengthen the rights of the ejidatario over his individual parcel, guarantee his liberty, and establish procedures to give the ejidatario use of his land and the right to pass it on to others" (Procuraduría Agraria 1993b, 2). "Libertad" was thus aimed at deconstructing collective decision-making rights held by the corporate unit of the ejido and emphasizing individual property rights. This emphasis was in line with the philosophy of neoliberal economic policy and NAFTA in particular. It also echoed some of the language in nineteenth-century liberal land reforms (described in more detail in chapter 4 on Chiapas and chapter 8 on Oaxaca).

The political scientist Deborah Yashar describes the shift to neo-liberal economic policy in Latin America as accompanied by what she calls "neoliberal citizenship regimes" (Yashar 1999, 80). Such regimes are characterized by some expansion of political and civil rights and the decline of social rights. Yashar states that neoliberal citizenship regimes shatter corporate-based methods of incorporating people into the state by sector (peasants, Indians, working class, etc.) and replace such cor-poratist integration with a more individuated set of state-society rela-tions. The result, however, can be that, when the individual rights that neoliberalism promises are not realized, local forms of autonomy that were fostered by corporate styles of governing (peasant organizations, for example) are challenged and politicized. This framework is useful for thinking about the nature of the reforms to Article 27, about the way they were packaged (as defending the rights of the individual ejidatario), and about response to the reform—particularly in Chiapas, where there were protests and, later, land invasions.

Rhetorically, the campaign to promote PROCEDE in the 1990s turned the 1930s effort to popularize the Mexican Revolution by the SEP and the CNC on its head. It is most instructive to compare the 1993 PROCEDE brochure cited above with a 1935 passage from *Simiente* titled "Land for All the Peasants," which directly opposed the sentiments of "individual liberty" promoted by PROCEDE. First, *Simiente* promised that every-one would have land to work and that this would bring freedom; sec-ond, it emphasized that it was important to form cooperatives and work collectively and discouraged individual ejidatarios from acting alone:

> There will come a day when not one peasant will not have a piece of land to cultivate.
>
> Land should be received with great affection, land brings independence to the workers on the countryside and thus can liberate them from the tyranny with which the large landowners exploited them. . . .
>
> The peasants should unite, forming cooperative societies, and in this man-ner they can acquire the agricultural machinery that will permit them to bet-ter cultivate the land; in addition, united they can also sell their product for a better price.
>
> What one man cannot acquire alone, can be achieved with the union of many men together. (Lucio 1935b, 65)[5]

The reform to Article 27 and the promotion of PROCEDE quite clearly inverted the messages of Cárdenas's 1930s agrarian program. In its promotional materials for PROCEDE, however, the government still uses 1930s language and images, providing a distraction from the new underlying messages of an "end to agrarian reform" and "individual liberty."

The marketing of PROCEDE involved extensive deployment of rhetoric and symbols from the Mexican Revolution, some reminiscent of the 1930s appeals to campesinos recruited to form ejidos and join the CNC. As part of PROCEDE marketing, two publications were made available to ejidatarios in Oaxaca. The initial brochure describing the Procuraduría Agraria had a five-color cover featuring a barefoot peasant wearing white *calzones* (cotton trousers associated with revolutionary-era indigenous peasants) bent over in the dirt, an image not far from the depictions of peasants by Diego Rivera that were used to illustrate 1930s SEP textbooks for rural schools. The brochure bore the headline "Procuraduría Agraria" and, below it, the slogan "Libertad y Justicia al Campo Mexicano" ("Liberty and Justice in the Mexican Countryside").

Under the question, "What Is the Agrarian Attorney's Office?" the brochure explained that this "is a new social service institution in charge of the defense of the rights of ejidatarios, communal landholders and their successors, and of ejidos, agrarian communities, small property holders, residential property owners and rural workers" (Procuraduría Agraria 1993b). One might ask whom the office is not in charge of defending in the countryside.

PROCEDE was deliberately promoted intensely in Zapata's home state of Morelos. It was the government's goal to have Morelos be the first state to finish incorporating all ejidos into PROCEDE. Morelos, as the home to Zapata's guerrilla movement and the supposed cradle of agrarian reform during and following the Mexican Revolution, is of obvious symbolic importance in getting ejidos to participate. It is also, not coincidentally, the state where the anthropologist Arturo Warman (head of the Procuraduría Agraria from 1992 to 1994) carried out extensive fieldwork.

A second widely disseminated national publication of the Procuraduría Agraria describes the certification process by highlighting a case study. The 43-page booklet, *Yecapixtla, Morelos: Crónica*, actually chronicles two stories. While its title suggests that it is going to tell the story of Yecapixtla's incorporation into PROCEDE, the margins of every page feature testimonials on topics such as the original struggle (shortly after the death of Zapata in 1919) to establish the ejido, the Plan de Ayala, and "a Zapatista memory" (Procuraduria Agraria 1993c, 12–18, 33–36). In this booklet, the story of Yecapixtla's incorporation into and successful completion of PROCEDE is sandwiched between snippets about and photographs of Zapata, details of the Zapatista land reform program, and fond memories of what Zapata represented.

The "sandwich" strategy represented in this publication seems to have been deliberately reproduced in the many dimensions of the marketing of PROCEDE. Most publications promoting PROCEDE feature images from the past, not modern ejidatarios with high-tech farming equipment. The government could not let go of the revolutionary symbolism, despite the actual content of PROCEDE. Nevertheless, underlying the classic agrarian symbols is the implication that although ejidos are part of its cherished past, to modernize and become a first-world nation, Mexico has to move on—to turn farmers into entrepreneurs.

These brochures, booklets, and posters were seen by a wide range of ejidatarios, who had to enter the Procuraduría's district and regional offices at various stages of their incorporation into PROCEDE. The interior courtyard of the Procuraduría Agraria in Oaxaca had a large bulletin board featuring photographs of events carried out by the agency. On most days that I was in the Procuraduría, the courtyard was crowded with ejidatarios waiting to see staff members charged with shepherding them through PROCEDE. While waiting, men and women often looked at the pictures, picked up brochures, and discussed their content or questioned one another about them.

This print-strategy linkage of PROCEDE to the Mexican Revolution and to Zapata was followed in the ceremonies carried out in the name of the Procuraduría. In 1994, Salinas de Gortari seemed in a virtual war of words with Subcomandante Marcos of the Zapatistas over who could gain the most press coverage linking him to the legacy of Zapata. The powerful national television network Televisa often followed Salinas de Gortari around the country and religiously broadcast his invocations of Zapata on 24 *Horas,* the national news broadcast anchored by Jacobo Zabludovsky.[6] When Salinas de Gortari inaugurated a dam in Morelos (conspicuously named "Tierra y Libertad"), which was supposed to benefit 977 campesino families, he said, "Yesterday's promise is today's reality for the benefit of the children of Morelos, the dignified descendants of General Emiliano Zapata" (Hallin 1994). On another occasion in Morelos, in the southern part of the state, when the president gave out twenty-five certificates to ejidatarios who had just completed PROCEDE, the act was broadcast on Zabludovsky's show, and, again, Salinas de Gortari directly invoked the memory of Zapata. As he handed out land titles to appreciative-looking campesinos, he said: "With these acts, we are realizing the ideal of Emiliano Zapata. We do honor to the memory of Emiliano Zapata because with peace and harmony, promoting acts of justice and progress, [that] is how we honor the memory of Emiliano Zapata and how we maintain his memory as he wanted—in favor of the peasant communities, towns and families. . . . Long live Morelos, my compatriots. Long live Emiliano Zapata" (Hallin 1994).

One of the biggest government homages to Zapata that was broadcast on national television occurred in April 1994. At that time, the Procuraduría Agraria launched a widespread campaign to commemorate the seventy-fifth anniversary of Zapata's assassination. The Procuraduría commemorated his death by handing out a record number of ejido parcel certificates in Morelos. This event coincided with a very different memorial sponsored by the EZLN in the Lacandon jungle (see chapter 6). Pictures of the government event were posted in Oaxaca, and it was featured in publications and national newspapers. Accompanied by Secretary of Agriculture Carlos Hank González, Secretary of Agrarian Reform Víctor Cervera Pacheco, Agrarian Attorney General Arturo Warman, and representatives of official peasant organizations such as the CNC, President Salinas de Gortari stated that "Zapata's struggle continues" and had not been set back by the recent reforms to the Constitution—presumably by the Mexican government—"in order to help out peasants" (Lomas 1994, 3). A ceremony was held in the municipal auditorium of Teopanzolco, Morelos—prime Emiliano Zapata territory—where, in his speech, the president emphasized that the struggle of Zapata remained alive, that there had been notable advances in the countryside, but that there was a lot of work yet to be done. He stated that he had come to Morelos to commemorate a date marked by pain and hope, "the seventy-fifth anniversary of the unjust and unacceptable death of Emiliano Zapata and seventy-five years of commitment and work carried out for the good of Mexican peasants" (ibid.). His words echoed those of annual homages to Zapata in most major Mexican cities and towns by the CNC since the 1930s.

The president's discussion of Zapata's memory and of work done to benefit peasants included a promise that the country would not return to latifundias, and his certainty that the constitutional reforms had strengthened the ejido. He informed the audience that PROCEDE had given out 200,000 certificates to ejidatarios, and that he was about to give out 200,000 more in Morelos, so that two out of three ejidatarios

in Zapata's home state of Morelos would have certificates. He also announced that 3.5 million peasants would receive direct support through
the PROCAMPO program in the spring (Lomas 1994, 3). In this speech,
Salinas de Gortari and the officials accompanying him tied the state's
claim to Zapata's struggle for land with PROCEDE and PROCAMPO
programs. Their rhetoric, focusing on the anniversary of Zapata's assassination, linked the revolutionary leader's legacy to the reception by
thousands of persons of land certificates and the future reception by millions of persons of farm subsidy checks. Consistent with PROCEDE's
marketing strategy, the government attempted on these occasions to continue to claim the symbol of Zapata, but in his new neoliberal form—
Emiliano as the defender of individual property rights, as was emphasized in PROCEDE's information campaigns in Oaxaca and Chiapas.

The formation and maintenance of the Procuraduría Agraria and of
the agencies working with it in administering the 1992 agrarian reform
law and PROCEDE has resulted in a new generation of bureaucrats
whose career advancement has been pegged to the success of the certification and titling program. They have also actively marketed a new interpretation of the land reform aspects of the Mexican Revolution, going into most rural communities, much as federal teachers and CNC
organizers attempted to do in the 1930s. They have been the bearers of
a new 1990s nationalism, in which the unifying symbols of the past are
used to justify the end of agrarian reform and the encouragement of privatization of previously inalienable, communally held land. Government
employees such as those in PROCEDE have also disseminated an economic and social message of the value of the individual and individual ini-
tiatives, private property, unfettered trade and commerce, and the needs
of global capitalist development—key ideological aspects of NAFTA.
These employees' sincere belief in the importance of this program for
saving the Mexican ejido as a legacy of the revolution, of promoting
democratic processes in ejido assemblies, and of guaranteeing individual
property rights were constantly communicated to Mexico's rural population in the 1990s. However, as will be seen, there were quite distinct
reactions to the state's attempt to employ the revolution's rhetoric to justify the end of agrarian reform and secure Mexico's place in the global
economy. In Chiapas, the announcement of the end of the government's
obligation to redistribute land to petitioning landless peasants was met
in some areas with rebellion and land invasions. There, PROCEDE did
not go far. In parts of Oaxaca, PROCEDE was passively embraced, but
with wariness about its ultimate outcome.

UNEVEN STATE FORMATION: THE 1930S AND THE 1990S

In the 1920s and 1930s, the creation of the Secretaría de Educación Pública, a system of rural federal schools, and a national curriculum emphasizing hygiene, consumption, production for the market, and making the rural campesino into a Mexican citizen with direct ties to the nation, who participated in celebrating Zapata and the Mexican Revolution, marked a significant period in twentieth-century state formation in modern Mexico. The campaign undertaken by Cárdenas in the 1930s to make good on the rights to land held by Mexican peasants according to the 1917 Constitution was also key in directly linking rural people to the centralizing government. The active formation of ejidos and the subsequent organization of new ejidatarios into the CNC concretely bound agrarian officials at the state and national levels to local ejidatarios and their elected authorities. The active involvement of rural federal teachers in helping communities to petition for land also, in some areas, strengthened these ties. What the comparative cases of ejidos in Oaxaca and in Chiapas suggest, however, is that this process of state formation was variable and was regionally and even locally contingent.

In communities such as Unión Zapata in Oaxaca, federal education programs and the organization of ejidos had some impact at the local level—if only by providing local intellectuals with linguistic fodder to pressure the government to provide them with land (and implements to work it, and other material items). Ejidatarios deployed the revolutionary rhetoric of the PNR (later the PRM under Cárdenas), the SEP, and the CNC in the 1930s to argue their cases (a topic further explored in chapters 9 and 10). In Chiapas, the impact of agrarian reform and federal education under Cárdenas appears to have been more limited, particularly in the indigenous highlands. The examples provided here confirm an already established trend in the characterization of postrevolutionary state formation in twentieth-century Mexico: this formation is decentered and uneven (Rubin 1997; Joseph and Nugent 1994; Purnell 1999).

The unevenness of state formation and of penetration of state ideologies, institutions—even the effectiveness of individuals representing the state—in the 1930s can be seen again in the 1990s in relation to the new national campaign designed to link each ejidatario directly to the state, by providing him or her with an individual certificate designating his or her particular plot of land as mapped and measured. The land certification program of the Agrarian Attorney's Office was specifically designed to prepare land held in nonprivate status for privatization, and, while many ejidatarios might not act on this possibility immediately, the ideological framework promoted by PROCEDE used the inheritance of the Mexican Revolution to try to legitimate positive values of private property and investment. Because this rhetoric was laid on top of varying local histories and experience, it had varying effects in Oaxaca and Chiapas.

PROCEDE IN OAXACA AND IN CHIAPAS

By mid 1997, about 51 percent of Oaxaca's ejidos had completed PRO-CEDE, with results varying significantly by region. By 1999, that number was up to 478 ejidos, or 65 percent of the total. At the same time, about another 36 percent of Oaxaca's ejidos and agrarian communities were involved in collective conflicts, primarily boundary conflicts. Until these were resolved, the ejidos and agrarian communities could not complete the PROCEDE process. Thus, in 1999, PROCEDE had proceeded as far as it could in Oaxaca without taking on cases of conflict.

In Chiapas, only about 17.5 percent of ejidos had completed PRO-CEDE by mid 1997. By mid 1998 (the last year for which I have information), 437, or 23.2 percent, of ejidos in the state had completed the process (Villafuerte Solís et al. 1999, 129).

This low number was significantly affected by the exclusion, by the Chiapas Office of the Agrarian Attorney General, of 500 of Chiapas's 1,873 ejidos from the "universe" of ejidos targeted for incorporation into PROCEDE. An official report on the progress of PROCEDE, dated May 1996, states, "[T]he so-called zone of conflict eliminates the possibility of carrying out PROCEDE in approximately 500 *nucleos agrarios* [ejidos]" (Procuraduría Agraria, Delegación Chiapas 1996a: 5). The report continued, "[T]he lack of activities of the program [PROCEDE] is in large part due to occurrences in the regions of Los Altos and the Selva [Lacandon region] with their respective social and political connotations" (ibid., 6).

PROCEDE's advance in Chiapas had been severely limited not only by the ongoing conflict there between the EZLN and the federal army, but also by conflicts between cattle ranchers and members of independent peasant organizations, political conflicts between the PRD and the PRI, the appearances of paramilitary groups, and vigilante violence in many parts of the state. In late June 1996, stories were circulating in the Chiapas office of the Agrarian Attorney General about violence committed against employees. "They burned three of our trucks outside of

TABLE 1

EJIDOS THAT HAD COMPLETED PROCEDE
IN THE STATE OF OAXACA AS OF APRIL 1997

Region	Total Number of Ejidos	Number Certified	% Certified
Papaloapam	261	150	57.5
Valles Centrales	137	68	49.6
Istmo	96	49	51.0
Mixteca	48	31	64.5
Sierra Norte	22	19	86.4
Sierra Sur	46	15	32.6
Cañada	27	15	55.5
Costa	95	24	25.3
Totals	732	371	50.7

SOURCES: Registro Agrario Nacional, Delegación Oaxaca 1997; Secretaría de Reforma Agraria, CORETT 1996, table 7.

TABLE 2

EJIDOS THAT HAD COMPLETED PROCEDE
IN THE STATE OF CHIAPAS AS OF MAY 1997

Region	Total Number of Ejidos	Number Certified	% Certified
Centro	264	83	31.4
Los Altos	118	3	2.5
Fronteriza	336	43	12.8
Fraylesca	105	12	11.4
Norte	206	46	22.3
Selva	436	55	12.6
Sierra	94	0	0.0
Soconusco	231	53	22.9
Istmo Costa	83	33	39.8
Total	1,873	328	17.5

SOURCES: Registro Agrario Nacional, Delegación Chiapas 1997, for numbers of ejidos that completed PROCEDE; Procuraduría Agraria, Delegación Chiapas 1996a, for total number of ejidos in each region.

NOTE: The Agrarian General Attorney's Regional Office in Chiapas published different totals in 1996 and 1997. In Procuraduría Agraria, Delegación Chiapas 1996a, the total number of ejidos in the state is given as 1,873. In 1997, however, the total number was given as 1,787. I have used the former figure, which is more widely cited.

the office in Ocosingo." "The people from INEGI refuse to go and measure and map the land. They are afraid to go where people don't want
them." And, according to the second-in-command at the office, "Our
work results in a lot of conflict here. They have kidnapped employees of
the Procuraduría. It is dangerous work." Such comments are certainly
not evidence of a smooth process of land regularization.

The advances of PROCEDE are lowest in the areas where the EZLN
has support and that have high levels of indigenous population. Resistance to the program is coordinated in areas that form part of self-
declared autonomous governments in rebellion controlled by the EZLN.
Beginning in 1994, the EZLN declared thirty-four different municipalities autonomous and in rebellion. In these municipalities, parallel governments were established with new officials sympathetic to the EZLN.
In self-declared autonomous municipalities, schools, clinics, and other
government installations were shut down and people refused to accept
any form of government assistance or to admit government officials,
including those from PROCEDE. While a series of military/police raids
in 1998, 1999, and 2000, along with continued militarization, have
wrestled control of parts of some of these communities from the EZLN,
tensions run high, and administrators from programs like PROCEDE
still find it difficult to operate. In addition to the autonomous Zapatista
municipalities, there are also five pluri-ethnic autonomous regions in
Chiapas where alternate systems of government also exist and government programs do not easily enter.

A formal report issued by the Chiapas office of the agrarian attorney
general stated, "we have not been able to reach these ejidos [within
the conflict zone] because the peace accords with the EZLN have not
yet been implemented. This obviously is slowing down our work in the
countryside, because of the risks implied for our personnel" (Procuraduría Agraria, Delegación Chiapas 1996a, 6). The report details the difficulties in moving forward with PROCEDE. According to the subdelegate
of the Procuraduría in Chiapas, in 1996, there were 172 ejidos that had
begun but not completed PROCEDE. In more than 25 percent of these,
the program had initially been accepted but then was rejected, and, pre-
dictably, the majority of these rejections (59 percent) were in the zones
of Los Altos and the Lacandon, where the EZLN has strong support
(Procuraduría Agraria, Delegación Chiapas 1996b). The next most frequent reason cited (26 percent of cases) for stalled completion of PRO-
CEDE was that personnel from the office and from INEGI were threatened with physical harm.

THE AGRARIAN BACKLOG
AND LAND INVASIONS IN CHIAPAS

Another major obstacle to PROCEDE in Chiapas has been the high number of ejidos with cases in the backlog of land petitions. In 1996, 25 percent of Mexico's backlogged land petitions related to Chiapas, involving over half of the state's ejidos (Procuraduría Agraria, Delgación Chiapas 1996a, 6). Much of this backlog was caused by the contestation of land claimed by multiple parties. After the mid 1970s, there was little unclaimed land left in Chiapas to give to petitioners to form new ejidos. As a result, the primary mechanism for gaining land was to invade—or reclaim (depending on one's perspective)—land and then petition the Ministry of Agrarian Reform for a resolution in one's favor. Often, indigenous peasants would invade land held in ranches, in private property, or by smallholders. State and federal rulings would then take a long time to be completed, if they ever were. In Chiapas, it took an average of more than seven years for the federal government to "approve claims that had been provisionally accepted by state authorities"; even if a land claim was unopposed, a 27-step completion process required two years of bureaucratic effort on the national level (Collier 1994, 47).

In 1984, the governor of Chiapas, General Absalón Castellaños Domínguez, set up the Agrarian Rehabilitation Plan to facilitate peasant colonization. The program was supposed to purchase lands from private owners to "turn over to peasants where peasants and ranchers were embattled over agrarian reform" (Collier 1994, 50). The program turned over 80,435 hectares to 9,283 families. Peasants affiliated with the CNC received much more favorable treatment than those affiliated with independent organizations (Collier 1994, 51; Reyes Ramos and López Lara 1994, 12–13). In many cases, the CNC even carried out its own invasions in zones targeted for inclusion in the Agrarian Rehabilitation Plan (Harvey 1996, 158). The governor also protected the landholdings of ranchers by issuing 4,714 *certificados de inafectabilidad*, which kept 70 percent of the area used by cattle ranchers legally beyond the reach of agrarian reform (ibid., 159; Reyes Ramos 1992, 119). Indeed, one of the chief forms of opposing a claim was to file a *certificado de inafectabilidad* (exemptions protecting property from expropriation). The "rehabilitation" did little for indigenous peasants, protected the holdings of large ranchers, and increased social and political tension by playing off the PRI's CNC against other independent organizations. The most solid evidence of the plan's failure can be seen in the number of land invasions.

In 1983, 203 pieces of land were invaded. By the time that Absalón Castellanos Domínguez left office, this number had grown to 428 (Reyes Ramos and López Lara 1994, 13).

From 1988 to 1992, a follow-up program, the Agrarian Agreement Program, recognized the agrarian problem as the most severe and unjust problem in Chiapas. In accordance with President Salinas de Gortari's model of *concertación,* or pacted agreements, peasant organizations, ejido authorities, and community leaders were invited to participate in diagnosing agrarian problems. The program turned over an additional 69,429 hectares, to 4,077 peasants, and attempted to promote the formation of associations of ejidatarios and comuneros, and to create better conditions for marketing and credit (Reyes Ramos and López Lara 1994, 15). Most of the land redistributed in this program was purchased by the state government. Thus, well before the emergence of PROCEDE in Chiapas, a pattern had been established of the state government attempting to short-circuit further agrarian conflict by buying land and handing it out.

A final factor inhibiting progress of PROCEDE in the mid 1990s was the high level of land invasions following the Zapatista rebellion in 1994. In the "conflict zone," it is estimated, more than 60,000 hectares of land were invaded between January and July of 1994 (Solis et al. 1999, 131). Most of the invasions were carried out by well-established independent peasant organizations with a long history of fighting for land. A second phase of land invasions, which began in September 1994, took place outside of the conflict zone and later spread across the state. Some invasions were also carried out by members of the CNC. Between 1994 and 1997, about 147,970 hectares were reported invaded in the state of Chiapas (Villafuerte Solis et al. 1999, 135).

ACCOMMODATING PROTEST

In an attempt to terminate the *rezago agrario* and resolve all land invasions in the state of Chiapas, a negotiation process and trust were set up to buy land to satisfy the organizations and communities with land in dispute or with outstanding agrarian petitions. Some cases were old, but some were new conflicts emerging since the Zapatista rebellion. Built on the model of the *concertación agraria,* the trust, or *fideicomisio,* headed by the state coordinator of the Ministry of Agrarian Reform was supposed to look at, and attempt to resolve, agrarian demands, case by case. While cases came primarily from communities and organizations, the trust granted settlements with limits of up to five hectares of land per person, or up to a value of Mex $4,000 per hectare. Thus the limit is Mex $20,000 (about U.S.$2,666) per person. Organizations and communities had to make decisions about land size and value in negotiating with the trust. Again, the government emphasized its relationship with individuals and not with communities.

While the reform to Article 27 that became law in 1992 firmly stated that no more land would be redistributed, the trust created in Chiapas was doing just that through purchase. In July 1996, the state coordinator of the Ministry of Agrarian Reform of Chiapas, José Becerra O'Leary, reported to me that he had signed agreements on two thousand separate points with sixty-nine different organizations as part of state-level Agrarian Accords. According to Becerra O'Leary, the trust had negotiated 243,191 hectares of land for 60,199 petitioners. By mid 1998, the state government of Chiapas had obtained 80 percent of the land it had promised and had turned over about 67 percent of this to the petitioners (Villafuerte Solis et al. 1999, 147). Chiapas was circumventing the 1992 change in agrarian reform law by purchasing land for petitioners involved in agrarian conflicts.

In discussing the purpose of the legal trust, Becerra O'Leary repeatedly emphasized that the government no longer had any obligation to grant land to those demanding it; the modification of Article 27 removes the state from this obligation. In emphasizing this point, however, he indirectly highlighted the central contradiction of the process he was involved in—ending agrarian reform by redistributing more land:

> In this process, we had a lot of new groups arriving with new demands. We told them, hey, you are new. If the group is new, we are not obligated to them, but we attended everyone, anyway. . . . We found that 90 percent of the people who came to us were people we had no legal obligation to give land to. But we are committed to buying land for them all. . . . Do you know what happened here in Chiapas? A lot of people say that the Revolution never reached Chiapas, that there was never agrarian reform here. That is a lie. Sixty percent of the territory of this state is ejidal and communal. . . . What happened is that there was a demographic explosion. There isn't enough land for everyone. So people can't keep expecting the state to give it to them.

Becerra O'Leary admitted that the buy-out of land was not a long-term solution:

> Agrarian struggle has to end so that we can work together to promote a model of economic production that works. We know that these negotiations and the *fideicomisio* will only buy us about five years of peace. We have to

make a more significant investment. If we can't promote economic development, then buying land doesn't work.

If the predictions of Becerra O'Learey are realized and some 58,000
peasants receive 240,000 hectares of land, then the negotiation process
that has undercut the "end of land redistribution" will certainly have
been more important to agrarian politics in the state of Chiapas than
PROCEDE. If his other prediction is correct, then the buying of land
will not solve the deep-seated agrarian problems in the state.

CONCLUSIONS

Just as Lázaro Cárdenas's campaign for rural socialist education and the
creation of ejidos was unevenly implemented in Mexico in the 1930s,
PROCEDE was unevenly implemented in the 1990s. In Chiapas, it was
unable to progress in light of the Zapatista rebellion, high levels of
conflict, land invasions, and the negotiation process of the state of Chiapas with agrarian petitioners. In both the 1930s and the 1990s, rural
development policy has been cloaked in different versions of postrevolutionary nationalism in an attempt to unify the Mexican countryside
behind a particular policy. What emerges of key interest for the rest of
this story is not only that the state's version of the Mexican Revolution
and the heroism of Emiliano Zapata has been unevenly and variably absorbed in rural Oaxaca and Chiapas through national educational and
agrarian programs in the 1930s and again in the 1990s, but that the
terms and symbols of the Revolution—land, peasants, Zapata, struggle,
and Mexican national identity (Mexican-ness) have been and continue
to be floating signifiers that become detached from, and then reattached
to, local histories and national histories in interaction.

To understand the variable resonance of Zapata and the Mexican
Revolution in the NAFTA era of the 1990s, we have to be willing to
eliminate the dichotomy between "national" and "local" histories and
cultures and look at how the elements of both work in interaction
through time. A good place to begin is by looking at, and then extending to the ideology-making apparatuses and culture of the state, the
definition of "popular culture" provided by Gilbert Joseph and Daniel
Nugent, who state that popular culture is processual in nature and is
constantly being refashioned and read within "(and upon) the subordinate imagination":

> At once "socially constituted (it is a product of present and past activity) and socially constituting (it is part of meaningful context in which activity takes place)" (Roseberry 1989: 42), popular culture is neither an autonomous, authentic, and unbounded domain nor a "little tradition" version of dominant culture. Instead, popular and dominant culture are produced in relation to each other through a dialectic of cultural struggle (S. Hall 1981: 233) that takes place in contexts of unequal power and entails reciprocal appropriations, expropriations, and transformations. (Joseph and Nugent 1994, 17)

While knowledge is constantly refashioned and reread in the "subordinate imagination," this is also the case, I would argue, in the imaginations of the architects and executors of state policy, such as those who worked in the educational campaigns of the SEP in the 1930s and the army of *visitadores* and *auxiliares* who combed rural communities in the 1990s to encourage these communities' involvement in the process of mapping, measuring, and certifying their land.

In the remainder of this book, I use four local cases, the ejidos of Guadalupe Tepeyac and, to a lesser degree, La Realidad in Chiapas, and the ejidos of Santa María del Tule and Unión Zapata in Oaxaca, to illustrate both the specific ways in which local histories, identities, and experiences are critical filters for national policy and, also, how such policy, once interpreted in communities, is redeployed back to the center. Such local histories constitute different views of the nation. These local nation views are the filters for how national policy is given meaning. In addition, such histories also suggest the multiple senses of citizenship and loyalties that people, such as the men and women in the ejidos studied, have had through time. While the term "flexible citizens" has been aptly applied to populations such as the transnational Chinese, as suggested by Aiwa Ong (1999), why not also consider indigenous men and women of Mexico as actively creating their own sense of "flexible citizenship" as well, as they participate in different sets of obligations and claims in relation to their communities, regions, and varying senses of the nation? I return to this idea in the concluding chapter.

Recent accounts of the evolution of development policy emphasize *the economy* not only as a material entity, but also as a cultural production (Escobar 1995; Kearney 1996). As cultural discourses, economies are influenced by cultural production in many forms and from many sites (Gudeman 1986; Gudeman and Rivera 1990). Students of public policy and development have long recognized that policy implementation often deviates from the intentions of policy makers. What anthropological and historical literature specifically highlights is how the actual outcome of state policy is strongly influenced by the historical and cultural context of the regions within which it is implemented (Mallon 1995; Joseph and Nugent 1994). To demonstrate this in Mexico is the explicit goal of the remainder of this book, but with one further aim—to suggest that what goes on at the margins of the state, particularly where its legitimacy is in dispute, also affects what happens at the center, as demonstrated by the case of Chiapas where the Zapatista rebellion and land invasions forced the state to renegotiate "the end of land reform" through the back door.

CHAPTER 3

Ethnic and Racial Categories in Mexican History

Chapter 2 describes government attempts to forge a discourse of unitary nationalism built around Zapata and the Mexican Revolution in the 1930s and again in the 1990s. The next four chapters relate the specific story of how indigenous men and women in eastern Chiapas ultimately claimed Zapata and Zapatismo as their own, beginning in the 1980s. To understand this contemporary story, we must first look at the distinctive colonial and postcolonial history of the region, strongly linked to the historical struggle for land, to the establishment of regional indigenous and peasant organizations, and ultimately to armed rebellion.

To tell this story, and that in subsequent chapters focused on Oaxaca, we need to clarify a set of terms and concepts. Both historical and current descriptions of social, economic, and political relations in southern Mexico are littered with terms referring to class relations, ethnic categories, and the intersection of these with biologically based notions of race. This is hardly unusual; often, racial and ethnic categories emerge as part of state discourses used to build nations and to empower certain sectors of a population and disempower others. Such discourse works through creating racial and ethnic categories from social difference, treating these categories as biological, fixed, and "natural," and codifying them in laws distinguishing different segments of the population.

INDIANS, MESTIZOS, AND LADINOS

Racial categories in Mexico began with the invention of the term *indio* (Indian), a homogeneous category used to classify everyone the Spaniards ran into in "New Spain" who were not "from Spain" and thus not "Spanish." The term *indio* lumped hundreds of ethnic groups into an invented racial category, thus denying, at the time of the Spanish invasion, the history and culture of distinctive peoples. The term "Spanish" also homogenizes many differences found among those who arrived from Spain, some of whom were of African, Middle Eastern, and other origins. From the inception of racial discourse in colonial Mexico, through the independence and contemporary period, the constructed "white Spaniard" was the norm. *Indio* and later *mestizo* were deviant and inferior categories.

Within a few decades of the Conquest, the growth of the population of mestizos (supposedly of mixed indigenous and Spanish blood) and *mulatos* (the offspring of Spaniards and female African slaves) turned into a source of anxiety for colonial authorities (Martínez 1997, 751). By the 1540s, the rights of mestizos to gain access to public office and to inherit *encomiendas* (grants of an Indian town or towns, carrying the right to assess tribute) were restricted on the basis that mestizos had impure lineages. By the 1600s, purity-of-blood statutes added mestizos and mulattos to categories considered impure castes. But as time passed, the "mixed bloods" steadily increased, despite efforts to control the sexuality of elite women and to encourage racial separation.

Initially, the Spaniards recognized six basic racial divisions in New Spain, based on appearance. White denoted light-complected persons of European appearance. *Mestizo* designated a person of mixed white-Indian racial appearance. *Pardo* defined an individual of black-Indian physical characteristics. *Mulato* identified someone of black-white racial background. *Negro* indicated African physical appearance. Finally, *indio* or *natural* implied a person having the physical characteristics of the region's indigenous populations (Carroll 1991, 87). Contact between the racial categories grew, particularly in urban areas, and new categories became necessary as racial and cultural traits became hopelessly confused. A minimum of sixteen different ethnic and racial types were identified during the colonial period (Meyer and Sherman 1995, 204), with dozens appearing in popular and artistic descriptions. The emergence of an elaborate system of racial hierarchies appears to have taken place in the second half of the sixteenth century, when mestizos and mulattos occupied a clear numerical presence (Martínez 1997, 751).

The overall shift in demographics in Mexico demonstrated that, by 1803, so-called mestizos had become more than one-third of the population. Even a significant number of the elite were of mixed racial heritage. Kay Warren writes that by the eighteenth century, the term *ladino* had displaced *mestizo* in Guatemala (1998, 10). Since Chiapas did not join independent Mexico until 1824, and until then was part of the colonial jurisdiction of Guatemala, the term *ladino* was also used there. Carol Smith (1990) proposes that *ladino* came to signify a person of nonindigenous descent and culture late in the nineteenth century; *ladino* no longer referred simply to a person of nonindigenous descent, but to a conscious effort to assimilate—to exchange indigenous dress, language, and custom for national or regional identity. Shannan Mattiace notes that during the colonial period in Chiapas, "the term 'ladino' referred to Indians who had adopted an urban, non-Indian lifestyle. This contrasts with the nineteenth century usage characterizing ladino as a lighter-skinned non-Indian. This usage continues today" (Mattiace 1998, 164).

MESTIZAJE AND INDIGENISMO

After the Mexican revolution, the promotion of *mestizaje* as a national ideology was pushed in tandem with policies focused on incorporating the indigenous population. Beginning with Manuel Gamio's call for the fusion of "races" in his *Forjando Patria* (1916), and continuing into the work of the better-known José Vasconcelos, the erasure of indigenous culture became a central part of state centralization and creation of uniform citizens. Anti-Chinese rhetoric, a part of Vasconcelos's writing about "the cosmic race," anti-Chinese eugenics publications, and the expulsion of hundreds of Chinese from Sonora in the early 1930s also reinforced the nationalist idea of Mexico as a one-race nation.

As stated by Vasconcelos, "[T]he Indian has no other door to the future but the door of modern culture, nor any other road but the road already cleared by Latin civilization" (1997, 16). The Ministry of Public Education and the establishment of a federal system of schools, particularly in rural areas, would be a key way to slowly but surely assimilate Mexico's indigenous population into the nation.

At the end of the Cárdenas administration, the government policy of indigenous incorporation was questioned, and, in 1940, Mexican delegates at the Interamerican Indigenist Conference in Pátzcuaro, Michoacán, signed onto a declaration calling for bilingual education and declaring that the theory of incorporation of "the Indian to civilization—a pretext used to better exploit and oppress the aboriginal peoples—had been discarded" (Lewis 1997b, 841; see also Aguirre Beltrán 1992). A new era in government race policy had begun that also planted the seeds for the reversal of the discourse on "the Indian problem" in Mexico. The creation of the National Indigenous Institute after the Interamerican Indigenous Conference in 1940 was the beginning of a counter-hegemonic discourse against assimilation that existed both within the state and in local and regional indigenous communities and movements, which emerged most strongly in the 1970s. These movements reached their maximum horizontal articulation through the National Indigenous Congress, formed in 1996 to push the Mexican government to implement the San Andrés Accords on Indigenous Rights and Culture, which the government of Ernesto Zedillo signed with the Zapatista Army of National Liberation in February 1996, but Mexico's government has yet to implement as of this writing. In March 2001, Subcomandante Marcos and a busload of Zapatista comandantes followed a circuitous route to Mexico City to press the Mexican Congress to legislate the San Andrés accords.

The work of Manuel Gamio, who organized the Inter-American Indigenist Institute in the 1940s, was followed in Mexico by the creation of the Instituto Nacional Indigenista (National Indigenous Institute), or INI. Founded in 1948, INI often represented contradictory policies toward Mexico's indigenous peoples—suggesting autonomy but also incorporation. The founding of INI, in creating a separate agency on indigenous peoples, made these the only racially identified members of the Mexican population to have their own government institution. The creation of such an institution suggests again that the central policy question was how Mexico's indigenous population should be described, identified, and positioned as citizens. Racial discourse in Mexico continued to revolve around the indigenous population; blacks were completely forgotten by the government until recently.

QUESTIONING DEFINITIONS AND DEBATING AUTONOMY

Much of the anthropological research initially promoted by INI, as well as research carried out by a host of anthropologists in Mexico from the 1930s onward, focused on particular ethnic groups, often identified by so-called "objective criteria," such as language, dress, territory, custom, and forms of social organization. Mexico was carved up into studies of particular indigenous peoples—such as the Zapotec, Mixe, and Mixtec of Oaxaca, and the Tzotzil, Tzeltal, Ch'ol, and Tojolabal of Chiapas. Most of these designations were based on linguistic affiliation, and using language to measure "Indianness" continues to this day. A 1995 census put the country's indigenous population at 5,483,555, or about 6.8 percent of the total population aged five years and over. To reach this number, the government counted all persons five and over speaking an indigenous language as "indigenous." In 1995, a separate count included all of the residents in households where the household head or spouse spoke an indigenous language. This yielded a count of 8,984,152, or 9.9 percent of the population. Others put the indigenous population in Mexico at 30 percent if children under five and persons who understand but may not fluently speak an indigenous language yet self-identify as indigenous are included. There are 56 different ethnic/language groups in Mexico. According to the language criteria of a 1995 census counting speakers aged five and over, Chiapas then had an indigenous population of 768,720, or 25 percent of the state's total, and the 1995 indigenous population of Oaxaca totaled 1,027,847, or 36.5 percent of the state's population aged five and over (Instituto Nacional de Estadística, Geografía e Informática 1996).

In terms of specific indigenous ethnic group designations mentioned in this book, in Oaxaca there were approximately 319,000 Zapotec speakers, 88,863 Mixe speakers, and 239,451 Mixteco speakers in 1990 (Consejo Estatal de Población 1994, 49). In 1990 in Chiapas there were approximately 35,3567 Tojolabal speakers, approximately 258,153 Tzeltal speakers, and approximately 226,681 Tzotzil speakers (Viquera 1995, 25–27). New census data by particular language were not available as of final editing.

Concepts of ethnicity used by the Mexican government continue to rely on trait recognition and the certification by experts of indigenous legitimacy. Obviously this method is about forty years behind anthropological concepts of ethnicity, which focus on the expression and practice of ethnic identity in action and on the processes of identity construction. Local and regional ethnic histories and power relations are the relevant criteria for how ethnicity is lived and experienced. Language is still critical to self-definitions and boundaries in many parts of Oaxaca, but not everywhere. And many speakers of indigenous languages in Oaxaca are bilingual in Spanish. Language is still a significant, but not necessarily the primary, ingredient of ethnic identity in eastern Chiapas, particularly in areas where indigenous and peasant organizing has grown over the past twenty years. Second- and third-generation Tojolabales may not speak Tojolabal, yet they have a strong sense of ethnic identity. In other areas of Mexico, indigenous people often understand but do not speak their language and use other measures of identity, most often rooted in community. The shared identity of people within the Lacandon region, for example, is not necessarily based on language or on generations of shared customs. Since many have come to the region within the past forty to sixty years, their shared culture and identity is built out of their political experience and participation in a range of peasant, indigenous— and now guerrilla—organizations.

Since the early 1990s in Mexico, proposals for structuring indigenous self-determination have ranged from pluri-ethnic regions (in which several indigenous groups, and perhaps even mestizos, coexist and control territory, resources, education, and government) to mono-ethnic communities granting self-determination at the level of community and allowing communities to affiliate into larger entities to coordinate governance. Indigenous autonomy in places like Oaxaca, for example, requires a self-conscious naturalization of the particular practices of everyday life in specific ethnically defined communities—Mixe, Huave, Zapoteco, and so on. This self-promoted ethnic essentialism on the part of a group like the Mixe is a historical reality that resonates with that group's people, and coexists with the more hybrid examples of pluri-ethnic regions in lowland eastern Chiapas. Historical and regional variation of what constitutes indigenous self-determination, and of how that self-determination should be realized more broadly in the Mexican nation, provides an important challenge to the hegemonic notion of the multicultural nation, a notion articulated in 1990 through the modification of Article 4 of the Mexican Constitution but currently having no legislative blueprint or set of laws for its realization. The specific stories of how neo-Zapatismo was created and spread in Chiapas, and later absorbed in Oaxaca, are tied to varying understandings of what indigenous identity is and how it relates to other struggles for land, access to productive resources, and relations with the government.

PART II

Zapatismo in Eastern Chiapas

CHAPTER 4

The Historical Roots of Indigenous Struggle in Chiapas

Colonial history in Chiapas, along with later trends in the republican period, set important precedents for indigenous loss of land and efforts to reclaim it. The system of *encomiendas,* put into operation between 1523 and 1531, laid the basis for the exploitation of the indigenous population. Some communities in the Tzeltal- and Tzotzil-speaking highlands, such as Chamula, Tenejapa, Oxchuc, and Huixtán, were able to retain a communal land base during the colonial era (Favre 1984, 46). Others almost completely lost their territorial base. Tojolabal, Tzotzil, Tzeltal, and Ch'ol people were conscripted to work on ranches and plantations in the lowlands. Others from the lowlands were resettled to the highlands around Ciudad Real (San Cristóbal de las Casas) to serve as laborers, particularly after lowland populations were wiped out by disease (Collier 1994, 19). Even those communities able to legitimize part of their land base under the Spanish crown paid high rates of tribute and participated in forced labor schemes. The Tojolabales of eastern Chiapas had their original land base around what is now the city of Comitán.

Founded in 1528, Comitán is the oldest city in Chiapas. Thirty years after its founding, Dominican priests founded the monastery of Santo Domingo de Guzmán in Comitán and took over surrounding indigenous lands. The monastery in Comitán came to control the majority of large cattle ranches in the municipalities of Trinitaria, Chicomucelo, Comalapa, and Socoltenango, as well as the ranches around Comitán and

Las Margaritas (Lomelí González 1988, 10). Thus, shortly after the arrival of the Spaniards, the Tojolabales were forcibly relocated to labor on large Spanish estates, outside of Comitán, owned either by the Church or by the Spanish elite. In this process, the Tojolabales went from being owners of communal land to peons (Ruz 1992; Gómez Hernández and Ruz 1992).

Chiapas joined independent Mexico in 1824. Early agrarian laws decreed in 1826 and 1832 defined the legal extension of village commons by population and opened up the lands surrounding indigenous communities for privatization. The so-called *terrenos baldíos* (vacant lands) could thus be appropriated by private citizens (Benjamin 1996, 13–14). The laws in fact encouraged the nonindigenous elite to claim title to what had been considered indigenous lands. "Arguing after independence that to leave such an immense resource unexploited would unnecessarily retard the state's development, successive governments between 1826 and 1844, liberal and conservative alike, progressively simplified the process by which private citizens could 'denounce,' or claim, them (*terrenos baldíos*). As a result, by 1850 virtually all the state's Indian communities had been stripped of their 'excess' lands" (Rus 1983, 131–32).

Elite *ladino* families, such as the Larráinzars, who succeeded in "denouncing" three-quarters of the Chamulas' land, were able to transform more than "a quarter of Chiapas's Indians from 'free' villagers into permanently—and legally—obligated peons and laborers" (Rus 1983, 133). As the number of private ranches and plantations grew and those of the Church were privatized under the Ley Lerdo of 1856, indigenous peoples, such as the Tojolabales near Comitán, continued to be attached to these large estates through forms of debt peonage (Montagu 1969, 227).

The transfer of Church properties largely into the hands of liberals in Chiapas was accompanied by the secularization of political control inside indigenous communities. Over the decades since independence in 1821, indigenous communities had increasingly lost access to the terrenos baldíos that had been held in protectorship first by the crown and then by the republican state. With secularization, indigenous communities lost whatever protection Church management of their properties had provided against tax collectors and labor contractors. In 1861, the state government of Chiapas appointed ladino municipal secretaries, who collected taxes and were supposed to be liberating Indians from the system of legal servitude (Benjamin 1996, 17). Liberal government attacks were also aimed at the control the Catholic clergy had had over indigenous religion for more than three hundred years. Religious *cargos* were abolished and Indians were encouraged to abandon churches altogether (Rus 1983). As priests fled churches and communities, or were ignored, indigenous religion flourished more openly.

In Comitán, the domination of the Dominican friars ended definitively with the Reform Laws of 1857, and their large cattle farms and ranches passed into the hands of the Spanish and criollo elite of Comitán (Lomelí González 1988, 12). Chief among those families who gained control of Church property were the Castellanos, who became the owners of new properties in both the highlands and the valleys. The Castellanos family came to possess thirteen large ranches, including Rosario Baja, Rosario Santiago, Rosario Jotaná, Rosario Chiptic, Rosario Bauitz, Saltillo, San Joaquín, Medellín, Soledad, El Momón, Napité, Bajuku, La Piedad, and Santa Rita (Lomelí González 1988, 12).

NINETEENTH-CENTURY INDIGENOUS REBELLION

After liberals gained uncontested control of the Chiapas state government in 1867, they assured indigenous people that they "were now free of onerous obligations to clergy, including religious taxes and registering vital statistics" (Rus 1989, cited in Eber 2000, 27). The Chamula, "when given the chance, withdrew from their churches and pueblos altogether, establishing an independent religious and marketing center of their own" (Rus 1983, 144). Celebrations such as Carnival, patron saint days, and other rituals were enthusiastically celebrated, and the Catholic Church claimed that such celebrations really aimed at eliminating ladinos. The Church increased its attacks on indigenous religion, but to no avail.

While in hindsight one may often analyze rebellions according to current categories and frameworks, the language and messages of indigenous movements often integrate a range of elements including culture, religion, land, and work. Just as the Zapatista rebellion of 1994 is a mixture of ideological elements, so too was a crucial indigenous movement in 1867–69.

Agustina Gómez Checheb, a Chamula woman, declared in 1867 that three sacred stones had fallen from the sky and communicated with her. Shortly thereafter, Pedro Díaz Cuscat traveled to see Agustina and declared that he too could talk to the stones. Cuscat, a major authority figure in the religious hierarchy of Chamula, had a shrine built and began actively to recruit believers, who came not only to see the shrine but also to hear his sermons (Rus 1983, 144–45). And many did come. The traffic in devotees, and the commercial activity that accompanied their journeys, made not only the Church, but also ladino politicians and economic elites in the highlands, nervous. The possibility of autonomous economic networks, markets, and cultural and religious spaces provoked attacks on the devotees and their families. Ladino highlanders invaded the religious site and tried to persuade the Indians to abandon their rebellion. Angered at the attempts to stop their activities, and fearful of ladino reprisals, indigenous people in a few towns took up arms and directed their wrath at a handful of landowners, a school teacher, and a priest (Rus 1983, 150). The ultimate response was brutal.

A first ladino offensive killed three hundred Indians camped north and west of San Cristóbal. A later offensive in Chamula territory killed three hundred more, and a militia action in Yolonchén, near San Andrés, resulted in the deaths of two hundred men, women, and children (Rus 1983, 155). Rus notes that, sadly, Indians themselves participated in these persecutions, eager to prove themselves "loyal" (ibid., 155). Several later attacks chased down exhausted families fleeing and living in the forest, resulting in the deaths of over a hundred more people. Although the rebellion is often portrayed as a "caste war" of Indians against ladinos, the ethnohistorian and anthropologist Jan Rus provides a more realistic interpretation of this movement from the perspective of its indigenous protagonists, as an attempt to defend access to land, markets, and religious and cultural practices of importance (Rus 1983; see also Harvey 1998, 46–47). "The Indian movement of 1867–69, when it was their movement, appears to have been a peaceful one. What they sought was to be left alone to farm their fields, conduct their markets, and worship their saints as they themselves chose," Rus observes (1983, 159).

This analysis could be extended to the Zapatista rebellion of the 1990s. What is important to note is that, while many accounts of Chiapas history for the earlier period focus primarily on the loss of indigenous lands, on the continuation of debt-peonage, and on servitude, there was clearly also a simultaneous countercurrent of indigenous refashioning of political, economic, and cultural spaces. This lesson is not to be lost in understanding processes in the Lacandon jungle from the 1950s to the present.

THE LACANDON FOREST AND NINETEENTH-CENTURY LAND PRIVATIZATION IN THE GLOBAL MARKET OF LIBERALISM

While agricultural land was privatized under a series of liberal laws that extended through the nineteenth century, the Lacandon forest was being integrated into a global market for hardwoods. This forest was first discovered as a reserve by Cayetano Ramón Robles, who asked for authorization to explore and exploit the basin of the Rio Jataté in 1822 in order to offer the new nation of Mexico "the exploitation of all the construction wood and tar that would be necessary" (de Vos 1995, 340).

The proposed project never reached fruition. Instead, the area remained virgin territory until 1859, when a Tabascan entrepreneur began timber exploitation for the global market. By the decade of the 1870s, there were about fifteen small-scale lumber businesses operating in the Lacandon. Average tree cutting at the time did not exceed two hundred trees per firm (de Vos 1995, 340). In the 1880s, the rate of timber exploitation increased with the entrance of three larger and more powerful companies, based in the city today called Villahermosa. With the financial support of foreign investors, these firms converted the logging industry into a large-scale operation that established logging camps on seven Lacandon rivers. The primary product was mahogany, shipped out through ports in the Gulf of Mexico and sold on the docks of London, Liverpool, Hamburg, and New York as "wood from Tabasco" (ibid.). Labor conditions were extremely difficult; "bound to the mahogany lumber camps by their debts and by more than 100 kilometers of uninhabited tropical vegetation, [workers found] it was difficult to gain freedom" (ibid., 342).

The 1890s were a boom decade, in which European, U.S., and Mexican investors established plantations in the tropical regions of Chiapas, Tabasco, and Guatemala to extract precious hardwoods, such as mahogany, from the forest, and to grow sugar, coffee, and cacao. Coffee production began in the Soconusco region, and by the end of the century, it had spread to almost every *municipio* in Chiapas. Spurred on by export markets for Chiapan products, the number of *ranchos* (small to medium-sized private plots) and haciendas (large private ranches and plantations) in Chiapas grew steadily from the 1870s to the 1890s. In 1877, the state had 448 haciendas and 501 ranchos (Benjamin 1996, 27); by 1896, this number had grown to 1,049 haciendas and 3,497 ranchos, a result of the privatization of indigenous communal land (ibid., 87).

In 1894, eager to be ahead of the liberalization program carried out
from the center of Mexico, Chiapas's governor, Emilio Rebasa, "en-
acted and vigorously enforced a measure . . . to divide all ejidos in Chiapas into parcels" (Benjamin 1996, 48–49). While the number of small
property owners did increase in particular localities, particularly in the
central valley, between 1893 and 1909 at least sixty-seven village ejidos
were negatively affected (ibid., 49). The liberal idea of creating a new
class of small farmers promoting productive agriculture through private
property primarily resulted in communities independent for hundreds
of years either disappearing or becoming *hacienda rancherías*—that is,
populations living inside the boundaries of an hacienda and bound to
it (ibid.). Many villagers who were supposed to get plots in the process
never did.

The process of deterritorializing indigenous communities that culminated before the Mexican Revolution was accompanied by the privatization of large tracts of land in the Lacandon jungle. An 1883 law gave
those who surveyed lands the right to keep one-third of what they surveyed as private property; the remaining two-thirds became national
lands suitable for subsequent sale. A revision to this law, in 1894, removed any stipulations requiring that the lands claimed by surveyors be
settled and cultivated, as well as eliminating any limit to the amount of
land an individual or company could acquire. After this revision, the
main lumber companies working in the Lacandon converted themselves
into surveying companies. When the dust settled, three major companies
became owners of land they had previously rented, each possessing as private property between 200,000 and 700,000 hectares (between 500,000
and 1.7 million acres) (Sullivan 1997, 1368). The rest of the jungle was
in the hands of three Mexico City businessmen and a Spanish nobleman,
Claudio López Bru, known as the Marqués de Comillas, whose name
the region still bears (de Vos 1995, 342).

Constitutionalist troops dismantled some logging camps in 1913 and
promised the laborers that their poor treatment and low pay would end,
but the promises were not kept. The major downfall of the logging industry was the loss of the European market for hardwoods during
World War I. After 1915, the extraction of hardwood from the Lacandon went steadily downhill (de Vos 1995, 345). Some firms continued to
log while in decline; the horrible labor conditions of the *monterias,* or
logging camps, were widely publicized in the 1920s.

Even after the Mexican Revolution, ownership of large parts of the
Lacandon remained legally in the hands of the firms of Romano, Valen-

zuela, Sud-Oriental, and Agua Azul, and of the Dorenberg, Dorantes, Martínez de Castro, and López Bru families (de Vos 1995, 342). The real populating of the Lacandon jungle was to come long after the revolution, beginning in the late 1930s and 1940s, when landless laborers who had been bound to plantations and ranches began to colonize the jungle and then petitioned the government for title to the land as ejidos.

DEBT SERVITUDE

The conditions of slavery in the lumber camps were part of a wide-ranging system of debt servitude, peonage, and share-cropping crucial to economic development in the state of the Chiapas in the late eighteenth and early nineteenth centuries. Systems of debt peonage or debt servitude developed as the number of large ranches and plantations multiplied steadily after 1890, when the price of coffee began to rise on the world market. While there were few coffee plantations in Chiapas in the 1880s, "by the end of 1927 there were 94 large ranches: 32 German, 13 Spanish, 10 North American, 7 French, 3 English, 2 Swiss, and 27 Mexican" (Rus, Rus, and Hernández 1990, 3). Although recruiting first in nearby communities, ranchers began, as the demand for labor grew, to recruit in the highlands and elsewhere, including the Tojolabal region around Comitán, a stopping point for those coming down from the highlands.

In the 1890s, some Tojolabales joined the stream of highland Tzeltzles, Tzotziles, Ch'oles, and others who worked seasonally on the coffee and sugar plantations of the Soconusco coast. In 1897, the department of Comitán, where the Tojolabal population was concentrated, had more people in debt servitude than had anywhere else in the state. In the department, 4,783 indebted servants owed 333,077 pesos (Benjamin 1996, 65). In the neighboring department of Chilón, with Tzeltal and some Tojolabal populace, there were 3,530 indebted servants. These two regions, along with the coffee zone of Soconusco, had the most indebted servants in the state at the end of the nineteenth century (Benjamin 1996, 65). Overall, the state's survey in 1897 found that there were 31,512 indebted servants, who owed more than 3 million pesos to their employers (ibid., 54). Government revenue for the state of Chiapas that year was approximately 450,000 pesos (ibid., 47).

The indigenous labor force was controlled in several ways. First, those who migrated to work on coffee and other plantations were enticed by the *enganche,* or advanced payment, system. Contractors would

travel to indigenous communities and offer a small sum of money to establish a debt, or large quantities of liquor to induce individuals to sign
a contract (Benjamin 1996, 77). Once on the plantation, indigenous laborers could run up debts through purchases at company stores. "[I]n
this way, workers rarely accumulated enough to pay back initial loans,
were obligated to accept new loans, and as a result, accumulated more
debt. Bosses could also increase their workers' dependency by financ-
ing religious ceremonies and selling cheap liquor at the company store"
(Harvey 1998, 50).

In an outstanding bilingual book of Tzotzil testimonies edited and
translated by Jan Rus, Diana Rus, and José Hernández, five Tzotzil laborers describe the *enganche* system and other aspects of life working
on the fincas:

> During that time, there were *enganchadores*—we called them "give money"
> —in San Cristóbal. Those who needed a loan, whether it was twenty or thirty
> pesos, went to look for them. "Okay, come back at such and such a day at
> such and such a time [with the borrowed money]," they said. Fine. The per-
> son would get their money and go home. When it was time for them to re-
> pay the loan, the *enganchador* would say, "Now you have to repay your debt,
> now you are going." And if you didn't show up when you had to pay back
> your debt, they would look for you. They also looked for people before they
> had to pay their debts because they had their photographs, they knew where
> their houses and their communities were. So that is how they would look for
> people, taking their *caporales* [headmen, or managers] with them as helpers.
> During that time, they knew to look all the way here in Chamula. The ladi-
> nos would come after us all the way into our hamlets where we lived. But one
> time a ladino came and the people got together and they cut off his head and
> threw it in the river. That was the end of that disagreement. (Rus, Rus, and
> Hernández 1990, 5; see also Guzmán López and Rus 1990)

In some areas, such as Simojovel, where migrants accumulated so much
debt that they were prohibited from leaving plantations, they became permanently indebted workers, or *peones acasillados,* and "were obliged to
work for their *patrón* in exchange for the use of a small plot of land"
(Harvey 1996, 50). This was the situation of most Tojolabales further
south.

THE MEXICAN REVOLUTION IN CHIAPAS

While some Tojolabales migrated to seek work on coffee and sugar plantations, many lived within the boundaries of large ranches and fincas,
where they labored as peones acasillados. These ranches were located

on prime agricultural lands in the corridor between Comitán and Altamirano to the north, and eastward and southward toward Guatemala. While Carrancista troops did arrive in Chiapas in 1914, and a military government in 1915 distributed flyers and sent translators throughout the state advising villagers to claim land stolen from them during the reign of Porfirio Díaz, between 1915 and 1920, only six ejido grants were approved to petitioners in Chiapas (Benjamin 1996, 130).

In the Soconusco region, soldiers spreading ideas about land reform also attempted to enforce the 1914 Ley de los Obreros (Workers' Law) outlawing debt servitude. This led to the politicization of some workers and professionals in the region, and in 1920, the Partido Socialista Chiapaneco (Chiapas Socialist Party) was formed. That same year, however, a conservative state government bent on reestablishing the Porfirian order ended enforcement of the Ley de los Obreros. "[S]ervitude, montería slavery, enganche, and *tiendas de raya*—abuses that had never completely disappeared—again became normal in the countryside of Chiapas" (Benjamin 1996, 150). It is thus no wonder that the "Mexican Revolution" had no meaning for most rural populations in Chiapas until well into the 1930s, when it became possible to petition for and receive ejido land under Cárdenas, and when debt servitude was definitively ended. A Cárdenas representative, Erastro Urbina, was put in charge of organizing highland Indians and indigenous workers into a coalition to help Cardenas's party take over the state. Urbina had previously served as part of a 1934 labor commission in Chiapas. In 1936, Urbina was named director of the Chiapas Departamento de Protección Indígena (Department of Indian Protection), or DPI (Rus 1994, 275). From this position he was able not only to influence the formation of an indigenous workers union but to take control of indigenous municipios through a new system of governance that included two municipal presidents. Since Urbina's Department of Indian Protection would only deal with municipal presidents who were bilingual, the bilingual scribes represented the communities in dealings with the state government. These scribes were further empowered in the late 1930s, when they were also made labor union officers, heads of municipal agrarian committees, leaders of the official party, and representatives of the Confederación Nacional Campesina (Rus 1994, 278). In contrast, in the lowlands, power dynamics continued to be concentrated in the haciendas, not in communities.

Even now, the oldest generation of founding Tojolabal ejidatarios in the Lacandon region have clear memories of life as peones acasillados.

The Tojolabales referred to this role as that of *mozos*—being bound servants who labored in exchange for access to a small plot of land. For many, moving off the hacienda and colonizing land of their own was a life-transforming event. Carlos Lenkersdorf and Gemma van der Haar are two anthropologists who have worked for many years in Tojolabal communities; their edited collection of testimonies from San Miguel Chiptic captures the memories of Tojolabal mozos bound to a large ranch belonging to the Castellanos family. Tata Pedro recalled what it was like to live and work under the Castellanos family:

> The owner was Don Pepe Castellanos. The Chiptic ranch was his. He had a lot of servants there. These servants did different types of work. There was one who was in charge of supervising the work.
> Others took care of the cattle. There was a lot of cattle. They wandered all over the place because the patrón had a lot of lands. . . .
> Others carried water, firewood, and *ocote* [pine used for tinder]. At the tender age of twelve, children became *porteros* [gatekeepers and guardsmen]. Their job was to see that the birds didn't eat the jocote fruits. . . .
> None of the people were paid, because the patrón gave them a small piece of land to plant their corn on and to gather firewood from. . . . [T]here were some people who had one or two heads of cattle, or horses, but during this time they belonged to the patrón. He wouldn't give them anywhere to pasture their cattle. (Lenkersdorf and van der Haar 1998, 53–54)

Women also bore a heavy burden of work in the household of the patrón. A Tojolabal ejido member from San Miguel Chiptic said: "Women were servants too. We also suffered. We had to prepare the food for the patrón. We each had to take a turn, one person per day. To start this work we had to get up at three in the morning, when the sky was beginning to turn. We worked until six in the afternoon" (ibid., 55). In the testimonies assembled by Van der Haar and Lenkersdorf, the Tojolabal authors clearly reflect on their past life and the need to ensure that they never return to a state of servitude. The current generation of ejidatarios, too, are determined to never return to this life their grandparents lived. One said: "They looked at our grandparents like they were mere puppets. Because of our grandparents, we don't want to ever see those patrónes again. Now we don't ever want to return to the time of being servants. Today we get angry at what they did to our ancestors. It is necessary for us to prepare ourselves to destroy all of that which was no good" (ibid., 55).

The Tojolabal *mozos* who worked on the Chiptic ranch eventually organized themselves into several ejidos. In 1952, thirty-two persons from Chiptic who founded the ejido of Florida were given 762 hectares when they petitioned the government for land. In 1963, fifty-one mozos and their families purchased 900 hectares from the Chiptic Finca, from Don Pepe Castellanos, and founded their community (ibid., 148).

The first ejidos in the Tojolabal region were granted in the 1930s. It was not until then that people even knew it was possible to petition for land. The formation of ejidos was a transforming moment, and people remember the time as a movement from a period of "slavery" to "freedom." This historical riff, which runs through many of the recorded testimonies of Tojolabal *mozos* who became ejidatarios, is a motif replayed in the 1970s by liberation theology as the theme of exodus. The search for liberty was repeated as the population of the original ejidos doubled, tripled, and quadrupled, and there was no more land. In the 1930s, however, "slavery" was a firsthand concept. As related by Casimiro Gómez and Lorenzo Gómez López, from ejido Veracruz and Estanislao García Pérez from Colonia Lomantan, whose testimonies are mingled in a 1988 publication:

> In 1930, the people started to realize that the slavery was ending. When the patrones heard this, they only laughed but their smiles were wrong because the slavery did end and the peasants remained free. This was in the years of 1935 and 1936. These were the years the people were freed and when they began to work their own lands and to buy their own animals to work on their land. During the time of slavery, the people couldn't own animals. . . .
>
> In 1938, the Engineer came to measure the lands and people knew that they would remain free from peonage. They began to allot parcels of land to people and they formed their *colonias*. Each ejido began to name its own commissioner and they moved forward. United and organized, they respected each other because they were the owners of their lands. (Lomelí González 1988, 40–41)

While some ejidos were formed in the 1930s in Chiapas, in other areas campesinos were not allowed to organize to petition for land. In 1935, Manuel Castellanos took charge as inspector of the fifth federal education zone in Chiapas, primarily covering the highlands. There, he worked not only to improve school infrastructure and facilitate the attendance of indigenous peasants in schools and organize social programs, but also to jump-start the federal agrarian reform program. (Using federal teachers to organize peasants and to help them petition for land was common under Lázaro Cárdenas.) In 1935, Castellanos wrote to the state inspector:

> This revolutionary promise has greatly disappointed the campesinos with the exception of a few places where with a thousand sacrifices agrarian colonies and centers have been established. . . . There have been cases where unscrupulous engineers have swindled them, like in Cancuc, Tenango, Tenejapa,

etc. . . . [I]n the valleys of Ocosingo, where the peasants have been thrown off the lands that they tried to solicit, they were denied land for sharecropping, they were blocked from occupying national lands under the pretext of conserving forests, and their leaders are persecuted and incarcerated, like Plácido Flores, who remains in the jails of Ocosingo along with other agraristas, all of this so that the campesinos might denounce the just rights that the Revolution has conquered for them and return to being submissive and resigned. . . . to the yoke of servitude. (Castellanos 1935, cited in Lewis 1997a, 397)

While some Tojolabal communities petitioned for ejidos in the 1930s, many did not receive formal recognition of their colonies until the 1950s. Policy changes at the national level would prove to be important in helping to legitimate ejido land claims. Beginning in 1950 or so, the Departamento de Asuntos Agrarios y Colonización (Department of Agrarian and Colonization Affairs), or DAAC, was preparing a new demarcation of the Lacandon jungle that would annul the Porfirian grants to families and businesses of title to large tracts of the forest (de Vos 1995, 348). In the northern part of the Lacandon, a large tract of land was expropriated in 1961. In 1967 and 1972, two other vast tracts of land were expropriated in the central and southern zones of the Lacandon and granted to many communities as original ejido land or ejido extensions (ibid., 348–49). Thus, beginning in the 1930s and continuing into the 1960s and 1970s, people who had been landless peones acasillados on the large cattle ranches and coffee plantations of the Comitán and Las Margaritas areas in "the time of slavery" colonized the Lacandon jungle in several waves. Population calculations for the Lacandon jungle confirm this. In 1950, there were 1,000 colonists; in 1960, there were 10,000; in 1970, there were 40,000; in 1980, there were 100,000; and in 1990, there were an estimated 150,000 inhabitants (ibid., 355).[1] The vital mix in the Lacandon forest of this population growth, liberation theology, independent peasant organizations, Maoist organizations, the clandestine Fuerzas de Liberación Nacional, and decades of frustration with state agrarian officials would ultimately produce the Ejército Zapatista de Liberación Nacional.

CHAPTER 5

The New Zapatismo in the Lacandon Jungle

Before, [during the times of] my mother and my grandmother, . . . the husband and the wife worked more because
they had a *patrón* to work for. They [the *patrones*] gave them
washbasins, we still have them, but they didn't pay them any
money. My mother and grandmother even made their own
soap, and they only had Sundays to do their own work.

We don't have a patrón now. We looked for a better life
without a patrón and we found our land. We continued to be
poor, but we had our products. When we would bring our
products to Las Margaritas, they bought them at a very bad
price. They told us, "Your coffee is no good." And because
we were really poor, we sold it to them cheaply. . . . I decided
to become a Zapatista so that our communities can improve.

> *Comandante Trinidad, Tojolabal leader from*
> *Guadalupe Tepeyac, daughter of one of the orig-*
> *inal ejidatario families of Guadalupe Tepeyac,*
> *quoted in Zúñiga and Bellinghausen 1997,*
> *340–41*

In her mid fifties, Comandante Trinidad cuts an imposing figure at a
press conference. Unlike the female comandantes who participated in
the second round of peace dialogues between the Ejército Zapatista de
Liberación Nacional and the Mexican government during 1995 and
1996, Trini is from an older generation. Her long white hair reaches her
waist as it flows below the red bandanna she wears over her face, a Zapatista trademark for those who regard ski masks as too hot or too ex-
pensive. While Trini herself did not work as a sharecropper on a finca, her
parents and grandparents did. Trini was part of a generation that grew up
in the Lacandon as part of a new ejido community that rapidly expanded
from the 1950s through the 1990s. She is also part of a generation who

have turned some of their children over to the armed struggle of the
EZLN, encouraging them to fight to improve their communities. Doña
Trini watched for many years as her community confronted a largely unresponsive and disrespectful agrarian bureaucracy while trying to secure
new lands for the expanding population of young people. She listened
as Marist priests preached the notions of "exodus" and "liberation" and
spoke of finding God in Indian culture. She also witnessed the community's participation in the marketing and credit programs promoted by
regional peasant organizations from the 1970s through the 1990s. She
watched as small farmers who had put their faith in independent organizations and the potential of coffee for a better future were devastated
by the collapse of coffee prices in June 1989. And she watched as her
children and grandchildren lost hope when the government announced
there would be no more land allotted after the 1992 reforms to Article 27
of the Mexican Constitution.

Sometime in the mid to late 1980s and the early 1990s, she and others in and around Guadalupe Tepeyac gave up on independent organizations as a means of procuring change, and decided to risk everything
and join the EZLN. She nodded her approval when at least one of her
sons went off to become a member of the EZLN and then returned to
work clandestinely for it in his community. She knew that, even as the
Mexican Army was conducting military exercises in and around the
community of Guadalupe Tepeyac in the early 1990s, many members of
her and other communities were secretly holding meetings in the first
Zapatista "safe house" located on ejido land from her community.
Doña Trini kept the military and militia training of the EZLN a secret, as
did thousands of others. Since February 1995, when the Mexican Army
organized a major offensive into EZLN territory, permanently occupied
the ejido of Guadalupe Tepeyac, and established a garrison there, most
of the ejidatarios of Guadalupe Tepeyac have been living in a new community. Doña Trini and others have returned to their roots, struggling
to eke out a living in the jungle. Forced to live outdoors there in the elements for months, the community eventually reestablished itself and
continues to be a bastion of the new Zapatismo.

What were the local and regional processes that gave way to whole
families from ejidos like Guadalupe Tepeyac joining the Zapatista Army
of National Liberation? What is the story of their ejido and others like
them? How did the words and images of Zapata, filtered through these
persons' own experiences and education in regional peasant organizations, and later through the EZLN, come to take on a new meaning?

Figure 2.   Zapatista comandantes with staff and advisors in San Andrés Larráinzar during the peace dialogues in 1995. Comandante Trinidad is in the
flowered dress. Photo by Lynn Stephen.

The purpose of this and the next two chapters is to answer these questions. I do not seek to provide an exhaustive account of events in eastern Chiapas over the past fifty years, or to explain the entire story behind
the story of the formation of the Zapatista Army of National Liberation.
Instead, I seek to offer an explanation for how contemporary Zapatismo
might have taken hold in the ejido of Guadalupe Tepeyac and in nearby
La Realidad, to explore Zapatismo's various meanings to people in the
region, and to explain—in later chapters—how the symbols of Zapata
and contemporary Zapatismo emerged from Chiapas and were absorbed
elsewhere in the nation—specifically in two ejidos in the state of Oaxaca. At a larger level, the story of the ejido of Guadalupe Tepeyac is a
window for understanding how concrete local experiences and histories
combine with more distant versions of history and national symbols to
produce a hybrid political ideology—contemporary Zapatismo—with
multiple levels of meaning.

   In 1994, I was able to visit and talk with people in Guadalupe Tepeyac. I returned to the community after it was occupied by the military in
1995, to find it completely abandoned. In and after 1995, I periodically

came into contact with individuals from Guadalupe Tepeyac, often in other communities or in the context of EZLN forums or the peace dialogues. I was also able to visit and talk with people in La Realidad on three trips, in 1995, 1996, and 1997. After February 1995, regular patrols through the town of La Realidad by Mexican Army convoys of humvees with mounted machine guns and soldiers with video cameras came to characterize daily life. The ever-increasing militarization of the interior of the Lacandon that began in 1995 made it increasingly difficult to visit and talk with people. In 1995, a permanent immigration post was set up just outside Las Margaritas, which monitored all movements to and from towns further into the interior, particularly movement to La Realidad. As conditions tightened and regular harassment became part of visiting La Realidad, it became increasingly difficult to return. I had originally hoped to conduct more extensive oral histories and interviews in these two communities, but the conditions of the low-intensity war, combined with the harassment by immigration officials, made it impossible to complete this plan. Instead, my accounts in the following three chapters are built on interviews and observations from 1994 to 1997, on archival records obtained from the National Agrarian Registry in Tuxtla Gutiérrez, and on published interviews with members of the EZLN. In many (not all) cases, I was not able to tape my interviews with EZLN members, and I was often requested not even to take notes, out of concern about what would happen if the materials were encountered by immigration officials or public security police. This was a very valid concern, since my documents and contents of my luggage were examined on several occasions. Thus, I wrote up conversations afterward, noting as much detail as I could. I learned much from these conversations, and have incorporated it into the narrative of these chapters. (The interviews contained in chapter 7 are from those instances in which I was granted permission to tape.) The archival records from the National Agrarian Registry contain all the correspondence between ejido officials and agrarian officials regarding Guadalupe Tepeyac and La Realidad since their formation as ejidos in the 1950s; while this correspondence is not an impartial record by any means, when read as it evolved over time, it provides a convincing outline of the mounting frustration, disillusionment, anger, and despair with which ejidatarios viewed the state and, ultimately, independent peasant organizations as well. (In the future, I hope to be able to share copies of this correspondence and of my written histories with the populations of Guadalupe Tepeyac and La Realidad.)

FROM PEONS TO EJIDATARIOS

On the eve of the Mexican Revolution in 1910, 71 percent of the population of Las Margaritas were living on large farms and ranches, primarily as laborers. By 1960, this had diminished to 8 percent, with 75 percent living on ejidos, ranchos, and private small plots (Leyva Solano and Ascencio Franco 1996, 74–75). In the 1930s, Tojolabales and others began to occupy parts of the Lacandon jungle, working their way eastward and northward from the fincas where many had been bound for generations as sharecroppers and servants. A significant number could trace their origins to the ranches of the Castellano family. There were few ejido petitions in the 1920s and 1930s; the greatest number of agrarian actions—including the allotment of original ejido lands, extensions to ejidos, constitution of new ejido populations, and restitution of communal lands—in the Lacandon jungle occurred from 1940 to 1970 (51 percent), with a significant number of agrarian actions from 1980 through 1989 (36 percent) (ibid., 81, table 12). In the municipality of Altamirano, with a significant Tojolabal population, the greatest number of agrarian actions occurred from 1950 through 1969. In the municipality of Las Margaritas, also with a significant Tojolabal population, the greatest number occurred from 1980 through 1989, with a steady level of activity for most other decades between 1930 and 1990 (ibid., 80, table 12). The total number of those (primarily heads of household) who benefited from agrarian reform in Las Margaritas from 1930 to 1991 was 8,714; for the Lacandon jungle as a whole, the number was 29,529 (ibid., 81, table 13).

The founders of the Tojolabal ejidos in the Lacandon began to move into the jungle in the late 1930s and early 1940s, according to documents in the files of ejidos held in the National Agrarian Registry in Tuxtla Gutiérrez. At that time, the area around Las Margaritas was used by ejidatarios for growing coffee and raising cattle, and for subsistence farming. The lowlands were used for growing sugarcane, tomatoes, and fruits. The few scholars who have carefully studied the migration of Tojolabales, Tzeltales, Tzotziles, and Ch'oles into the Lacandon write that the pioneers who arrived in the late 1930s and 1940s had few choices (Leyva Solano and Ascencio Franco 1996; Ruz 1992). Either they could work as wage laborers on surrounding ranches and farms, in combination with seasonal migration to the Soconusco coastal area, or they could take a risk and colonize. Unlike the Zapotec in Oaxaca, the Tojolabales had no long history of land struggle in which they were, at least partially, the victors. Their connection to the land came primarily from a long history of debt peonage under large landowners. Once they received land to form ejidos, beginning in the 1930s, the structure of the ejido became an important cultural and social part of daily life—a perspective argued by Shannan Mattiace (1998, 184).

Because most of the Tojolabal population had long been dispossessed of its original lands, and had for centuries been attached to large ranches, the internal social-political structure of many Tojolabal communities differed significantly from that of indigenous highland communities, where civil and religious cargo systems were often the backbone of community life—albeit as these systems had been colonized by teachers and educated scribes sympathetic to the PRI (Rus 1994). Those Tojolabales in the Lacandon who did not belong to any community were known as *vagabundos* (vagabonds), *laboríos* (laborers), or *baldíos* (tenants) (Ruz 1992, 31, cited in Mattiace 1998, 165–66). People in these categories had also come to work on large ranches during the mid to late colonial period. From the mid nineteenth century until the formation of ejidos, many Tojolabales worked as baldíos, a kind of tenant required to work three or four days each week for the landlord (Wasserstrom 1983, 261, cited in Mattiace 1998, 167). Once communities were granted ejido land, the governance structure of the ejido—including the ejidal commissioner, treasurer, secretary, security council, and ejido committee members—formed a central part of community life. The ejido structure was also incorporated into the regional peasant organizations that began to operate in the Tojolabal region in the 1970s and 1980s, such as the Central Independiente de Obreros Agrícolas y Campesinos (Independent Confederation of Agricultural Workers and Peasants), or CIOAC; Lucha Campesina (Peasant Struggle); and Tierra y Libertad (Land and Liberty).

To understand the process that these pioneering men and women—as well as several generations of their offspring, some of whom joined the ranks of the EZLN in the 1980s and 1990s—went through, I shall trace their engagement with the state through almost four decades of interaction with agrarian officials. Woven into this story is that of the rise of a regional peasant organization, the Asociación Rural de Interés Colectivo–Unión de Uniones (ARIC–Unión de Uniones), as a major force in the area, one that eventually came to have much more credibility and presence than the government. The primary community that this story focuses on is Guadalupe Tepeyac, with comparative comments on La Realidad. These two Tojolabal ejidos emerged as among the strongest supporters of the EZLN in the region of Las Margaritas. They also interfaced with Tzeltal, Tzotzil, and some Ch'ol populations through the canyons stemming from Altamirano and Ocosingo, and in a number of areas of the Lacandon, where communities are multi-ethnic.

GUADALUPE TEPEYAC

On 24 January 1955, twenty-four Tojolabal men and one woman formally petitioned the governor of the state of Chiapas for land to form an ejido (*Periódico Oficial* 1955). In May, Manuel Gutiérrez Meneses, representing the Ministry of Agrarian Reform in Chiapas, was asked to go to Guadalupe Tepeyac to hold an election for a community census representative. Isidoro Jiménez Cruz, one of the twenty-five persons to sign the first official ejido petition, won the election. Isidoro and his census workers reported that there were 117 persons, consisting of 24 household heads (*jefes de familia*—referring to men) and 27 individuals, who qualified to receive ejido land. Collectively, these people possessed 9 head of cattle, 98 head of goats, sheep, and pigs, and 135 turkeys and chickens (Comisión Agraria Mixta 1955). The group soliciting ejido land came from two populations, Guadalupe Tepeyac and El Carmen Villaflores. At the time of the original petition, both communities were living on lands labeled *terrenos nacionales* (national lands). According to the report turned in by Manuel Gutiérrez Meneses to the commission, "The principle crops grown by the petitioners are corn, beans, bananas, sugarcane, and coffee—all with very low yields" (Comisión Agraria Mixta 1955). At that time, Guadalupe Tepeyac was connected to the town of Las Margaritas only by horse paths, and from there to the city of Comitán only by an unpaved road.

According to the same report, those petitioning for ejido land in 1955 had already been occupying that land for up to twenty-five years. The report revealed that in 1939, one of the people petitioning for ejido land had asked the government for the right to occupy a parcel of 300 hectares, which had become Carmen Villaflores. In 1949, Alejandro Hernández, together with most others requesting ejido land, had petitioned for the right to occupy an additional piece of national land. By 1955, the populations of these two settlements had cleared about 4 hectares of land for coffee.

The Mixed Agrarian Commission recommended that the people from Carmen Villaflores and Guadalupe Tepeyac be granted 1,400 hectares of national lands, which they already occupied, as ejido lands. This translated into 28 parcels of ten hectares, "which could theoretically be irrigated," plus an additional parcel for the school (Comisión Agraria Mixta 1955). The vast part of the land granted was classified as "mountainous lands that are only 40 percent cultivable." Much of it was not usable for farming and was still uncleared and remained in reserve. In 1956, the population of Guadalupe Tepeyac received a favorable presidential resolution for the 1,400 hectares of ejido land, and took official possession more than a year and a half later, on 26 June 1957 (Aviso de posesión 1957).

The original map outlining the ejido lands allotted to Guadalupe Tepeyac shows two population nuclei scattered on a path along the Río Caliente. The entire area around the ejido consisted of national lands, but, in the course of twenty years, these national lands would largely disappear, occupied not only by the initial colonizers, such as those in Guadalupe Tepeyac, who had arrived as early as 1939, but also by two generations of their offspring. It was the grandchildren of the original ejidatarios of Guadalupe Tepeyac who would form the local base of the EZLN—those most removed from the pioneer experience but most prepared to reclaim the legacy of Zapata. Many among the older generation, however, would also prove loyal Zapatistas.

The stories of several women among the pioneering edjidatarios who founded Guadalupe Tepeyac were recorded by the Spanish journalist Guiomar Rovira. She talked with the women in February 1995, shortly after the community fled to the interior of the jungle following an army invasion. The conditions they were living under formed eerie reminders of what life had been like when they first settled in the area—minimal shelter, a limited food supply, few tools and implements. To begin again in 1995 brought back memories of the founding of the ejido. Doña Chole recalls:

> The men began to clear the jungle. . . . We didn't have anything, not beans, coffee, or salt. We were without anything. That is why I am telling you that we gave up so much originally that I don't want to be suffering any more. Now it is the same, but I am much older. . . .
> [In the time of founding the ejido] people were sick with a fever and they died. We were left as widows. Our husbands were doing fine but they got sick and we didn't have any way to cure them. We were pure women and children. . . . Then other people came to join us, family members who didn't have anywhere to live. We certainly were poor, we were just embracing each other without anything. But we already had the land. . . .
> When we were left widows, we went to harvest coffee at the ranchos around here. They paid us and that was how we were able to buy clothing

for our children. They paid us two reales[1] for each carga that we harvested. When we started out in this place we were suffering, but now not long ago [referring to the army incursion and flight in 1995] I am seeing this suffering again. (Rovira 1997, 58)

The difficulties remembered by Doña Chole and others who helped to found the ejido reflect the name that many from this region have given themselves—*los olvidados,* "the forgotten ones." While the government encouraged people to colonize eastern Chiapas, and ultimately granted a significant number of land petitions, this was the sum of state assistance for more than four decades. Those, like Chole, who struggled in the 1950s to found the ejido began with nothing; only through cooperation and through working part-time as laborers for small and medium ranchers could they earn any cash income. Not until the 1970s could ejidatarios from places like Guadalupe Tepeyac begin to produce products like coffee, hogs, cattle, and corn for local and regional markets. Even then, their production was plagued with problems such as the lack of roads, of transportation to get their goods to market, and of credit.

IGNORED BY THE STATE, ENCOURAGED BY THE CHURCH

While the Mexican government ignored the growing colonies in the interior of the Lacandon jungle, providing no infrastructure or social services, another group did not. In 1960, Samuel Ruiz took over as bishop of the Catholic diocese of San Cristóbal de las Casas, where he remained until his retirement in late 1999. He is best known today for his role in the 1990s as an intermediary in peace talks between the EZLN and the Mexican government. Ruiz began as a traditional bishop who viewed indigenous peoples as potential subjects for pastoral action, but once he began to tour his diocese and saw the incredible poverty and marginality of indigenous communities, the impact on him was tremendous. When he saw dozens of children dead from measles, diarrhea, and other preventable diseases, he came to know what reality was for much of indigenous society (Fazio 1994, 57). Ruiz began working in the Tzeltal zones of Ocosingo, Bachajón, and Simojovel. In 1961, in collaboration with Marist monks and the nuns of the Divino Pastor, he opened up catechist schools in San Cristóbal, to the east of Ocosingo, in Bachajón, and in Comitán, first to Christianize Indians. From 1961 to 1968, the catechist movement flourished, growing to six hundred people (ibid., 78), and by 1965, it had taken on more radical tones. Marist priests who learned to speak Tzeltal began to understand the feelings of the colonists for their land and their past. Grasping that many saw theirs as a promised land, an escape from their past as sharecroppers and self-labeled "slaves," the Marists harnessed this vision to the story of Exodus—the journey from slavery to freedom—and diffused the resultant concept throughout the jungle regions of the San Cristóbal diocese. As seen by the testimonies (detailed above) of "life under slavery," for those pioneers who founded ejidos and remembered life on the fincas, the theme of liberation struck a chord. In these testimonies, related in the 1980s and 1990s, the themes of slavery and liberty illustrate the ways in which current historical memory has incorporated the notion of liberation. When this was joined with the notion of liberation through receiving land and the means to make it productive, the basis was laid for a new kind of Zapatismo.

In 1972, two brothers, Mardonio and Ignacio Morales Elizalde, began translating the Bible into Tzeltal, focusing first on Exodus. The Book of Exodus was titled *We Are Looking for Liberty*. One passage read:

> God tells us that as a community we should leave and look for liberty. If we go out and look for ways to improve our lives and for our liberty, God will be with us. When the Israelites lived as slaves, they had to leave and go and fight for their liberty. When our ancestors lived as slaves, they also had to unite and fight to win back their lands. They were people of great faith. But true liberty still hasn't arrived. We have to find the force in our hearts to fight and suffer even more. We have to fight against poverty, hunger, and injustice. (Rovira 1994, 23)

During the 1960s and 1970s, the Marists in the Ocosingo-Altamirano Mission worked up and down the Tzeltal-Tojolabal corridor that connects Comitán and Altamirano. Marists also worked out of Las Margaritas. The message of Exodus made its way to Guadalupe Tepeyac and surrounding ejidos and was partially incorporated into the populace's own experiences of struggle; some in the ejido no doubt identified with the story as it reflected their struggle to establish themselves and improve their lives. Furthermore, the organizational and educational style used by the Marists validated people's own sense of history and knowledge, encouraging them to articulate their own visions rather than imposing an outside notion of liberation.

Perhaps the Church's most radical impact came from the education of thousands of catechists, first through the school in San Cristóbal and, after 1970, through regional courses. But, while the Catholic Church began to actively train catechists in the Lacandon, the population grew steadily, and the original lands received for ejidos such as Guadalupe Tepeyac were proving insufficient.

POPULATION GROWTH AND A NEW LAND PETITION

The first tensions inside the new ejido of Guadalupe Tepeyac emerged in 1960, when the General Assembly of Ejidatarios initiated action against five ejidatarios who had been absent for two years and had not farmed their parcels. This action preceded petitions for additional land for the ejido and may have been an early signal of population growth and impending shortages of land. The five ejidatarios had their rights to ejido land terminated in 1963 by presidential resolution; five other ejidatarios received rights in their place (*Periódico Oficial* 1963, 5–6).

The following year, 1964, the people of Guadalupe Tepeyac petitioned for additional lands (*ampliación,* or enlargement) for their ejido, demonstrating that they had an additional 34 persons who could qualify for land. The overall population of the community had grown to 240 — doubling in less than a decade (from 117 in 1955). The census carried out for this request revealed an increase in animal population, too, with 60 head of cattle and 131 goats, sheep, and pigs (Comisión Agraria Mixta 1965a). In this census, ejidatarios continued to report that their primary crops were corn, beans, and coffee sold in Las Margaritas. This petition for additional lands in 1964 was to be greatly helped by the government declaration of 401,959 hectares as national lands in the municipalities of Ocosingo, Trinitaria, La Independencia, La Libertad, and Las Margaritas in 1967 (de Vos 1995, 349, map 31, 351); from these lands came the expansion to the ejido of Guadalupe Tepeyac.

In what now seems a stroke of historical irony, President Gustavo Díaz Ordaz (1964–70) granted the Tojolabal ejidatarios from Guadalupe Tepeyac additional ejido lands, in the amount of 2,266 hectares, about eight months before the Mexican Army massacred an estimated three hundred persons who had gathered for a peaceful demonstration at the plaza of Tlatelolco in Mexico City in 1968. Six years later, some of those inspired by the student movement of 1968 and deeply affected by the massacre would work with some ejidatarios of Guadalupe Tepeyac in independent peasant organizations—as well as in what ultimately became the EZLN. The additional lands granted to the ejido of Guadalupe Tepeyac in 1968 worked out to 34 parcels of about 20 hectares each, plus addition marginal mountainous (Díaz Ordaz 1968); these additional ejido lands were measured in August 1969.

In the meantime, the presence of the Church continued to grow in the Lacandon, as did the number of catechists. What stands out in the training of the catechists, in particular as reflected in the philosophy of Samuel Ruiz, was the idea that in every cultural community, the seed of God can be found.[2] Rather than implanting an entirely new theological idea in indigenous communities, the job of the clergy as outlined by Samuel Ruiz was to validate indigenous cultures and build on their insights. Taking indigenous cultures seriously was an important part of the pastoral work in the *cañadas*—from conducting services, discussions, and classes in indigenous languages to drawing out local customs, ideas, and histories that could be integrated into the word of God. This perspective permeated the work of the diocese and the priests working with it from the mid 1960s on.

While the thinking of Samuel Ruiz certainly incorporated some classic aspects of liberation theology—including the "preferential option for the poor," the concept that poverty is a sin and its solution not something that should wait until the hereafter—his perspective not only emphasized class analysis but, equally, was engaged with critically evaluating the role of indigenous culture in religion. These two tendencies are best reflected in his diocesan plan, published in 1986 but written earlier in the 1980s, which begins with a referential framework outlining the struggle in the state of Chiapas. Ruiz clearly invokes a framework of class analysis that blends well with the type of analysis carried out by organizers of regional peasant organizations in the 1970s and 1980s:

> [A] first and perhaps fundamental node of the Chiapan problematic is the continuous production of laborers. For some, this has been a constant in Chiapas's social formation for the last five centuries. These are the laborers who if they got a piece of land were exploited by commerce and manipulated by the National Peasant Confederation, and if they did not get land, had to pick coffee on the Fincas of Soconusco or who now migrate in search of work. . . . These are the same laborers who have made protest marches to the state capital and to Mexico City, who do sit-ins and roadblocks on the highway. . . .
>
> Thus the peasants, finca peons, farm workers, and Indians have remained at the center of class struggle in Chiapas, and it is this accumulation of laborers, impoverished and taking hard beatings, that points towards a new explosion and social change. (Diócesis de San Cristóbal 1986, cited in Womack 1999, 203)

Ruiz's 1986 plan advocates "contact with independent popular organizations, dialogue with them, promotion and support of them" (Diócesis de San Cristóbal 1986, cited in Womack 1999, 206). This statement indicates the bishop's disposition to work with activists outside the Church, a plan he actively pursued in the 1970s and the 1980s, including unknowingly with the first cadres of what became the EZLN. Along with his class analysis and proclivity to work with popular organizations, the bishop also espoused a deep respect for indigenous cultures. They would, he wrote, provide liberating knowledge. In his 1986 plan, he stated, in relation to the "the critical reevaluation of cultures":

Goals

>   To insert ourselves into the culture of our people, to take on ourselves the social utopia hidden there, and to accompany them on their historic path.

Criteria

>   That we reevaluate the liberating content of cultures.

Actions

>   To learn the language.
>   To know the history of the ethnic groups.
>   To promote cultural expressions.

Diócesis de San Cristóbal 1986,
cited in Womack 1999, 207

These words written in the 1980s reflect a commitment that first became manifest in a historic event in 1974.

THE FIRST INDIGENOUS CONGRESS

The work of Bishop Ruiz and his team of priests was critical in laying the foundations for the First Indigenous Congress "Fray Bartolomé de Las Casas" of 1974, referred to by many as a landmark event in the development of civil-society organizations in Chiapas. Originally conceived by such persons as Angel Robles, director of the Program for Socio-Economic Development for the Highlands of Chiapas, and Gertrudis Duby, an anthropologist in San Cristóbal de las Casas, to celebrate the five hundredth birthday of Bartolomé de las Casas,[3] the idea of the congress was endorsed by the governor of Chiapas, Manuel Velasco Suárez, who asked Bishop Ruiz to assist in the preparations (Mestries 1990, 473; Harvey 1998, 77). Committed to building the congress through a "bottom–up" process, Ruiz took the idea to his team of priests and nuns, who worked with staff from places such as the National Indigenist Institute (INI) School for Regional Development to promote initial meetings in the towns (Harvey 1998, 77; Mestries 1990, 473; Pérez Castro 1995, 311). According to the historian John Womack, the initial six organizers of the congress included a priest in Chamula, a priest in Chenalhó representing the Tzotzils, a Jesuit in Bachajón, a young ex-

Marist schoolteacher in Ocosingo for the Tzeltal zone, and a young Marist sociologist representing the Tojolabales (Womack 1999, 148).

Before the 1974 congress, local and regional meetings were held, run in a style characterized by "planting and harvesting the words of the people [*sembrar y cosechar la palabra*]," in which all issues were discussed first in small groups, of six to eight, that worked by consensus (García de León 1994, ii). After these groups reached consensus, democratically elected leaders would make a periodic synthesis of what had been decided by the groups and would call for a general consensus. The teams that led these meetings were made up of indigenous leaders, usually trained as catechists and put together largely by the Church; they also included advisors from the Maoist Unión del Pueblo (People's Union), or UP, such as Chapingo-trained agronomist René Gómez and his wife, Marta Orantes, invited by Samuel Ruiz to help prepare for the congress (Harvey 1998, 79). Those arriving in 1973 in Chiapas to help prepare for the congress were Maoists who wanted to establish mass organizations and broad support before launching a popular struggle. Two of the UP activists gave courses for the pre-deacons, catechists, and ejido officers who formed Chiapas's first union of ejidos (Womack 1999, 175).

Methods used by the UP and later by other Maoist *linea de masas* (mass line) organizers were designed to decentralize and democratize decision-making. The degree to which the organizing style and context of the First Indigenous Congress and subsequent organizations were influenced by the decision-making style of Church and UP-based organizers, as opposed to the styles of indigenous people participating in the congress, is unclear. What is interesting is that this style of consensus building seems characteristic of decision-making within Zapatista-controlled communities, such as La Realidad, where I have observed this process.

One of the most important features of the Congress was its multiethnic nature. There was representation from the four chief Mayan linguistic groups in the state. While language was not, nor is, the only or all-defining feature of ethnicity in Chiapas, it remains a unifying symbol for certain shared collective experiences, which may have nothing to do with language. For example, Mattiace writes of the Tojolabales that their identity as a people is not tied to speaking an indigenous language, wearing traditional dress, or even having a common territory; it is linked instead to a "common history and experience of oppression" (Mattiace 1998, 169, 192). Thus, representation by linguistic group should not be read as a one-dimensional statement of indigenous identity, but as a symbolic space with shifting content tied to the particular and ever-changing experience of an ethnic group. Filling that symbolic space identified by language affiliation involves change, not just "loss" of culture (see Warren 1992, 203; Mattiace 1998, 192–201). Self-identifying as "Tzotzil," "Tzeltal", "Ch'ol," or "Tojolabal" at the First Indigenous Congress was as much a means of identifying oneself as part of a particular shared struggle as of specifying linguistic affiliation.

There were 1,230 delegates present, including 587 Tzeltales, 330 Tzotziles, 152 Tojolabales, and 151 Ch'oles, representing 327 communities (García de León 1994, ii). The Tzeltales and Tojolabales were the first to take on the organizational work for the congress, probably reflecting the strength of the Catholic Church and the presence of large numbers of catechists in these regions. Four thematic areas were worked on at all levels of the meetings: "land, commerce, education, and health" (Mestries 1990, 474; Morales Bermúdez 1992, 292–352).

While the first small meetings to prepare for the Congress were often monolingual, subsequent local and regional meetings were multilingual and multi-ethnic. At these regional meetings, a team of multilingual translators was trained for the congress. Most were from colonization zones such as the Lacandon area, or from linguistic border zones such as Altamirano, where Tzeltal and Tojolabal overlap (García de León 1994, ii). The multi-ethnic and multilingual experience of the preparatory meetings influenced the culture of the congress and of subsequent organizing.

The demands of the congress, and the platforms given and published in Tzotzil, Tzeltal, Ch'ol, and Tojolabal, focused on land and land conflicts; labor rights, including provision of the minimum wage; issues in indigenous education, including language instruction, problems with teachers, and a demand for an indigenous newspaper to be published in four languages; credit, and issues of commercialization of coffee and other products; and health issues, including the preservation of indigenous systems of healing, the establishment of clinics, and the eradication of chronic diseases (García de León 1994, iii–viii; Harvey 1998, 77–78; Mestries 1990).

Ethnic autonomy and political representation were reflected not in the formal documents of the congress but in speeches such as that delivered by the Tzeltal leader Sebastián Gómez of San Francisco, Altamirano. The content of his speech pointed to the deep history of indigenous rights in Chiapas and foreshadowed many of the pronouncements on indigenous rights articulated in the communiqués of the EZLN and by the

Congreso Nacional Indígena (National Indigenous Congress), or CNI, formed in 1996. His words were a call for indigenous peoples to organize themselves and defend their own rights, not to depend on others. The speech was dedicated to Fray Bartolomé de las Casas:

> Where is the freedom that was left by Friar Bartolomé? We have been suffering injustice for five hundred years and things are the same as ever. We continue receiving the same unjust treatment. They are always trying to control us because we are indigenous and they think that we don't have any rights and we don't know how to think. Well, compañeros, Fray Bartolomé is not alive anymore and we are only remembering his name with this congress. He is dead and we can't wait for another person like him. Who is going to defend us against the injustice we suffer and help us to win our liberty? . . . I don't think the ladinos are going to defend us. Will the government? Maybe yes, maybe no. . . . Who is going to defend us? I think that our only defense is to organize ourselves so that we can have liberty and work better. We all have to be the new Bartolomé: we will reach this goal when we are all capable of forming and defending our own organization. Because unity is what gives us power. (García de León 1994, ii)

Gómez's call for organization and unity across ethnic groups hints at the possibility of a new concept of ethnicity that does not focus on individual ethnic traits but is rooted in a common sense of struggle and in taking political control over decision-making processes affecting indigenous communities. It is a clear call to self-defense.

The 1974 congress also brought out many testimonies to the inefficiency and disrespectful behavior of agrarian officials. The Mixed Agrarian Commission and the Departamento de Asuntos Agrarios y Colonización (Department of Agrarian Issues and Settlement), or DAAC, came in for bitter criticism (Mestries 1990, 476–79). "There are many cases in which agrarian authorities have deceived us—especially the topographic engineers who ask for money in order to carry out their work," a Tojolabal representative said (ibid., 478). There were many complaints about people's lack of control over the marketing of their products. Tojolabales denounced the presence of monopolizing merchants, or *atajadores,* who parked in the roads and markets and insisted that indigenous farmers sell products to them at low prices. The Tojolabales also spoke against the pig and chicken merchants who would put pebbles into the hoofs of pigs and then say that they were sick and therefore worth less. "They buy our things from us at low prices and sell things to us at high prices" (ibid., 480). These words echo those of Doña Trinidad when she remembered the difficulties in founding the ejido and how the people of Guadalupe Tepeyac could not get a fair price for their coffee and other products in the markets of Las Margaritas.

REGIONAL PEASANT ORGANIZING
FOLLOWING THE 1974 CONGRESS

Following the congress, grassroots organizing efforts took off in several directions, supported by the Church and by leftist activists, although the two groups did not always see eye to eye. According to Womack, after the 1974 congress an executive council was formed to bring the demands of the congress into action, with the council president the Marist sociologist who had first organized the Tojolabal zone for the 1974 event (Womack 1999, 149). Shortly after the 1974 congress, the Confederación Nacional Campesina concocted a parallel congress and apparently attempted to co-opt some of the original congress leaders. Womack reports that, by 1976, the Las Casas Indigenous Congress was in crisis and, despite efforts to organize around issues of land, commerce, education, and health, it disbanded in 1977 as a result of internal differences and outside political pressures (ibid., 149–50). While the organizational structure of the congress did not endure, several regional peasant organizations were formed in the wake of its failure to consolidate. Outside organizers from the Maoist Linea Proletaria (Proletarian Line), or LP, also stepped in to fill the void.

Encouraged by the 1971 Federal Agrarian Reform law, which allowed ejidos to join together in larger productive units known as *uniones de ejidos,* or unions of ejidos, the catechists and activists who had come together in the 1974 congress set out to take action on the many complaints that emerged about lack of control over the productive and marketing process in the highlands and in the colonized areas of the Lacandon jungle. In 1976, bringing together at least two communities each, three regional ejido unions were formed: Ejido Union Quiptic ta Lecubtecel (United in Our Strength), or UEQTL, in Ocosingo; and Ejido Union Tierra y Libertad (Land and Liberty), or UETL, and Ejido Union Lucha Campesina (Peasant Struggle), or UELC, both in Las Margaritas (Harvey 1994, 29; Harvey 1998, 79–83). Members of the Maoist Linea Proletaria arrived in the Lacandon in 1977 at the invitation of Bishop Ruiz, who had met them in Torreón (Harvey 1998, 81–82).

The LP had been started in 1968 by economics professors and students at the National Autonomous University of Mexico (UNAM). It had originally been called the Coalición de Brigadas Emiliano Zapata (Coalition of Emiliano Zapata Brigades) and had published a pamphlet, "What Is the Proletarian Line?" that called for a decentralized people's politics, saying, "The working masses in their struggle are those who make history, not leaders or employers or government officials" (Womack 1999, 177). Later, the Coalición had split into two groups, one of which, Linea Proletaria, became involved in Chiapas. This faction was led by Adolfo Orive, who became a key actor in the formation of a new type of regional peasant organization focused on production. Much later, in the 1990s, he went to work for the government.

In Las Margaritas, the agrarian legacy of Emiliano Zapata began to surface in a significant way in the late 1970s. Two unions of ejidos bore his name or a slogan attributed to him ("Tierra y libertad"), and the LP activists in the region regarded Zapata's name as part of their organization's genealogy. Comandante Tacho, a Tojolabal ejidatario from Guadalupe Tepeyac who was one of the earliest members of the EZLN, relates his experiences in organizing the ejido and the first independent organizations. The notion of peasant struggle, or *lucha campesina,* tied to the legacy of Zapata was part of his experience:

> We are people who tried *la lucha pacífica* (nonviolent struggle). We tried the unions—well, first we tried the ejido organization . . . solicitation of land, official transactions, and different things . . . the same government encouraged us to make unions of ejidos. They said that we would have more facilities, more credits, roads, loans, better prices, export prices; in that moment, that was what the government wanted. . . . We tried all of this. I—well, in fact, most of us—formed ejido unions. The first in 1979 was a union called Lucha Campesina. This union emerged among others as the first with the objective of soliciting better roads, more transport—this was the objective of the unions of ejidos. (Reza 1995)

The beginnings of regional independent organizing in the Lacandon area coincided with ongoing population growth. As national lands were allotted to new ejidos and to growing older ones, it became evident that the struggle of Zapata meant more than simply having land; it involved having much greater control over the marketing and distribution of the products from that land.

THE CONTINUED GROWTH OF INDEPENDENT ORGANIZATIONS

In 1980, one year after the ejido union Lucha Campesina was formed, 39 ejidatarios from Guadalupe Tepeyac submitted a second petition for additional ejido land. By 1978, the local population had grown to 378, almost doubling again since the previous decade. The number of animals had grown as well, with 248 head of cattle and 884 turkeys, chickens, and other domestic birds. Ejidatarios were not only raising cattle but were also expanding coffee production, as were many others in the region (Comisión Agraria Mixta 1980). By this time, much of the national land surrounding the ejido had been granted to other communities, in response to petitions for ejido land and/or as extensions to already existing ejidos.

For example, the bordering Tojolabal ejido of La Realidad had been granted 1,930 hectares of land by presidential resolution to form an ejido in 1966. In 1964, La Realidad reported a population of 141 people (Comisión Agraria Mixta 1965b). Just nine years later, the community made its first petition to extend its ejido. By then, the population had grown to 273 (Comisión Agraria Mixta 1978). The community had to wait twelve years for the extension petition to be finalized, and finally accepted 421 hectares less than promised in its presidential resolution of 1981, because "[T]here are no more vacant lands, property of the nation, which can be allotted to benefit our town" (Acta que se levanta en el poblado "Realidad Trinidad" 1985). The need for new land every eight to ten years in ejidos like Guadalupe Tepeyac and La Realidad was an indication of the rapid growth of the population, and of the lack of viable alternatives to rain-fed agriculture in the region. The second request from Guadalupe Tepeyac for land led to a long and frustrating encounter with the Chiapas agrarian bureaucracy, and coincided with the incorporation of the ejido into the Unión de Uniones in 1980.

Born of the three independent organizations formed after the Indigenous Congress, the Union of Unions of Chiapas was built from the struggle not only to regularize—by obtaining official recognition through ejido grants—land occupied in the Lacandon jungle, but also to help people to market their coffee and other goods. In 1979, the Union of Ejidos Quiptic ta Lecubtesel (UE Quiptic) organized to alleviate the problem of the high cost of transporting coffee, a cost carried by the producers. UE Quiptic also wanted to end the delayed payment system used by the Mexican Coffee Institute (INMECAFE) to compensate producers (Harvey 1998, 83). In 1979, UE Quiptic and several other organizations negotiated an agreement with INMECAFE that provided for credit, construction of coffee warehouses in isolated places, payment for the cost of air transportation where there was no ground transportation available, naming of peasant representatives to check the

INMECAFE books, training courses for producers, and direct purchase of coffee from the producers (Hernández Navarro 1992, 83–84). The campaign to improve the terms of coffee marketing resulted in the unification of three ejido unions, along with smaller producer groups, to form the Union of Ejido Unions and Solidarity Peasant Organizations of Chiapas, often known as the Unión de Uniones, or UU, which focused primarily on peasant appropriation of the production process. It was "the first and largest independent campesino organization in Chiapas, representing 12,000 mainly indigenous families from 170 communities in 11 municipalities" (Harvey 1994: 30). The emergence of the UU as a force in Las Margaritas suggested a strategy for dealing with unresponsive agrarian officials, and indicated that people could cooperate with, but also bypass, the government as they tried to improve their lives by taking greater control over marketing and distributing their products.

The struggle of the younger ejidatarios of Guadalupe Tepeyac to try to gain all of the land promised to them in a presidential resolution in 1981 was similar to struggles waged in other ejidos, including that in neighboring La Realidad. All were competing for increasingly scarce land. As long as the government was not willing to expropriate from surrounding ranches (which had significantly declined in overall acreage by the 1970s), the only economic options were to obtain more land or to better use the land the ejidos controlled. While the land titled as ejidos had grown tremendously between 1950 and 1970, it was primarily for subsistence agriculture, with an ever-increasing proportion dedicated to coffee. Privately owned land was concentrated in areas with natural pasturage and used primarily for raising cattle; from the 1970s through the 1980s, ejidatarios also began to convert from subsistence crops to cattle-raising and coffee-growing in an attempt to raise their standard of living (Leyva Solano and Ascencio Franco 1996, 89).

A few years after the ejidatarios of Guadalupe Tepeyac filed their second petition for additional lands, problems emerged over demarcating the boundaries. Land that was promised could not be had. Even though the governor of the state of Chiapas had granted the ejidatarios' request for additional lands, and this was published in the *Periódico Oficial del Gobierno del Estado* in 1981, only 480 (or about 27 percent) of the promised 1,760 hectares were turned over to the community. The additional lands were not turned over because it was reported that 829 of these hectares had been invaded by the neighboring ejidatarios of La Realidad and the remaining hectares were judged useless (López y Velasquez 1985). In reality, the situation was even more complicated.

On 25 April 1985, in response to an apparent stream of requests, Ingeniero José Adrian Ordoñez, representing the technical office of the Subdelegation of Priority Programs of the Ministry of Agrarian Reform Delegate in Chiapas, traveled to Guadalupe Tepeyac to meet with the ejidatarios and to study the situation, as a step toward resolving the ejidatarios' second petition for additional lands. His mission included contacting all the property holders whose land lay within the legal radius of land supposed to be granted to Guadalupe Tepeyac as part of its second petition. He was to verify the quality, extent, and use of the land and the number of cattle on it.

This was a big job, particularly given the earlier memos stating that a significant part of the land to be given to Guadalupe Tepeyac had been invaded by La Realidad ejidatarios. A month later, he turned in his report, which documents the difficult conditions for moving coffee, cattle, and other products out of Guadalupe Tepeyac for marketing. It also underscores the continued isolation of the community. "To arrive at this population, Guadalupe Tepeyac, you take bus transportation from the Municipio of Las Margaritas, traveling for some five hours on a dirt road. Once arriving at a rancho called San José, where the road ends, it takes another three hours on horseback to arrive. There is also transportation by small airplane to this place" (Ordoñez 1985). These were the same conditions producers confronted for getting their coffee and cattle to market. The report also provides interesting details on the patterns of private property purchase, the presence of coffee-growing and cattle ranching in the area, as practiced by both ejidatarios and small and medium private ranchers, and the increased occupation of national lands by surrounding ejidos. Two pieces of private property and six pieces of national lands occupied by other ejidatarios, detailed in the report, were planted with corn and coffee and included small to medium herds of cattle. Both the human and the cattle populations were growing.

From Ordoñez's 1985 report and a follow-up report in 1987, it is abundantly clear that there was no coordination or careful surveying of the land promised to Guadalupe Tepeyac or to other ejidos. The Ministry of Agrarian Reform Delegate's Office in Chiapas appears to have arbitrarily made promises to one community after another without ascertaining whether the promised lands overlapped with those being granted at the federal level by presidential decree. The result was a legal, human, and political nightmare called *sobreposición de planos,* or "overlapping maps."

Overlapping they were. Of the 1,760 hectares promised to a third generation of ejidatarios in Guadalupe Tepeyac in 1980, a full 1,153 hectares had *also* been promised to the ejido of Poblado Francisco Villa in 1973 and to the ejido of San Carlos Veracruz in 1980 (Ordoñez 1985). On 2 April 1980, by presidential decree, the community of San Carlos Veracruz was granted 553 hectares of land that had also been promised to Guadalupe Tepeyac, planting the seeds of the frustration, anger, and sense of government betrayal felt by the ejidatarios of Guadalupe Tepeyac long before the end of land reform in 1992.

While the office of the Chiapas delegate of the Secretary of Agrarian Reform was "studying" the land situation in Guadalupe Tepeyac and dozens of other communities, regional peasant organizations continued their activities. In 1983, the Unión de Uniones split, and shortly thereafter a new organization was formed, the Unión de Ejidos de la Selva (UE de la Selva), which Neil Harvey describes as "the most important organization prior to the EZLN" in the cañadas of Las Margaritas (Harvey 1998, 193). The Unión de Ejidos de la Selva came to represent eight hundred mestizo and Tojolabal peasant families from Las Margaritas (ibid., 258, n. 14). In 1988, UE de la Selva participated in the formal creation of ARIC–Unión de Uniones. This organization became the de facto subterranean government of the region.

COMMUNITY AUTHORITY STRUCTURES IN THE JUNGLE

In the best discussion to date of relations among the catechists, indigenous deacons (*tu'uneles*) elected as part of ejido community government structures beginning in the 1970s, and ARIC–UU, Xochitl Leyva Solano (1995) documents the ways in which catechist education and training worked in conjunction with peasant organizing in many Tzeltal and Tojolabal cañadas of the Lacandon. Community authority structures consisted of, first, the communal assembly, which held ultimate authority over, second, elected officials—including the ejido commissioner, the municipal agent, the *tu'unel*, or deacon, the catechist, and the delegate to ARIC–UU or other independent organization. Below these elected officials was a series of local committees (Leyva Solano 1995, 382).

When the EZLN began to organize in these communities in the mid 1980s and the 1990s, the picture got more complicated. In an unusually candid interview with the French sociologist Yvon Le Bot, Subcomandante Marcos confirmed Leyva Solano's outline of community governance, noting that while Zapatista influence became strong in some communities, in others the three sources of local government authority caused a split:

> From 1990 to 1993 is when there was friction with the authorities of the local church. . . . Here I am talking about the *tu'uneles*, the deacons, the catechists. . . . When the EZLN and above all the women of the EZLN begin to make some noise . . . this creates disagreements in the communities, especially among the local clerical authorities, who accuse us of putting bad ideas into the heads of women and young people. . . . In this case in the zone of the Jungle, in the most interior Tzeltal region . . . the *principales* (religious authorities in the religious cargo system) and the local authorities of the Church were the same. In some cases, there was agreement and acceptance and this struggle [between the EZLN representatives and local Church authorities] didn't occur. The Church authorities, the local authorities—the ejido commissioners and the municipal agents—and the Zapatista authorities were all the same. . . . But in other parts, there were three distinct types of authorities: the authority of the ARIC–Unión de Uniones, that of the Church, and the Zapatista authority. (Le Bot 1997, 183–84)

People elected to positions of authority had to serve the community in a spirit popularized through the EZLN as *mandar obedeciendo*, or governing through obedience to the will of the communal assembly. In his study of the Tojolabal language, Carlos Lenkersdorf notes that the term in Tojolabal for elder or *presidente* (referring to the elected president of a community or municipal agent) is *ja ma' 'ay ya 'tel*—literally, "he who has his work" (Lenkersdorf 1996, 80); "Legitimate leaders receive respect because they know how to articulate community sentiments and in this sense they obey the community" (ibid., 81). The Tojolabal language emphasizes intersubjectivity, and Lenkersdorf suggests that the culture of community decision-making is well captured by the phrase "governing through obeying." Decision-making thus does not depend on any one person but on consensus. Whether these were traditional Tojolabal ways of thinking, as Lenkersdorf suggests, or the result of participating in catechist education, of the governance structures of ejidos with assemblies, or of the structures of organizations like the ARIC–Unión de Uniones and EZLN, the local governing concepts suggested by Leyva Solano, Lenkersdorf, and Subcomandante Marcos formed part of what people like the ejidatarios of Guadalupe Tepeyac came to see as part of their cultural inheritance. The political scientist Shannan Mattiace, who has studied the role of Tojolabal communities in the process of organizing for indigenous autonomy in Chiapas, also suggests that the ejido continues as an important reference point in local

Tojolabal identities, and that governance structures of ejidos have continued to influence local political culture (Mattiace 1998, 178).

LOCAL AND REGIONAL SOURCES OF ZAPATISMO

As outlined in Harvey (1994; 1998), many sources of independent peasant organizing besides the ARIC–UU and the organizations attached to it historically, emerged in the 1970s and 1980s in Chiapas. Many of these brought a language and symbolic system that reclaimed Emiliano Zapata and the struggle for land. The Coordinadora Nacional "Plan de Ayala" (CNPA), which takes its name from Zapata's 1911 plan to redistribute land, was founded in 1979 with ten regional peasant organizations. Their principle demands included "the legal recognition of longstanding indigenous land rights; the distribution of land exceeding the legal limits for private property; community control over and defense of natural resources; agricultural production, marketing, and consumption subsidies; rural unionization; and the preservation of popular culture" (Paré 1990, 85). CNPA participants included indigenous peoples with communal land or no land, minifundia peasants, peasants soliciting land, and groups of small producers and agrarian wage workers.

The CNPA had twenty-one member organizations in the early 1980s, including the Organización Campesina Emiliano Zapata (Emiliano Zapata Peasant Organization), or OCEZ, formed in 1982 by community members from Venustiano Carranza, Chiapas, who fought a long battle to recuperate three thousand hectares of land from local ranchers. Indeed, many people have died between 1982 and the present in the struggle to recuperate land. Although at the end of the 1980s, OCEZ split, with one faction dropping out of the CNPA and another working with the rival Frente Nacional Democrático (Popular National Democratic Popular Front), or FNDP, the OCEZ was a pivotal member of the CNPA during the 1980s and represented a politics of direct confrontation with the state in the struggle for land (Hernández Navarro 1994, 53; see Harvey 1998 for a detailed description as well). OCEZ banners of the mid 1980s, placed throughout Chiapas, had graphics of Emiliano Zapata and a clenched raised fist, and stated: "'Free land for all, without overseers and bosses, this is the war cry of the Revolution'—Emiliano Zapata" (Harvey 1998, 137). CNPA's marches in Mexico City also featured large banners and portraits of Zapata, some of which have been recycled in the 1990s, in the new Zapatismo of the EZLN (see Moguel 1990, photos between pp. 340–41). In terms of regional presence in Chiapas, the OCEZ was a major importer of Zapata as a figure for contemporary agrarian struggle.

CIOAC was another important regional peasant organization that developed in the 1970s and had an increasing presence in the 1980s in Chiapas, where it initially organized Tzeltal and Tzotzil agricultural workers into unions on coffee and cattle ranches in the municipalities of Simojovel, Huitiupán, El Bosque, and Pueblo Nuevo Solistahuacán. CIOAC was based in Comitán and also became a strong presence in the Tojolabal cañada (Mattiace 1998). Like those of OCEZ and CNPA, CIOAC's name did not signal ethnically based demands, but its documents reflect an awareness of indigenous identity and politics through acknowledgment of indigenous claims to lands historically denied, defense of indigenous forms of government and religion and language, and recognition of the need to struggle against efforts to assimilate indigenous peoples.[4] While indigenous identity within CIOAC was still framed by "class struggle," its organizing efforts brought indigenous peoples together across ethnic boundaries to form labor unions, resulting in a multi-ethnic organizing model that forced participants to break down the cultural barriers of particular ethnic identities. CIOAC developed a presence in Las Margaritas after 1984, when a faction of democratic teachers split from the Supreme Tojolabal Council, one of the many supreme councils of indigenous peoples that the Mexican government had organized to buttress discontent with the CNC in the late 1970s (Mattiace 2001, 79). In Las Margaritas and elsewhere, the Supreme Tojolabal Council became a site of opposition. During a 1984 election for council president in Las Margaritas, the local CNC, refusing to accept the candidate of the independent teachers group, called in the state police to impose its own candidate (ibid.). The teachers left the Supreme Council and formed their own ejido union, the Union of Ejidos and Tojolabal People, which later affiliated with CIOAC. "[T]his break represented the beginning of longstanding political cleavages among the Tojolabal people into three political camps," Mattiace notes. CNCistas affiliated with the PRI, members of CIOAC–Union of Ejidos and Tojolabal Peoples, and members of Lucha Campesina affiliated first with UU and then with ARIC–UU (Mattiace 1998, 178). While Lucha Campesina and UU were oriented toward production in the 1970s and 1980s and focused on issues like credit and marketing, CIOAC and CNC incorporated an agrarianist discourse into their focus on land reform, often invoking the symbolism of the Mexican Revolution and Zapata. These cleavages can be partially seen even in 1990s political divisions, with some of those from Lucha Campesina / ARIC–UU going into the EZLN, CIOAC leaders becoming active in the movement to establish autonomous pluri-ethnic regions in Chiapas, and the CNC continuing to support the government (ibid.).

As discussed by Harvey (1998), both OCEZ and CIOAC were visible public presences between 1983 and 1988, organizing demonstrations and marches to Tuxtla Gutiérrez and to Mexico City. These efforts were met with escalating repression from the governor of the state, Absalón Castellanos Domínguez (a descendent of the Castellanos ranch-owning family from Comitán who was governor from 1982 to 1988). "The most common response was repression and persecution of independent leaders. . . . [T]he expansion of the military only strengthened the position of the governor, who proceeded to protect private landholdings from the threat of land redistribution" (Harvey 1998, 155). One of CIOAC's most important public actions was the March for Dignity and Freedom from Chiapas in 1983, in which Tojolabales from Comitán and Las Margaritas joined with contingents from Simojovel and El Bosque and headed to Tuxtla Gutiérrez. They demanded the release of CIOAC activists from prison, an end to repression, and land redistribution (Uno Más Uno 1983, 2, cited in Harvey 1998, 158). When they were not received by Governor Absalón Castellanos Domínguez, about six hundred of the marchers decided to go to Mexico City. There, they were able to negotiate with an interministerial commission to resolve land petitions, to obtain credit for CIOAC-affiliated communities in Simojovel and Comitán, to obtain an official *registro* (license) for CIOAC, and to secure the release of twenty-nine prisoners and the cancellation of three hundred arrest warrants (Harvey 1998, 158). CIOAC activists returned to the state empowered, but "set up" to become the victims of escalating repression, a turn that made a deep impression on many members. CIOAC organized subsequent marches in 1984 and 1985 to Tuxtla Gutiérrez to press that the accords negotiated in Mexico City be honored.

In Comitán, home of the governor, repression against CIOAC leaders increased. On 4 October 1985, Andulio Gálvez Velásquez, a CIOAC advisor elected to the local congress as a deputy of the Partido Socialista Unificado de México (Unified Socialist Party of Mexico), or PSUM, was assassinated by CNC groups linked to the governor's brother (Harvey 1998, 159). CIOAC organized another protest a year later in Tuxtla, on the anniversary of his death, with more than two thousand participants. CIOAC leaders continued to receive death threats and to be subject to repression. The reign of Castellanos Domínguez as governor of Chiapas from 1982 to 1988 was distinguished by an average of two politically motivated killings per month (ibid., 160).[5]

For some who watched—like Comandante Tacho, still a CIOAC sympathizer in the mid 1980s—the death of Gálvez Velásquez became a turning point in developing strategies of political activism. Tacho recalls of the incident:

> I remember Andulio Gálvez Velásquez. . . . [The issues he fought for are] what we are struggling for now. The problem then was that there was a lack of understanding and people didn't have arms to respond. There were only words. So we went through all of these struggles. We know how to form an ejido association, how to make an ejido union, how to group ourselves together in other constellations, the Union of Unions. What happened there was that the advisors began to divide the organization, the UU. That is why there is . . . the Unión de Ejidos de la Selva. We made it.
>
> We began to see that these organizations were not able to follow through with their demands. The Unión de Uniones only went after economic demands, for coffee export. But for those who live further in the jungle that doesn't work, because they don't produce coffee. They live in *tierra caliente* (the lowlands) . . . they only produce cacao, cattle, and wood, but there wasn't much interest in these products. . . .
>
> First the advisors [of the Unión de Uniones] fought with the bosses of INMECAFE and then they became just like them. . . . We watched all of this.
>
> There were more deaths, disappearances, tortures, people were put in jail as political prisoners. We saw that it wasn't possible [to work peacefully]. We saw that there was a stronger and stronger presence of the Mexican Army in the communities. Why, we asked? Why are they here? We thought that we could just assault the Mexican Army and get our arms. We didn't even know about the Zapatista Army. We just had these ideas. We were very ingenuous. We weren't manipulated by anything, but were motivated by what we were living through.
>
> We took prisoners from INMECAFE. We demonstrated, we tried all this . . . that is how we really didn't have any other path left than to integrate ourselves into *filas armadas* (armed struggle). So for us the EZLN was a *pan caliente* [something desirable—literally, a fresh loaf of bread]. This was the solution. That is what we were looking for. . . . In the organizations, we couldn't get anything. The only thing was that we learned how the government worked, how it deceives people. (Reza 1995)

The thickening of the bonds between ejidatarios and independent organizations in the 1980s provided an important contrast for people in Guadalupe Tepeyac as they continued their struggle with agrarian officials. For some, however, independent organizations also proved a dead end, and they began to look for a way to pursue armed struggle.

THE STORY OF INGENIERO JULIO CÉSAR SOLIS RUIZ

By 1987, the situation of the ejidatarios of Guadalupe Tepeyac had not changed. More studies, surveys, and visits by engineers and officials had no result. The people of Guadalupe Tepeyac could not get the 1,760 hectares promised as an extension to their ejido. Ingeniero Julio César Solis Ruiz was commissioned in 1987 by the Chiapas delegate of the Ministry of Agrarian Reform to bring to a close the second petition for lands from Guadalupe Tepeyac. His real job, however, as he set out for Guadalupe Tepeyac in July of 1987, appears to have been to convince the ejidatarios once and for all that they could only get a small part of the land they had been promised. Eventually, he reported that "although at first they refused to receive the land offered," the ejidatarios of Guadalupe Tepeyac finally agreed to accept the 450 hectares offered as a result of their second petition (Solis Ruiz 1988). To confirm the agreement, Solis Ruiz wrote a legal document, signed by him and by the ejidatarios, that "the majority of ejidatarios of this place have agreed to accept the 450 hectares of national lands that belong to them by order of the Governor as lands that can be affected within the legal limit of annexation" (ibid.).

Such letters of agreement can be found in the files of many ejidos in the 1980s, as the government of Castellanos Domínguez "helped to protect private landowners from possible expropriation by issuing more documents of nonaffectability [*certificados de inafectabilidad*] than all the previous state governors combined" (Harvey 1998, 155). Under the national Agrarian Rehabilitation Program, from 1984 to 1987, the states were supposed to purchase those lands belonging to private owners and occupied by peasants whose land claims had not been resolved by the Ministry of Agrarian Reform (ibid., 153). According to Harvey's analysis, the real outcome of the program in Chiapas was to transform conflicts between peasants and landowners into conflicts between independent peasant organizations and the government-controlled CNC. The primary benefactors were landowners who received "payment for land they had resigned themselves to losing anyway" (ibid., 154). To those like the ejidatarios of Guadalupe Tepeyac who were forced to sign "agreements" to accept a small part of the land previously promised, the outcome of the Agrarian Rehabilitation Plan must have been laughable.

The community's continued interactions with Ingeniero Solis Ruiz confirmed the feeling that he, like most agrarian officials, was disrespectful and wished in no way to be of assistance. Although, later in 1987, Solis Ruiz requested information about other private ranches in the area to determine whether they could be annexed as part of the lands promised to Guadalupe Tepeyac, he appears never to have forwarded his report to the state delegate of the Ministry of Agrarian Reform. (Most of the properties in question were between 150 and 350 hectares and were dedicated to corn, coffee, fruit trees, and cattle.) Meanwhile, some of the ejidatarios of Guadalupe Tepeyac were running out of patience.

In December 1988, Jorge Jiménez Pérez, secretary of the Guadalupe Tepeyac Executive Agrarian Committee of the Second Solicitation of Land, went to the office of the Ministry of Agrarian Reform in Tuxtla Gutiérrez. He had made the trip often. To get to the office, he had to walk several hours, then take a bus for five to six more hours on a winding dirt road to Las Margaritas, crossing small rivers, so that only if he was lucky could he arrive without delay. Then he had to take a series of buses to Tuxtla Gutiérrez. The road was hot and dusty, and he would have to bring water and food or purchase his meals. If he left at three in the morning, he might arrive by late afternoon. By that time, the agrarian officials would most likely be gone for the day. Most likely, he would spend the night sleeping on the floor of the house of a friend or camped on the office floor of an independent organization in Tuxtla.

On the December 1988 trip, he carried a letter addressed to Lic. Cancino Cortines, secretary of the Mixed Agrarian Commission, saying that although Solis Ruiz had carried out his technical work relating to the second petition for lands in Guadalupe Tepeyac in July 1988, five months later, the results of that work were still not available. After repeated trips, the ejidatarios were going to someone higher up. The letter stated:

> The previously mentioned Ing. Julio César Solis Ruiz always tells us to come on a particular date, and with this trip I have come more than ten times to see this ingeniero, and he doesn't take into consideration that we are workers in the countryside and we cannot always be traveling. When we present ourselves to him, he always comes up with excuses, like there is no official paper available in the Ministry of Agrarian Reform and because of this he can't write his report. (Jímenez Pérez 1988)

Getting no result from his visit, Jiménez Pérez returned the following month (January 1989) with the president of the Ejidal Commission of Guadalupe Tepeyac, Caralampio Hernández Pérez. This time they went to the top, going directly with a letter to the state delegate of the Ministry of Agrarian Reform in Chiapas, the ministry's highest authority there. In their letter, the two expressed their repeated frustration with Solis Ruiz and again detailed the difficulties of making the long journey:

> The previously mentioned Julio César Solis Ruiz always tells us to come on a particular date, and today this is our eleventh trip, and this public servant [Solis Ruiz] does not take into consideration that we are people from the countryside and we can't always be traveling. . . . [F]or this reason we solicit your intervention so that Julio César Solis Ruiz will make his report so that our case can proceed . . . to a decision.
>
> Mr. Agrarian Delegate in this state, we hope that you will take us into consideration and remember that we are people with few economic resources and we can't always be constantly traveling. The work that Ing. Julio Cesar Solis Ruiz carried out was done more than six months ago and he hasn't informed us of the results. (Hernandez Pérez and Jiménez Pérez 1989a)

In February, the same two men made a twelfth trip, with another letter for the state delegate, detailing how they had been told by Ingeniero Solis Ruiz that he had lost a crucial document needed for their case to proceed, and that Solis Ruiz had told them that *they* would have to determine how to get the missing document to its proper place. It was, they write, "because of this that we again solicit your intervention. . . . [It] is not the responsibility of the campesinos who solicited the land [to see to it that the proper documents are sent to move forward their case]." They end the letter with a reminder that they still have not received the 1,700 hectares of land promised them (Hernández Pérez and Jiménez Pérez 1989b). The January and February letters were copied to the governor of Chiapas.

The story of Ingeniero Solis Ruiz and the letters documenting the mounting frustration of the ejidatarios with his treatment provides an important window on the view of the government from Guadalupe Tepeyac in the 1980s. Agrarian officials such as Solis Ruiz were regarded as disrespectful, uninterested, and probably violating the spirit of the office they were supposed to represent—that is, of agrarian reform, the distribution of land to those who need it. Such experiences were augmented by events such as the assassination of Andulio Gálvez Velásquez.

In 1989, just five years before Guadalupe Tepeyac emerged as a stronghold of the Zapatista rebellion, ejidatarios were struggling to get legal possession of even the 450 hectares they had "accepted." The frustration of ejido leaders with officials of the Ministry of Agrarian Reform was accompanied by a silent movement building in some parts of the community. Comandante Tacho joined the EZLN in the 1986–87 period, along with five others. The five began military training and went to Mexico City and other urban areas as part of this education. They also began to work in the communities of the Lacandon, including Guadalupe Tepeyac. Slowly, they built up a base of supporters in the community, while also recruiting insurgents (those living in isolated camps and training to become part of the Zapatistas' permanent army) and, later, training militia members (those receiving training with arms but residing in their communities of origin, prepared to mobilize for emergencies or specific actions).

THE COFFEE CRASH

By 1989, many ejidatarios in Guadalupe Tepeyac were small producers of coffee and depended on the crop as a source of income. The year 1989 was devastating for coffee producers; world coffee prices fell by 50 percent when the International Coffee Organization failed to agree on production quotas. During the same year, the Salinas de Gortari administration began to privatize INMECAFE, as its accumulated debt was approximately U.S.$90 million (Harvey 1998, 177). For the almost 17,000 coffee producers in the Lacandon forest, most with very small plots, this was not good news.

According to Neil Harvey (1998, 193), the Ejido Union of the Jungle (UE de la Selva / Unión de Ejidos de la Selva, which had a strong presence in Las Margaritas), was initially able to offset the results of the crash in coffee prices through a Dutch alternative trading company that agreed to pay 40 percent above international market prices. While this arrangement allowed UE de la Selva to repay principal and interest on loans, it still meant that coffee producers were paid less than promised. This "led to a general loss of confidence and decline in participation in the UE de la Selva in 1989 to 1990" (ibid.). UE de la Selva and other producers joined to form the Unión de Productores de Café de la Frontera Sur (Union of Coffee Producers of the Southern Border), or UNCAFESUR, in 1990, but clandestine organizing currents had begun to pull people away from such groups.

THE EZLN IN THE LACANDON JUNGLE

According to most sources, the origins of the EZLN can be traced to two earlier guerrilla forces: the Ejército Insurgente Mexicano (Mexican Insurgent Army), or EIM, secretly organized in the 1960s and disbanded after unreported action in Chiapas in 1968 and 1969, and the Fuerzas de Liberación Nacional (Forces of National Liberation), or FLN, organized in Monterrey in 1969 (Womack 1999: 190; Ortega 1994). An FLN safe house was raided by police in Monterrey in 1971, and a few who survived the raid escaped to Chiapas, where they trained as the Emiliano Zapata Guerrilla Nucleus (Womack 1999, 190). In 1974, in Chiapas— the same year as the First Indigenous Congress—federal police and the army captured the guerrilla training camp of the FLN, killing five people (Ortega 1994). According to Womack, several survivors escaped to Mexico City to rebuild the FLN, which by 1979 had cells in the Federal District and in six states, including Chiapas (Womack 1999, 190; see also Tello Díaz 1995, 8). In 1980, the FLN published its statutes and, in this document, stated its plans to form the Zapatista Army of National Liberation (discussed in the next chapter). By 1982, several FLN cadres were working secretly in San Andrés Larráinzar on social programs, and the EZLN's original indigenous recruits were Tzotzils who accompanied Subcomandante Marcos and other FLN organizers to the Lacandon cañadas in 1983 (Womack 1999, 191; Tello Díaz 1995).

According to their oral history, Marcos and his compatriots began military training in the caves in the Sierra of Corralchén near Ocosingo and in the jungle above Guadalupe Tepeyac near the Guatemalan border. (According to Marcos's statement, they arrived in approximately 1983.) The group undertook campaigns promoting vaccination and began to encourage people to engage in military training. They thus established themselves quickly in the Tzeltal-Tojolabal territory that includes the ejidos of Guadalupe Tepeyac and La Realidad. According to Marcos, Tacho belonged to a small but dedicated local group that worked with the EZLN. Many local leaders active in peasant organizing around issues of credit and production in the 1970s eventually moved over to the EZLN. Many of these probably engaged in so-called *doble militancia* for a long time, participating in local and regional peasant organizations as well as working clandestinely with the EZLN. Major Moisés, an early Tzeltal recruit to the EZLN, told how, having participated in the Unión Quiptic ta Lecubtesel, he remained in the organization after 1983 when its northern Maoist leaders were expelled and the Unión de Uniones split:

> At that time we knew the history of Zapata, of Villa, but we couldn't go any further because it was about fighting, about confrontation. That is when this guy, this muchacho arrives [one of the original outsiders arriving in Chiapas to form the EZLN] and I say to him, "[W]e see that this struggle we are in

[for land and control over productive processes] doesn't have a good answer, but we haven't entered into another form of struggle because we haven't found a way to do that." . . . I start to talk with this person and he gives me a pamphlet that is called *El Despertador.* . . . [I]t spoke of the history of Mexico, and how the rich rob, exploit, and deceive. . . . One day I just had to ask him, so I said, "[L]ook, I understand what this pamphlet is trying to say. But the problem is how, in what form and with who? I want you to explain things to me clearly." It wasn't until that moment that he said to me, "If you are ready, then you will have to look for other people." I said to him, "I need you to explain to me what this is all about so I know how we will do this." Then he told me. "It is a guerrilla group that is called the Zapatista Army. They are clandestine," and he explained to me the issue of security. (Le Bot 1997, 172)

In many communities where the EZLN began to organize secretly, women were specifically recruited, along with youth. In winning covert converts to the EZLN, women were key. In many cases, those militating secretly in the EZLN while also working in other organizations first worked to recruit women. Tacho recalled the EZLN organizing process he participated in:

We started to see the necessity of the participation of women. We trained women who were like political delegates, and because we had indigenous women, peasants, who were already working with us, we would come into town with them and have secret meetings at night with the women outside of town. They would act as if they were going to get some corn or firewood, but in reality they would come to a meeting. They would persuade their husbands to stop drinking. Then, when we had two, or three, or four compañeras in one town, we would put them in charge of seeing who else they could get to work with us, and little by little, we would grow, until finally a whole town was with us. That is how we developed ourselves, very delicately, and doing truly clandestine work. (Le Bot 1997, 164–65)

The health and literacy campaigns of the EZLN, which included simple projects such as digging latrines, giving vaccinations, and teaching women to read, were critical in winning support in communities.

The Zapatistas also offered armed training to many young peasants in a range of organizations, particularly those in ARIC–UU, which split in 1988 into a reformist side focused on markets and negotiations with the government and a faction more closely affiliated with the Church and utterly distrustful of the government, which stuck to demands for land. In 1989, after the collapse of the coffee market, probably more than half of the communities affiliated with the ARIC began to participate secretly in the EZLN. In the early 1990s, probably around 1991, the EZLN built its first safe house on the ejido lands behind Guadalupe Tepeyac. Comandante Tacho observed:

At that time we needed to maintain security, as we called it, because in this place of Aguascalientes[6] . . . when the majority of the community was joining the bases of support of the EZLN, we came to an agreement on building this first *casa de seguridad,* where the town met as well as those of us who were local Zapatista leaders. . . .

We also formed the ranks of the Mexican Militia Forces. This safe house, the first house here in Aguascalientes, was built some time ago. This house was not discovered in the mountains here in what is now known as Aguascalientes. . . . So we started to meet here . . . at that time the headquarters of the EZLN or of the communities that were the bases of support was here. . . .

We [in the organization of the EZLN] had to take care that the enemy didn't discover us quickly. The Mexican Army always came here to carry out military exercises in this community. We had to maintain secrecy . . . with the people whom we spoke with. We told them that they had to keep very quiet about what we had commented on, what we had spoken about, that it was critical to do this. So we made sure that nothing would come out of the meetings. We had this responsibility, because it couldn't fall into the enemy hands. Everyone knew that if what we were doing fell into the hands of the enemy, that people would have to defend it to the death. . . . We said that it was necessary to take care of it like a growing child. We had to take care of its development. This was the struggle. (Reza 1995)

Even as the EZLN was making strong inroads into Guadalupe Tepeyac, the community's second petition to extend its ejido dragged on, now represented by ARIC–UU. Several memos from the Agrarian Delegates Office of the Ministry of Agrarian Reform in Chiapas suggest that the report required to move the case forward (requiring key information from Solis Ruiz) was never written. In 1991, ARIC–UU representatives from Las Margaritas went to Tuxtla Gutiérrez to again push an official from the Ministry of Agrarian Reform to move on the case (Countiño Farrera 1991). By the end of 1991, the ejidatarios of Guadalupe Tepeyac had been waiting fourteen years for the final resolution of their second request for additional lands already promised them. They had seen several studies made of their situation, had sent local authorities to Tuxtla Gutiérrez more than a dozen times in less than a year, and had seen a powerful regional peasant organization intervene on their behalf. Still nothing had changed. By this time, the EZLN was firmly entrenched in the ejido.

THE END OF AGRARIAN REFORM AND THE GROWTH OF ANCIEZ

The announcement, in early 1992, of the amendment to Article 27 of the Constitution calling for the end of land redistribution and the regularizing of all landholdings was the final straw for some indigenous peasants in Chiapas—certainly for the Guadalupe Tepeyac ejidatarios who had waited fourteen years for more land. With over 25 percent of Mexico's unresolved land disputes—including the case of Guadalupe Tepeyac—in Chiapas at that time, news of the end of agrarian reform was not well received there. Marcos later told the press: "[T]he government had the brilliant idea of reforming Article 27 of the Constitution, and this was a powerful catalyst in the communities. These reforms got rid of any legal possibility for obtaining land. . . . This slammed the door shut for indigenous people to survive in a legal and peaceful manner. This is why they took up arms" (Petrich and Henríquez 1994).

It is not hard to imagine the reception of the announcement of the changes to Article 27 in Guadalupe Tepeyac, where the population had been doubling every ten years and people had waited so long for land promised but never delivered. With no survival plan available beyond subsistence farming and coffee-growing, the ejido must have been startled to learn that no more land could be obtained, and that even land in the so-called agrarian backlog might not be distributed.

Small coffee growers and corn farmers from Guadalupe Tepeyac participating in ARIC–UU through the Unión de Ejidos de la Selva were being exposed to changes within that organization. In 1991, significant parts of the leadership were clandestinely militating in the EZLN. About the same time, another organization, the Alianza Campesina Independiente "Emiliano Zapata" (Independent Peasant Alliance "Emiliano Zapata"), or ACIEZ, was quickly attracting ejidatarios from a wide range of communities in the cañadas, the highlands, and the Northern Zone of Chiapas. ACIEZ began to pull people away from ARIC and to establish an independent presence. By some accounts, ACIEZ received a high percentage of its recruits (up to 40 percent, by one account) from ARIC–UU (Ross 1994: 280). In 1992, adding "Nacional" to its title, ACIEZ became the Alianza Nacional Campesina Independiente "Emiliano Zapata" (Independent National Peasant Alliance "Emiliano Zapata"), or ANCIEZ, a name change possibly prompted by a secret congress in the Sierra Negra of Puebla where ANCIEZ joined with radical peasant organizations from six other central and northern states that advocated an armed option (ibid.).

In January 1992, ANCIEZ organized its first mobilization in Chiapas, with over four thousand attending in the plaza of Ocosingo. The rally focused on the forthcoming NAFTA agreement and on changes to Article 27, emphasizing opposition to both and demanding a resolution of the agrarian backlog in the state (Tello Díaz 1995, 137). The demonstration included both members of ANCIEZ and many who were not. Certainly, news of the demonstration got back to Guadalupe Tepeyac, and it is quite likely that the community was represented there as well through the Unión de Ejidos de la Selva.

At the time that this protest against the agrarian reforms took place, the Secretaría de Agricultura y Recursos Hidráulicos was busy circulating information packages that tried to represent the positive side of the reforms. For those in Guadalupe Tepeyac, however, there was nothing positive to be found in these packets.

A few months later, three thousand gathered in Ocosingo to protest NAFTA and the counterreforms to Article 27 on the anniversary of Zapata's assassination, 10 April. A letter was read, addressed to the government of Salinas de Gortari, stating, "In four months, you have eliminated our most precious historical conquest, the right to land" (Tello Díaz 1995, 149). As the Zapatistas consolidated their movement, public events on 10 April commemorating Zapata and connecting him to current agrarian struggles became a central arena for celebrating the new Zapatismo of the 1990s.

COLUMBUS DAY, 1992: THE POLITICS OF SECRECY

On 12 October 1992, a meeting was held in Guadalupe Tepeyac, during which the results of yet another study and recommendations from the Ministry of Agrarian Reform were made known and supposedly agreed upon. This meeting happened at precisely the same time as a major demonstration in San Cristóbal de las Casas protesting the celebration of five hundred years of conquest. Although it is not possible definitely to document who from the ejido of Guadalupe Tepeyac participated in this demonstration, some members of the community were there. It was a contradictory and ironic Columbus Day. Some ejidatarios were marching in San Cristóbal de las Casas in a demonstration that culminated with the toppling of the statue of a Spanish conquistador; others remained in their community and signed a document acknowledging once again that they would never get most of the land promised by the government.

Indeed, 12 October 1992 was marked by a protest coalition called "500 Years of Indigenous, Black, and Popular Resistance in Chiapas" and elsewhere in Mexico. Several days earlier, a new statewide coalition of seventeen organizations, the Frente de Organizaciones Sociales de Chiapas (Front of Social Organizations of Chiapas), or FOSCH, had been created, including ARIC, OCEZ, CIOAC, ANCIEZ, UNORCA (Unión Nacional de Organizaciones Regionales Campesinas Autónomas), CRIACH (Consejo de Representantes Indígenas de los Altos de Chiapas), and others. On 12 October, the expectations of march organizers were far surpassed when ten thousand people arrived in San Cristóbal, most of them indigenous. About half were ANCIEZ militants, whoreportedly arrived in buses and trucks they had expropriated from throughout the Lacandon (Ross 1994, 81). Many marchers had their faces painted, carried bows and arrows, and shouted slogans. As described by John Ross, the march culminated when

> the marchers abruptly halted in front of a statue of the conquistador Diego de Mazariegos, exterminator of Chiapas. Ropes were fastened around the Spaniard's neck and ANCIEZ members smashed at his pedestal with sledgehammers. Within ten minutes, the Indian killer was pulled to the ground as thousands of indigenous cheered. . . . After repeated attempts to melt the old man were unsuccessful, de Mazariegos was so charred by the experience that he never again stood on his still vacant pedestal. (Ross 1994, 81–82)

Observers of this march, such as Amado Avendaño, a journalist and lawyer in San Cristóbal before becoming "governor in rebellion" at the head of the movement for indigenous autonomy in Chiapas on 8 December 1994, remarked on the disciplined nature of many of the marchers, saying: "There were columns of men and women at this march who were very disciplined. They carried a bow and arrow in order to identify themselves and they were marching in formation. . . . This was the first time I saw the indigenous insurgents in San Cristóbal . . . until two years later."[7] The downing of Diego de Mazariegos's statue by the ANCIEZ militants, which was followed by their disappearance in April 1993, is believed by many to be the first manifestation of the EZLN.

In a 1996 interview, Subcomandante Marcos, who watched the demonstration and is even said to have videotaped it, erased any doubt that those participating had belonged to the EZLN, saying:

> In 1992 we perceived a question that was very important for the indigenous communities, which was the character of the Conquest, what the Discovery of America signified. Inside the indigenous movement at the local level—I'm not sure of the national level—there was a concern about what this signified and of the necessity to have a demonstration. . . . The process of radicalization had precipitated and the communities had reached a point of no return about the question of war that was expressed by the indigenous leaders, the leaders of the communities and regions that later became the Comité [Clandestine Revolutionary Indigenous Committee]. So the indigenous leaders proposed that we begin the war in 1992. . . . We told them that the conditions

were not right yet, and that the international situation was not favorable, and that the national situation was also very unfavorable for any kind of attempts at change, especially for armed struggle. So we decided together that we needed to consult, and this was the first consultation of what came to be a regular style of organizing of the Zapatistas in the communities.

This happened in the second half of 1992 and coincided with the mobilization that the indigenous peoples were making to celebrate the five hundred years, the grand march that was to happen on the twelfth of October in San Cristóbal. The indigenous proposed it as the last civil presentation of the indigenous movement that is already Zapatista. . . .

. . . During this time we were carrying out the consultation, with an explanation in each town about conditions in the community among the ethnic groups, about the international situation, the national situation, and asking whether or not the time was right to begin the war. In the months of September, October, and the first two weeks of November, we carried out the consultation in something like four hundred or five hundred communities, among Tzotziles, Ch'oles, Tojolabales, and Tzeltales. In the North, the highlands, and the cañadas, a majority of the people participated in this consultation. (Le Bot 1997, 190–91)[8]

Meanwhile, as some members of Guadalupe Tepeyac were marching through San Cristóbal, others were quietly meeting with agrarian officials, going through the motions again of "accepting" a small portion of the promised lands. The document from the 12 October meeting in Guadalupe Tepeyac, entitled "The Act of Conformity to the Second Expansion of the Ejido of the Population of 'Guadalupe Tepeyac' of the Municipio of Las Margaritas, Chiapas," stated that in 1989, a recommendation had been approved that granted Guadalupe Tepeyac 1,024 hectares of land, distributed in three parts: 498 hectares from the national land known as "Las Delicias" that had already been provisionally turned over to the community's ejidatarios; a second piece of 450 hectares of what was presumed national land; and a third piece of 76 hectares, also national land. The document pointed out that the 450 hectares of "presumed national land" did not exist: "the first extension of Guadalupe Tepeyac and the recent extension of the ejido of La Realidad overlap in the precise area where this land is, therefore it doesn't exist." Overlapping maps again, this time with La Realidad! "Therefore," the document added, "the only thing that is accepted [by the ejidatarios] is the 498 hectares that were given to them provisionally, knowing that there are not any more lands available" (Acta de conformidad 1992). The document was signed by thirty men. In the end, Guadalupe Tepeyac had to settle for what it had provisionally been given in 1980 after a comedy of bureaucratic errors, delays, and misinformation. With large numbers of ejidatarios already committed to the EZLN and the path of armed struggle, the outcome of the meeting must have been laughable, particularly to those who returned from the successful demonstration in San Cristóbal and focused with increased urgency on the upcoming war.

This time also marks the consolidation of the EZLN politically in some communities, when formal votes were taken on whether to go to war.

COMMUNITIES VOTE FOR WAR

According to Subcomandante Marcos and to the oral histories of other EZLN comandantes, at the end of 1992, communities working with the social organization of the EZLN voted in assemblies to give the Zapatista military wing one year to prepare for war. Marcos said in an interview:

> We made the decision by means of a kind of referendum. After the October [1992] march, we started the count. . . . The vote was approved by a major- ity of those inside of the EZLN. The areas where we were operating included the highlands, the North, and above all in the jungle. The majority of the pop- ulation voted for war. . . . We asked them to send us arguments about why or why not so that the authorities (military and civil) of the EZLN could eval- uate the situation. Among the Zapatistas who voted against the war [there] was the argument that the repression would be very severe, that people were not ready, that there were divided communities and that it was better to wait. These were serious arguments. In conclusion, a wide majority of people stated that they were in favor of beginning the war now [at the end of 1992], and the communities gave a formal order to the EZLN to fight the war to- gether with them. (Le Bot 1997, 192)

A majority of the Tojolabales of La Realidad voted affirmatively, along with those in neighboring Guadalupe Tepeyac. There were definitely dis- senting votes, but the exact numbers are not known. Those not in agree- ment most likely left. By this time, more than half of the community was completely committed to the Zapatista movement. Guadalupe Tepeyac served as a key Zapatista base community and contributed young people to the army as insurgents. Experienced ejido members also worked as EZLN military and political leaders. The safe house constructed on the ejido land behind the community hosted frequent meetings and at times, according to Comandante Tacho, up to eight hundred combatants from the area would come to the site to practice maneuvers (Reza 1995).

By 1993, more than half the ARIC reformists, previously reluctant to join, had signed up for Zapatista military training and joined ANCIEZ, the semi-clandestine peasant organization affiliated with the EZLN. In- digenous leaders and EZLN military commanders met more and more frequently. In early 1993, when indigenous representatives and authorities at the community level supportive of the EZLN shared the results of the referendum on the war, the Clandestine Revolutionary Indigenous Committee was formally constituted. After several days' discussion, according to Subcomandante Marcos, all agreed that the political-military wing of the EZLN had to be subordinated to a democratic decision-making mechanism that would represent the majority of the organization. Since the majority of the EZLN consisted of indigenous people living in communities, rather than full-time insurgents, these would determine what the army would do. The leaders who represented the four primary ethnic groups within the EZLN—the Ch'ol, Tzeltal, Tojolabal, and Tzotzil—were made commanders (*comandantes*) of the Zapatista Army of National Liberation and constituted the Clandestine Revolutionary Indigenous Committee (Le Bot 1997, 195–96). As mentioned earlier, these ethnic affiliations represented not so much shared linguistic affiliation as shared experiences of struggle and local history (although in many cases linguistic affiliation was part of that experience). This structuring marked a turning point in the EZLN, Marcos said: "We had to go through an internal transition: a politico-military, urban organization is displaced from power by a collective, democratic, indigenous, plural organization" (Le Bot 1997, 202).

According to Zapatista accounts, there are three distinct groups in the EZLN. The first are insurgents, or *insurgentes,* who live away from their communities in military camps, where they train. They are the most highly disciplined members of the EZLN, and it is among the insurgents that equality of women has been most intensely discussed and debated. The existence of insurgents in the EZLN is mentioned in the 1980 statutes of the FLN: "combat troops [to] be made up of professional militants from the FLN and those Mexican or foreign combatants who, although not FLN militants, are disposed to subject themselves to military discipline and to respect the succession of commands set by the National Leadership" (Fuerzas de Liberación Nacional 1980, cited in Womack 1999, 197). By 1994, the EZLN insurgents were indigenous people of Chiapas commanded from Chiapas.

The second level of EZLN participation involves the militia members, or *milicianos,* who are mobile reservists who live in their communities, receive training, and participate in armed actions. Finally, the third level, and largest group, includes the bases of support (*bases de apoyo*) consisting of civilians who subscribe to Zapatismo, carry out Zapatista social programs, and support the Zapatista Army on a material level. The community assembly is the most important first-level decision-making organ in the base communities. Each community elects its own officers responsible for communal safe houses, education, health, and other concerns. These form a sort of local Clandestine Revolutionary Indigenous Committee. Women and youth are represented, and organized as groups at the local level. However, as noted by Christine Eber (1999), in the Tzotzil Zapatista base communities of San Pedro Chenalhó, single women are often the only ones elected leaders in their communities, because it is too hard for married women and those with young children to travel several times a month to regional meetings lasting more than a day; local gender roles often continue to constrain women's political participation in their communities. Community elected officers meet regionally to coordinate campaigns and initiate new ideas (Ross 1994, 287; interviews with Zapatistas in 1994, 1995, and 1996).

Local assemblies elect delegates to one of four Regional Clandestine Revolutionary Indigenous Committees, organized around the four Zapatista language groups. Each regional CCRI has sixteen to forty members. Eleven delegates from each regional CCRI are chosen to sit on the CCRI–General Command, the highest political authority of the EZLN— the group constituted in January 1993 as the Clandestine Revolutionary Indigenous Committee (Ross 1994, 287).

Subcomandante Marcos has been identified as the leader of the EZLN's military wing, serving on the CCRI–General Command in this capacity. In numerous interviews, Marcos has stressed that he has been and is under the orders of the CCRI–General Command. He has also been identified as the mouthpiece of the EZLN, its ambassador, because of his excellent spoken Spanish. Beginning in 1995–96, indigenous leaders such as Tacho, Moisés, Ana María, Trinidad, David, and Zebedeo also emerged as eloquent spokespeople in the second round of peace accord dialogues and in large national and international gatherings in Chiapas. In later years, when the EZLN sent out hundreds of delegates throughout Mexico, many different leaders emerged, including in February and March 2001, when a busload of comandantes went to Mexico City and addressed throngs of people in many cities and towns along the way.

In 1993, the EZLN and many of its community members were preparing for war. That year, President Salinas de Gortari briefly visited Guadalupe Tepeyac to dedicate a new clinic for the Mexican Social Security Institute, complete with a new ambulance. All indications were that he knew about the EZLN and realized he was visiting the Zapatista heartland.

The year was one of silence and hard work. The world might have known what was coming had the Mexican government not worked so hard to cover up what it knew about EZLN military training and planning. On 14 May 1993, a column of the Mexican Army clashed with an EZLN battalion in a battle in which at least two people died. The army issued a communiqué at the end of the month stating that it had engaged in combat "against a group of individuals of indeterminate number that were presumably involved in illegal activities" (Tello Díaz 1995, 168). In reality, it had attacked a major EZLN training camp, destroyed valuable infrastructure, and captured key documents. The EZLN commander in charge of the camp was relieved of command and sent back to Mexico City. Shortly thereafter, the EZLN consolidated its Chiapas-based command structure.

While the Salinas de Gortari government denied the existence of a guerrilla movement, thousands of indigenous people prepared for war in the highlands, northern zone, and Lacandon jungle. In the Tojolabal ejidos of Guadalupe Tepeyac and La Realidad, people prepared as well. The decision to go to war frightened many. Not everyone was in agreement, and those who were afraid began to leave EZLN strongholds— including Guadalupe Tepeyac and La Realidad—for surrounding cities such as Comitán, Las Margaritas, and San Cristóbal. Those not in favor of the war were not welcome in Zapatista strongholds. Those who stayed behind in places like Guadalupe Tepeyac were united behind the cause of the war, which was proclaimed on the first day the North American Free Trade Agreement went into effect, 1 January 1994.

THE JANUARY 1994 REBELLION

On 1 January 1994, Mexico awakened to news of an armed rebellion by the Zapatista Army for National Liberation. The troops were Tzeltal, Tzotzil, Tojolabal, Ch'ol, and Mam Indians from the central highlands of Chiapas and the Lacandon jungle bordering Guatemala. The group's name, methods, and message clearly invoked the spirit of the Mexican Revolution, advancing a simple platform of work, land, housing, food, health, education, independence, liberty, democracy, justice, and peace in the names of Emiliano Zapata and Pancho Villa.

The initial message of the Zapatistas proclaimed that they would march to Mexico City and demanded the overthrow of the "dictator" Salinas de Gortari. The response of the Mexican government was somewhat delayed, but within thirty-six hours after the Zapatistas had occupied five county seats in Chiapas, a military response came. Ocosingo became the primary site of military confrontation. The army next proceeded to shell civilian populations on the outskirts of several communities, detained large numbers of people, summarily executed at least six (and probably many more) suspected Zapatistas, and committed other human rights violations (Human Rights Watch / Americas 1994, 1995). Torture and degrading treatment against detained persons was carried out by the army in an attempt to extract confessions of membership in the EZLN. Casualty figures have ranged from a low of about one hundred, provided by the government, to the estimate of more than four hundred given by Bishop Samuel Ruiz.

Twelve days into the confrontation, the government agreed to negotiate, appointing Manuel Camacho Solís its negotiator. From January until early June 1994, when the Zapatistas formally rejected the government's 34-point peace plan, the EZLN engaged in a complex dialogue with the government, which continued to receive coverage, if low-level, in the Mexican press. When negotiations ceased, in the cathedral in San Cristóbal, in March, the peace plan received a lower profile until June, when the date for presidential elections drew near and Chiapas again became a national issue. The presidential elections took place in August, with Ernesto Zedillo of the PRI elected president.

By this time, most of the country, including ejidatarios in Oaxaca, had become familiar with the EZLN to some degree. In Oaxaca (as will be seen in chapter 11), the demands of the Zapatistas and their invocation of Zapata as a historic symbol resonated with parts of local history and experience—especially with that since the 1930s, when Lázaro Cárdenas established personal contact with some ejidos and positioned himself as a link to the agrarianism of Zapata. To understand how parts of wider Mexican society connected with contemporary Zapatismo emanating from ejidos in Chiapas such as Guadalupe Tepeyac, it is necessary to look more carefully at the origins and strains of Zapatismo in the cañadas and to see how the movement was translated in other parts of the country.

CHAPTER 6

Zapata Vive!

Local Lacandon Zapatismo and
Its Translation to Larger Mexico

Article 27 of the Magna Carta should respect the original
spirit of Emiliano Zapata: the land is for the indigenous
peoples and peasants who work it. Not for latifundistas.
We want the huge amounts of land that are in the hands of
ranchers, national and international landowners, and other
people who occupy a lot of the land but are not peasants to
pass into the hands of our communities where there is an absolute shortage of lands, as is established in our revolutionary
agrarian law. . . . The Salinas reform to Article 27 of the Constitution should be annulled and the right to land should be
returned to our Magna Carta.

> *Comité Clandestino Revolucionario Indigena–*
> *Comandancia General del EZLN, point 8*
> *of the first set of Zapatista peace proposals,*
> *March 1994 (Ejército Zapatista de Liberación*
> *Nacional 1994, 181)*

Since its first appearance in the press in Mexico, the EZLN has used the
figure of Emiliano Zapata as a central symbol in communiqués written
by its supreme authority, the Clandestine Indigenous Revolutionary
Committee, constituted in early 1993. This chapter seeks in part to establish how ejidatarios who formed and joined the EZLN in the Lacandon region of Chiapas appropriated the dominant symbol of Zapata,
claimed for decades by the Mexican government, and reworked it for
the purposes of resistance and armed struggle. This general story is not
particularly unique in history. Many groups have reclaimed dominant
symbols for their own purposes, often against established governments
or groups in power. What stands out about Lacandon Zapatismo is not
only its local development in eastern Chiapas, but also its projection and

presence outside the boundaries of its origins—throughout Mexico and even throughout the world.[1] What distinguishes the Zapatista rebellion from prior indigenous revolts in Mexican history is that so many knew about it instantly and continued to follow its changes. The presence of the media (television, radio, and newspapers) in Chiapas on the first and subsequent days of the rebellion, as well as the consistent transfer of EZLN communiqués from printed to internet versions, made a critical difference in the impact of neo-Zapatismo outside Chiapas. "This 'third army' of news reporters, as they were called in Chiapas, made the difference between an uprising that exposed the impoverishment of the majority of Mexicans to a world audience and a skirmish that could be buried by a government dedicated to a course of neoliberal 'modernization' and entry into international investment markets," June Nash wrote in reference to a story that might have appeared on the first day of NAFTA, 1 January 1994 (Nash 1997, 48).

The successful projection of neo-Zapatismo outside Chiapas since 1994 has also affected the struggle over how the Mexican nation is to be defined—over which nation views are to be part of wider hegemonic and counterhegemonic discussions transcending local and regional contexts. While the governments of presidents Salinas de Gortari (1988–94) and Zedillo (1994—2000) consistently put forward a vision of a new Mexico integrated into the global economic order built on free trade agreements and foreign investment (a vision some might argue is an *anti*-nationalist view of the nation), the new Zapatismo projected from Chiapas has put forward a different nation view—one based on looking inward, on fixing social and economic inequality, on returning territory and resources to indigenous peoples, and on not accepting the rules of global economics that disadvantage those on the bottom.

This chapter suggests how the refashioning of government-claimed nationalist symbols, such as the transforming of Emiliano Zapata into Votán Zapata (a hybrid Tzeltal/nationalist figure created by Marcos and the EZLN), and the projection of the local struggle represented by Votán Zapata back to the rest of the nation, resulted in a new version of nationalism projected from the margins—neo-Zapatismo. Because the nationalist vision of the Chiapas Zapatistas resonated for others outside Chiapas—particularly the organized left, labor, students, indigenous movements, debtors' movements, human rights movements, and progressive sectors of the Catholic Church—this vision became another nationalist discourse, legitimized for its believers by the government's steadfast opposition. As contemporary neo-Zapatismo gained both supporters and virulent opponents at the national level, it became sanctified as a competing nationalist discourse, a vision counter to that projected by the framers of NAFTA.

The First Declaration from the Lacandon Jungle, "Today we say enough," established Zapata and the Mexican Revolution as central to the new Zapatista struggle:

> We are a product of five hundred years of struggle: first against slavery . . . and finally, after the dictatorship of Porfirio Díaz refused to fairly apply the reform laws, in the rebellion where the people created their own leaders. In that rebellion, Villa and Zapata emerged—poor men, like us. (Ejército Zapatista de Liberación Nacional 1994, 33)

How Zapata was converted into the icon of an indigenous army and political organization is related to the initiation and growth of the EZLN even before that entity became a reality in Chiapas. The use of Zapata's name is deeply tied to the symbolism of the Mexican left in the 1970s and 1980s, and to the use of Zapata's image, name, and words (such as the slogan "Tierra y libertad," often attributed to him) in regional peasant organizing during those decades in Chiapas. At some level, ejidatarios in Chiapas, outside organizers from the People's Union and Proletarian Line, and members of the FLN (Fuerzas de Liberación Nacional) all in different ways absorbed the Mexican government's promotion of Zapata as a symbol of revolution. The local Zapatismo of the Lacandon jungle is therefore a hybrid, a mix of local and national elements, of ideas poured forth by many persons and cooked in the particular stew of eastern Chiapas at a particular time. The Zapatismo that emerged in 1994 was something still in process. As Subcomandante Marcos puts it:

> When we made our appearance on the first of January of 1994, we had only vaguely defined what Zapatismo is. It was a very vague initial synthesis, a mixture of patriotic values, of the historical inheritance of what was the clandestine left in Mexico in the decade of the 1960s, of elements of indigenous culture, of military elements of Mexican history, of what were the guerrilla movements of Central and South America, of national liberation movements. . . . All of this was reflected in the First Declaration of the Lacandon Jungle. (Le Bot 1997, 199–200)

THE ROLE OF ZAPATA IN PEASANT ORGANIZATIONS AND THE FLN

Like many longtime indigenous leaders in the EZLN, Comandante Tacho from Guadalupe Tepeyac and Major Moisés, rumored to be from the Tzeltal rancho La Huasteca, participated in independent peasant organizations in the late 1970s and the 1980s. Moisés participated in the Unión Quiptic ta Lecubtesel until the mid 1980s, while Tacho was an activist in the UE de la Selva and the Unión de Uniones (Reza 1995). Both have spoken at length about their involvement with such movements, their frustration, and their sense of needing to find another path of struggle after watching many fellow activists imprisoned, kidnapped, tortured, and assassinated for their work. Comandante Tacho said in a 1994 interview: "We saw that, instead of advancing us, in *la lucha pacífica* the leaders sold out and some died. They were killed, in the case of CIOAC. I saw all the work of these good people and how they fought for indigenous people and, yes, they died" (Reza 1995).

The symbols of agrarian struggle in the 1980s in these movements clearly included the person of Emiliano Zapata—and, more important, the message associated with his name, "Land for those who work it," and a general message of the rights of *campesinos* to the same opportunities and support for the productive and marketing process that larger farmers got: credit, roads, transportation for goods, fertilizer, good prices, and so on. Tacho, Moisés, and many others participated during these years in dozens of strikes, marches, demonstrations, sit-ins, and other actions in which the image of Zapata and demands for land and the rights of ejidatarios and other small farmers were central.

Ejidatarios in the Lacandon were clearly exposed to government use of the symbols of the Mexican Revolution through interaction with agrarian officials. Because such interactions came long after the revolution, and after the 1930s, when the Cárdenas government had reignited the fire of Zapata-style agrarianism through its brigades of socialist educators and its promoters of the formation of ejidos, the interactions lacked the intensity found where ejidos had been founded during the 1930s such as those described in Oaxaca. As discussed in chapter 2, government use of the symbols of the Mexican Revolution through promotion of socialist education also had minimal impact in indigenous parts of Chiapas. The primary source of Zapatismo in the Lacandon jungle in the 1980s was through the ideological messages of the Mexican urban left and through those organizers from the left who went out into the Mexican countryside after 1968 to work with the rural population.

In addition to advisors and organizers who arrived in the 1970s from groups like the People's Union and Proletarian Line (Harvey 1998), others, such as Subcomandante Marcos and Subcomandante Pedro (who was to be killed in the January 1994 EZLN offensive in Las Margaritas),

arrived in Chiapas in the early 1980s with the explicit purpose of organizing a guerrilla army and promoting armed struggle. They arrived just
as some Proletarian Line advisors to independent peasants organizations
were leaving or being expelled. Marcos and a few others from an urban
guerrilla organization known as the Fuerzas de Liberación Nacional, or
FLN, brought nationalist discourses about Mexican history to put in the
service of building armed struggle.

Urban intellectuals and organizers (including Marcos) shared a common educational background and set of national symbols with those
who ultimately formed part of the Mexican state—people like Carlos
Salinas de Gortari. The education that urban intellectuals and organizers received in Mexico City and other major urban areas in the 1950s
and 1960s built on the nationalist legacy created by the Department of
Education in the 1930s and fashioned it toward a changing image of the
Mexican Revolution.

Marcos brought this education and a love for history. He obviously
deployed his education to different ends than did many of his counterparts who became part of the government. In an interview recounting
the birth of the EZLN, he said:

> I went to teach what the people wanted: literacy and Mexican history. In
> 1984, I joined the first group of indigenous *guerilleros* in the mountains.
> They had a lot of political experience already, having participated in mass
> movements, and they knew all about the problems of the left political parties.
> They had also been in prison, suffered torture, all of that. But they demanded
> what they called "the political word" [*la palabra política*]: history. The his-
> tory of this country and of the struggle. So that was the task I arrived with.
> (Gilly, Marcos and Ginzburg 1995, 129–43, cited in Harvey 1998, 165)

The presence of the image of Emiliano Zapata, and the use of his
name in the EZLN, was spelled out by the FLN in its 1980 statutes, published in Mexico City. Under Article 26, describing its "organic structure" (Fuerzas de Liberación Nacional 1980, cited in Womack 1999,
196), the statutes specify that the organisms forming the FLN are:

    a.   The National Leadership: organism of political-military leader-
ship at the national level.

    b.   Zapatista Army of National Liberation, in rural zones.

    c.   EYOL (Estudiantes y Obreros en Lucha): clandestine organiza-
tions and networks and cells of "Students and Workers in Struggle," in
urban zones.

Under Article 30, the statutes explain why Zapata's name is used for the FLN's guerrilla army. "The Zapatista Army of National Liberation is so called because Emiliano Zapata is the hero who best symbolizes the traditions of revolutionary struggle of the Mexican people" (Fuerzas de Liberación Nacional 1980, cited in Womack 199, 196). Almost fourteen years before the EZLN made its appearance in 1994, the formation of a Zapatista army had been envisioned in a document apparently written by the FLN in Mexico City. The choice of Emiliano Zapata as a symbol for the FLN guerrilla army was carefully thought out. The urban leftist intellectuals who wrote the FLN statutes in the 1980s shared the nationalist socialization of many Mexicans in venerating Zapata as a national hero representing revolutionary struggle. What the original cadres of the FLN did not bank on was how the meaning of Zapata that emerged through the indigenous army that came to make up the EZLN in Chiapas would completely transform the 1980s language and vision of the then-urban-based FLN—eventually discarding its national leadership and running its army through an indigenous command structure from Chiapas.

ZAPATISTA REVOLUTIONARY AGRARIAN LAW AND AGRICULTURAL PRACTICES

When, during 1993, the Zapatistas prepared their rebellion, they published a series of Revolutionary Laws accompanying the First Declaration of the Lacandon Jungle. The legacy of Zapata figures strongly in the Revolutionary Law of Agrarian Reform, which, with the other laws, was published in the December 1993 issue of the EZLN newspaper *El Despertador Mexicano* (The Mexican Alarm Clock):

> *Revolutionary Agrarian Reform Law*
>
> The struggle of poor peasants in Mexico continues to claim the land for those who work it. After Emiliano Zapata and against the reforms of Article 27 of the Mexican Constitution,[2] the EZLN takes up the just struggle of rural Mexico for land and liberty. With the purpose of establishing a general rule for the new agrarian distribution of land that the revolution brings to the Mexican countryside, the following REVOLUTIONARY AGRARIAN LAW is issued. (Ejército Zapatista de Liberación Nacional 1994: 43; Womack 1999, 253)

This opening paragraph clearly establishes the EZLN as following in the path of Emiliano Zapata and suggests a new agrarian redistribution of land that will perhaps undo the perceived evils of the 1992 reform of Article 27. In its specificities, the Zapatista agrarian law puts strict limits on the amount of land that can be held—"all tracts of land that are more than 100 hectares of poor quality and more than 50 hectares of good quality will be subject to revolutionary agrarian action"—and advocates that land redistributed to landless peasants and farmworkers be worked collectively: "The lands affected by this agrarian law will be redistributed to landless peasants and farm workers who apply for it as COLLECTIVE PROPERTY for the formation of cooperatives, peasant societies, or farm and ranching collectives. The land affected must be worked collectively" (Ejército Zapatista de Liberación Nacional 1994, 43; translation in Womack 1999, 253). The Zapatista agrarian law calls for much stricter limits on the quantity of land that may be held in private tenancy without being affected by redistribution than did the 1917 constitution (which specified from 100 hectares of good land to 200 hectares of poor land), and also mandates that production of redistributed land be done collectively, contrary to the custom, found in many areas of the *cañadas* of the Lacandon, of each family working its own ejido plot.

In a discussion of the Zapatista Revolutionary Law of Agrarian Reform, Womack points out that the EZLN, like most of Mexico, believes that the original Zapatista program of agrarian reform of 1911–16 was incorporated into the Mexican Constitution under the original Article 27 (Womack 1999, 251). This idea was heavily propagated by the Mexican government for decades through the educational system, the formation and maintenance of the Confederación Nacional Campesina (CNC), and annual celebrations of Zapata's death and birthday. It should thus come as no surprise that this absorption of nationalist ideology is reflected in EZLN documents. It is unclear from the EZLN agrarian law whether its framers literally thought their plans stemmed directly from Emiliano Zapata's 1911–16 program; what is clear is that they felt that Zapata's name historically justified their demand for continued redistribution of land and that their detailed outline of collective production techniques, which focuses on satisfying "the primary needs of the people," would promote national well-being. In addition, the despair of thousands of young people from the cañadas ejidos who could not petition for land after the 1992 reforms, and who felt that they would not benefit from any of the productivist-oriented organizations operating in the Lacandon, can be seen in the agrarian law.

A conversation I had in 1994 with a Zapatista insurgent officer in Guadalupe Tepeyac reflects many of the fine points of the Zapatista agrarian law. Major Eliseo was happy to talk about the changes to Article 27 of the constitution in 1992 and had brought it up earlier. Our conversation suggests more clearly what might have been in the minds of those who framed the Zapatista law. Major Eliseo clearly identified the original Article 27 with the struggle of Emiliano Zapata and the right of rural people to land, following national socialization, but he also had ideas that went beyond land redistribution. Perhaps reflecting experience in agriculture prior to joining the EZLN, he had specific ideas about the kinds of inputs, such as fertilizer, necessary to make land productive. Eliseo could not be mistaken for an organic farmer, and based on his negative experience with slash-and-burn agriculture, he advocated using tractors and improved seeds and fertilizers. Finally, he also discussed the struggle to collectivize agriculture in Zapatista communities. While the collectivization of production is working in some places, in his description it is a struggle against individualism and something that will take a long time to accomplish. The conversation went as follows:

LYNN: One of the articles of the constitution that you have commented on . . . has been Article 27, which was changed significantly. What is your political objective with regard to this change? Ideally, how would you like to see it changed again?

MAJOR ELISEO: What we have always said about the change to Article 27 of the constitution. . . . We have spoken many times about this article because it comes from the struggle of Zapata. Thus it was the only hope that people had in recent times. So a lot of governments came and went and they maintained this, not so well, but nevertheless they left it alone. And now that there is an even worse government [that of Salinas de Gortari], it has disappeared completely. Now they don't want to honor it. So it doesn't seem good to us. It can't be like that. You can't have a provision that exists for a long time and then just get rid of it. For us it has a very bad significance. Because, as Zapata said, the land belongs to the person who works it.

LYNN: Do you want to return Article 27 to the way it was before 1992?

MAJOR ELISEO: Yes. This is our principal demand. For a lot of people, their principal demand is for land. This is one of our demands. It isn't so much to have a large amount of land, but to have high-quality land. Peasants often have a lot of land. The government will say, "They have land." But we can't plant on these lands [pointing up to mountainside in Guadalupe Tepeyac]. What are we going to produce? The government has to keep that in mind.

LYNN: So it isn't just a question of leaving Article 27 as before. You also need to have programs to develop and invest in the land?

MAJOR ELISEO: This is what is needed. We don't just need to have Article 27 as it was before, but to change it the best way that we can. Because, as I said, we may have a lot of land, but if it is a piece of land where you can't grow anything, then it's not worth anything. You can improve the land through help that the government could give, but now they aren't offering it. So it isn't so much necessary to get a lot more land, but if there were all of the inputs of production that would help.

LYNN: What kind of land use are you proposing?

MAJOR ELISEO: We want to use it for everything.

LYNN: What kind of model would you use for production? Would you propose multiple uses—like one part for cattle, another for corn and beans, another part for fruit? Commercialization?

MAJOR ELISEO: What we think is that the government should support us with the inputs that we need, like tractors, improved seeds, fertilizers—well, just everything you need so that you don't get hit with pests and you can get a better harvest.

LYNN: Did you grow up with the hope of having land?

MAJOR ELISEO: In the place where I grew up, I was going to have my piece of land, but it wouldn't last because, as we work, we turn over the land, we burn it, and in two years it wouldn't give anything. Everything is burned, it burns up the land—the good part of the land—and then after corn is planted, it doesn't yield anything.

LYNN: So what do you propose? Using fertilizers?

MAJOR ELISEO: On the one hand, yes, so that it helps production. It is also possible that production isn't just rain-fed. Because if we have the means, we won't just harvest corn in one season but there can be more . . . but only with irrigation. This has to come from the government. This is what we need to develop better production.

LYNN: Have you experimented with agriculture? Or with different kinds?

MAJOR ELISEO: In the form of how we are? We have a form that we use in working in communities. We think that there can be a certain amount of land, but that in time it won't provide good yields. The crops won't grow. . . . Every year there are more people. Everyone can have land, but what happens when there are more people? So the way we think that people can work [is] collectively. We also want to keep people from burning down so much of the forest.

LYNN: So what does it mean to work collectively?

MAJOR ELISEO: The collective is the way that we work with the communities.

LYNN: Were there communities this year where you planted with this collective model?

MAJOR ELISEO: Yes. There are some that are functioning. But not in all parts, just in some areas.

LYNN: So you are experimenting in some places?

MAJOR ELISEO: Yes.

LYNN: How is it, trying to convince people to change from an individual way of farming to a collective model?

MAJOR ELISEO: It is really hard. Think about what happens. They all have a lot of individualism. They say, what is mine, is mine, I can't give it to someone else. It is really hard to challenge this idea. We have to challenge our people this way, even people in our own army, giving them the idea, showing them what can happen with time. Part of the communities we have organized this way because of the war. Because, when it is time to go to war, we can't have one person here, and another person there, and another person there. Because that way they [the enemy] can enter very easily. We have people all working in one place together so that there is better security. Any woman can arrive to work and know that there will be people around. So we are carrying this idea out little by little. . . . In one ejido, sometimes there would be twenty people who would work collectively and the majority would be working individually. When [the individual farmers] saw that [the collective] worked, then another ten would join. And that is how the town was won.

LYNN: In the collective work that you are doing, are the women participating in agriculture? In planting?

MAJOR ELISEO: Women also participate. They have their own collective work. Of course they are not working in the cornfields but do other work. They do vegetable farming collectively, bakeries collectively. There are doing small things, but they are learning.

LYNN: And is this as difficult to implement as it is to get the men to work collectively?

MAJOR ELISEO: Yes, because the women have what we said—individualism. What they have, they don't want to give to everyone else. But little by little this idea is changing. And finally people are convinced, the whole town is convinced. That's how it is. Little by little, but this takes time. It isn't going to happen overnight. . . . You have to keep trying various times in order to succeed. That's how it is. That is the way that we are fighting for the land.

My conversation with Major Eliseo suggests that the EZLN was attempting to implement certain parts of their Revolutionary Law of Agrarian Reform, particularly those encouraging collective forms of production. What the conversation also reveals, however, is that collectivization
is not just an economic strategy. It is also a strategy of war that keeps
people together in one place and provides safety in numbers. In addition, structuring ejido agriculture collectively has served as an organizing strategy for the EZLN. Beginning with small groups of people who
would make a commitment to work their ejido plots as a group, EZLN
organizers have slowly tried to expand the number committed to this
model. Major Eliseo makes it clear that the objective of collective production is very hard to achieve and is only partially realized in Zapatista
strongholds.

One other aspect of the conversation is worth noting. While both
women and men are organized collectively to the extent possible, according to Major Eliseo there are differences in the type of collective
work that men and women do. According to him, women do not work
in the cornfields, but in vegetable farming, bakeries, and other small-
scale projects. This suggests that the gendered division of labor in agriculture is left intact in some Zapatista base communities, even in those
trying to change from individual to collective production. While another revolutionary law spells out broad areas of equal rights for women
(discussed in the next chapter), Zapatista gender roles (including those
in agriculture) in some base communities are lagging. In many Zapatista
base communities, traditional gender roles in agriculture have continued
even with collective production.

The revolutionary agrarian law and my conversation with Eliseo both
confirm the role of Emiliano Zapata as an important symbol in contemporary Zapatista discourse and written law. The use of Zapata by those
in the urban left who came to work in Chiapas is also clear. What still
remains to be explained is how the symbol of Zapata came to be embraced as a meaningful symbol of local and national liberation for indigenous men and women in the Lacandon jungle. Since indigenous people
from ejidos such as Guadalupe Tepeyac clearly had their own ideas,
plans, and visions for the future—as well as more than two decades of
organizing experience with the diocese of Samuel Ruiz and regional peasant organizations—it makes little sense to think that they were "brain-
washed" by Marcos and the other FLN cadres. What is more interesting to contemplate is the ways the specific, local, historical experiences

of ejidatarios—including confrontations with government officials—
formed part of how they understood and interpreted the ideology of the
FLN and, ultimately, remade it into a hybrid Zapatismo with specific local meaning. One clue to this process may be found in the invention of
the figure of Votán Zapata.

THE HYBRIDITY OF LOCAL ZAPATISMO: VOTÁN ZAPATA

Most people in the Lacandon jungle had completed little more than one
or two grades in elementary school, where they had no doubt heard of
Emiliano Zapata and celebrated his birthday. Within the embryonic
group that would form the EZLN (a group that included not only FLN
cadres such as Marcos but also indigenous recruits), a local interpretation of Zapata was forged through the melding of that revolutionary
figure with a supposedly Tzeltal mythical figure. The result was a hybrid—Votán Zapata—who appears to have been fashioned by Marcos
and some indigenous EZLN founders in Chiapas. The figure of Votán
Zapata became a local icon embodying the spirit of the new indigenous
Zapatismo there.

Subcomandante Marcos attributes the origins of Votán Zapata to an
elderly Tzeltal man whom Marcos, in his writing, came to call "el viejo
Antonio." Marcos says he met Antonio in 1984, and that the old man
died of tuberculosis in June 1994 (Le Bot 1997, 153). "El viejo Antonio" may refer to the historian Antonio García de León (1994), who is
the only academic I could find who writes of Votán as a Tzeltal deity.
While many credit Marcos with being the intellectual author of Zapatismo, according to him the real intellectual author of the core of Zapatismo was Antonio. Marcos refers to Antonio as the bridge between the
small group of guerrillas, both urban mestizos and indigenous Chiapans,
who trained in the mountains in the mid 1980s, and the indigenous
communities who became the heart and base of the EZLN. The figure
of el viejo Antonio becomes the chief vehicle through which the "indigenous" origins of Votán are documented, according to Marcos, who
states:

> Initially, the dream of a guerrilla is to encounter a peasant and to explain pol-
> itics to him and to convince him. So I started to talk to him [Antonio] about
> the history of Mexico, about Zapatismo, and he answered me with the his-
> tory of Votán and Ik'al. The first community we took in 1985—or, I should
> say, that first community that we entered as Zapatistas—was old Antonio's
> community. He acted as a kind of translator, explaining to us what we were

Figure 3.   Subcomandante Marcos in 1996 at the EZLN forum on Political Reform in San Cristóbal de las Casas. Photo by Lynn Stephen.

and what we should do. . . . At the same time we are going through an internal process of change regarding Zapatismo. It is Old Antonio who serves as a bridge so that the guerrillas in the mountains arrive in the communities. His final contribution was to make the Zapatistas understand the specificity of the indigenous question in the mountains of southern Mexico. . . . In the end, this is the tool that Marcos appropriates to join the indigenous world with the urban world. Old Antonio is the one who contributed the indigenous elements to the Zapatista discourse that we present to the outside. I am a plagiarist. (Le Bot 1997, 154–55)

In December 1994, Marcos wrote a "Letter from Marcos to all of those who have written and have not yet received an answer." (During 1994, he had addressed letters to a variety of writers, artists, intellectuals, and others.) In his letter, he details how old Antonio taught him the meaning of Zapata in the mountains of southeast Mexico. I quote the story at length because it is a crucial link in seeing how the hybrid figure of Votán Zapata emerged in Zapatista ideology (at least, according to Marcos). Votán Zapata, it should be noted, has a particularly strong presence in Zapatista celebrations on 10 April, the anniversary of Zapata's death in 1919. Excerpts from the letter follow:

> The cold is oppressive in these mountains. Ana María and Mario accompany me on this exploration, ten years before the dawn in January [1994]. The two of them have just been incorporated into the guerrilla group. I was a lieutenant in the infantry, and it is my turn to teach them what others had taught me: how to live in the mountains. Yesterday I ran into old Antonio for the first time. We had both lied. He told me that he was checking his cornfield and I told him that I was hunting. We both knew that we were lying, and we knew that the other knew it as well. I left Ana María to follow the route we were exploring and I returned near the river to see . . . if I would run into old Antonio again. He must have been thinking the same thing, because he appeared in the place where we had run into each other before.
>
> Like yesterday, old Antonio sat down on the ground; he reclined on a mound of moss and started to roll a cigarette. I sat down in front of him and lit my pipe. Old Antonio started the conversation:
>
> "You were not hunting."
>
> I responded, "And you were not checking your cornfield." Something makes me speak to him using *Usted* [formal term of address], with respect, to this man of undefined age, with a face that looks like the bark of a cedar tree, who I am seeing for the second time in my life.
>
> Old Antonio smiles and says, "I have heard of you. In the canyons, they say that you are bandits. In my town, people are nervous because you could be walking around in this area."
>
> "And do you believe that we are bandits?" I ask. Old Antonio lets out an arch of smoke, coughs, and shakes his head no. I am encouraged and I ask him another question. "Who do you think we are?"
>
> "I prefer that you tell me," responds old Antonio, and he keeps looking me in the eyes.
>
> "It's a very long story," I say, and start to tell about Zapata and Villa and the revolution and the land and the injustice and the hunger and the ignorance and the disease and the repression and everything. I end with "And so we are the Zapatista Army of National Liberation." I am looking for some sign in the face of old Antonio, who hasn't stopped looking at me during my talk.
>
> "Tell me more about this Zapata," he says, after more smoke and a cough.
>
> I start with Anenecuilco, then I move on to the Plan de Ayala, the military

campaign, the organization of the communities, and the betrayal at China-meca. Old Antonio keeps looking at me while I finish up my story.

"That's not how it was," he says. I make a gesture of surprise and only manage to stammer "No?" "No," insists old Antonio. "I am going to tell you the real history of that Zapata.

"A long time ago, when the very first gods were making the world and they were still rolling around in the night, they spoke of two gods who were Ik'al and Votán. They were two as one. If you turned over one, you would see the other, and vice versa. They were opposites. One was the light, like morning in May on the river. The other was dark, like a cold night or a cave. They were the same. . . . But they couldn't walk. "What will we do?" asked the two? "Life is sad because we are in this state." "Let's walk" said one. "How?" said the other. "To where?" asked one. And they saw that they could move a little bit, if they first asked how and then asked where. . . . First one popped his head out and then the other, and they moved around a little bit. And they realized that if one moved first, and then the other, that they could indeed move, and they reached agreement so that one could move and then the other, and they began to move and then no one remembered who was the first to move because they were so happy that they were moving. "What does it matter who moved first if we are moving?" said the two gods who were one, and they laughed, and their first agreement was to dance, and they danced. . . . Later, when they got tired of dancing and they were decid-ing what to do next, they saw that their first question of "How do we move?" was answered by the response, "together but separated and in agreement." . . .

"So that is how the true men and women learned that the questions help us to walk, not to just stay stuck in one place."

I am biting the already short stem of my pipe, waiting for old Antonio to continue, but he doesn't look like he intends to. With the fear of interrupting something really serious, I ask him, "And Zapata?"

Old Antonio smiles. "You already learned that in order to find things out and to move forward, you have to ask." He coughs and lights another ciga-rette that I have no idea when he rolled, and words fall like seeds to the ground between the smoke that comes from his lips.

"It's *that* Zapata that appeared here in the mountains. He wasn't born here, they say. He appeared, just like that. They say that he is Ik'al and Votán, that they came here to end their long journey and, in order not to scare good people, they became one. Because they spent a long time walking together, Ik'al and Votán learned that they were the same, and that they become one in the day and night, and when they got here they made themselves one and called themselves Zapata. And this Zapata said that he had arrived here and here he was going to find that answer to where the long road led. And he said that sometimes there would be light and sometimes there would be darkness, but that they were all the same, Votán Zapata, Ik'al Zapata, white Zapata, and black Zapata, and that the two were the same road for all real men and women."

Old Antonio takes a plastic bag out of his *morral*, or carrying bag. Inside the plastic bag is a picture from 1910 of Emiliano Zapata. Zapata's left hand is grabbing the hilt of his sword, at the height of his waist. In his left hand, he has a pistol; two belts of bullets are crossed on his chest— a two-tone band of black and white crossing from left to right. He has his feet placed like someone who is remaining calm or walking, and his gaze says something like "I am here" or "Now I am going." There are two stairways. On one of them that ends in darkness, more Zapatistas with brown faces can be seen, as if they are coming out of the background; on the other stairway, which is lighted, there is no one and you can't see where it is going or where it comes from. I would be lying if I said I saw all of these details. It was old Antonio who called my attention to them. On the back of the photo it read:

> Gral. Emiliano Zapata, Jefe del Ejército Suriano
> Gen. Emiliano Zapata, Commander in Chief of the Southern Army.
> Le Général Emiliano Zapata, Chef de l'Armée du Sud
> c. 1910. Photo by: Augustín V. Casasola.

Old Antonio said to me, "I have asked this picture a lot of questions. That's how I got this far." He coughed and flicked the ashes off of his cigarette. He gave me the photo. "Take it," he said, "so that you can learn to question . . . and to walk." (Ejército Zapatista de Liberación Nacional 1995: 153–65)

Marcos's rendition of this story highlights the melding of Tzeltal mythical figures with the personage of Emiliano Zapata. Votán is associated with the third day of the Tzeltal calendar and represents the heart of the people, according to the historian Antonio García de León (1994, 1), who may have gotten his information from Ramón Ordoñez y Aguiar.[3] Enquiries to anthropologists, linguists, and a Tzeltal-speaking priest who had worked with the Tzeltal population for the past twenty years yielded no recognition of Votán as an existing figure among the Tzeltal currently living in contemporary Chiapas. In fact the v sound doesn't even exist in contemporary Tzeltal, according to one source. Votán will most likely turn out to be an invented figure, successfully fused to Zapata by Marcos.

In Marcos's narrative, the gods Votán and Ik'al go through the steps of learning how to walk, to co-exist, and to move forward together, not only acting as a metaphor for the Tzeltal people but also suggesting a path for others who want to know the answers to their question: how do we move together? The answer they provide is: together, but separated and in agreement. Votán and Ik'al's question is, of course, crucial for the building of any social movement.

Zapata enters the story, not only by merging with the personas of Ik'il and Votán, reborn in the mountains of southeastern Mexico, but through the photograph Antonio presents to Marcos. Such photographs of Za-

Figure 4. Picture of Zapata on wall of a Zapatista-controlled municipal building in San Andrés Larráinzar. Photo by Lynn Stephen.

pata circulate widely in Mexico. They are found on the walls of most *casas ejidales* (ejido meeting houses), on the office walls of independent peasant organizations and unions of ejidos, on the walls of local government buildings, and often in people's homes.

I have met many elderly ejidatarios in Mexico who carry pictures of Zapata or who have them in their homes, sometimes on the altar next to the images and statues of saints and virgins. The image of Zapata in rural Mexico is not unlike the image of John F. Kennedy in the United States; they are both national heroes sainted by death and martyrdom.

The way that Antonio carried around the picture of Zapata is identical to the way many indigenous Mexicans carry small photographs of saints in wallets or bags. Usually, these photographs are wrapped in plastic, like Antonio's image of Zapata. The relationship that indigenous Mexicans have with their saints is very personal. Visits to local chapels and churches are usually focused on direct conversations with and prayers to particular saints. Throughout Oaxaca and Chiapas, community patron saints are the most meaningful religious symbols. Saints often represent natural forces or problems as well as particular personages. For example, St. John is associated with rain and fertile soil for planting. In the Lacandon jungle, people who formed new ejidos brought images of their saints with them. These were critical symbols in founding new communities. The cultural packaging of Zapata suggested by Antonio to Marcos (and by Marcos to others) turns a national figure into a saint and localizes him, blending him with supposed Tzeltal deities.

While we must approach Marcos's story of Antonio and his picture of Zapata as a testimonial rather than a proven fact, the importance of the story is its illumination of a possible path for the construction of the ideology of Zapata in the cañadas of the Lacandon. Votán Zapata, as projected first by Marcos and then by others around him, is a unifying figure with local meaning that cuts across ethnic groups and helps bind together thousands waging the Zapatista struggle. It may help to explain the fervor of Zapatista recruits who, in conversation, acknowledge that facing the Mexican Army is a suicide mission. "Sí, así es, pero ya estamos muriendo. Mejor vamos a morir por una causa justa que morir de hambre o diarrea." ("Yes, it is, but we are already dying. It is better to die for a just cause than to die of hunger and diarrhea.")

The story of old Antonio, as told by Marcos, suggests how the national symbol of Zapata was given local meaning in the cañadas of the Lacandon jungle, where Tzeltal, Tojolabal, and Tzotzil people had more than a decade of organizing experience in multiethnic organizations. The synthesis of Votán, Ik'al, and Zapata into one figure, Votán Zapata, provided a focal point for the emerging Zapatista movement when it first consolidated among an isolated multiethnic group of mestizo, Tzeltal, Ch'ol, Tojolabal, and Tzotzil guerrillas and then was exported to surrounding communities through indigenous leaders and political operatives of the EZLN. It should be noted that Ik'al is recognized by contemporary Tzeltal as the god of the Underworld. Although it seems that the current Tzeltal population does not recognize Votán as a significant mythical figure, what is of more significance is that Votán was promoted by the EZLN as Tzeltal, thus providing recognition for the Tzeltal indigenous experience in one key EZLN symbol. The "Zapata" sense of Votán links the regional Zapatista movement to larger Mexican history and makes the content of the movement accessible to many different Mexicans. Because of this mixture of meanings and symbols, the icon of Votán Zapata appeals not only to indigenous peoples of the cañadas, but to most Mexicans, and clearly "Zapata" is Votán's primary link for most Mexicans.

The creation of Votán Zapata provided the emerging Zapatista movement with a moral and religious focus centered on a new national/religious icon. Just as Agustina Gómez Checheb and Pedro Díaz Cuscat built a movement from sacred stones, the Zapatistas used Votán Zapata to build their movement and accommodate a range of participants.[4] As noted in the previous chapter, other indigenous rebellions, such as the Indian movement of 1867–69 in Chiapas, have been characterized by a mixture of cultural, religious, territorial, and production-related demands. The contemporary Zapatista movement is no different. And by claiming and redefining Zapata in local and regional terms, Marcos, Antonio, and subsequent Zapatistas wrote a counterdiscourse to the government's claim to Emiliano Zapata and the Mexican Revolution.

The lessons learned by followers of Votán Zapata are open to all *hombres y mujeres verdaderos*—"true" or "genuine" men and women. This linguistic notion of "genuine" men and women is contained in the Tojolabal language as well as in Antonio's story. The name for Tojolabal breaks down into *àb'al,* or word/language, and *tojol,* meaning real, genuine, authentic. Speakers of the language are *tojolwinik*—real or genuine (*tojol*) people (*winik*) (Lenkersdorf 1995, 22–23). Thus, the notion of *hombres y mujeres verdaderos* that accompanies the icon of Votán Zapata built on linguistic categories from the Tojolabal language.

The translation and projection of Votán Zapata from eastern Chiapas to the larger Mexican public developed through invoking Votán Zapata at public Zapatista celebrations, such as the 10 April anniversaries of Zapata's assassination. The inclusion of statements and stories about Votán Zapata on this occasion began before the Zapatistas emerged publicly in 1994 as the EZLN. "Zapata" made an appearance in Ocosingo on this anniversary of Zapata's death in 1992 (this appearance was interpreted by some as also representing Votán, and indeed Votán always appears simply as an image of Zapata). Marcos described this day as follows:

> In the municipal seat of Ocosingo, four thousand indigenous campesinos march from different points in the city to the ANCIEZ [offices]. Three of the marches converge on the municipal palace. The president of the municipality does not know what is happening and flees; a calendar left on the floor of his office shows the date: April 10, 1992. Outside, the indigenous campesinos of Ocosingo, Oxchuc, Huixtán, Chilón, Yajalón, Sabanilla, San Andrés, and Cancuc dance in front of a giant image of Zapata, painted by one of them. . . . The campesinos show that Zapata lives and that their struggle continues. One of them reads a letter to Carlos Salinas de Gortari accusing him of destroying the agrarian reform won by Zapata, of selling out the country through the North American Free Trade Agreement, and of returning Mexico to the time of Porfirio Díaz. They forcefully declare that they do not recognize Salinas's changes of Article 27 of the Constitution. (Subcomandante Marcos 1995, 49)

When Votán began to be deployed as part of the public discourse projected by the EZLN through the press, he became a hybrid local/national symbol played back, at the national level, to garner support for the EZLN outside its territory. The larger public first became aware of Votán Zapata when Marcos read a text released by the Clandestine Revolutionary Indigenous Committee of the EZLN's general command, on 10 April 1994. Marcos has consistently been the one to deploy Votán Zapata. He read the text at an event in the Lacandon jungle featuring hundreds of Zapatista troops marching and offering homages to Zapata, which was covered by the national and international press and captured in a number of video productions. Part of the homage to Zapata follows:

> Brothers and sisters, we want you to know who is behind us, who directs us, who walks in our feet, who dominates our heart, who rides in our words, who lives in our deaths. . . . From the first hour of this long night on which we die, say our most distant grandparents, there was someone who gathered together our pain and our forgetting. There was a man who, his word traveling from far away, came to our mountain and spoke with the tongue of true men and women. His step was and was not of these lands; in the mouths of our dead, in the voices of the old wise ones, his word traveled from him to our heart. . . .
>
> It was, and is, his name in the named things. His tender word stops and starts inside our pain. He is and is not in these lands; Votán Zapata, guardian and heart of the people. . . .
>
> He took his name from those who have no name, his face from those with no face; he is sky on the mountain. Votán, guardian and heart of the people. And our road, unnamable and faceless, took its name in us: Zapatista Army of National Liberation.
>
> This is the truth, brothers and sisters. This is where we come from and where we're going. Being here, he comes. Dying, death lives. Votán Zapata, father and mother, brother and sister, son and daughter, old and young, we are coming. . . .
>
> Salud, Mexican brothers and sisters!
> Salud, campesinos of this country!
> Salud, indigenous people of all lands!
> Salud, Zapatista combatants!
> Zapata, being here, he comes!
> Dying he lives!
> Long Live Zapata!
> Democracy! Liberty! Justice! (Ejército Zapatista de Liberación Nacional 1994, 210–13)

While the EZLN held its commemoration in the Lacandon jungle of the death of Zapata, similar events were held in almost every state in Mexico and were collectively called "The National Days of Liberation,

Zapata Vive." All over the country, the EZLN and peasants marked Zapata's assassination with marches, hunger strikes, and roadblocks; in Mexico City, fifty thousand peasants and Indians marched to the Zócalo, reclaiming the ideals of Zapata for peasant and indigenous movements. Marchers opposed what they called the "neo-liberal anti-peasant development plans" imposed by the government, and called for an alternative development project (Pérez 1994, 5). The principal statements of all of these actions included condemnation of the end of land redistribution and of the privatization of ejido land, and rejection of private landholding corporations in the countryside (Correa, Corro y López 1994: 36). The Zapatistas sent a special communiqué to Mexico City, which was read in front of the fifty thousand demonstrators and a large press corps. It stated, in part:

> Today, 10 April, is the seventy-fifth anniversary of the assassination of General Emiliano Zapata. His betrayal by Venustiano Carranza was an attempt to drown out his cry of 'Land and Liberty'! Today, the usurper Salinas de Gortari, who claims to be "president of the Mexican Republic," lies to the people of Mexico, saying that his reforms to Article 27 of the Constitution reflect the spirit of General Zapata. The supreme government lies! Zapata will not die by arrogant decree. The right to land of those who work it cannot be taken away and the warrior cry 'Land and Liberty!' echoes restlessly through these Mexican lands. . . .
>
> Our hearts are joyful; Emiliano Zapata has come again to the Zócalo of Mexico; he is in you; he walks in you. We, the small and forgotten, raise up the image of Zapata in the other heart of the country, in the mountains of the Mexico Southeast. (Ejército Zapatista de Liberación Nacional 1994, 208–10)

Since this occasion, the export of Votán Zapata and the Zapatismo he represents by the EZLN has been ongoing. One year later, on 10 April 1995, the Zapatistas repeated their sponsorship of 10 April events paying homage to Emiliano Zapata. In the communiqué released on that date by the CCRI–General Command, a clear evolution can be seen, in which the figure of Votán Zapata is projected as a symbol of struggle not only for indigenous peoples in Chiapas but for all people living in misery, without rights, justice, democracy, or liberty, and who support the struggle to obtain these goals. Votán Zapata is universalized into an icon for all who support the cause of Zapatismo, while also used to promote the EZLN's particular struggle. The theme of martyrdom and resurrection is strong in this communiqué, which ultimately is addressed not only to Mexico but to "all the peoples and governments of the world":

> To the insurgent compañeros and militia members of the EZLN
> To the bases of support of the EZLN

Figure 5.   Image of a Zapatista incorporated into a mural in Mexico City in
May 2000. Photo by Lynn Stephen.

To the people of Mexico
To the peoples and governments of the world
Brothers and sisters:
Today we remember the struggle that gave us our name and our face. We
remember the day in which treachery killed General Emiliano Zapata when
he was fighting for justice. Emiliano Zapata died, but not his struggle nor his
ideas. A lot more Emiliano Zapatas were born, and now his name is not just
for one particular person. His name invokes the struggle for justice, the cause
of democracy, and the notion of liberty. In us, in our weapons, in our covered
faces, and in our truthful words, Zapata is united with the knowledge and
struggle of our oldest ancestors. United with Votán, the Guardian and Heart
of the people, Zapata has risen again to struggle for democracy, liberty, and
justice for all Mexicans. Although he has indigenous blood, Votán Zapata is
not just fighting for the indigenous, he is also fighting for those who are not
indigenous but who live in the same misery, without rights, without justice
for their work, without democracy for their decision-making, and without
liberty in their thoughts and words.

Votán Zapata is everyone who marches behind our flag. Votán Zapata is
the one who walks in all of our hearts and in each and every one of the genuine men and women. We are all one in Votán Zapata, and he is one in all
of us. . . .

To be indigenous today is to be dignified and truthful. Your color and language doesn't make you indigenous; it is the desire to struggle and become better [that does].

Votán Zapata includes all of the colors and all of the languages; his past includes all of the roads, and his words grow in all of the hearts. Today his loudest word is through the words of the genuine men and women, the indigenous who in southeastern Mexican raise their voices and their hands to speak with great and truthful words.

Brothers and sisters, we are all Votán Zapata, we are all the Guardian and the Heart of the People. . . . Our voice will continue to be raised through many and various channels, from the mountains to the hearts of all Mexican brothers and sisters; our truth cannot be hidden because it is the truth of everyone. . . .

Long live Emiliano Zapata!
Long live Votán Zapata!
Long live the forever dead!
Long live the indigenous Mexicans.
Long live the EZLN. (Ejército Zapatista de Liberación Nacional 1995, 306–9)

TRANSLATION AND TRANSVALUATION
OF CHIAPAS ZAPATISMO

In his work on ethno-nationalist conflict and collective violence in South Asia, Stanley J. Tambiah has coined the term "transvaluation," which refers to "the process of assimilating particulars to a larger, collective, more enduring, and therefore less context-bound, cause or interest" (Tambiah 1990, 750). The deployment of the figure of Votán Zapata from the Lacandon jungle to the larger Mexican public and the world through the Internet illustrates the process Tambiah describes. The re-imagining of Zapata through the figure of Votán Zapata, with his inclusion of "all of the colors and all of the languages" and his presence in everyone ("we are all Votán Zapata, we are all the Guardian and the Heart of the People"), takes the localized version of Votán created in Chiapas and makes him accessible to everyone, in Mexico and throughout the world. Through identifying with the struggle and goals of the "genuine" men and women of southern Mexico, the indigenous of the EZLN, we can all—we are told by the communiqué—become symbolically indigenous through joining in this struggle and making it larger than the issues found in Chiapas. Of course, the transvaluation of Votán Zapata and Chiapas-based Zapatismo to a national and international context also promotes a simple, unified image of Zapatismo that papers over local differences and increasing conflicts within communities in Chiapas (issues discussed below).

The 10 April 1995 communiqué highlighting Votán Zapata (partially reproduced above) provides clues to the strategies used by the EZLN to build national and international grassroots support. The transvaluation of local Zapatismo was key in this process. Zapatista strategies for connecting the larger world with Zapatismo have included: (1) inviting numerous people from many sectors of society (labor, students, indigenous organizations, teachers, artists) to Chiapas and to the Lacandon region for a series of meetings; (2) sending Zapatista delegates throughout Mexico; (3) conducting referenda at the national and international levels on what the future direction of the EZLN should be and, subsequently, on whether there was support for the 1996 San Andrés Accords on indigenous rights; (4) developing international networks of solidarity and support groups; (5) encouraging the publication of Zapatista communiqués and information on the Internet (a process facilitated by others).

In these processes of transvaluation, the Zapatistas have themselves become visual and literal icons of the new Zapatismo, linking with and galvanizing indigenous movements, student movements, labor movements, and others in struggle, both in Mexico and in other countries. When Marcos and twenty-three comandantes traveled to Mexico City in March 2001, partially retracing Zapata's route to the capital in 1914, the trip received international press coverage. The hybridity of Votán Zapata thus serves as a way to make Zapatismo meaningful to Tojolabal ejidatarios from Guadalupe Tepeyac as well as to nineteen-year-old, urban, mestizo students in Mexico City. While this has clearly been one of the great (and unanticipated) successes of the EZLN, what are the limits and negative consequences of Zapatismo in Chiapas?

THE LIMITS TO HYBRIDITY AND TRANSVALUATION

Tambiah (1990) argues that the process of transvaluation can contribute to a progressive polarization and dichotomization of issues and partisans. While the embrace of Zapatismo by parts of larger Mexican society can certainly be seen to contribute to the increasing polarization of national politics, as the PRI lost its grip both nationally and in more and more places, some negative consequences of hybrid Zapatismo have occurred in Chiapas. These negative consequences are intimately linked to the government's strategy for eliminating the Zapatistas as an armed movement and forcing them to become a formal political presence.

When Zapatismo consolidated in the Lacandon region in the late 1980s and early 1990s, it brought a powerful movement incorporating thousands of individuals living in hundreds of communities. At the same time, the adoption of Zapatismo in a community resulted in specific changes, built upon other complex local divisions. In some communities, Zapatismo was laid on top of religious divisions among traditional Catholics, liberation theology Catholics, evangelical Protestants, and mainline Protestants. In others, religious divisions coexisted with political divisions among the PRI, PRD, and smaller political parties. And in some communities, there were additional divisions between those affiliated with the official government peasant federation (CNC) and those affiliated with independent peasant organizations such as ARIC, CIOAC, or OCEZ. When the Zapatismo of Chiapas consolidated as a pan-ethnic movement in eastern Chiapas, divisions were added in many communities, Zapatista or not.

All of this has created a current situation in Chiapas where there is no neutral position. Every single person has a political identity and these identities can result in life and death circumstances, as when individuals are singled out by paramilitaries as Zapatista sympathizers and harassed, kidnapped, or even killed.

As the strategy of low-intensity warfare promulgated by the Mexican government to defeat the EZLN has dragged on in Chiapas, it has become a state of normalcy, no longer a time-bound emergency. It has also affected everyone, both Zapatistas and non-Zapatistas. Since the Zapatista uprising in 1994, more than a third of Chiapas has been heavily militarized. The army completed a major road project connecting previously inaccessible communities to main population centers and facilitating troop movement, built permanent installations in dozens of communities, and significantly altered the local economy and culture. In mid 2000, there were forty thousand to sixty thousand soldiers permanently installed in the Altos, Cañadas, and Northern regions of the state, which are Zaptista strongholds. The army has taken over the state police forces of Chiapas. In some regions of Chiapas, there may be eight different police forces including Rural Police (local), Municipal Police (local), State Public Security Police, State Judicial Police, Federal Judicial Police, Federal Fiscal Police, Federal Preventive Police (initially army members), and Federal Transit Police.

In January 2001, President Vincente Fox ordered the withdrawal of soldiers from some military checkpoints and encampments in an effort to entice the Zapatistas back to the negotiating table. In early March 2001, the Zapatista refused to reenter negotiations until three conditions were met: (1) withdrawal of troops from army bases in seven

Zapatista strongholds; (2) release of all Zapatista political prisoners in all parts of Mexico; and (3) ratification of the San Andrés Accords on Indigenous Rights and Culture by the Mexican Congress as signed by the EZLN and the Mexican government in 1996.

On 28 March 2001, Zapatista comandantes who had completed a two-week trip to Mexico City addressed the Mexican Congress in a mass committee meeting, not a formal joint session. This had been the objective of their trip. The comandantes were led by Esthér, an indigenous woman. Marcos did not speak in the Congress, because he is a military, not political, leader. During this special congressional meeting, the Zapatistas argued for the passage of the San Andrés Accords. The day before, troops had begun to tear down the last army base the Zapatistas had demanded be closed as part of an effort to restart peace talks. All EZLN political prisoners in the state of Chiapas had also been released. With their address to the Congress, the closure of the final bases, and release of prisoners, the Zapatistas agreed to reopen peace talks in late March 2001. However, the original accords were not passed and peace talks did not begin.

There was approximately one soldier for every three or four inhabitants, in many communities. In mid 2000, a newspaper story by the prize-winning reporter Herman Bellinghausen stated that there were "more than seven hundred different military installations, [which] include bases, mixed operations bases, living quarters and commercial centers, encampments, and roadblocks, particularly concentrated in the Tzotzil region of Los Altos, the Lacandon jungle, and those that are today inserted in Montes Azules [ecological reserve]" (Bellinghausen 2000). The presence of armed police and military units on constant patrol, the constant checking and harassment of all local persons and vehicles at roadblocks, and the permanent presence of thousands of young soldiers living in indigenous communities dramatically altered the landscape and daily lives of many inside the conflict zone.

As of January 1998, twelve different paramilitary groups operated in the conflict zone in Chiapas (Centro de Derechos Humanos Fray Bartolomé de las Casas 1998, 77, 80–84). In the two months prior to elections in July 1997, dozens were killed and wounded in local confrontations between the PRI and the PRD, and as victims of paramilitary forces and federal police forces. In December 1997, forty-six Tzotzils, primarily women and children, were gunned down in a five-hour killing spree that began with the storming of the village church in Acteal, where men, women, and children were kneeling in prayer. A paramilitary group, armed and trained by state police and by an ex-soldier from the Mexican Army, carried out the Acteal massacre. In the spring and early summer of 1998, State Security Police, along with the army, carried out raids in four Zapatista communities that had declared themselves to have autonomous governments. In one of these raids, nine Zapatista sympathizers and one federal soldier died. In May 2000, two local PRI members and a member of the pacifist civil society Las Abejas (The Bees) were killed while riding in a car. Low-level violence continues on a daily basis in the Altos, Northern, and Lacandon regions.

Such conditions do not encourage freedom of expression. Existing divisions within communities have deepened, and Zapatista individuals and communities have hardened in their resistance. Christine Eber notes, for example, that by 1996 in the highland area of San Pedro Chenalhó, people were divided into four fairly distinct groups: (1) supporters of the PRI, (2) Las Abejas, a pacifist, liberation theology–based group supporting EZLN demands, but rejecting armed struggle, (3) Zapatistas, and (4) independents (Eber 2001, 55). The utopian segments of the Zapatista vision—collective agriculture, rights for women, rights for children, appreciation for all cultural and individual perspectives—have had to compete with the reality of daily survival in what has become a long-term war. Where local differences and flexibility might have been possible under more relaxed circumstances (and indeed seemed possible in 1994), the strain of war has resulted in uniformity and a certain conformity to a program of resistance and survival.

Acceptance of Zapatismo at the local level requires letting go of some local cultural practices. This makes for divisions and unhappiness in some contexts. For example, Christine Eber cites resistance to short, sometimes harsh punishments administered by Zapatistas, such as being tied to a tree for several hours after a third instance of public drinking, which are preferred to jail time in the Chenalhó area (Eber 2001, 67, n. 16). She also reports local discomfort with a perceived lack of EZLN support for traditional healing practices (ibid., 59). This she interprets as evidence that Zapatista base members "continue to struggle with the reality that the Zapatista rhetoric and agenda would have them reject or subordinate some aspects of their culture that they value, in order to fit into the larger frame of class struggle" (ibid.). At the local level in Chiapas, largely as a result of the military and police response of the Mexican government, Zapatismo has resulted in rigidity among Zapatista supporters as they struggle to survive, hold to their vision, and recruit new supporters. This is probably truest in areas like Chenalhó where daily tension is extremely high. This area continues to be highly polarized among communities and individuals loyal to the PRI, supportive of the military presence, and involved in paramilitary groups; the Autonomous Municipality of Polhó, with a self-declared autonomous parallel government run by Zapatistas; and the pacifist civil association Las Abejas, which continues to support the basic demands of the EZLN but remains completely opposed to armed action.

What is important to consider, however, is the larger political opening that Zapatismo has brought to Mexico, which has helped to consolidate other social movements. Perhaps the most important way the transvaluation of Zapatismo has been effective has been in providing support and political space for a national indigenous autonomy movement, something directly relevant to the indigenous peoples of Chiapas. While regional indigenous rights networks have existed in Mexico since the 1970s, in the wake of the Zapatista uprising—and spurred by the Mexican government's rewriting of Article 4 of the Mexican Constitution to recognize the country as "multi-ethnic"—a national network of indigenous groups has formed for the first time. The National Indigenous Congress has been an important actor, with several others, in advancing the cause of indigenous rights throughout Mexico (Stephen 1997a, 1997b; Mattiace 1997, 1998, 2001). In addition, as will be seen in chapter 11, Zapatismo has resonated with indigenous communities outside Chiapas as well.

The contradictory effect of the transvaluation of Chiapas Zapatismo may be linked to the nature of Votán Zapata. Because he is invented in part from a shared national symbol that was localized and then redeployed at the national level, the image of Votán Zapata inherently embodies the ability to both unite and divide. He, and the ideology of Zapatismo he represents through Emiliano Zapata's image, can call on the nationalist socialization that many Mexicans have received through their education and interactions with the government. This common socialization has the potential to unify. Yet to unify people locally in Chiapas around a central symbol such as Votán Zapata / Zapatismo, a certain level of local cultural uniqueness is sacrificed, resulting in the homogenization or elimination of local cultural differences (as suggested by Eber 2000).

Because of the instant publicity and continued attention paid to the Zapatistas by the media, Zapatismo has also become a global discourse most often projected as anti-neoliberalism, both by the Zapatistas and by others. Thus, ironically, while the Zapatistas have provided Mexico with a reworked nationalism built on the traditional symbols of the Mexican Revolution, they have used the same symbols to promote a global discourse. The media and the Internet are what have made what would have been a local rebellion into a global event.

CHAPTER 7

Conversations with Zapatistas

The Revolutionary Law of Women
and Military Occupation

In eastern Chiapas, Zapatismo has been experienced in different ways by communities and by individuals. The process of becoming a Zapatista involves profound challenges and sacrifices for the young men and women who make up the armed ranks of the insurgentes who live full-time in military training camps, as well as for the men, women, and children in Zapatista base communities, who, having kept the movement a secret as it grew, now defend it in the midst of army occupation, low-intensity war, and growing numbers of local paramilitary organizations seeking to intimidate and slowly eliminate, or convert into deserters, Zapatistas and Zapatista sympathizers. This chapter uses a series of conversations I had from 1994 to 1997 with self-identified Zapatistas at various levels of participation in the movement (comandantes, insurgents, militia members, base community members) to profile the passion, ideas, analyses, and visions of a range of individual men and women. The conversations took place during two distinct periods: (1) in 1994, when a hopeful EZLN had control over the territory it had defended in the 1 January 1994 rebellion, and (2) after February 1995, when a massive military operation by the government resulted in the restriction of Zapatista troops to a limited area backing onto the Guatemalan border, the creation of thousands of refugees, and—for those who stayed behind in communities sympathetic to the EZLN—adjustment to life under military and police occupation.

A major theme in some of these conversations is whether greater equality has been achieved in relationships between men and women within the Zapatista army and in Zapatista base communities. Such equality has been referred to as "the revolution within the revolution." This revolution is ongoing and far from over. While significant experimentation in gender roles may be taking place among the groups of men and women who live completely separated from their communities while training as full-time armed insurgents in special camps, women in Zapatista base communities often continue to struggle for recognition and participation in decision-making. At the same time, civilian women who support the Zapatistas actively confront and attempt to drive out the military in their communities. One of the most famous Zapatista images of the late 1990s is a woman pushing back a soldier who is among a large group attempting to install a military encampment in X'oyep, Chenalhó. Women also mobilize in large numbers to resist men from paramilitary groups and from the PRI attempting to terrorize their communities.

The government's implementation of a low-intensity warfare strategy since 1995 has complicated the context for experimenting with gender roles. Because safety and security are first priorities, the struggle to merely persist and survive frames the "revolution within the revolution." While fear for women's safety, as well as the notion that women should not travel alone outside their communities (always a source of worry, even before 1994), prevents some women from participating in regional Zapatista leadership, the rumored threat of rape by the military, police, and paramilitaries to discourage women from such participation has resulted in discussions of the topic in some communities—a novel occurrence. Zapatista women are clear that they are threatened with rape precisely because of their political activity; this threat confirms their importance as effective political actors (Stephen 2000: 835; Hernández-Castillo 1997).

What has emerged in the conflict of low-intensity war is the "in-your-face" role women have come to play when physically confronting soldiers and police and attempting to force them to leave invaded communities. Women have also assumed a public political role in relaying stories to reporters, videographers, anthropologists, and other outsiders of how they repelled the army from their community, or tried to. And the ongoing presence of hundreds of young men living inside indigenous communities in encampments has brought prostitution and the increased sale and use of alcohol and drugs. The lines between forced, coerced, and "voluntary" sexual interactions between women and occupying soldiers and police in such circumstances are not clear. All of these changes have generated new topics of discussion and action in some communities, and have opened new spaces for the discussion of topics and "rights" not previously considered—such as a woman's right to decide how many children she has, and the desire to punish men who rape and mistreat women. Rape was also an issue in indigenous communities before the arrival of outside soldiers and police. These topics and others became part of a critical dialogue mounted by indigenous women from Chiapas and elsewhere, in relation to the content of the San Andrés Accords on Indigenous Rights and Culture signed by the EZLN and the Mexican government in 1996. Thus both Zapatismo and the conditions of the low-intensity war have produced new openings for questioning gender roles at the local level, but have also generated conditions that shape the ways such changes are explored. The result is contradictory and varied, as seen in the conversations that follow.

The second theme that emerges in these conversations is the experience of living under military and police occupation. Since the government's failed attempt to capture the Zapatista leadership in February 1995, and the militarization of many Zapatista communities, daily life has become permeated by the ongoing presence of soldiers, by a feeling of being watched twenty-four hours a day, and by a fear of leaving communities to travel, work, or even weed in the cornfields. These narratives of occupation provide eerie insights into the dynamics of being constantly on display, constantly watched. There is also a gendered dimension to the watching, as those doing the watching are men and many of those watched daily in communities are women and children. The sense of always being watched, of never being alone, has had a profound effect on women in militarized zones of Chiapas. It has heightened the constant fear of rape and harassment and created high levels of intimidation that can isolate women within their communities and homes. At the same time, it has produced a dynamic of entrenched resistance and brought out the determination of the Zapatistas to continue their struggle and eventually win through perseverance.

My approach in the construction of this chapter has been to highlight the voices of the people I spoke with. While the ideas and visions of the Zapatistas interviewed here may not match up with some sort of "general reality" in any given community, it is extremely important their individual stories be heard. The ideas of these men and women are useful, not as a check on "the real Zapatista world"— there is no such thing— but as a window on what particular Zapatistas imagine and think, given their specific experience and histories. What matters most in these conversations is the passion, conviction, commitment, and moral authority with which these Zapatistas speak.

Each conversation is prefaced by general comments about the topics covered and by relevant contextual information providing background on when, where, and how the interview took place. I am under no illusion that, by including long quotations from these people I spoke with, I might be enabling them somehow to "speak for themselves." I have had full control in deciding what interview material to include, how to edit it, and how to frame it. The ordering and editing I have done certainly reflects my ideas about what readers need to know. However, I have deliberately structured these excerpts as conversations, since they were. Rather than snip the prose of subjects out of a conversation and insert it into analytical text to underline a point, I have represented the conversations as such. Thus they include myself, as an active participant in fashioning these conversations. Since none of the information that follows was simply announced to the public, with the exception of the testimonials from the youth group of Guadalupe Tepayac, I have represented it in relation to some of its context, both social and physical. Those in the Zapatista movement have done more thinking about and analysis of their experiences than has anyone else, and I hope that providing their words free of extensive analysis of "what they mean" will allow the reader to accept their analysis and their explanations of their meaning. They are the experts on the meanings of Zapatismo. Nevertheless, my perspective is obviously woven into this text. More than anything, I want to highlight the variety of experiences and viewpoints I encountered among Zapatistas. This more than anything should serve to show the variety of perspectives represented within Zapatismo and some of the tensions and divisions that exist, particularly on topics such as changing gender roles.

THE REVOLUTIONARY LAW OF WOMEN AS VIEWED BY EZLN COMANDANTES AND INSURGENTS

When the EZLN burst onto the international scene on 1 January 1994, a few observers noted that there were significant numbers of women among their ranks and that the temporary takeover of San Cristóbal had been directed by a woman whose nom de guerre was Major Ana María. It was not until sixteen days after the now-famous "Declaration from the Lacandon Jungle" was released that the newspaper *El Financiero* made mention of the "Women's Revolutionary Law" distributed simultaneously with the Lacandon declaration (Castellanos 1994, 4). That law states:

> First, women have the right to participate in the revolutionary struggle in the place and at the level that their capacity and will dictates, without any discrimination based on race, creed, color, or political affiliation.
>
> Second, women have the right to work and to receive a just salary.
>
> Third, women have the right to decide on the number of children they have and take care of.
>
> Fourth, women have the right to participate in community affairs and hold leadership positions if they are freely and democratically elected.
>
> Fifth, women have the right to primary care in terms of their health and nutrition.
>
> Sixth, women have the right to education.
>
> Seventh, women have the right to choose their romantic partners and should not be obligated to marry by force.
>
> Eighth, no woman should be beaten or physically mistreated by either family members or strangers. Rape and attempted rape should be severely punished.
>
> Ninth, women can hold leadership positions in the organization and hold military rank in the revolutionary armed forces.
>
> Tenth, women have all the rights and obligations set out by the revolutionary laws and regulations. (Ejército Zapatista de Liberación Nacional 1994, 45–46)

The wide-ranging issues discussed in the laws point to the importance of the EZLN as a political organization, and suggest an underlying conception of democracy that includes women's rights to full political participation and control over all decisions that affect their lives, whether in their sexual lives, in raising children, in work, in politics, or in their participation in a revolutionary organization. The issues highlighted in the Revolutionary Law of Women did not emerge spontaneously in the wake of armed struggle, but came out of a sustained organizing context in which women slowly articulated the need for attention to their life experience as well as that of men.

Nevertheless, the writing of a revolutionary law for women is one thing; its implementation is another. This law is, of course, implemented variably (or not at all) in the varying levels and types of Zapatista organizations. In many Zapatista base communities, the ability of women to participate equally with men is constrained. Local gender roles often limit women's activities to the domestic arena or require that women ask their husbands for permission to leave the house or the community, and the division of labor makes it difficult for women to attend distant meetings (and easier to attend local ones). The law was more heavily discussed in the Lacandon lowland regions of EZLN support than in the highlands, where it arrived later.

The following passage is from an interview recorded with Captain Maribel in October 1994 after the second meeting of the National Democratic Convention in Aguascalientes, located on the ejido land of Guadalupe Tepeyac. Captain Maribel is Tzeltal, from further down the canyons toward Altamirano and Ocosingo. She was stationed close to Guadalupe Tepeyac at the time of the interview, which was recorded by Eduardo Vera. I include portions here to illustrate the awareness that some women at the higher levels of the EZLN military command have of what life is like for women in indigenous communities. Maribel describes the changes that she and others went through when they became hard-core militants of the EZLN and armed insurgents. The contrast between the descriptions of life in the communities and among the militants is striking and provides insight into the gap that may exist for what women in insurgent camps experience and what those who remain in Zapatista base communities experience.

CAPTAIN MARIBEL: A compañera who lives in her community, she has to do the same work every day until she dies. This is what has always happened in the indigenous communities. She has to get up, to make her *pozol,* she sweeps the house, she has to maintain her children and the animals. She attends to her husband. She has to make meals for her husband when he goes out to the cornfields. She has to carry firewood. She has to make tortillas. She has to go and wash the clothes. . . . It is a series of jobs that leave her really tired. She doesn't have any time to rest, or any entertainment. She doesn't just have to take care of one child, but she may have several—as many as life has given her, as they say.

So we see that these compañeras suffer a lot. They don't have any support. They don't know what a stove is, or a washing machine. They don't know about a lot of things. They don't have any support, and we see that they work very hard and at the end of the day they are very tired. They sleep a little bit and then they have to get up again and repeat the same thing. That is how life is.

We women changed a lot [once we got here with the EZLN]. When we become militants of the EZLN, we begin to learn a lot of things that are new for us. If we don't know how to read and write, the first thing we do is learn to read and write. We also learn what politics is, why we are struggling, who we are struggling against, and who we are working with. We learn the history of Mexico, and they teach us as a group. We learn according to our levels of preparation. We are also subject to the laws of the EZLN. We learn what the laws of the Geneva Convention are, and we also have other laws for women that we have discussed with the women in the communities. We have more experience about how to do different kinds of work because they have taught us, we have taken courses. In terms of military training we learn the same things as the men . . . military tactics, the arming and disarming of a weapon. When we make progress and advance, we also achieve military ranks inside of the army. Women have the same right to hold military rank as men.

This is a big change that a woman in a community would not be able to make. In the communities, the mothers wouldn't let young women participate together with young men in anything. Here in the EZLN, we have the right to do this. We do that. We do everything with the compañeros. They help us, they teach us, they support us. There is a relationship of solidarity. This is really different from the life we had before.

That part of the Zapatista army offering the best possibilities for radical changes in gender roles is the *insurgentes,* those men and women who are full-time EZLN army members, like Mirabel, and have the possibility of creating a new kind of gendered culture in their military training camps. Often training camps combine young men and women from different ethnic groups, bringing together Tzeltal, Tojolabal, and Tzotzil speakers. For all men and women who leave their natal indigenous communities to train and become full-time Zapatista army members, the changes required are difficult—but perhaps most difficult is the idea that men and women are equal, that they can achieve equal rank within the military hierarchy of the EZLN, and that women can and have become high-ranking military officers with responsibility for hundreds of other soldiers and militia members.

The Revolutionary Law of Women was discussed and debated among the insurgentes, but was also discussed and voted on in Zapatista base communities such as Guadalupe Tepeyac and La Realidad. The struggle behind the Revolutionary Law of Women was and is one of the most intense the EZLN has faced internally, at least as testified to by some of its members (see Rovira 1997, 105–17). This struggle has not just involved men. Quite the contrary. The strategy for changing gender roles has involved educating men and women together and having both come to agreement on the content of the Revolutionary Law and then, more important, work to implement it.

The mere existence of a Revolutionary Law for Women in no way guarantees a major change in gender roles and hierarchies in indigenous communities, Zapatista or not. Nevertheless, its existence and the process attached to its creation are ideological markers for future possibilities. Talking about the struggle to create the law with high-ranking female comandantes provided a chance to see some of the political frontiers of the EZLN and to hear from some of its thinkers who are most radical—at least in terms of gendered issues.

COMANDANTES MARISELA AND CONCEPCIÓN: MAKING THE REVOLUTIONARY LAW OF WOMEN

In July 1996, I had a conversation with seven women comandantes of the EZLN, representing various segments of the Clandestine Revolutionary Indigenous Committee. Two were Tojolabal speakers from Guadalupe Tepeyac and nearby; the others were primarily Tzotzil speakers from the highlands. The two women comandantes most fluent in Spanish spoke the most, while others remained silent who perhaps understood Spanish but did not feel comfortable speaking it. We were all in San Cristóbal de las Casas attending a forum the EZLN organized on "Reforming the State," which brought together a wide range of grassroots political activists, including Cuauhtémoc Cárdenas of the left-center Party of the Democratic Revolution (PRD) and representatives of the much smaller Labor Party (PT). The forum aimed, in part, to solidify communication and plans between the EZLN and wide sectors of Mexican society, to push harder on the government to implement the Accords on Indigenous Rights and Culture that it had signed in San Andrés Larráinzar in February 1996, and to fortify the grassroots organization of the Zapatista Front of National Liberation (FZLN), the EZLN's national civilian support movement. The topic at hand was how to reform the state and foment participatory democracy.

I was there as an international observer credentialed by the National Intermediation Commission (CONAI) and the National Commission of Concord and Pacification (COCOPA), made up of members of the Mexican Congress. (From 1994 to 1997, I made many trips to Chiapas invited and credentialed as an international observer by different Mexican entities—an experience that was a significant part of my fieldwork and in addition to work I did as an individual.) On this occasion, in 1996, the seven women comandantes were participating in the different round-tables of the forum, offering their perspectives but mostly listening and observing, watching and learning from what others in Mexican society had to say.

One evening, after the official sessions for the day were over, several of us sat down with the comandantes to discuss the Revolutionary Law of Women. We asked two general questions: "How was the Revolution-ary Law of Women formed?" and "Was there any resistance to it?" I have put Comandante Marisela's response first because it synthesizes much of the discussion:

COMANDANTE MARISELA: What we did was to organize ourselves. We didn't create the Revolutionary Law of Women among those of us that are here today, but we made it with all of the women, all of them that struggle with us. And when we decide to do something, or have a task that we want to accomplish, then we have to consult with all of the other compañeras. We have to ask all of the other women to see if they are in agreement or not, to see if something is missing or if they want to add something. When the Revolutionary Law of Women was created, everyone had to be in agreement—everyone.

Why did we think it was necessary to have this revolutionary law? Because the women have never been respected. The participation of women has not been taken into consideration. The govern-ment never took our participation into consider-ation, and neither did anyone else. But we think that women also have the right to have laws, not just men. Women can think about this too, women together with men. That is how we were able to achieve the revolutionary law of women. Because women have the right to participate in different kinds of work and different types of activities.

As was said, there are a lot of women who haven't had the right to decide how many children they want to have, or who they want to marry or have a relationship with. A lot of women have never had these kinds of rights. Women have had a lot of problems; and a lot of times women are

Figure 6. Women comandantes after our conversation in 1996. Photo by Lynn Stephen.

obligated to couple up with a man even though they do not like him, but that's how it is. That is why we made this law, so that they respect the rights of women. Women should also have a space to participate in, and have the right to do work. This is what we have achieved with the rest of the compañeras. And women have the right to participate as well. When we have a meeting or a big assembly, women participate in everything, everything. You won't just see seven or eight women arriving, but thousands and thousands of women will participate and decide whether not the points brought forward are good or bad, and we will discuss them. That is what we do.

The response from Comandante Concepción that follows illustrates a somewhat different perspective. She addresses the repression of women, but also takes the opportunity to talk about the more generalized struggle for freedom that the Zapatistas are undertaking—men and women together. In addition, she uses the conversation to publicize the conditions people are living under as a result of the low-intensity war and military occupation of many communities. She commented afterward that she thought this information is rarely reported outside Mexico.

COMANDANTE CONCEPCIÓN: This question takes me back to the times when I first joined this struggle, because we women are also oppressed and the government doesn't recognize our rights. . . . There is repression of men but it is much worse for us. So it is because of this that, together with other women, we have organized ourselves together, men and women so that we can achieve what we want: peace, justice, dignity, and respect for the rights of men and women. And we didn't just organize ourselves because of this repression, but also because of the mistreatment, the beatings that go on.

Well you probably know how the government sends people here, bad people . . . who are paid. And they are sent arms and they use all of this to intimidate society. There is no respect for women and men. So we have taken on all of this in order to achieve what we are looking for.

More than anything, we want to be free. But because we are looking for our freedom now, all we see there is repression. We see persecution more than anything. This is what has existed for our people, in our communities and this is why there have been massacres and more. We have women and children who are living in the mountains, homeless. . . . Those of us that can are using this opportunity to make people aware of this situation and to denounce this type of problem. As you can see, we are also making an effort to help men and women achieve equal rights. That is all I can say now.

LIEUTENANT NORMA: LIFE AS A YOUNG REVOLUTIONARY WOMAN

In mid June 1994, the Zapatista Army of National Liberation rejected the Mexican government's first 34-point peace plan, which was the result of a dialogue between EZLN representatives and the government negotiator, Manuel Camacho Avila, in the Cathedral of San Cristóbal de las Casas. The Zapatista rejection came after a two-month grassroots consulting process. Many felt that the peace plan did not adequately address questions of political democracy. These questions came to be the focus of the first large national meeting the Zapatistas called with representatives of Mexican civil society. Called the National Democratic Convention, this historic meeting brought together more than six thousand delegates from across the nation to discuss a wide range of national issues, particularly how to change the Mexican Constitution and political system and push for democratization from below. I was there as an invited international observer credentialed by the national organizing committee of the National Democratic Convention.

Visiting Guadalupe Tepeyac at the time of the convention allowed me to share the infectious optimism that abounded in many EZLN communities from January 1994 to February 1995. During that period, the EZLN controlled a clear territory and was busy implementing Zapatista ideas and plans at the local level. Communities organized campaigns against alcoholism, rape, and wife-beating. Women and children had their own organizational groups and attended all assemblies. Many people were dreaming, debating, and struggling for change. Corn and vegetable growing were being organized collectively.

Making contact with six thousand Mexicans from all segments of society was an important step for the EZLN, and the context of the convention generated a great deal of excitement for all who attended. This was the context in which I spoke with Lieutenant Norma, a young Zapatista officer bubbling with enthusiasm and energy. I met her amid a wider conversation and asked if I could speak with her personally. She motioned me to one side and said yes. I pointed to my tape recorder, and she said, "Yes, you can turn it on." I did. Her conversation with me perhaps best captures what it was like to come into the Zapatista army as a very young person and to remake most aspects of one's life as a revolutionary. Most striking was our brief discussion of contraceptives, which I found a number of young Zapatista soldiers willing to talk about.

LYNN:	One of the most interesting things that has surfaced in the Zapatista struggle. . . .
LIEUTENANT NORMA:	When our struggle started, it was clandestine. They told us not to tell anyone except our parents. . . . Because if the government arrived. . . . [she implies by her hand movements that people would be caught and punished]
LYNN:	I see. I also wondered about the Revolutionary Law of Women. Why did this law come to be?

LIEUTENANT NORMA: We decided that women could join the struggle. We women don't have everything that we need. We need a good place to live, we need food. Women didn't have that. We didn't have anything. So we decided to integrate ourselves with the [Zapatista] army to fight with the men. . . .

The government says that women are not worth anything. They are worth shit, as we say. The federal army comes and makes fun of us, but women are worth the same as men. Because everything a man does a woman can do too. If a man has military politics, then so does a woman. If a woman gets to be a captain, a major, a Lieutenant or sergeant . . . she is in charge.

LYNN: Why was it necessary to make a law like this?

LIEUTENANT NORMA: Why was it necessary? Because they didn't take us into account in the [Zapatista] army.

LYNN: Who actually organized the law? Men or women?

LIEUTENANT NORMA: The people who worked on it were elected by us in areas that were controlled by the [Zapatista] army—that is, areas that were already under our control. That is where women decided on the law.

LYNN: Subcomandante Marcos has publicly stated that getting this law passed was one of the biggest struggles that took place among the Zapatistas because it was controversial. . . .

LIEUTENANT NORMA: Yes, yes it was. Because in a lot of places women were worth nothing. Why? Why? Because women just aren't valued. But this law is really necessary. . . .

LYNN: One of your compañeros just told me that there are men who are very machista. He said, "I also had this idea that they are not going to have a woman in charge of me." He said it is hard the first time when a woman is in charge of a man. Did you have to struggle to be respected?

LIEUTENANT NORMA: Yes. Because of being women, we have to struggle. Because, between women there is not respect either. We don't take each other seriously because we see that we are women. So we all began to study.

LYNN: What kind of things did you study?

LIEUTENANT NORMA: We began to study about politics, about military tactics . . . and a lot of other pamphlets that they gave us. And we studied about the advances and the ways of thinking we are going to have as women, thinking among ourselves. We asked, why is it that they don't take us into account? Why do they say that women can't do anything? Why do they mistreat us? We began to think.

LYNN: Did the men make fun of this education?

LIEUTENANT NORMA: Yes, yes.

LYNN: How did you defend yourselves in this process?

LIEUTENANT NORMA: In the [Zapatista] army we formed two to four battalions. In the army we can't say anything against anyone. Nothing, nothing. Let's say someone says, "A compañera is worth shit." No, no, nothing like this can happen. This isn't permitted at all. It is there [in the Zapatista army] where women and men are worth the same.

LYNN: The army had to work on this point?

LIEUTENANT NORMA: Just the same as men and women.

LYNN: Of course. The women also had to work on this, as well.

LIEUTENANT NORMA: Yes, absolutely. . . .

LYNN: A lot of people say that it is only men who put down women, but women can also put down each other.

LIEUTENANT NORMA: Yes, that's how it is. We had to think about how it is in relation to the men, and also in relation to one another. And the men had to think about how to relate to women and also to think about themselves so that we could all get along. . . . We had to think about the discipline, the inequality, and how to build solidarity between men and women. All of this.

LYNN: Was the tradition of women very different where you grew up?

LIEUTENANT NORMA: Yes, different. Very different. When I was a civilian, my mother would say that I should respect a compañero [man] not a compañera [woman]. And we would walk around as girls gossiping about how we weren't worth anything. But when I joined the [Zapatista] army, they taught me discipline, they taught me how to think about everything—about how a woman is, how a man is.

LYNN: So you went through a period of self-development?

LIEUTENANT NORMA: Yes, a whole lot.

LYNN: How old were you when you joined?

LIEUTENANT NORMA: I was twelve years old when I joined.

LYNN: How old are you now?

LIEUTENANT NORMA: I am eighteen years old.

LYNN: In your battalion, how many people are there?

LIEUTENANT NORMA: Us? I am not sure. There are a lot of people here now. Right now there are a lot of men and women. And because we are always moving around from group to group . . . it's hard to know. Here is a group where we have twenty women and thirty men, but I don't know how it is in other groups.

LYNN: So it changes . . . but in general there are more men than women.

LIEUTENANT NORMA: Yes, there are more men than women [in the battalions].

LYNN: Maybe we could say that, for each woman, there are three men [meaning ratios of women to men, but in Spanish this could imply multiple male sexual partners for each woman].

LIEUTENANT NORMA: Yes, but not because, if I am a woman and I have a husband, I am going to go with another man. This is not permitted in the army. People have to respect women even if they are just with one compañero who is not their husband. Other men don't have the right to come on to her. She is respected.

LYNN: So people who are in couples are respected.

LIEUTENANT NORMA: Yes, there is a lot of respect. The husband or the wife is very much respected by the other [spouse].

LYNN: So a woman can have a compañero [partner] in the army even if they are not married?

LIEUTENANT NORMA: Yes. It is permitted. . . . But in the army you can't have a child. You are in training. We constantly move around and walk. You can't carry a child. . . .

LYNN: So part of the education of a woman is education about her own body?

LIEUTENANT NORMA: Oh yes.

LYNN: About contraceptives? Would women who are *civiles* know about contraceptives?

LIEUTENANT NORMA: No, only those who are in the army. Those who are civilians, if they want to have children, that is up to them. . . . It is only in the army [where you can't]. . . .

LYNN: Do you have other family members who joined up?

LIEUTENANT NORMA: I have two siblings who are also here.

LYNN : I imagine that helps out. Are there a lot of women who join up with their cousins and their sisters or brothers?

LIEUTENANT NORMA: Yes, most of them do. There are times when there are three siblings who join, four siblings, six or eight siblings who join up.

MAJOR ELISEO: BEING A REVOLUTIONARY MAN

One of my most interesting conversations about the Revolutionary Law of Women was with a high-ranking man, Major Eliseo (introduced in the previous chapter). I first heard Major Eliseo speak when he addressed a journalist from a Mexican newspaper in Guadalupe Tepeyac during the National Democratic Convention. Afterward, he motioned to me to join him on a large rock facing the warm rays of the late afternoon sun. He was on a break from working a security point across the river with a group of ten or twelve people. I sat down next to him and asked if I could interview him. He said, "Of course." I started to talk and he responded, "Do you want to tape-record this?" "I would love to if it is OK." "Yes," Major Eliseo replied, "That way you will get it right." What I remember most from our conversation was his willingness to talk honestly about the difficult aspects of trying to treat women as equals. His analysis of gender was also interlaced with ideas on how women are exploited in capitalist economic systems. His willingness to blame *all* exploitation of women on capitalism, however, suggests a reluctance to face some of the exploitation of women that occurs within indigenous communities that has little to do with capitalism—the realities discussed by Captain Maribel. He is still avoiding some of the local cultural norms that pushed some women to organize the women's law. From my conversation with him, as well as from that with Norma, I felt that at least among the limited group of insurgents I was able to talk with in 1994, significant discussions and struggles had taken place about gender equality. What follows is part of my conversation with Major Eliseo.

LYNN:	What ideas do you have about the Women's Revolutionary Law? What do you think about it?
MAJOR ELISEO:	I need to explain so that you can understand. There used to be a lot of messed-up ideas that were different from what the Revolutionary Law of Women says.
LYNN:	What were the different ideas?
MAJOR ELISEO:	The different ideas were that—well, one could say that women in the capitalist system aren't worth the same as men. And the woman is seen to be worth less and the man worth more. Men are more in charge and women can't do this. This is a big difference. This is what a lot of people thought. So we asked, why? Why weren't women worth much and men were?
LYNN:	And how do you feel about the part of the law that says that a women should decide how many children she could have,

that she should have martial relationships with whom she wants, that she shouldn't be obligated. . . .

MAJOR ELISEO: . . .The decision should be up to a man and a woman. It should be up to the two of them. They shouldn't be obligated. What you said is also true. The decision to have a family should also be a decision made by both. A man wants one thing and a woman wants another and then what happens is that they do what the man wants. It shouldn't be like that. Women should have their point of view, too. That is what I think. There should be agreement between the two.

LYNN: I don't know if it is true, but I read . . . I think it was in a statement of Marcos, that this was the thing . . . most debated internally among you . . . this was the real revolution because there were months and months of conversations and debates. Is this true?

MAJOR ELISEO: Yes. . . . We had to talk about this a lot because some people didn't agree with it.

LYNN: Why? Was it what some people call machismo, what others call "tradition?"

MAJOR ELISEO: I think that it is this . . . it is in part because of this, of what they call being "machista." Because someone who is a man feels that he is superior. For example, he has his woman, and she can't do anything until he tells her too. It also comes because of the capitalist ideas, as well. This is what we have. . . . We had to combat this idea, because a revolutionary idea can't be this way. We are looking for an equality, for justice. Thus equality means that one person is worth the same as the other. . . . They are the same. We didn't understand this. We had to be convinced that women can be in charge, as well as men. This was the principal discussion we had.

LYNN: It is very interesting that you [plural, in Spanish] disseminated the Revolutionary Law of Women with other communiqués, but the press didn't pick it up or print it? Why do you think that this law didn't get much publicity?

MAJOR ELISEO: Well, one part may be because they don't want to publish the truth that was our law, which continues to be the case. . . . It's also because the damn bourgeois takes advantage of women. . . .

LYNN: We have talked about the law. How is the law implemented? How do you guarantee that this law is implemented inside of your [Zapatista] army?

MAJOR ELISEO: The law is a rule for all revolutionaries. We already said that the decision to have a family is the decision of both [man and woman]. It is a law that has to be obeyed. Another thing

	that I want to say is that the woman shouldn't be dominating the man. The work should be equal, because the woman needs to eat as well.
LYNN:	Can you give me an example of how the law is implemented?
MAJOR ELISEO:	We, can I say we? We insurgents follow the law. As we say, as men in the army, sometimes a woman is making a decision for us.
LYNN:	How does this work out in the physical labor that you carry out?
MAJOR ELISEO:	Well, there is one thing. Because women don't have the same physical force as a man. So when we do a job we don't give the same jobs to a woman as to a man. So we give them less work or less to carry because it is a woman. But to receive something, everything should be equal. This is what we do.
LYNN:	Within the structure of the organization, are there comandantes who are women, as well as men?
MAJOR ELISEO:	Well, to talk about this signifies something else, because in the structure that we have, in our hierarchy, we have women who are ranked officers and men who are ranked officers. Women can become lieutenants, majors, even higher. And men, as well. For example, if a woman has a higher rank than I do, I have to obey her. This thus signifies the reversal of how people thought before. The idea before was, why would a woman tell me what to do? That is what they said. Now in the new structure, it's not like that. If the woman has a higher rank, she is going to be in charge. There is an equality.
LYNN:	I imagine that this hasn't been so easy and that people had to get used to it.
MAJOR ELISEO:	Yes, little by little, because there were people who didn't want to accept this idea.
LYNN:	Was it a struggle for you?
MAJOR ELISEO:	For me, at the beginning it was. You don't understand it. But then after you think about it, it is true what they are saying . . . they [men and women] should be equal.

Eliseo's words capture the contradictions of trying to implement profound changes in gender roles within the ranks of the Zapatista armed insurgents. For young men and women coming from communities where men were used to being in charge of their own lives and dictating many aspects of women's lives as well, taking orders from women was difficult and some resisted. And, as suggested by Norma, women also had to learn to take each other seriously as well.

FROM THE REVOLUTIONARY LAW OF WOMEN TO ENGENDERING
INDIGENOUS RIGHTS IN THE SAN ANDRÉS ACCORDS

At another level, there have been significant differences between expected
behaviors for men and women within the ranks of armed insurgents and
in their home communities. At the level of Zapatista base communities,
an even greater potential gap persists between the ideas expressed in the
Revolutionary Law of Women and the daily life of women. These differences were highlighted in a 1994 women's gathering in Chiapas that
preceded the National Democratic Convention held by the EZLN in August 1994. The Chiapas Women's Convention brought women from
Zapatista communities but also brought many others who had reflected
on the Revolutionary Law of Women. Delegates to the Chiapas Women's
Convention sought a model of government that was democratic and participatory, not patriarchal, vertical, discriminatory, or corporativist (Rojas 1994, 190–95). While the summary document of the 1994 Chiapas
Women's Convention mentioned the need for laws to guarantee women's
equal participation in a range of arenas, the most detailed proposals came
under the heading "family life." Some highlights included:

- [We want] men to change, to respect us and to learn that we have
  rights and that they should help us so that everyone respects our
  rights.
- [We want] to be respected for our choice of marriage partner, and we
  want those who sell women [into marriage] to be punished.
- [We want] mothers and fathers to teach their sons and daughters how
  to do domestic work at a young age, and that the work of women
  matters as much as that of men.
- [We want] both parents to decide together how many children to
  have, and we want men to help women with the responsibility of family planning.
- [We want] men who don't respect women, who rape and mistreat
  women, and who don't carry out their responsibilities to be punished.
- [We want] women's rights to inherit property to be recognized, and
  [we want] their rights to land to be respected whether or not they are
  widows. (Rojas 1994, 194–95)[1]

In this summary, the notion of participatory citizenship at the level of
the home is clearly expressed. While the document is the outcome not

only of the participation of indigenous women, but also of mestiza advisors from a variety of organizations, it contains the seeds of ideas followed through in discussions women participated in about the meaning of indigenous autonomy at the national level. These subsequent discussions were part of the process leading to the formulation and signing of the San Andrés Accords on Indigenous Rights and Culture in 1996.

In two subsequent forums—in October 1995 and January 1996—to prepare the accords, the most contentious issue for women was the meaning of *usos y costumbres,* roughly translated as "uses and customs in indigenous culture." While one central point of proposals for autonomy was that indigenous systems of justice and political decision-making be respected, some "customs" included under the loose terminology of *usos y costumbres* did not promote gender equity. Quite the opposite. For example, while the inclusion of men, women, and even children in community assemblies has been the practice in some Zapatista base communities, it was not a common occurrence in most parts of Chiapas or in other indigenous communities in Mexico. "Customary" political decision-making has often involved community assemblies attended by men between the ages of eighteen and seventy. In such assemblies, the majority of men present would not speak, but would listen and simply vote silently with their hands when a specific resolution was put forward.

Thus, for many indigenous women, "customary" community decision-making processes have meant exclusion. Other "customs" could include men beating women, parents negotiating the marriages of their daughters (and sons) without respecting their wishes, and divisions of labor in which women worked many more hours than men. While such patterns were not universal, they appeared common in a significant number of households in rural Chiapas. In a national forum on indigenous rights held in October 1995, indigenous women from Chiapas, Oaxaca, Puebla, Querétero, Mexico, Hidalgo, and Mexico City, along with their advisors, put forward a key modification of the term *usos y costumbres.* They declared, "We demand that our customs and traditions be respected if and when they do not violate women's rights" (*Ce-Acatl* 1995, 22). This wording was more or less adopted in the signed accords.

In the preparation of the Accords on Indigenous rights and Culture, indigenous women attempted to influence several arenas of citizenship at once and to integrate concerns of ethnicity and of gender with those of nationalism. The notion of autonomy articulated by indigenous women and their advisors through almost three years of meetings and workshops in Chiapas and elsewhere in 1994–96 was expansive. It referred to economic autonomy—women's rights to have access to, and control over, modes of production; political autonomy—women's basic political rights; physical autonomy—the right to make decisions concerning one's own body and the right to a life without violence; sociocultural autonomy—the women's right to assert their specific identities as indigenous women (Hernández-Castillo 1997, 112).

A translation follows of the summary of the women's resolutions from the 1996 Congreso Nacional Indígena (it is written first in passive voice and then switches to active voice):

> The women demand recognition of their right to equality in homes, community, and all the spaces of the nation. . . . They demand that their citizenship rights be recognized: their right to equal political participation with men, their right to property and land and to participate in decision-making in their communities. Because of these rights, they demand legislation that equalizes the position of indigenous women and guarantees their right against being violated physically, psychologically, sexually, or economically. In terms of the undeclared war, . . . they demand an end to the rape of indigenous women; women cannot continue to be war booty. We demand an immediate and careful investigation of all of the acts of violence against indigenous women and exemplary punishment for those responsible. (Meneses 1996)

In documents produced by women in the CNI, the physical and psychological integrity of women's bodies and reproductive decision-making are linked to the rights to land, property, and participation in political decision-making in all arenas. This integrated vision makes visible the systematic marginalization of indigenous women and suggests specific remedies for correcting it.

In October 1996, the EZLN and the Comisión de Concordia y Pacificación (National Commission of Concord and Pacification), or COCOPA, composed of representatives from Mexico's three leading political parties, announced that a joint commission had been formed for the verification and follow-up of the Accords on Indigenous Rights signed in February 1996. Following formation of the joint commission, a proposal for legislation was elaborated by COCOPA and endorsed by the EZLN. In the COCOPA legislative proposal, women's rights are stated as follows: "[Indigenous peoples] have the right . . . to apply their own normative systems in the regulation and solution of internal conflict, respecting individual rights, human rights, and the dignity and integrity of women." Women's political rights in this proposal are stated as "[the right of indigenous peoples] to elect their authorities and exercise their own forms of internal government in accordance with their norms . . . guaranteeing the equal participation of women" (Cuadro comparativo de la iniciativa de COCOPA y las observaciones del ejecutivo 1997). The words "customs" and "traditions" have been subtly replaced in the COCOPA draft with "own normative systems," indicating the volatility of the notion of "uses and customs" from a gendered point of view. The draft thus subtly addresses women's political participation where "according to custom" they have often been absent, and also discourages internal forms of conflict resolution that do not respect women's rights—such as, perhaps, forms applicable to choice of partner in marriage.

However, other issues highlighted in the women's roundtables that were part of the preparatory meetings, including women's lack of equal rights to land, unequal division of labor in households, domestic violence, and rape were downplayed in the accords signed by the EZLN and the government, and in the COCOPA legislative proposal. The actual signed accords drop all women's demands concerning the democratization of the home and sexual violence, and only address women at the community level by the statement that women should participate in all legislative processes and be involved in choosing local leaders. This outcome suggests another instance where the gap between the Women's Revolutionary Law and reality is quite substantial. In this case, it is a legal, not merely a social, gap.

For Zapatista women who participated in the process leading up to the signing of the accords, the act of coming together with others from throughout the nation—in this case, other indigenous women—has provided networks beyond the back and forth of the EZLN and the government. Ultimately, these networks may prove more important than the accords. Women within the national movement for indigenous autonomy have begun to carve out a space and political vision that takes the three levels of home, community, and nation and binds them to a new framework for being indigenous in Mexico—autonomous in economic, cultural, and political decision-making, but part of the Mexican nation. This vision, with the political culture it represents, has the potential to begin opening up new political spaces not only for indigenous women in Chiapas, but for other women in Mexico as well.

FIGHTING FOR ZAPATISMO AMID MILITARY
OCCUPATION: TESTIMONIES FROM GUADALUPE
TEPEYAC AND LA REALIDAD, 1995–1997

Since February 1995, the Mexican Army has occupied the territories
where the Zapatista Army of National Liberation has been supported.
The utopian period of Zapatista territorial control, experimentation,
and optimism was replaced by a struggle to resist, to survive, and to
maintain Zapatista ideals in increasingly difficult circumstances. Per-
suaded by hard-liners, President Ernesto Zedillo issued judicial orders
on 9 February 1995 for the arrest of the EZLN leadership. The army
moved quickly into Zapatista-held territory and ransacked the villages,
causing thousands of community base members to flee into the mountains. Between ten thousand and twenty thousand people became refugees at that time. Some, like those from the community of Guadalupe Tepeyac, became permanent refugees. As of April 2001, they still had not
returned to their original community but lived in a new community site.

In 1995, the Mexican government initiated a double-edged strategy:
negotiation coupled with increased militarization of areas that were Zapatista strongholds. The government entered into a second round of negotiations with the EZLN in San Andrés Larráinzar in that same year. I
attended two of these negotiation sessions. In February 1996, the EZLN
and the Mexican government signed the San Andrés Accords on Indigenous Rights and Culture, which laid the groundwork for significant
changes in the areas of indigenous rights, political participation, and
cultural autonomy (these are described in detail in the Conclusion).

While the government refused to implement the accords, the Mexican Army engaged, beginning in 1996, in a strategy to win the "hearts
and minds" of people in Zapatista communities through actions like
giving haircuts, distributing candy, and providing food, farming inputs,
and other necessities to those who would support the government. This
strategy had several results. The "hearts and minds" campaign had begun in 1995 after the Mexican Army had pushed thousands out of their
communities in its unsuccessful efforts to capture the EZLN leadership.
This created a flow of refugees in areas where the army occupied lands,
drove people out, and destroyed schools and clinics, as in Guadalupe
Tepeyac (see below). In communities already polarized between those
sympathetic to the EZLN and those sympathetic to the government, the
"hearts and minds" campaign furthered the splits and weakened community cohesion and social organization. In unified Zapatista commu-

nities, it resulted in the emergence of thirty-six autonomous municipal governments, which acted in parallel to the "official" governments and refused all government help. These municipalities, referred to as "autonomous municipalities in rebellion," decided to self-implement the San Andrés Accords on Indigenous Rights and Culture that the government refused to honor. From 1995 to mid 2001, this has resulted in continued confrontations between autonomous and official government bodies. The division of communities has also served as a basis for a paramilitary strategy of recruiting supporters of the PRI into organized armed groups, trained and supported by public security police and sometimes by ex-army members. The use of paramilitaries permits the army to act as border guards and as a security force in indigenous communities, while leaving the dirty work of the war to paramilitaries, who are locals. The most extreme act of violence wrought by paramilitary groups was the massacre of forty-six women, men, and children in the Tzotzil community of Acteal in December 1997 (see Stephen 1999b).

In Zapatista history, February 1995 marks a turning point in the daily life of the rebellion in indigenous communities. The EZLN lost physical control of large amounts of territory, and communities had to move into defensive positions. They began what has become a long-term struggle to cope with the daily effects of militarization, refusing any government funding or services.

The threat of rape and the psychological control exerted over communities through a male army presence is probably the strongest weapon used against indigenous women. The physical presence of the army is augmented through their surveillance tactics, which involve intimidating every-other-day patrols, with video cameras, through communities. These patrols passed through La Realidad on a regular basis; I witnessed them several times.

In 1995, visitors approached La Realidad from a road that wound through Guadalupe Tepeyac, past a huge military garrison where the first National Democratic Convention was held. La Realidad is surrounded by small coffee plots as well as some subsistence plots of corn. A river runs through the center of town, and houses are arranged along a few dirt streets on both sides of it. Like other Zapatista cultural centers, La Realidad has its own Aguascalientes Center, which has hosted many large meetings; it is off to the side of the community. Most homes are of wood with tin roofs. Some are thatched. A few horses graze in the middle of town. Public latrines for men and women sit in the center of town. There are also several buildings used for public meetings and to

Figure 7.   The center of La Realidad in 1995. Photo by Lynn Stephen.

house visitors. Most people wash and bathe in the river, observing local rules about who can bathe where and when. The early mornings are
often shrouded in mist, but can heat up rapidly once the sun breaks
through. It is at this time that the military patrols begin to come through.
What follows is a description of one such patrol.

At about nine o'clock in the morning, just when the sun is beginning
to heat up the mud, a very slow-moving caravan of about sixteen "humvees" and a few tanks moves through La Realidad. Most people hide in
their houses, peering through windows and doors. A few continue their
activities, ignoring the army's presence. Machine guns are mounted on
top of the humvees, and about four to eight soldiers sit in each vehicle.
While one soldier stands behind the machine gun, another one or two in
each vehicle are snapping photographs with still cameras, while others
are videotaping. The faces of the soldiers holding the still cameras and
the video cameras are not visible, hidden behind the cameras. They appear as human machines mounted on the humvees, filming all that comes
into their line of sight. These machines extend a very slow, deliberate,
and intimidating gaze over the community. They travel at about two miles
per hour and slow to a standstill periodically in their journey through
the village. When they stop, everyone ceases moving and stands frozen.

Figure 8.   Humvee with mounted machine gun in La Realidad. Photo by Lynn Stephen.

In about fifteen minutes, the humvees have passed through the two-block town.

Once they leave, people come out of their houses to resume work and to complain about their presence. Some break the tension by joking about whether the soldiers were really taking pictures: "They would have to spend thousands and thousands of pesos on all their film and pictures of La Realidad." Others talk about the army being able to watch them on video even when they weren't there. Such a suggestion leaves a chilly pall over conversations.

The effect has been quite startling, over the long term. While men, women, and children in La Realidad became accustomed to the video-taping and picture-taking, they never forgot about it. Women in the town talked about "always being watched" and the "eyes of the army being everywhere." This sense of always being watched, of never being alone, has had a profound effect on women in these militarized zones. While it has frightened them, it has also strengthened their resolve to hold firm in their communities and to communicate the injustice of their situation to anyone willing to listen.

The following conversations reflect the situation in Guadalupe Tepeyac and La Realidad following the militarization of the region in 1995.

Figure 9.   Soldiers on daily patrol in La Realidad, with cameras and video
equipment. Photo by Lynn Stephen.

Before proceeding to the interviews, I give a description of Guadalupe
Tepeyac that I wrote on a visit in March and April of 1995, after members of the community fled following the army incursion.

Field Note: Army Invasion of Guadalupe Tepeyac in February 1995

From Comitán to Guadalupe Tepeyac, where there were previously large numbers of EZLN sympathizers who came out in force to greet the caravan going
to the National Democratic Convention at Aguascalientes in August 1994,
people now looked at passing vehicles with fear, some with anger, and a few
weakly held up their fingers in the V sign. Where hundreds had gathered to
shout EZLN slogans before, only two people now shouted "Viva Marcos!"
Beginning in Las Margaritas, communities are clearly divided and marked by
houses with white flags and those without. These flags indicate support for
the army and what is now called the "official" part of the ARIC—those who
have aligned with the government as opposed to those who call themselves
"independent." They are not flags of surrender or of neutrality. There is
no neutral position. Conflicting graffiti can be seen on the walls, from "Viva
el Subcomandante Marcos" to "Muere asesino EZLN," ("EZLN assassins
should die") and "Samuel Ruiz no quiere a la Virgen de Guadalupe, Obispo
asesino" ("Samuel Ruiz doesn't love the Virgin of Guadalupe. Assassin
bishop"). Only in one town close to Guadalupe Tepeyac did people come out
to greet us and actually shout "Zapata Vive!" although somewhat quietly.

Figure 10. Ransacked home after 1995 army invasion of Guadalupe Tepeyac. Photo by Lynn Stephen.

People who had fled Nuevo Momón, Cruz del Rosario, Vincente Guerrero, and San Pedro in the wake of the army's February offensive had begun to come back, although not all of them. Some houses were empty, those with white flags occupied. In Nuevo Momón, several of the signs announcing land reclamations for the CEOIC [Consejo Estatal de Organizaciones Indígenas y Campesinas, or State Council of Indigenous and Peasant Organizations], dated March 1994, appeared to be abandoned, as was an occupation claimed by the CNC [the government-affiliated Confederación Nacional Campesina].

Guadalupe Tepeyac was abandoned. The only people who appeared were from nearby San Pedro and Vincente Guerrero to sell *refrescos* and tortillas.

Some of the houses in Guadalupe Tepeyac were completely ransacked. Everything had been pulled apart and destroyed. The army appeared to be trying to fix up some of the houses closest to the road, hanging clothes out to dry where there were no people. People fled without having time to bring anything. In many cases, work implements, *comales* [griddles], ovens, etc. were destroyed. Some animals returned. In one house, a corner was full of eggs where a hen continued to lay despite the fact that no one was there to collect them.

The most difficult sight was the destruction of the Aguascalientes installations on the ejido land of Guadalupe Tepeyac, where we had all stood at the threshold of optimism just seven months before, in August 1994. The theater, the library, the dormitories, the latrines, the kitchens were all destroyed. Instead, it had become a major military garrison, with rows of trucks, tanks, and dozens of humvees parked inside. An army officer came to speak with us and told us that there was no was no way we could tour the inside or see the "work" that the army had done in the area. Several helicopters were sitting on an open field, and the entrance to what had been the Zapatista capital was now ringed with barbed wire and a sign that said "MILITARY ENCAMPMENT." Not only was the community abandoned, but the physical heart of the Zapatista movement had been torn out and its people scattered.

But not for long. A year later, the Zapatistas built five new Aguascalientes, which have since served as political and cultural gathering places in the regions of the Zapatista movement, and have held subsequent large national and international gatherings (see Stephen and Collier 1997). What follows are testimonies from Guadalupe Tepeyac recorded shortly after the community fled in 1995 and ultimately reestablished itself in the Lacandon jungle. These testimonies were given by the youth of Guadalupe Tepeyac.

TESTIMONIES FROM THE ZAPATISTA YOUTH GROUP
OF GUADALUPE TEPEYAC: 29 MARCH 1995

ROSIBEL: On the ninth of February 1995, Guadalupe Tepeyac was completely invaded by the federal army and by uncountable numbers of helicopters. When they saw so many helicopters, the children began to cry and scream. So the population fled to the rural hospital, which was occupied by the International Red Cross, thinking that the rights of the International Red Cross would be respected. When we arrived at the hospital, an ejidatario stayed in his house because he was sick. He couldn't walk. We haven't seen him any more. Between 11:00 and 11:30 in the morning, General Ramón Rieta entered the hospital to take us out, saying these words, "Good morning, compatriots. We recognize your just struggle. Don't be afraid, because we have come to protect you." But we didn't believe him. And we stayed there without eating, with all of our children. At four in the afternoon the general came in again. He came in again without respecting the International Red Cross. He was menacing, writing down the names of all the people ... pounding on the doors, searching through everything.

When we heard that they had taken the hospital and they told us it was their barracks, we withdrew at five o'clock in the afternoon because we saw that the Federal Army didn't respect the International Red Cross. So if they didn't respect the International Red Cross, they certainly were not going to respect us. Without thinking, we had to flee to the mountains, walking day and night under the moon and the weight of the jungle with only the sound of the crickets to console us. Without eating, without drinking, we finally arrived in a secure place, where you find us.

MARCOS [not the subcomandante]: I want to tell you the real words of General Ramón Rieta. He told us, "We come to protect you, to take care of you. Don't be afraid of us. Return to your houses." But we didn't trust him, because what he is doing is a big mess. The compañero who stayed in his house and couldn't even walk was with a family member. That family member told us that the army captured the compañero, and began to threaten him. They hit him on the left foot (which was injured) until he confessed everything. They said, "Turn in your weapon. If you don't, we will find it in your house." They asked if he is Mexican or Guatemalan. Afterward, they tied his hands and his feet. They shut him up in the bathrooms of the DIF [Desarollo Integral de la Familia, a federal family-assistance program] building without anything to eat or drink. They kept him there for five days. They told him, "We are going to take you to Las Margaritas to free you." And he answered, "I don't have anything to do in Las Margaritas without money." He asked them to leave him in a place where he could get help to cure his wound. It was infected. He stayed in this town until he got here and found his family.

MARISÓL: Today we are somewhere in the mountains of the southwest of Mexico, suffering from hunger and cold. The children have a lot of illnesses and we are without medicine or doctors, but we continue to resist. We are going to continue to resist as long as the Mexican Army doesn't retreat from where it is positioned in our community. We are ready to die even though we are all poor. . . .

TESTIMONIES FROM LA REALIDAD: ARMY
OCCUPATION AND THE STRUGGLE TO ORGANIZE

I arrived in La Realidad with a humanitarian aid caravan about seven weeks after the army occupied Guadalupe Tepeyac on 9 February 1995 and pushed people temporarily out of La Realidad. After the army invasion, the population of La Realidad was cut off from food for about three weeks. By the time we arrived, the community had become a corridor for aid going far into the jungle to people of other communities, some of whom had fled their homes. The people of La Realidad reported daily helicopter buzzings and low-flying planes over the community. Community members also reported that the army drove heavy trucks and earth-moving equipment up and down past the town. In their public dialogue, many enumerated the reasons why *el pueblo se levantó* ("the people rose up") in January 1994 and said they would not give up until their demands were met.

My conversations began with Juan, who was standing around watching the unloading of several truckloads of aid that we had brought for distribution to refugee communities in the jungle. At first he hung back, but later he moved closer to our group to begin a conversation. I asked if I could tape our conversation and he said, "Fine. You should tell people what is going on here."

JUAN: The army came here after it went to Guadalupe Tepeyac, to various communities. They came in and, when they arrived, they took over the town and went into people's houses. They stole animals, machetes that we use to work in our cornfields. They arrived on that day that they took over Guadalupe Tepeyac. The people were frightened . . . especially the children and old people. So we had to leave, to flee, something that we have never had to do. The army concentrated itself in our community. So because of this the children got really scared.

LYNN: Now there are some people who claim that the army isn't here any more, that it is fine now. But others have told me that they can't leave to work in the fields.

JUAN: That's how it is. It isn't true. The army is here. We always work, but with difficulty. We are afraid of their presence. We aren't used to having the army around on a daily basis in our community or when we are working. That doesn't seem right to us.

LYNN: Let's talk a little bit about the history of this town. Your grandparents. . . .

JUAN: My father always told me about the suffering they underwent when there was no transport. They had to walk all over. They suffered a whole lot . . . since they were little. My father got old and he still hasn't been able to get ahead. We have always been screwed over. When we grew up, suffering was a part of our parents' and our grandparents' lives. They told us about the suffering they went through.

LYNN: Did your parents speak Tojolabal?

JUAN: Yes, my parents did. My father came from Carmen Yashalá. He came from there, in the direction of Ocosingo and Altamirano. They came to live here. They came here, but those who were the first ones here aren't alive any more. Those who lived continued to work here.

LYNN: When did they begin to organize this community?

JUAN: I think it would be about three or four years ago. When I was twenty-five years old. That was when we started to organize some work here.

LYNN: How is the community organized?

JUAN: The work is organized communally. In terms of our work, we work our cornfields together.

As my conversation with Juan wound down, a woman approached us. Ruth was in her early forties; she told us that she had two children, already grown. She was holding her first grandchild as we began talking. She had been designated to speak for the women, and others followed her to where I was taping. Juan, who turned out to be a local authority, had sent the women over upon learning that we were interested in speaking with them about their experience in the army occupation. When the Mexican military invaded EZLN-held communities, women had taken an active role in driving out and controlling the military in many communities, and in representing community defense efforts to the press and other media. Ruth had become an official spokesperson from La Realidad, representing women. She told her story with finesse, then inquired where and how the information would be used. She was a sophisticated leader, willing to talk to get her point of view across and publicize what was happening in her community. She also held those to whom she provided information accountable for publicizing what she shared. This was my obligation, as well, understood from the moment she motioned me to turn on my tape recorder.

LYNN: Can you tell us a little about how the army arrived on 9 February 1995.

RUTH: The soldiers who arrived here told us that they were offering medicine and were going to provide medical care for our children. That is what they shouted at us so that we would come together in a meeting in order to see that they had come for peace, that they didn't come to do us harm. But we, as indigenous people, we didn't accept this because we still are frightened when the civilian doctors come here, so we are even more frightened by the army that says that we should trust them and let them enter our community in order to provide medical care for us. . . . We came together and we decided we didn't want them here. We didn't accept their presence. We want the government to accept what we want, what we need.

LYNN: What is it that you want?

RUTH: We want the basic necessities. We don't have soap, we don't have money to buy things we need for our homes, we don't have good health, we don't have good housing. That is everything we need. We don't want the Mexican Army to come here and offer us a few things, because they don't even give out the little amount of what they bring. Because of this, we organized ourselves, the women. We don't want them here. We aren't in agreement to receive things from the army.

LYNN: How were the women organized?

RUTH: We organized ourselves. We said that we don't want them here. We pushed up against them and told them to retreat because our children get frightened when they see the weapons, when they see their vehicles. They come with tanks, with machine guns, this is what we don't accept. So we shouted, "We don't want you to come here." The whole town was shouting. We had to shout at them.

LYNN: Have they left? Or are they still here?

RUTH: They are still around but not in the community permanently. It's because the first time that they came through and shouted that they were going to give us medicine, we were in the mountains. We were not in the community. We weren't here. The next day they came again, they returned. They broke all the fence pickets that surround the community and threw them all away. They were going to meet here, to fill it up with the army. But because we organized ourselves . . . we didn't let them into our community. If we had let them in, we would have had to leave. I don't know where they would have sent us.

LYNN: You have to plant now, don't you? And gather firewood? Is it a problem for you to go to the countryside to get firewood, now?

RUTH: Yes, it is. That is what we shouted at them. We need our firewood, little stalks of wood, that is what we burn here. They told us that they would even provide us with firewood, that they would help us collect it, but we told them no. Because we don't want the Mexican Army to help us. They are walking around with weapons. No, we don't trust them.

LYNN: As we discussed before, is there a message you would like to send to the United States?

RUTH: Well, we would like to get support. . . . We would like more support, if you want to help us, we need more strikes. We need you to help us to shout that we don't want the army here any more. For example, they say that they are here for peace, but how can they be asking for peace? How can we have peace when the army is here? The dialogue can't happen while the army is here.[2] Before, they used to come once a week, but now they are here on a daily basis, night and day they come through. . . . They treat us like we don't know what we are talking about. We aren't as stupid as the way they treat us. They don't respect us.

LYNN: Before the army arrived last month, was it peaceful here?

RUTH: Yes, yes. Of course. We were organized, working, peaceful, happy to walk around. But now we hear, "Here they come," and the kids say "Here they come again," and we hear their vehicles and the soldiers. The kids get frightened, and even we the women . . . we are so frightened. He who has a little courage doesn't get as frightened. They don't get scared. But the person who does get frightened. . . . We were trembling here with fright.

LYNN: What kinds of hopes do you have for the future?

RUTH: We hope that we are tranquil, that we are organized, that we can get out of this. The government doesn't understand us. They don't take us into account. They offer us so many things, but all they do is make demands. They didn't give us the things that we needed. So the people rose up, they organized. Now all of us are organized. But we want things for all of us, not just for one of us or one community. We don't want just one community to be liberated, but all of them. We want the whole country to be liberated. . . .

   What I wanted to know is, how can you help us? What kind of support can you offer us and in what form? You come to get this information from us? We also want to know where you are going to take this information? Where are you going to put it? What kind of support can you offer us?

LYNN: I am going to try to answer the best we can. This group here is a caravan from a group called Pastors for Peace. This caravan passed through one hundred towns in the United States telling about the situation here, calling together meetings, and asking for humanitarian aid—rice, beans, other types of food. The help is important. But just as important is organizing the people there and telling them about the situation here.

RUTH: You have to organize people.

LYNN: Yes. That is what I know. This interview and things I write can be a resource so that people who get interested have information to work with. So that they believe what is going on, by listening to your words. Maybe, then, when they read about something in the paper and it says that everything is fine in Mexico, they will say, "That isn't true. That is a lie, because Señora Ruth told us a different story." They are going to say "I believe the Señora, not the newspaper."

We chatted with more people and then rested. The story of Ruth stayed with me as I watched more and more women in a great variety of communities stand up to the presence of the Mexican Army. In the midst of low-intensity war and continued army occupation, women became more and more vital to allowing Zapatista sympathizers to maintain some control within their communities and to open up small spaces for continued resistance.

Women like Ruth are clearly overstepping the boundary of acceptable female behavior in the face of a military invasion. The fact that Ruth is indigenous Tojolabal adds another dimension to her challenge. Defiant acts, such as shouting at the soldiers until they leave the community, work sharply against stereotypical images of indigenous women. Through their actions, women such as Ruth are redefining historical images of indigenous women. By being active, women like Ruth provide an important countertrope to the inherited colonial images of indigenous women as passive victims.

THE LOW-INTENSITY WAR CONTINUES IN LA REALIDAD

I returned to La Realidad in July 1996, and again in July 1997, to follow up on the longer-term effects of army occupation. What I found was continued militarization and a disturbing sense of permanent alarm that had become part of daily life. The emergency conditions of 1995 had been extended into a permanent occupation. The road to La Realidad had been graded and greatly improved by the army, which was preparing to connect it to another improved road section, which ran through the Tzeltal canyon joining San Quintín with Ocosingo. The army was tightening its circle around Zapatista communities and was about to complete a triangle of improved roads linking Ocosingo, Altamirano, Comitán, Las Margaritas, and San Quintín. With this infrastructure in place, the army was coordinating actions with the Public Security Police of Chiapas, as well as the Federal Judicial Police, to gain even tighter control of the population. Roadblocks multiplied; more immigration posts appeared to monitor the activities of foreign human rights workers, observers, and others. Local populations were stopped and searched each and every time they left their communities to travel to a neighboring city to attend to a medical need, sell produce, or purchase basic goods. In a word, the army had become a permanent part of the landscape.

On a hot morning in La Realidad, I met with a group of community authorities, men and women, to discuss the current situation. Pedro, the designated community authority, began our meeting by discussing the effects of the occupation.

LYNN: What has been the impact of the army's presence here?

PEDRO: They are cutting down the forests. They use wood without thinking
           about the community. They don't ask permission if they are chop-
           ping down a tree. They make whatever they want to build and they
           destroy the mountains. . . .

           The army comes through here, one day yes, one day no. So the
           women don't really want to walk in the road. They are afraid. If
           they have to move their firewood from one place to another . . . they
           always run into the army. The army completely occupies the road.
           They frighten the children. The children see them walking by with
           machine guns. Before, the children hadn't seen this type of weapon.
           . . . The army arrived, and, up to today, they haven't left. So this has
           affected us. . . .

           [President] Zedillo isn't concerned about the people. He doesn't
           think about the people, women, children. The army is still here. We
           don't know when they are going to leave or when the government
           will take this army out. We never saw anything like this before.

           The army came in when the armed movement emerged. They told
           us that they were watching out for the communities, that they sup-
           ported us. But truth is that today it is 505 years later and they still
           haven't begun to be concerned about the people. There are some
           children who are sick from *susto* [magical fright] from the presence
           of the army. They come down the road, they stop there [pointing].
           The children are afraid they are going to take over the town. . . .

           Last Monday of this week, a driver from the Mexican Army al-
           most hit a passenger bus from here. It was full of people coming
           from Las Margaritas. There was going to be an accident because the
           Mexican Army doesn't slow down in the curves. . . . They go tear-
           ing down the mountains, and it doesn't matter to them whether or
           not other vehicles are coming or not. The army vehicle would have
           hit this civilian bus. Fortunately, the chauffeur who was driving the
           bus saw the army [vehicle] and he swerved into a ditch. He just man-
           aged to save the bus, but barely. This is the kind of thing that hap-
           pens here. Even the passenger buses who carry those going to the
           city have to face this as part of daily life. The ugly thing is that the
           army causes all of these situations. Dozens of compañeros, dozens
           of compañeras, or dozens of children who ride on the bus are at risk
           because the army goes tearing around. They get into accidents.
           Nothing will happen to the people in the army vehicles, but the civil-
           ian vehicles will suffer damage. In this case, it was lucky because
           there was a place for the bus to go. But if they had encountered each
           other in a dangerous curve with a steep canyon below, the driver of
           the bus couldn't have saved the people.

           This is what the Mexican Army is doing. Instead of taking care of
           people like the government says, this is what they do. They aren't
           helping people at all. They want to cause accidents. . . .

I want to say something about the Mexican Army. The EZLN—
that is, the Zapatista Army of National Liberation—shows that it
doesn't want war, but wants the participation of society. But Zedillo
doesn't understand this. So we don't trust him. The army is here in
the jungle and even they are confused, because we are struggling for
their families as well. We know that they work in the army because
they don't have land. They are poor like us. Because of this, they are
giving their life for money. It isn't because they are doing it for their
people. Because of this, the EZLN doesn't want to kill the army.

We don't want to kill the army, because what we are really doing
is supporting them—their mothers, fathers, brothers, sisters, their
in-laws, their aunts and uncles, their children, their grandchildren.
We are asking that the children of the people in the army have food,
that they have land, that they have good health, that they have education, that they have the ten points that we have talked about. Our
struggle is for everyone—that there is justice, liberty, democracy,
peace.

But we see that there isn't peace now. Because, in 1994, Carlos Salinas de Gortari brought Swiss airplanes here. He brought airplanes
equipped to bomb, he brought helicopters. Now Zedillo is arming
and militarizing the country. He defends a small group of the rich.
We don't say "rich" for someone who has ten or fifteen cars. We
don't call them rich. Those who are rich are those who have power,
the big businessmen, big landowners—latifundistas. That is why the
soldiers are there—defending the interests of the bourgeois of the
monopolies, of the oligarchy. What we want at the international and
national level, all over the world, is that everything has life. We don't
want to destroy our life as humans. Because we all have the right
to live.

Another woman, María, joined in the conversation. She was about thirty-
five years old and had been designated to speak for the women in the
community. She began by telling about the occupation of the community on 9 February 1995. (The date had become a significant marker in
local history, and any assessment had to begin with a retelling of that bad
moment.) María began talking without responding to questions, sure of
herself.

MARÍA: When the army came to take this community it was the ninth of Feb-
           ruary 1995, and we fled, we ran away. We took all of the kids with
           us. The children were really afraid when the army took over on
           9 February. . . .
           We fled, we ran to our ejido land. We went on one side and settled
           there. Then the army came after us and screamed at us that we
           should return to our community, that they wouldn't do anything.
           They said they came for peace. They said they hadn't come to bother
           the people.

We didn't come back. But the next day we came back and we started to yell at them. We ran them out with all of the women. A group of women stood and we screamed at the army to leave, that they get out of here. The army doesn't belong here in our community.

We are the owners here. We are in charge of the community. The army belongs in the city, in their barracks. They only came here to frighten the women.

People are getting sick with fear from their presence, right to this very day. It is still going on. You saw today in the morning [when the army crawled through town on patrol]. We aren't telling lies about what the army does, like Zedillo says. He says that we are telling lies. Now you realize, those of you who come from different countries, that the army continues to come into our communities. But we can't do our work.

For example, we have coffee fields that are off of this road. But we can't even walk there, because the Mexican Army is going back and forth, watching us to see what we are doing to make sure we don't do anything. They say they won't do anything to us, but then they will come and they will betray us. In the moment when we are in the road, they say, "We won't do anything" so that we will go by them, but afterward they will come. . . .

The government says that we don't have the right to participate, but we do have that right—to talk, to say what our needs are. We suffer a lot of hardships with our children. We have children dying of diseases. We don't have good schools, we don't have good education, we don't have good health. But the government doesn't care about this. They don't take us into consideration. It is true that many of us are dying of diseases.

They don't see how we are living in our community. They don't come to see whether or not we have good medicine. Our children die of simple diarrhea. They die vomiting, of worms. But the government doesn't take this into consideration. But we have this experience and we have reflected on what kinds of necessities our children have. We know what we are fighting for, as women. We want those basic necessities. We have to struggle for these basic things as women. We have to participate. . . . We have to go out and shout at them. . . . These are the things we have to talk about. It isn't just here in this community where we need these things, but everywhere. All over Mexico, people need these basic things.

CONCLUSIONS

The insights of Comandante Concepción, Comandante Marisela, Captain Maribel, Lieutenant Norma, Major Eliseo, Rosibel, Marcos, Marisól, Juan, Ruth, Pedro, and María suggest a deeply entrenched social movement with many committed participants with varying experiences. They offer insight into the individual experiences of self-named Zapatistas and suggest what some key issues have been both within the military wing of the EZLN and in base communities. The struggle to implement changes in gender roles as prescribed in the Revolutionary Law of Women is an ongoing one, which operates in fits and starts and will no doubt continue in this style. While some members of the EZLN have begun to change their behavior to accommodate a model of equality for men and women, others have not yet begun. The struggle to implement some ideas of the Revolutionary Law of Women is not only found at the community level but also at the highest levels of negotiation between the EZLN and the Mexican government. While the presence of women is acknowledged in the San Andrés Accords on Indigenous Rights and Culture, and minimal protections are offered to women to guarantee their political participation at the community level, many issues brought forward by Zapatista women (and contained in the Revolutionary Law of Women), by some of their advisors, and by other indigenous women in Mexico—such as equal land rights, sanctions for sexual violence and rape, more equal division of labor in the home, and the democratization of domestic gender relations—are absent. These more fundamental issues remain invisible in the formal documents signed by the government and the EZLN.

The pressure of low-intensity war has provided the framework for daily life in many Zapatista communities and has fallen on everyone in the region, Zapatista or not. Those who supported the PRI now get extra government benefits, such as new housing materials, but many who are neither Zapatistas nor government supporters have also suffered greatly in the war. While the first priority in EZLN communities has remained survival, this situation has also brought women to the forefront of their communities, where they have actively participated in pushing the army out, defending their communities against paramilitaries, and representing this struggle to the outside world. This has been a change for many women. At the same time, many have remained constrained by "uses and customs" that keep them at home, discourage their independence, and prevent their participation as local and regional leaders.

War and radical change often produce contradictory effects, in the arena of gender relations and elsewhere. The testimonies offered here provide personal interpretations of some of these contradictions. At another level, they are also meant to bring forward the personal passion and integrity that I found in so many I talked with in EZLN communities. It is this integrity and moral conviction that, along with the figure of Emiliano Zapata and the media, carried Zapatismo to other corners of Mexico. In the next section of this book, we shall move to the neighboring state of Oaxaca to understand how Zapatismo played in two ejidos in the central valleys.

PART III

New and Old Zapatismo in Oaxaca

CHAPTER 8

The Historical Roots of Land Conflict and Organizing in Oaxaca

While both support for and opposition to the Zapatistas is well documented in the case of Chiapas, little attention has been paid to the reception to Zapatismo in other parts of rural Mexico. The next three chapters are written as a historical comparison to the stories of the ejidos of Guadalupe Tepeyac and La Realidad and to describe in detail the ways ejidos formed in other primarily indigenous parts of Mexico resulted in different local experiences with the government and agrarian officials. In these chapters, I discuss the particular cases of the Zapotec ejido of Santa María del Tule, formed in 1917, and the Zapotec and mestizo ejido of Unión Zapata, formed in 1936, both located in the central valleys of Oaxaca.

I begin in this chapter with a historical description of Oaxaca, focused on the period marking Mexican independence and soon afterward, to provide background for the stories of the two ejidos. There are important historical differences between central Oaxaca and eastern lowland Chiapas with regard to land distribution and conflict over land, which significantly affected the experiences of local ejidatarios in their interactions with agrarian officials. While eastern Chiapas came to be dominated by large coffee and cattle ranches, along with logging operations, central Oaxaca consisted primarily of small-scale subsistence farming, with relatively few haciendas. The land conflicts that emerged in Oaxaca during the colonial period and later were most often between indigenous communities.

Differences in the political history of the two states with regard to the nature of relations between indigenous communities and government officials are also important on a general level. State-community interactions, through the granting of ejido land and, more recently, in the treatment of independent and autonomous peasant organizations by the government have differed somewhat in Oaxaca and Chiapas. It is important, too, that, notwithstanding general trends in Oaxaca and Chiapas, there were also important regional differences within each state. This book focuses on a specific part of Chiapas (the canyons of the Lacandon jungle in eastern Chiapas) and on a specific part of Oaxaca (the central valleys), and the government-community interactions depicted for these regions are not meant to represent those in either Oaxaca or Chiapas as a whole.

In eastern Chiapas, even after people received land through the granting of the ejidos (often in the 1960s and later), when they organized independently to improve the conditions of production, they were severely repressed by state police and the army. In the central valleys of Oaxaca, because of friendly historical relations with the government, Zapotecs often joined state-run peasant organizations like the Confederación Nacional Campesina and did not suffer repression.

The different experience of the Isthmus Zapotecs with the government is also described in this chapter, to underscore the point that even in the same state and among the same ethnic group, distinct political experiences and identities can coexist. In the Isthmus, where open rebellion had ignited several times during the past two centuries, independently organized Zapotecs did suffer repression, both when they tried to secede from the state of Oaxaca in the mid 1800s and when they organized an opposition government in the 1970s. The level of repression was less than in the state of Chiapas, but quite significant. The Mixtec region of Oaxaca, in contrast to the central valleys, was also the site of significant indigenous rebellions in the eighteenth century. Understanding these local historical differences in relations with the government through time is important for understanding contemporary reactions to government policies and even to political campaigns and voting.

INDIGENOUS STRUGGLES TO CONTROL
LAND IN COLONIAL OAXACA

Historical studies of Oaxaca during the colonial period reveal that there, as opposed to other parts of Mexico, indigenous individuals and com-

munities were able to resist Spanish encroachment on their lands. Spaniards led by Gonzalo de Umbría arrived in Oaxaca in 1519 by way of the
Mixtec region. Another year passed before other expeditions reached
further into the area and into the central valleys. Although the Spaniards
were able to consolidate their presence in some parts of Oaxaca, such as
Tehuantepec and the central valleys, where they made alliances with local rulers, they did not have a constant presence elsewhere in the region
until after 1530, and some indigenous groups continued to resist (Romero Frizzi 1988, 111). The Mixe fiercely defended their territory until
the end of the sixteenth century (Cortés 1983, 147)

Most of the land in Oaxaca remained in the possession of indigenous
communities for the first part of the colonial period, because indigenous
communities held more land grants than did the Spanish in many areas
through the sixteenth century (Romero Frizzi 1988, 137). In the Mixteca,
central valleys, and Isthmus regions, indigenous holders of land grants
outstripped the Spanish in terms of the number of cattle-ranching properties held from 1540 to 1610, for example (ibid., 130, graph 1). Because the crown insisted on respecting the rights of indigenous rulers
and their descendants, only lands that were royal patrimonies were officially granted to Spanish immigrants. The land grants held by indigenous people gave them rights over their lands, which could be defended
in Spanish courts. Indigenous peoples in Oaxaca used colonial courts to
retain their land. Spanish courts respected land held by individual indigenous rulers or caciques, as well as that held by communities. In the
Spanish courts, caciques and communities would often battle over land
rights. Thus, land battles in colonial courts were not only between indigenous communities and Spanish immigrants but also between indigenous caciques and communities. Nevertheless, aided by epidemics, which
were even worse on the coast than in the central part of the state, and
despite the insistence of Spanish colonial law that lands granted to Spaniards were in no way to affect indigenous holdings, the Spanish did
acquire some large land grants, which were eventually converted into
haciendas. Because the coast of Oaxaca was almost depopulated by epidemics of measles and smallpox, the Spanish acquired more land there.

In colonial Oaxaca, a majority of the land battles took place between
indigenous peoples, not between Spaniards and indigenous peoples. Such
battles could be between indigenous communities, between indigenous
caciques who continued to accumulate land grants and communities, or
between competing caciques; most often they were between competing
indigenous communities. William Taylor found that of fifty-two docu-

mented land disputes in the central valleys during the eighteenth century (at a time when haciendas were expanding), thirty-seven were between indigenous communities and only thirteen between indigenous communities and haciendas (two pitted an indigenous town against an indigenous individual) (Taylor 1972, 84). Five of these disputes went on for nearly a century. Several towns, such as Tlacochaguaya and Tlalixtac, were notorious for gobbling up the common lands of smaller surrounding communities (ibid., 88). Sometimes settlement was reached by kidnapping leading citizens from a rival town until agreement came about (ibid., 85).

The Tlacolula arm of the central valleys of Oaxaca escaped the major changes in land tenure experienced elsewhere. This is the area in which the two ejidos studied in the next chapter are located; in this region, the only large estate granted was the Guendulain Mayorazgo (see chapter 9). Other than that, most land was held by indigenous communities, with the exception of some small agricultural properties held by the Church, called *labores*. Most land was relatively infertile and only rain-fed, decreasing its value. Indigenous towns such as Tlalixtac grew at the expense of others, including Santa María del Tule. Tlalixtac included two sheep ranches and had fertile land and well-kept houses, in comparison to some of its poorer neighbors (Taylor 1972, 104) (see chapter 9). In evaluating the state of indigenous landholders in the central valleys at the end of the colonial period, Taylor states:

> They worked the best of the Valley's cropland in the sixteenth century and in general were still self-sufficient farmers on the eve of the independence movement in 1810. Only a handful of communities became dependent on lands they did not own. . . . The Indian peasant actually had more communal and personal land at his disposal in the colonial period than he has today, owing to the recent growth of Oaxaca's population and the limited possibilities for land redistribution after the Revolution of 1910. (Taylor 1972, 107)

Taylor also concludes that, although there were private and Church-owned haciendas, Spanish estates in the valleys of Oaxaca were very different from conventional haciendas. In general, they were small and fragmented; there were as many farms as haciendas (ibid., 200). At the end of the colonial period, non-Indians held less than half the land in the central valleys; individual Indians and indigenous communities controlled about two-thirds of the agricultural land during the last one hundred years of Spanish rule; and the priesthood made the most significant gains in landownership, usually at the expense of Spaniards (ibid., 201). Thus, many indigenous peoples of the central valleys of Oaxaca had a very different colonial experience than had those in eastern Chiapas.

COLONIAL REBELLIONS IN OAXACA

If indigenous communities often battled with each other during the colonial period over land, they also rebelled against unreasonable authority, just as in the highlands of Chiapas. In a study that included nineteen judicial investigations of the Mixteca Alta and thirty-two from the Valley of Oaxaca from 1680 to 1811, William Taylor found that most rebellions were "against individuals who personally embodied the abuse of authority in specific local cases of perceived deprivation of tyranny: the alcalde mayor [the Spanish official in charge of a district], his lieutenant in charge of the village, the royal tax collector, or the parish priest" (Taylor 1979, 133–34). Most of these rebellions involved arms that were basically work implements, such as shovels, pickaxes, hatchets, machetes, hoes, iron bars, knives, lances, and powdered chili peppers, used to blind and immobilize the enemy temporarily. While few rebellions involved the use of firearms, more serious endeavors did involve spears, javelins, horses, and bows and arrows (ibid., 115).

Most often, protests and rebellions were begun because of the imposition of tribute, forced work, certain kinds of punishments applied by hacendados and government officials, or intervention in community affairs. In 1719, an indigenous woman named Mariana, from Santa Lucía near the city of Oaxaca, led a mob of men and women against a "group of royal officials, priests, and militiamen who had come to mark the town's boundaries" (Taylor 1979, 116). She took on one of the Spaniards in hand-to-hand combat, and eventually the Spanish officials were driven out of the community by a rock-throwing barrage. Taylor notes that women were quite active in uprisings in Oaxaca.

In the Sierra Norte, three communities joined together in the 1770s to rebel against local officials who had demanded that they turn in their cochineal dye and who wanted to impose a local liquor tax (Reina 1988, 205). Other towns in the Mixteca Alta joined in an armed movement against officials in 1738, when a Spanish alcalde ordered locals to receive fifty lashes and imposed other harsh punishments (Taylor 1979, 89; Reina 1988, 205).

INDIGENOUS REBELLIONS OUTSIDE THE CENTRAL
VALLEYS DURING AND AFTER INDEPENDENCE

Oaxaca did not fully enter the independence movement until 1812, when a Mixtec muleteer named Valerio Trujano headed up a guerrilla struggle in two communities equipped by an arms shipment from Veracruz (Reina 1988, 213). The Mixtecos continued to fight against royalists under the banner of José María Morelos, the most important military commander and politician of the independence movement. In Cuatula Amilpa, rebel forces under the leadership of Morelos survived a lengthy siege by royalist troops. Later, after suffering severe starvation, Morelos, the Mixtec rebels, and others fled. Morelos occupied Oaxaca and Acapulco in 1813. In 1815, however, a reorganized royalist army defeated Morelos, and he was captured and tried. In 1816 he was executed, but the guerrilla war continued (Archer 1997, 1597–98). Leticia Reina argues that the experience of the Mixtec rebels and their communities under Morelos was transformative:

> What the communities learned during this war—the motto of Morelos which said that land should be turned over to communities and the experience of living with relative autonomy during those years—all of this transformed the communities. From this point on, the communities coalesced ever more strongly in the face of outside aggression, and they never stopped struggling to survive as a corporate group and to have their autonomy respected. (Reina 1988, 245)

While the revolution for independence in Mexico was carried on in the name of "the people," the outcome for indigenous people who had actively participated was not good. The new administrators who came to power in Oaxaca and elsewhere in 1821 were committed to building a "modern nation." This vision of the "modern nation" largely excluded indigenous people, who in Oaxaca were still a major part of the population. By 1857, Oaxaca was still 87 percent indigenous, 12 percent mestizo, and 1 percent "other," including 4,500 "Africans" and 156 Europeans (González Navarro 1958, 176, cited in Reina 1988, 245). Among the changes that would most affect indigenous communities were attempts to eliminate colonial legislation used by indigenous communities and individuals to defend their land rights (Reina 1988, 221). The Agrarian Law passed in 1826 in the state of Oaxaca removed the right of community officials to represent their communities in court. After independence, indigenous rebellion continued in Oaxaca, focused first in the Mixtec region and then in the Isthmus Zapotec area. The central valleys remained an area of relative support for the new government of independent Mexico.

The Mixtecs and others in the Mixtec region continued to use their experience in guerrilla warfare after independence. From the 1830s until the 1850s, a series of rebellions that included Mixtecs and Triquis took place in the Mixtec region. In 1842, President Antonio López de Santa Ana imposed a head tax of one real (a monetary unit equivalent to one-eighth of a peso) a month on all adult males between the ages of sixteen and sixty years of age. Mixtecs, Triquis, Amuzgos, and Tlapanecos joined together to fight the tax and defend their lands. By the end of 1843, there were eight thousand rebels in the region (Reina 1988, 251). Federal troops were sent, and the confrontation continued. The conflict lost steam when U.S. troops entered Mexico and the rebels were invited to fight against the United States. What this episode in Oaxacan history suggests—as do later revolts in Chiapas such as the Indian movement of 1867–69—is that the liberal reforms that began after independence, and that deprived indigenous peoples of control over their culture, resources, and patterns of economic development, were not met passively. In some areas, such reforms were actively contested, as they have been again at the end of the twentieth century. A further example from the Isthmus area confirms this.

The Isthmus Zapotecs of southern Oaxaca had a long history of struggle for autonomy. Isthmus colonial history was marked by periodic armed rebellions against the Spaniards (Tutino 1993). After Mexican independence, the Isthmus Zapotec town of Juchitán became the center of rebellions against Oaxacan state government authorities in 1827 and in 1847–51. The Zapotecs of the central valleys of Oaxaca did not rebel in the same manner, focusing more on local issues (see the next chapter); in fact, they worked with state officials. Zapotecs from the central valleys lost some communal lands under the liberal reforms of 1856, but never proposed seceding from Oaxaca. The Isthmus Zapotec post-independence rebellions against the state authorities were grounded in changes in laws so as to allow the privatization of corporate property. When what had been considered communal property was given as an individual concession to an entrepreneur, protests mounted and eventually escalated into a move to secede from the state of Oaxaca.

In the Isthmus, the salt pans and salt-water lagoons lining the seacoast were a major source of livelihood for Zapotec, Chontal, and Huave coastal populations. In 1825, the governor of Oaxaca passed a law that proposed giving a monopoly of the salt lagoons and pans to "an individual who could exploit the salt much more economically than the Indians could" (Reina 1988, 255). After the monopoly was granted to an individual, Francisco Javier Echeverría, the Zapotecs of Juchitán rose up in arms to defend their rights to use the salt beds, and also to protest the centralization of rents imposed by the government. In addition to continuing to exploit the salt beds, the Zapotecs of the Isthmus were planting on the lands of haciendas that had long formed part of the estate of the Marqués del Valle. In 1836, the haciendas of the Marqués del Valle were sold to two Europeans, who wanted the Zapotecs off the land. The foreigners turned to the government authorities to defend their cause. In 1842, the Zapotecs of Juchitán expelled some of these authorities.

The conflict that began in 1842 subsided with negotiations in 1845, when the national government offered to recognize at least some Zapotec land claims. For a few years, the dispute languished while Mexico was preoccupied with the war provoked by the United States. But in 1848, when Benito Juárez took office as governor, he determined to stabilize what he saw as chaos in the Isthmus. He appointed a local leader of the previous resistance, José Gregorio Meléndez, to lead the militia charged with enforcing state power.

Unfortunately for Juárez, Meléndez refused to become a representative of the state and declared the separation of the Isthmus from Oaxaca (Tutino 1993, 57). For the next two years, Meléndez and others defied state authority, using the salt beds and continuing to cultivate disputed lands. They also jailed a local official responsible for the earlier sale of community lands. State officials freed the captive and jailed several Zapotec leaders. In retaliation, Meléndez organized a large force of angry Juchitecos (ibid.).

Determined to enforce his liberal agenda of privatization and to honor the claims of the hacendados and the salt monopolist, Juárez sent in four hundred troops, as well as light artillery. In one battle outside Juchitán in 1850, seventy indigenous rebels were killed. Nevertheless, the government could not pacify the rebels of Juchitán with guns. Meléndez evaded government control, sacked several haciendas, and remained hidden in the area. Cholera then struck hard at the occupying troops, and the army collapsed. Meléndez and his troops claimed control of Juchitán, and, for the remainder of 1850 and most of 1851, Juchitecos ruled themselves (Tutino 1993, 58). In 1851, however, Juárez assembled a large army, secured the immediate surrender of most Juchitecos, and then installed a new municipal council loyal to the state. The liberal state thus regained control, but Juchitán remained a site of future resistance, rising again in the 1970s.

The indigenous rebellions of Juchitán and of the Mixtecos demonstrate the contested nature of the implementation of liberal reforms in Oaxaca. While such rebellions did not occur in the central valleys, they suggest the variety of ways in which incipient liberal state formation was received by indigenous communities in Oaxaca.

BENITO JUÁREZ AND THE REFORM PERIOD: PRIVATIZATION OF LAND

During his second term, from 1856 to 1857, the indigenous governor of Oaxaca, Benito Juárez, implemented laws to radically reorganize rural land tenure. In 1856, during the reform period, a sweeping law, the "Ley Lerdo," abolished the property rights of all corporate organizations. The decree did not call for the "expropriation of property, but rather aimed at converting corporate wealth from real estate to liquid assets" (Berry 1981, 31). The law also endorsed the principles of economic individualism, advocating that only individuals should own properties. The primary targets of the law were properties controlled by the Church and administered by town councils and indigenous communities. John Tutino suggests that the economic liberals who promoted the Ley Lerdo had the conscious goal of ending community landholding and were clear about their objectives (Tutino 1986, 259). Indeed, liberal leaders such as Juárez believed that the Ley Lerdo would create a pattern of free enterprise that would bring prosperity to Mexico. With Church and indigenous property moving into the market, liberal leaders thought they would spread prosperity throughout Mexico. Their predictions did not come true, however. Rather than Mexico becoming a nation of small to medium-sized farms, the results were varied. Although large landowners and speculators acquired Church and village properties in some regions of Mexico, elsewhere the reform had little effect. The impact at regional and local levels varied significantly. In Oaxaca, important changes in landholding patterns did occur, but these varied by region, with some areas having a much higher percentage of former communal lands privatized than had others. The largest amount of land was not privatized immediately after the reforms, but much later, from 1880 to 1910.

The central valleys of Oaxaca were the only locations in that state where some indigenous land was converted to individual, privately owned plots immediately after the announcement of the Ley Lerdo. According to Charles Berry (1981, 176), there were villages that quickly sold some of the common lands dedicated to the support of *cofradías* (religious brotherhoods that conducted the ritual celebrations for the local saints), or divided these lands among community members, asking each to pay a small sum to the municipal government for the plot received. Manuel Esparza (1988, 287) notes that although practically every district in Oaxaca had initiated the process of dividing common lands in 1856, most did not culminate that process until later (if ever), some in the 1870s and more in the 1880s. Esparza (ibid., 288) confirms Berry's observation that the municipalities closest to the control of the liberals in the capital city were those least able to resist the legal dispositions of the reformers. These were the lands of Zapotec communities in the central valleys. In contrast to those in other parts of the state, however, the communities of the central valleys already had a higher percentage of land in private holdings than in communal holdings in 1856. Many of the private holders were indigenous. Thus in many central valley Zapotec communities, indigenous citizens were already private landholders before the 1856 law was written. Elsewhere in Oaxaca, indigenous authorities were suspicious of the law and ignored it (Berry 1981, 177–78).

Citing what he calls a somewhat superficial review of more than one thousand land documents (*expedientes*), Esparza states that, in Oaxaca, "from 1880 to 1910 the largest amount of land was privatized in the greatest number of districts and in greater quantities than in previous decades" (Esparza 1988, 289). While Esparza agrees with Berry that the central valleys had more private holdings held by indigenous people than elsewhere, he also states that in the central valleys, as in other districts, there were communities that showed great interest in privatizing their land through either *repartos* (land distributed to community members with no charge) or *adjudiciaciones* (sales made—often forced—to tenants and other individuals who claimed the right to buy communal land for reasons stipulated by the Lerdo law or by state or other law). In 1889, the state government of Oaxaca passed a law requiring municipios to declare the income received from the sale of land to individuals. The law also reiterated that local authorities had to provide documentation of their division of communal lands in accordance with an earlier regulation (from 1862) that specified that all communal lands should be divided up among local citizens, including widows and single men. The lots were not to exceed 200 pesos in value and were not to involve any charge for the benefactors (ibid., 283).

In 1890, another state law explicated which lands specifically were subject to division and asked municipal authorities to provide documentation of who had claims to which parcels and to specify lands not claimed. Unclaimed lands were thus available for purchase after a three-month period. While this 1890 law was the most draconian, in that it required the privatization of all communal land except the *fundo legal* (the townsite to which every community was entitled), it was abrogated by a 1894 law that reinstated the exclusion of *ejidos,* or communal lands, and *montes,* or uncultivated mountainous regions surrounding communities. The existence of a legal exclusion did not guarantee that privatization of such lands did not take place, however. The period from 1880 to 1910 saw the greatest quantity of indigenous land privatized in Oaxaca, through division within local communities and through sales. By 1910, 53 percent of the state's territory had been privatized. The top three areas of privatization included the Cañada-Tuxtepec region, where 2,493,538 hectares were privatized between 1889 and 1903; the Isthmus and south coast, where 1,714,689 hectares were privatized in the same period; and the central valleys region, where 510,792 hectares were privatized during this time (Esparza 1988, 290). These areas include the best agricultural land in the state. Most of this land, however, probably went to community members, not to outsiders.[1]

With 53 percent of the state's territory privatized by 1910, Oaxaca's land tenure system underwent significant change. Francie Chassen-López (1994, 33) maintains, with Esparza (1988), that the land tenure system in Oaxaca underwent an important transformation: *comuneros* became private owners of small plots and some private interests established fincas on larger tracts. Because indigenous communities and individuals had retained much more land before independence, however, the outcome of the reforms for indigenous communities in central Oaxaca was not nearly as devastating as in eastern Chiapas, where most indigenous land had been privatized by 1910, when as much as 50 percent of the rural workforce was made up of indebted, landless servants (Harvey 1998, 59).

THE MEXICAN REVOLUTION AND
THE FORMATION OF EJIDOS IN OAXACA

While some analysts, such as Ronald Waterbury, have stated that during the Mexican Revolution, indigenous peasants in Oaxaca defended the status quo (Waterbury 1975), others have documented currents of Za-

patismo in Oaxaca, tied to specific locations such as Silacayoapan, Za-
potitlán Lagunas, Huajuapam de León, and La Pradera, all located in
the traditionally rebellious region of the Mixteca (Ruiz Cervantes 1990,
274). And a regional rebellion in Juchitán, led by Che Gómez, is viewed
by many as an important part of what happened in Oaxaca during the
years of the Mexican Revolution.

In the winter of 1911, Che Gómez's mobilization against an imposed
mayor who had replaced him became the largest armed rebellion after
Zapatismo in Morelos during that same year (Knight 1986, 376; Campbell 1990, 156–62). The imposed mayor for Juchitán in 1911, Francisco
León, was accompanied by two hundred government soldiers. Thousands of Gómez supporters came out to meet León's military escort and,
after battling with the federal troops and killing a judge, a tax collector, and many soldiers, some five thousand *Chegomistas* retreated to
allied villages (Campbell 1990, 161). Gómez called for independence
from Oaxaca and for the establishment of a sovereign Isthmus territory. Gómez was later killed by agents of the governor, but twenty-five
hundred Juchitecos continued the uprising for another eight months
(ibid.).

Probably the most important statewide movement in Oaxaca during
the period from 1915 to 1920 was the state's declaration, on four occasions, of its sovereignty and autonomy from the Mexican nation. A succession of occupations by troops from the Sierra Juárez, led by Guillermo Meixueiro, General Isaac Ibarra of Oaxaca City, and others, led
to continued instability in the state (see Ruiz Cervantes 1985). Those
who were part of the state's sovereignty movement declared the Reform
Constitution of 1857 to be valid. Those who ruled the state as part of
the Carrancista regime had to devote their time to military actions attempting to contain the sovereignty movement, and had little time for
legislative action (Martínez Vásquez 1985, 331). The sovereignty movement in Oaxaca did little to endear the state to the national government;
the state's unfavorable position at this time was reflected in the small
number of favorable resolutions to petitions for ejido land. (Such petitions were sent to the National Agrarian Commission through its state-
level branch, the Local Agrarian Commission.)

In 1916, the Local Agrarian Commission was created in the city of
Oaxaca. Its purpose, according to the 1915 law calling for the formation
of such a commission at the state level, was "to restore to the communities of this state the ejidos and common lands that belong to them and

[that] they were dispossessed of, and to grant land to those ejidos that are lacking" (Ruiz Cervantes 1988, 390). The Local Agrarian Commission depended on the National Agrarian Commission in Mexico City. In Oaxaca, the Local Agrarian Commission was working in a hostile climate, caught between the sovereignty movement and the national government.

Nevertheless, between 1915 and 1920 there were 123 petitions for land, of which 57 percent were from the central valleys (Ruiz Cervantes 1988, 393, table 13). Those areas of the state controlled by the Carrancistas were first to have solicitations for land. Those that were part of the sovereignty movement, such as the Sierra Norte and parts of the Mixteca, did not have solicitations for land until later. The central valleys also were where the heaviest efforts were put into encouraging campesinos to solicit land, through the work of labor organizations such as the Casa del Obrero Mundial (House of the World Worker) (Ruiz Cervantes 1988, 391).

Because petitions for land were personally decided by the president of the nation—at this time, Carranza—there were clear patterns in whose petitions were granted and whose were denied, and the entire state of Oaxaca was unpopular with the national government because of the sovereignty movement. From 1915 to 1920, only 11 of the 123 petitions for ejido land from Oaxaca received favorable presidential resolutions. Among these was the petition from Santa María del Tule; this presidential resolution was challenged (as will be seen in the next chapter) by a neighboring community under the leadership of a key figure in the Oaxaca sovereignty movement, Isaac Ibarra.

Oaxaca's state constitution was not changed to match the national constitution of 1917 until 1922. Petitions granted at the presidential level for ejido lands in the state, for example, were seldom carried out at the local level, or faced considerable opposition from hacendados reluctant to give up their land (see chapter 9). In the early 1920s, local hacendados grouped themselves into the Agrarian Chamber of Oaxaca. This group worked to stop expropriations of hacienda lands, seeking legal protection against actions carried out by the federal government, the state government, and local and national agrarian commissions (Ruiz Cervantes 1988, 412). The period from 1920 to 1923 saw a slight increase in petitions for land, with a total of 133, including areas outside of the central valleys. However, as already noted, only 11 of these 133 received positive presidential resolutions, indicating that the state of Oaxaca was still in the doghouse (ibid., 411).

THE SEEDS OF ZAPATA IN OAXACA: PEASANT
ORGANIZATIONS AND CONTINUED EJIDO
LAND GRANTS AFTER THE REVOLUTION

Many Oaxacans continued to distance themselves from the revolutionary national government in the 1920s, still dreaming of seceding from
Mexico. In the 1930s, under Cárdenas, however, the central valleys and
the Oaxacan state government became more sympathetic to the national
government and were often enthusiastic boosters of Cárdenas's educational and agricultural policies. It was under Cárdenas, with his promotion of socialist rural education and ejidos, that Zapata became a popular and cherished figure in Oaxacan rural communities. In Oaxaca, the
formation of the Confederación Nacional Campesina (CNC) in conjunction with other labor unions was crucial in the incorporation of Zapata into local historical canons.

Oaxaca served as the site for the consolidation of the Federación de
Sindicatos Obreros y Campesinos de Oaxaca (Federation of Worker and
Peasant Unions of Oaxaca), or FSOCO, and other labor federations that
were important precursors to the CNC, formed in 1938. FSOCO formed
some of the first peasant organizations structured as unions and was affiliated with the Regional Confederation of Mexican Workers, the most
important labor organization in the country between 1918 and 1928.
The federation was influential in the central valleys, in the Isthmus, and
in the Mixteca, and played an important role in connecting rural citizens of Oaxaca with government programs and ideologies. Nine local
peasant organizations were formed in 1923; their demands included sal-
ary increases, schools for campesino children during the day, and night
schools for campesinos (Ruiz Cervantes 1988, 422; Arellanes Meixuiero
1999, 137).

It was not until 1932 that, at the behest of the governor, a statewide
organization for peasants was formed in Oaxaca, the Confederación
Oaxaqueño de Campesinos (Oaxacan Peasant Confederation), or COC,
known as COCO. The first convention included delegates from 128 locations. Most consisted of the administrative committees of ejidos. The
official *memoria* of the congress describes these persons as "238 delegates that are in their majority indigenous" (Arellanes Meixuero 1988,
65). Two years later, the COC included 472 peasant organizations in the
state. Archival data from 320 of these shows a total of 33,334 members,
in local committees that ranged in size from 30 to more than 1,000 mem-

bers. Most of the organizations were made up of "agrarian committees" and "ejido committees" (Arellanes Meixueiro 1999, 173).

In December 1934, the leaders of the COC accused officials of the Agrarian Department in Oaxaca of having been converted into an instrument of control for another group, which, they said, wanted to divide the peasants of Oaxaca. This other group was the Confederación Campesina Mexicana (Mexican Peasant Confederation), or CCM (Arellanes Meixuiero 1999, 218). The CCM began an intense recruitment campaign throughout Mexico that year, with the support of the Cárdenas government. Several key members of the COC were drafted into the CCM, but, as the CCM grew, confrontations emerged between it and the COC. The CCM had the vast resources of the Agrarian Department at its disposal; the COC did not. In 1935, the CCM declared unconditional support for Constantino Chapital's candidacy for the governorship of Oaxaca, and after he took office, the CCM received his endorsement and support. The confrontations continued. In 1937, eight members of the CCM were killed by members of the COC in a central Oaxacan town (Arellanes Meixueiro 1999, 219–20). By this time, however, the CCM had become the predominant peasant organization in Oaxaca. Ultimately, after the founding of the Confederación Nacional Campesina under the Cárdenas government in 1938, the COC disappeared.

Thus the period 1923–38, which involved a quantitative leap in the number of rural citizens incorporated into labor organization structures, became an important chapter for understanding how national ideology entered the local circuits of community history in Oaxaca. Another major means for the diffusion of government ideology and the promotion of Cárdenas's claim to the legacy of Emiliano Zapata was through the granting of favorable presidential resolutions to petitions for ejido land. The period of growth in the number of rural citizens incorporated into labor organizations (1923–38) was paralleled by an increase in the number of ejido petitions filed and granted.

The period 1923–32 saw a significant increase in petitions for lands filed from Oaxaca. A total of 340 petitions were submitted in this period, the majority from the central valleys region, followed by the Mixteca and Tuxtepec regions (Arellanes Meixuero 1988, 121, table 24). The resolution rate for the petitions was considerably better than before 1923, with approximately 40 percent receiving favorable presidential resolutions (ibid., 120). Oaxaca was gaining favor at the national level as the sovereignty movement lost steam and the state government began to cooperate closely with the national government.

With the presidency of Cárdenas (1934–40), the number of land petitions from Oaxaca that were granted increased dramatically. This process was aided by official visits Cárdenas made to Oaxaca in April 1934 while a presidential candidate and in March 1937 as president. On both these trips through the central valleys, the Sierra of Ixtlán, and the Mixteca, he attended numerous meetings, met with commissions, and had direct exchanges with communities on how to expedite petitions for land, how to get buildings for schools and libraries, and how to get irrigation, water, and telegraphic equipment to communities (Arrellanes Meixuero 1988, 141). This is confirmed by descriptions of both visits in the newspapers *El Oaxaqueño* and *Oaxaca Nuevo*. After the 1937 visit, rural teachers and such organizations as the Oaxaca section of the CCM and the COC continued the discussions that Cárdenas had initiated with Oaxaca's rural inhabitants. After the president's 1937 visit, the rate of land grants to ejidos was slated to increase vastly, as "brigades of engineers left for all regions" of the state to survey land and write up land petitions with local ejido committees (*Oaxaca Nuevo* 1937d). At the same time, the engineers would also work to help promote leagues for peasant women (ibid.). Many elderly ejidatarios in places like Santa María del Tule and Unión Zapata still remember Cárdenas's visit and the spurt of activities that followed it (see chapters 9 and 10). Student groups joined in the Cárdenista programs, as did the Partido Nacional Revolucionario (PNR), and a sympathetic governor. There was a great mobilization in Oaxaca to carry out the programs. In contrast to the state of Chiapas, important sections of Oaxaca embraced the programs, which were particularly influential in the central valleys. This era was key in consolidating the legacy of Emiliano Zapata as promoted through Cárdenas's government. The nation view of Mexico exhibited in the local histories of ejidos like Santa María del Tule and Unión Zapata (see chapters 9 and 10) was solidified during this period.

Between 1935 and 1940, the Oaxaca delegate of the National Agrarian Commission received 586 petitions for land, as a result of the work of Cárdenas sympathizers (Arellanes Meixuero 1988, 143). This number was 113 more than the total petitions received in 1916–32. Between 1916 and 1934, 114 communities had received 108,213 hectares of land, with 3 receiving additional lands. This represented an annual incorporation of 1,202 ejidatarios, a total of 22,846 ejidatarios (Arellanes Meixuero 1988, 144). In the period 1935–40, 432,869 hectares were redistributed to 256 communities, resulting in an average 4,547 new ejidatarios per year —a total of 27,281 ejidatarios in 1935–40 (Arellanes Meixuero 1988, 144). Thus, in just five years, the number of ejidatarios in the state of Oaxaca doubled, and most were organized into what became the CNC, providing an impressive rural base for Cárdenista politics. In Santa María del Tule, Unión Zapata, and other communities that had spent many years in conditions of landlessness, the granting of ejido land radically changed lives and endeared state agrarian officials to the people, at least for a time. Additional ejidos were formed in the 1960s and 1970s, particularly in the Isthmus. Oaxaca at present has a total of 732 ejidos.

INDEPENDENT INDIGENOUS AND PEASANT ORGANIZING IN CONTEMPORARY OAXACA

The preceding historical discussion has documented the development of government-linked peasant organizations in Oaxaca since the Mexican Revolution, but the geography of agrarian politics in Oaxaca is much more complex. The CNC may have been the predominant peasant organization in the state from 1938 until the 1960s, but in the 1970s, Oaxaca saw a flowering of popular protest that generated many indigenous and peasant organizations. These organizations assumed a political stance independent of the PRI and often in opposition to the official peasant organization, the CNC. The following discussion of a few of these organizations will provide a sense of their variety in the state and will contrast the experience of the two ejidos in the central valleys highlighted in the next two chapters. These ejidos belonged to the CNC and were supportive of the Mexican government, by and large, until recently.

One of the most important organizations formed in the 1970s and active in the politics of indigenous autonomy both in Oaxaca and at a national level has been the Coalición de Obreros, Campesinos, y Estudiantes del Istmo (Isthmus Coalition of Workers, Peasants, and Students), or COCEI. Formed during the popular organizing of the 1970s, COCEI established a grassroots movement that "succeeded in defending claims to land, credit, wages, benefits, and municipal services" (Rubin 1990, 250). The presence of COCEI, centered in the city of Juchitán, has continued the tradition of Isthmus Zapotec autonomy and resistance to national and state government intervention. According to the anthropologist Howard Campbell, who has studied COCEI extensively, its "use of Isthmus Zapotec ethnic identity . . . is an active, overt form of resistance occurring in indigenous territory. . . . [I]ndigenous identity is strengthened by opposition to exploitative forms of capitalist development and government domination" (Campbell 1993, 215).

In the 1980s, COCEI was the first leftist opposition group to succeed in having its victory recognized by the dominant Partido de la Revolución Institutional (PRI) in municipal elections. When COCEI won municipal elections in 1981, Juchitán became the first and only city in Mexico with a leftist and indigenous government. During its initial two-and-a-half year reign of *ayuntamento popular* (people's government), COCEI embarked on an ambitious cultural program centered on the Zapotec language, attempted to regain land lost by peasants to large landholders, formally organized the peasantry, and developed public works projects benefiting the city's poor majority. In 1983, COCEI was impeached by the state legislature, then forcibly removed from office by army and police forces. In 1986, COCEI entered municipal elections and joined a coalition municipal government.

In 1989, after again winning in municipal elections (held every three years), COCEI governed jointly with the PRI, but in the majority role (Rubin 1990, 250). During the 1980s, COCEI withstood major political pressure and military repression to emerge firmly entrenched in the municipal government. In 1990, the COCEI mayor Héctor Sánchez welcomed President Salinas to Juchitán with a speech highlighting dialogue, conciliation, and cooperation (Campbell 1990, 426). COCEI won further victories in 1992, 1995, and 1998 and is a major (but not the only) political influence in Juchitán (Rubin 1997). Historically, COCEI changed the course of relations between indigenous people and the state in Oaxaca and provided a model for indigenous, peasant, and workers' organizations of an organization that could maintain a stance of independence yet also periodically negotiate with the state. Jeffrey Rubin argues that COCEI offers concrete evidence of the vulnerability of the Mexican state, suggesting that its hegemony is uneven and is constructed and contested regionally and culturally (Rubin 1997). Negotiation with the state by independent organizations in Oaxaca contrasts strikingly with the nonstop repression unleashed against independent organizations in Chiapas.

Another important organization formed in the early 1980s was the Asamblea de Productores Mixes (Assembly of Mixe Producers), or ASAPROM, which was established to address the economic concerns of the Mixe people as producers. In 1988, an NGO (nongovernmental organization) linked to the Asamblea was created that more recently focused on ethnically based demands, emphasizing cultural mechanisms and traditions that distinguish the Mixe, such as communal work and local forms of justice. Called Servicios del Pueblo Mixe (Services of the Mixe People), or SER, it went from concentrating on local processes of economic development, such as granting community-based credit, to considering ways to create a national indigenous movement and exploring how to participate in such a movement. SER has justice, economic, education, cultural, women's, and political development projects. In the year 2001, SER collaborated with seventeen Mixe communities and other organizations, such as the Assembly of Mixe Producers.

Other indigenous organizations were created in the 1980s in Oaxaca that based their claims on the rights of indigenous peoples to maintain themselves as culturally distinct populations. In a few communities, such as Villa Alta and Guelatao, Zapotec leaders consolidated their positions in local government and began participating in indigenous coalitions as indigenous governors (*gobernadores*). More militant organizations called for a new government that would be "multinational"—that is, inclusive of the many indigenous nations—democratic, and populist (Hernández 1996, 10). Another important regional organization, the Unión de Comunidades Indígenas de la Zona Norte del Istmo (Union of Indigenous Communities of the Northern Zone of the Isthmus), or UCIZONI, includes more than one ethnic group, having both Mixe and Zapotec members.

A major difference between Oaxaca and Chiapas, which has also affected the nature of indigenous organizations formed in each state, has been the role of binational migration, along with the existence of what Michael Kearney (1996) calls transnational communities. While many in Chiapas have worked as migrant laborers in the United States, many others have remained in the state of Chiapas, or at least in Mexico. Oaxaca has had a historical pipeline to the United States since the 1940s, when the second U.S. bracero program (launched by the Mexican and U.S. governments during World War II to replace laborers drafted into the U.S. military) reached down into the state. Workers were recruited from throughout the central valleys and elsewhere. Many continued to migrate to the United States after the program officially ended in 1964. Continued migration of a range of ethnic groups, most prominently the Mixtec and the Zapotec, but recently also the Triqui, has resulted in transnational communities with active members not only in the United States and in Mexico, but also in transnational Oaxacan indigenous organizations.

In the late 1970s, migrant Mixtec farmworkers began to be recruited in significant numbers to work in California. In 1994, it was estimated that in peak summer seasons, there were roughly fifty thousand Mixtecs in California, representing over two hundred communities in Oaxaca (Runsten and Kearney 1994). Kearney (1996, 176) estimates that over twice that number cycle in and out of California every few years.

In the mid 1980s, Mixtec leaders from Oaxaca began to experiment with "forms of associations that combined members from various communities into fronts, which are organizations of associations" (Kearney 1996, 178). Many Mixtec and Zapotec migrants living in southern California formed community associations that raised money and other kinds of aid to send to their hometowns. Zapotec leaders worked to form hometown associations and to bring these together into fronts. In the 1990s, some of these transnational organizations came together to form a multi-ethnic organization, the Zapotec–Mixtec Binational Front, which evolved into the Frente Indígena Oaxaqueño Binacional (Oaxacan Binational Indigenous Front), or FIOB, in 1994 and came to include other ethnic groups such as Triquis, Mixes, and Chinantecos. This organization changed from a loose coalition of hometown associations to a more tightly structured membership organization, with offices on both sides of the border and binational leadership. Currently, FIOB carries out community work in the Mixtec region of Oaxaca, in the San Quintín Valley in Baja California, and in the San Joaquín Valley in California. Members in each region are affiliated with community committees, representatives of which make up the FIOB regional council (Rivera Salgado 1999, 61). The experiences and political agendas of independent peasant and indigenous organizations in Oaxaca offer an important contrast to the experiences described in the next chapter. In the year 2001, Oaxaca remains a state of contradictions, with significant numbers of communities still loyally affiliated with the CNC and the PRI—albeit with interesting interpretations—but with others having established what is now a long record of opposition to the PRI and government agrarian and indigenous policies.

CONCLUSIONS

Both the colonial and the postcolonial experiences of Zapotec peoples in the central valleys of Oaxaca were different from those of the Tojolabals, Tzeltals, and Tzotzils of the Lacandon jungle and highlands of Chiapas. The Zapotec were able to hold on to much more of their land through the colonial period than were the indigenous peoples of eastern lowland Chiapas. They used the Spanish court system to defend their land rights, and, even in the postcolonial period, indigenous farmers did not always lose their land under reform laws. Some, indeed, purchased land and became private property owners. The other major characteristic of the Zapotec of the central valleys was their relative cooperation with government authorities—with the exception of the sovereignty movement of the state as a whole. While Mixtec and Isthmus Zapotec communities repeatedly challenged both state and federal government authorities, the Central Valley populations were more focused on local land disputes among neighbors.

The next chapter looks in depth at a land conflict of the Zapotec ejido of Santa María del Tule with both its Zapotec neighbors and local hacendados. In this case, as well as in the case of the ejido of Unión Zapata, described in chapter 10, national and Oaxacan state agrarian officials emerged as helpful in resolving the conflicts and in ultimately assisting communities to obtain new and additional ejido land. This experience contrasts sharply with that of the Tojolabal ejidatarios of Guadalupe Tepeyac and La Realidad. Ejidatarios from Santa María del Tule and Unión Zapata were also members of the COC and frequently used it as a channel to pressure the government for action. Through their participation in the COC and, later, the CNC, both ejidos were directly linked to the national government and had continual interaction with its agrarian officials. In other parts of Oaxaca, such as the Zapotec Isthmus and the Mixe Sierra, opposition peasant and indigenous organizations emerged, providing a different experience and a stronger sense of conflict with the government; thus, what happened in the communities of Santa María del Tule and Unión Zapata does not represent what happened in all Oaxacan communities. Nevertheless, the positive historical memories ejidatarios in these two communities have of the government could strongly influence the reception of government policies ending agrarian reform. Historical memory also affected responses to neo-Zapatismo in the 1990s.

CHAPTER 9

The Story of Santa María del Tule

Zapata, Cárdenas, and "Good Guy" Officials

In the ejidos of Santa María del Tule and Unión Zapata in Oaxaca, the figures of Lázaro Cárdenas and Emiliano Zapata came to assume almost familial status in local histories. Cárdenas personally visited both communities during two trips to the region. As president of Mexico from 1934 to 1940, he was personally involved in either providing initial and additional land grants, as in the case of Unión Zapata, or in resolving a long-standing conflict over ejido land, as in the case of Santa María del Tule. In both places, his actions are today seen as an extension of the legacy of Emiliano Zapata and the Mexican Revolution.

In moving from the archival record of the interactions in these Oaxacan communities between local authorities and state agrarian officials in the 1920s and 1930s to people recounting community and personal histories in the 1990s, one has a different sense of how ejidatarios have positioned themselves in relation to the government, both historically and at present, than one does in eastern Chiapas. In eastern Chiapas, the figure of Cárdenas has little currency, and Zapata has been reinvented as a religious/political figure, in the personage of Votán Zapata. Votán Zapata has no connection with the Mexican government and offers a spiritual center to the Zapatista movement; Zapata is an antigovernment symbol in the ejidos of Guadalupe Tepeyac and La Realidad. However, in the two communities in Oaxaca profiled in this chapter, the twin symbolic figures of Zapata and Cárdenas serve as positive personal connections to a government that, for a while, was viewed as very helpful.

This and the next chapter record local stories of the formation of the ejidos of Santa María del Tule and Unión Zapata, respectively, by highlighting the relationships that ejidatarios in the two communities developed over time with the Mexican government and with the symbolic figures of Cárdenas and Zapata. From their particular historical and regional circumstances, and in particular the role government officials played in securing ejido land in both communities, many in the two have come to view the government as largely helpful. In Santa María del Tule, the land was secured after almost four hundred years of conflict with a neighboring Zapotec community and, later, with a family of Spanish hacendados. In Unión Zapata, ejido land was secured swiftly by a group of landless laborers, who succeeded in having land expropriated from haciendas where they had worked as laborers.

The redistribution of hacienda land as ejido land is a turning point in the local histories of these two communities. For those who are still ejidatarios today, the formation of the ejidos is a high point in their sense of local identity and in their assessment of community interactions with the government. Following the Mexican Revolution, particularly beginning in the 1930s with the Cárdenas administration's initiation of national education and labor organizing campaigns to incorporate rural Mexicans into government structures, the men and women of Santa María del Tule and Unión Zapata began to tie their local histories to national figures and symbols—most prominently to Zapata and Cárdenas. In this process, they began to claim these figures as their own and to reconfigure nationalist ideology disseminated from institutions of the central government—the Ministry of Education (SEP), the National Peasant Confederation (CNC), and the government party (PNR and later the PRI)—to suit their own needs and experiences. Even though the stories of the two communities reveal important differences—Santa María del Tule is at least 470 years old and Unión Zapata is only about 60 years old; Santa María del Tule is a Zapotec indigenous community, whereas Unión Zapata's population is of mixed origin, consisting primarily of Spanish-speaking mestizos and Zapotecs; and residents of Santa María del Tule have a significantly higher standard of living, owing to employment in the service sector of Oaxaca and local tourism, than the people of Unión Zapata do—they share a history of loyalty to the government, and a sense that, overall, the government has been good to them. (As we shall see in chapter 11, however, that loyalty is flexible and allows for the possibility of simultaneous sympathy with antigovernment positions such as that of the EZLN in Chiapas.)

In the larger picture, the historical relationships between these two communities and the postrevolutionary governments of Mexico confirm the importance of paying close attention to regional and historical specificity (and variation) in assessing the ability of governments to impose uniform, nationalist imaginings of community equally in all places. This finding is consistent with the work of scholars such as Daniel Nugent (1993), Ana María Alonzo (1995), Jeffrey Rubin (1997), Jennifer Purnell (1999), and the authors of the essays in Joseph and Nugent (1994), all of whom document varying local and regional responses to postrevolutionary nationalism in Mexico. Collectively, this work suggests that the image of a leviathan corporatist, all-controlling Mexican government running the country from the center should be seriously questioned. In addition, this work also suggests that the nation views held by those at the margins of the state influence how people act in the center.

THE NARRATIVE STRUCTURE OF THE HISTORY OF SANTA MARÍA DEL TULE: MAIN EVENTS AND KEY PROTAGONISTS

The history of Santa María del Tule is a long and complex one. From how ejidatarios currently remember and talk about their community's history, six key episodes emerge, at least in most narratives:

1. The founding of the community by thirty-two couples from Tlalixtac. The separation of the population of Santa María del Tule from that of Tlalixtac was marked by ongoing conflict between the two communities from the colonial period until the late 1940s.

2. The founding of the hacienda of Guendulain by a Spanish family and its establishment as a center of exploitation and power that controlled many lives and ruled the community until the hacienda land was expropriated after the Mexican Revolution.

3. A dispute between the enemy community of Tlalixtac and the owners of the Guendulain hacienda over three hundred hectares of land, which was later used by Tlalixtac to try to prevent the people from El Tule from receiving this land as part of their ejido in 1917.

4. The granting to Santa María del Tule of ejido land expropriated from the Guendulain hacienda and the seventeen-year struggle with

the neighboring community of Tlalixtac to gain full control over all of that land, including the three hundred hectares that Tlalixtac residents claimed had been stolen from Tlalixtac in 1857 by the Guendulain family and were therefore theirs and not part of El Tule's ejido grant.

5. The key roles played by government agrarian officials—making them emerge as local heroes—in helping the community win against Tlalixtac.

6. The final conflict in 1945, when six people from El Tule were shot to death, presumably by residents of Tlalixtac. This reignited a conflict over Tlalixtac's claim to half of El Tule's communal land. In the 1950s, El Tule ceded half its communal land to Tlalixtac and the conflict ended.

The key protagonists in the history as told by ejido members are (1) the people and community authorities of Santa María del Tule; (2) the antagonistic people and community authorities of Tlalixtac; (3) the Guendulain family and subsequent owners of the hacienda; (4) Isaac de Ibarra, a Oaxacan general who was briefly governor and tried to block Santa María del Tule from occupying all of the ejido land it had been granted, by granting half to its historical enemies from Tlalixtac; and (5) government officials from the Agrarian Department who helped the ejidatarios of Santa María del Tule receive a favorable answer to their initial petition for ejido land and then sided with the community against Tlalixtac, securing all of their land for them after a seventeen-year legal struggle.

In their narratives of local history, ejidatarios paint themselves and government agrarian officials as the heroes, and their Zapotec neighbors from Tlalixtac and the Spanish hacendados of the Guendulain ranch as the enemies. As becomes clear when we look at more specific conversations about the formation of the ejido, the figures of Zapata and Cárdenas are aligned with the good guys in the local story—the ejidatarios of Santa María del Tule who petitioned for land and fought to occupy it, and the government agrarian officials who helped them. The final result is a local version of history that appropriates the nationalist heroes of the Mexican Revolution and makes them belong to the community of Santa María del Tule; they become a part of the history of the ejido.

We now turn to the story of the ejido as relayed by those in the community. I recorded more than a dozen narratives of this story, primarily with the oldest men and women who are original members of the ejido, but also with several persons whose parents were original ejidatarios. (Note that many of the narratives use "El Tule" to refer to Santa María del Tule. This is the name used by most people in the community and in the central valleys.) What follows is a reconstruction of the history of the ejido, based on the narrative structure provided by ejidatarios, but supplemented by other historical documentation.

THE FOUNDING OF SANTA MARÍA DEL TULE

In discussing the origins of Santa María del Tule, and its relationship to the neighboring Zapotec community of Tlalixtac de Cabrera, most elderly people in the community recite a similar story, reiterating their long subordinate status to Tlalixtac, which they call "the big town" (*el pueblo grande*). Initially, this is a story of warring indigenous neighbors. The founders of the community settle in a holy spot and proceed to establish a separate community (no one provides a precise date for this). To begin, Genaro Domínguez de Cabrera, aged 82, states:

> This town here of Santa María del Tule was formed when thirty-two couples settled here. They came here from Tlalixtac de Cabrera, the big town. They made a living extracting lime from the big mountain you see in front of you. Before that time, the entire mountain range you see there belonged to Tlalixtac. They gave us that land as communal land. We continued to fight with them about that land and other pieces. We were always in conflict with them.

Esperanza Méndez, aged 75, adds the important detail of why the thirty-two couples moved to the specific spot the community occupies—it was designated by a local virgin. She also notes that the people in El Tule labored for an indigenous ruler in Tlalixtac—clarifying not only the hierarchical relationship between Tlalixtac and El Tule, but also that there were indigenous nobles who forced laborers to work in their fields and households:

> You know that Tlalixtac de Cabrera used to rule us. We worked for them and their cacique. They used to be like our municipio. We had to obey what they said. Then the Virgin de la Asunción appeared here in El Tule and about thirty-two couples of men and women came here from Tlalixtac to live.

The strongest element in community histories relays continued conflict and confrontation with Tlalixtac and a perpetual defensive position with regard to land. José González, aged 55, repeats the familiar story of how the community was founded, with an emphasis on conflict:

> You know this town got started when thirty-two couples came here from Tlal-
> ixtac. All of the land we have was theirs. From the beginning, there was a lot
> of conflict. This continued until 1944 or 1946, when six people from here
> were shot on the mountain in front of our town. They gave us that mountain,
> but they always wanted it back.

If these local narratives are taken as a basis for further exploration of
colonial land and labor relations between Tlalixtac and El Tule, William
Taylor's research indicates that *terrasguerros,* or landless sharecroppers,
who worked for a cacique of Tlalixtac were found around Santa María
del Tule by the mid 1600s (Taylor 1972, 43). This suggests that even as
early as the mid 1600s, people in El Tule faced a shortage of land. In
1663, in what is the earliest documented case of rebellion against caciques, these *terrasguerros,* who lived in and near El Tule, and others from
Tlalixtac refused to perform their duties of cultivation and domestic service for the indigenous cacique of Tlalixtac (ibid., 54). The strong feelings of hostility and conflict with neighboring Tlalixtac found in the historical narratives are thus also documented in other sources.

The defensive position regarding land found in community narratives
is borne out in written history. Santa María del Tule seems never to have
had secure documentation dating from the early colonial period for its
communal lands. For example, in 1917, El Tule presented authorities
from the local agrarian commission of Oaxaca with documents dated
from 1529 testifying to the existence of communal lands. But these documents did not clearly specify the boundaries of communal land. The
presence of landless sharecroppers, their confrontation with a Tlalixtac
cacique about the legitimacy of his claim to *caciazgo* land, and the accepted history of migration from Tlalixtac to El Tule suggest that the
community's boundaries may have been in dispute since 1529.

Taylor suggests that Tlalixtac enjoyed considerable landholdings at
the expense of El Tule and other neighbors (Taylor 1972, 104). A 1776
survey of 28 towns, recording the size of the *fundo legal,* reported that
Santa María del Tule occupied a town site smaller than the official fundo
legal of one square league (ibid., 69). Ejidatarios' sentiments that their
lands were usurped first by Tlalixtac and then by the formation of the
Guendulain Hacienda are further borne out in other documentation.
While the village of El Tule in 1615 received a royal grant for land to graze
sheep and goats, which incorporated about three square miles of land,
by 1700, most residents of the community were sharecroppers on the
hacienda of Guendulain (ibid., 104n). In local histories, the establish-

ment of the Guendulain ranch in the colonial period is the next significant event in the life of the ejido.

THE GUENDULAIN HACIENDA: CENTER OF EXPLOITATION

Local accounts of the history of the Guendulain hacienda peg its establishment as "a long time ago," and designate the community's relationship to the hacienda as remaining consistent throughout nearly three
hundred years. The hacienda is represented in most narratives as exert-
ing controlling influence over most of the community, being responsible
for the community's continued poverty, and being run by a succession of
persons who mistreated laborers and ruthlessly exploited them. María
Cortés, a widowed ejidataria, aged 85, sat up straight and gestured in-
tently as she described the hard labor men and women performed for the
owners of the Guendulain ranch:

> Everyone from El Tule and many from Tlalixtac and Santo Domingo worked
> on the Guendulain hacienda. We had nothing. We just had miserable little
> houses made of cane. We didn't have any land at all. The hacienda controlled
> everything and made all of the rules. The men went and worked in the fields
> and the women went and made tortillas for the big house in the hacienda and
> to feed all of the workers. . . . Sometimes they even sent out their dirty laun-
> dry from Oaxaca to be washed by women who worked on the hacienda.

Ninety-year-old Rufina Manuel, also an ejidataria, remembered doing similar labor on the hacienda:

> Many of the women from here went to the hacienda to make tortillas for
> the hacendados. I was a *molendera* [corn grinder] there. I would go at three
> o'clock in the morning to make *atole* [a corn drink] for the laborers in the
> hacienda. A lot of women from Tlalixtac went there as well.

María's and Rufina's statements detail the gendered division of labor
for *peones* on the hacienda, making it clear that women rose as early as
men and worked as hard or harder. María also hints at how gendered
labor relations on the hacienda incorporated tasks stemming from the
owner's urban residence in the city of Oaxaca. Many Spanish owners of
estates in the Valley of Oaxaca, being prominent figures in government
and society who kept residences for their family in the city (Taylor 1972,
158), had no hesitation about sending dirty laundry out of the city to be
washed by women from El Tule working on the Guendulain ranch.

Another ejidatario, Juan Ramírez, had strong words to describe the exploitative labor relations that extended even into the community's ritual participation:

> The hacienda belonged to the Guendulain family, and that was created a long time ago, not that long after the Spaniards got here. I'm not sure exactly when. It grew from lands that belonged to other communities around here. My father, who was the *síndico* [community trustee] when the ejido was formed in El Tule, told me that those people who worked as peones from here and from Tlalixtac for the ranch owners were treated like slaves. They would go to work at four in the morning and, if they arrived late, they weren't even allowed to work.[1] They left late at night after they finished their day's work. One of my uncles, José Dolores, was what they called a *mandador*. He was in charge of the laborers. He and others would ride around on horseback beating the laborers if they didn't work fast enough.
>
> Almost everyone was really poor. Those who had teams of oxen could be sharecroppers with the hacendados. But most people didn't have oxen. They would go to the hacendado and ask, "Can I have some land to sharecrop?" The hacendado would say, "You don't have anything to work the land with. You should just work as a laborer." Nobody had anything except the hacendados. The only other work was to mine lime from the mountain in front here.
>
> One way that the hacendados got land from people was when they were named mayordomos.[2] After they are named as a mayordomo, they would borrow money from the hacendado to pay for their mayordomía. When they couldn't pay it back, the hacendado would get their land, their oxen—or sometimes people would even have to indenture their children for years in the house of the ranch owners to pay back their debts.

In describing the hacienda, those interviewed state that it grew from the communal lands of surrounding communities. The hacienda's exploitation assumes such force in these narratives that the historical conflict between El Tule and Tlalixtac fades temporarily into the background, as both populations assume the same subordinate position of day laborers. Other historical evidence suggests that the Guendulain family was indeed a major force in the central valleys.

During the 1600s, the Guendulain family became one of the largest landowners in the valleys. The entailed estate of the family, which included the ranch near El Tule, was founded in 1677 by Pedro de Guendulain, who served as a Spanish official (Taylor 1972, 155). The Guendulain estate included the Hacienda Asunción (called El Guendulain by locals) near Santa María del Tule, as well as a sugar mill near Teotitlán del Camino and at least three houses in Oaxaca (ibid.). The Guendulain family, like many others, maintained the unity of their large extensions of property under the title of entailment, or *mayorazgo*, a Spanish institution that guaranteed that properties could not be divided at the death of the owner among several sons, but would be passed intact to the eldest son (Romero Frizzi 1988, 156).[3] The Guendulain ranch near El Tule, like many dating from the colonial period in Oaxaca, would eventually be characterized by low profitability. The central valleys of Oaxaca were home to about forty haciendas in 1643. Subsequently, the land converted to large private holdings in the area did not grow significantly until much later, during the Porfiriato.

CONFLICT BETWEEN TLALIXTAC AND THE GUENDULAIN
RANCH OWNERS OVER THREE HUNDRED HECTARES

The conflict over land between Santa María del Tule and Tlalixtac fades somewhat where the narratives focus on the communities' mutual exploitation at the hands of the Guendulain ranch during the colonial period and until the Mexican Revolution, but an intervening event in the life of the hacienda indirectly foregrounds this conflict again. According to the ejidatarios of El Tule, a major land dispute emerged in 1857 between the people of Tlalixtac and the ranch owners. The dispute is important to these ejidatarios because after the Mexican Revolution, this piece of land became the object of their dispute with the people of Tlalixtac de Cabrera. The story of the conflict was told to me by Raimundo Bautista, a 55-year-old ejidatario:

> There was a big dispute between the people from the big town of Tlalixtac and the Guendulain hacienda. They say that the land was originally from Tlalixtac. One day, the community authorities from Tlalixtac went to Guendulain. They brought the land titles with them because the hacendados said they wanted to clarify something. The community authorities got drunk and left the documents with the hacendados. When they came back the next day to retrieve their documents, the hacendados laughed and told them, "What documents? We don't have them." That is how they lost their land to the hacienda.

Documentation found in the records, outlining how the ejido of El Tule was formed in 1917, date the conflict between Tlalixtac and the owners of the Guendulain ranch to 1857 and place the land in dispute at three hundred hectares.

The documented claim by community authorities of Tlalixtac of losing three hundred hectares to the Guendulain ranch in 1857 (Secretaría de Reforma Agraria, Delegación de Oaxaca 1926a, 3) makes sense in the context of state policy, aimed at privatizing communal lands, during that time under the Ley Lerdo (see chapter 8). It is unclear exactly what the process was by which the Guendulain family took possession of land claimed by Tlalixtac. Ejidatarios in El Tule attribute it to carelessness on the part of community authorities from Tlalixtac, greed on the part of the hacendados. Community authorities from Tlalixtac claimed the land had first been plundered from the community in 1856 by the Guendulain family, and that in 1857, Sra. Dolores Guendulain illegally transferred the title to her husband, Joaquin Romero (ibid. 1926b, 3–4). The existence of the Ley Lerdo, and Tlalixtac's proximity to Oaxaca, undoubtedly made community authorities aware of the law facilitating privatization of communally held land. It seems unlikely that the community authorities of Tlalixtac would simply turn their titles over to the Guendulain hacendados while drinking. Later legal investigations of the process by which the Guendulains acquired title indicated that neither the Guendulain family nor Tlalixtac had sufficient proof of ownership of the land in question (ibid.), as is seen in records among the documentation of El Tule's awarded ejido land. Copies of these records are found in the community, and were first housed in the Oaxaca branch of the Secretaría de Reforma Agraria and later in the Registro Agrario Nacional in Oaxaca.[4]

THE FORMATION OF EL TULE'S EJIDO

The long-standing animosity between El Tule and Tlalixtac continued past the Mexican Revolution and resurfaced in 1918. In 1917, El Tule submitted a formal petition for ejido lands. When the community was awarded six hundred hectares through a positive presidential resolution in 1917, most was to be expropriated from the Guendulain ranch. This was seen as a just outcome in view of the suffering caused by the hacienda's owners. On the day before the people from El Tule were to be given official possession of the land, in 1918, the community authorities of Tlalixtac petitioned the state's local agrarian commission to disqualify the land grant to El Tule because it included the three hundred hectares that Tlalixtac de Cabrera claimed as having been stolen in 1857 by the Guendulain hacienda (Secretaría de Reforma Agraria, Delegación de Oaxaca 1926b: 3). The conflict between the two communities resurfaced, just when the landless laborers of El Tule were about to be given a new chance at survival by receiving their own land after centuries of landlessness. Ninety-one-year-old Hilario Vásquez related how the ejido was organized:

> In 1917 a presidential announcement came to us that said that those who didn't have lands could get them by taking them away from the latifundias.

We were interested, so we sent some people to Oaxaca to ask about it. After that, a whole legion of engineers arrived here. My father was named as president of the Executive Committee for Boundaries [to be established for the ejido]. We sent a petition to Mexico City to the Agrarian Department for Land. In 1917 we received a positive presidential resolution that awarded us six hundred hectares. . . . After the government gave the order for our ejido, we went to occupy the land of the hacienda. I was only fifteen, but I grabbed my machete and we all went with arms. We drove the hacendados and all of the hacienda managers off the land. Later, we had a meeting with the representative from the State Committee for Agrarian Reform and we divided up the land. . . .

Our biggest problem came later, with the people of Tlalixtac. They received part of our ejido through a deal they made with General Ibarra.

The final part of Hilario's narrative refers to the dispute with Tlalixtac in 1918 and to the enlistment of a local political figure, General Isaac Ibarra, by the community authorities of Tlalixtac to help defeat the land claims of El Tule. A district judge supported the appeal of the community authorities from Tlalixtac who had petitioned the local agrarian commission to disqualify the land granted El Tule because it included land belonging to Tlalixtac (Secretaría de Reforma Agraria, Delegación de Oaxaca 1926b, 3). In 1919, when the appeal reached the supreme court of the state of Oaxaca, three hundred of the six hundred hectares to be granted to El Tule were put under special protection, to remain in the possession of Tlalixtac. El Tule was thus officially allowed to occupy only half the lands granted.

According to the remaining original ejidatarios in El Tule, the legal suit that Tlalixtac brought against the community authorities of Santa María del Tule did not prevent people from taking possession of the three hundred hectares not under dispute. Even this land, however, was being defended by the owner of the Guendulain ranch at that time, Miguel Cobo. José Flores, aged 55, relayed what his father told him of the struggle to possess this land and drive off the hacienda owners, with reference also to Ibarra's intervention on behalf of Tlalixtac:

They went to find Miguel Cobo to get him to sign the papers saying he would turn over his land. There was a battle for his land. People went there with machetes. There were people protecting the hacendados. They cut off people's arms and wounded people. We had to occupy the land by force. The hacendados wouldn't give up. We were supposed to get 628 acres from the Guendulain ranch, but Miguel Cobo wouldn't give up. For years, he continued to try and farm the land he lost possession of. Then, later, there was another intervention in the ejido from General Isaac Ibarra.

Ibarra, who was one of the key figures in Oaxacan state politics after the Mexican Revolution, came from the town of Lachatao in the Sierra Juárez. After fighting in Guerrero and Morelos with the revolutionary forces of the south, aligned with Zapata, he returned to the Sierra Juárez region, where he became an extremely important political and military figure (Ruiz Cervantes 1985, 262–64). He led several military missions against the Constitutionalists in the state and became interim governor in 1924. The community of Tlalixtac had long-standing political ties with the Serrano Zapotecs of the Sierra Juárez whom Ibarra had led. Locals tell of how the people of Tlalixtac cooperated with the rebel Serranos in the Sovereignty movement that shook Oaxaca until the early 1920s (see chapter 8).

In 1920, Ibarra occupied the city of Oaxaca with two thousand troops, called "the heroic forces in defense of the Sovereignty of the State." They passed through the streets and markets of Oaxaca and convened a meeting in the town square, which all local notables attended. There, they elected an interim governor, who won with forty-six votes, and pledged to respect the Constitution of 1857 (Ruiz Cervantes 1985, 305). The integration of 150 men from Tlalixtac into the troops Ibarra had brought into Oaxaca provides clear confirmation of the political and military ties between the general and that community. These ties come to light again in the fact that, in 1924, as interim governor, Ibarra engineered an agreement between Santa María del Tule and Tlalixtac regarding their respective ejido lands, without involving the National Agrarian Commission. The agreement formalized Tlalixstac's claim to half of the land granted to El Tule in 1917. The illegality of this agreement was later rectified, but Ibarra seemed to the people of El Tule to have betrayed them, because many had supported his Sierra troops earlier during the Mexican Revolution, when they were aligned with Zapata and Villa. When Ibarra supported El Tule's historic enemies in Tlalixtac, the level of conflict intensified. The outside agrarian officials who helped them win back their ejido land emerged as local heroes.

OFFICIALS FROM THE AGRARIAN DEPARTMENT HELP SANTA MARÍA DEL TULE

According to the ejidatario José Flores, the agreement arranged by Ibarra held the community of El Tule hostage. As Flores told it, Santa María del Tule returned to its long subordination to the "big town" of Tlalixtac—and now to its patron, Ibarra, the betrayer. Officials from the Federal Agrarian Reform Commission and the Oaxaca state delegate of the Agrarian Department became supporters of the community and emerge as the good guys:

> Part of the ejido land we were ceded from the Guendulain hacienda goes by a river called the Zogocho. A general who fought with the Serranos named Isaac Ibarra intervened on behalf of those from Tlalixtac. He came here with his people. They were heavily armed and told the community authorities of El Tule, "Listen, there are a lot of people in Tlalixtac who didn't get any land through the Agrarian Reform. Why not give them the piece of land behind the river? We have a lot of arms and it wouldn't do you any good to die for this land. Why not agree to this proposal?" So, the community authorities didn't say anything because Ibarra and his people had so many guns. Eleven years later, we were able to get this land back from Tlalixtac. We had to do it by going all the way to the Agrarian Department in Mexico City. The people from Tlalixtac were not happy with this. They continued to resist and get angry until sometime in the mid 1940s. That is when they shot six people from here. They wanted our communal land as well.

Another ejidatario, Eugenio Vásquez, who witnessed the events, told a similar story. Here, his narrative picks up with how the community finally obtained all of the land they had been granted. This happened under the administration of Cárdenas, which most ejidatarios have never forgotten. In 1934, Cárdenas visited the ejido personally while a candidate for the presidency:

> . . . so after Ibarra intervened, half of our ejido went to Tlalixtac. They took possession and worked the land. This kept on going for eleven years, until we went to Mexico City and there was an Agrarian Congress called by the Oaxaca delegate of the Agrarian Department. It was held in a place called Ixcotel, near the city of Oaxaca. The community authorities of all of the ejidos in the state were invited.[5]
>
> The community authorities of El Tule presented their case against Tlalixtac in that congress, to get support. After the congress, we got some kind of notification from the government. It said that the community of Tlalixtac never sent a formal application to the government requesting the lands that they had taken away from El Tule. Tlalixtac never filed an application for ejido lands. So the federal government said that our ejido had to be reconstituted. The government said that Tlalixtac had to give back the lands. They didn't resist.
>
> After we heard this, we held a big meeting. We said, "We have to demand full restitution of our lands. We formed a commission and sent them to Mexico City." In 1935, under Cárdenas, the order for the restitution of our lands came.

On 28 October 1935, the community authorities of Tlalixtac de Cabrera and Santa María del Tule, along with the Oaxaca delegate of the Agrarian Department, signed a document, witnessed by most of the men and women of El Tule, which finally gave them full possession of the ejido lands granted in the presidential resolution dated 15 November 1917. The ejido commissioner of Santa María del Tule promised, in the name of all ejidatarios, to respect the crops that had been planted by people from Tlalixtac until 27 November. After that date, the ejidatarios of El Tule had permission to tear up anything planted on their lands and to proceed with their own planting (Secretaría de Reforma Agraria, Delegación de Oaxaca 1935). After seventeen years, they finally had full possession of their ejido land, and after hundreds of years of landlessness, they would finally be working on land they had the rights to.

RENEWED VIOLENCE: EL TULE CEDES HALF ITS
COMMUNAL LAND TO TLALIXTAC AND THE CONFLICT ENDS

From 1935 to 1945, the ejidatarios in El Tule enjoyed a relatively peaceful existence. Then, suddenly, early in the morning on a day in 1945, six people from El Tule were shot to death as they walked up the mountain in front of the community. Ninety-one-year-old Hilario Vásquez remembered the incident:

> Six people died in a path that goes up into the mountain there in front of the community. Tomás Matias and some other people fought there with those from Tlalixtac. Tlalixtac won the fight and they took away half the mountain from us. Since then, the most important land we have is the ejido. That's why we want to keep it. We won't ever give it up.

The violence in 1945 was followed by more than five years of tense encounters between people from the two communities. Tlalixtac reignited a legal process to claim half of El Tule's communal land. In the 1950s, El Tule decided to cede about half of its communal land to Tlalixtac to guarantee peace between the two communities. Like many indigenous communities in Oaxaca that have ejidos, Santa María de Tule also has communal lands dating from the colonial period; thus, many in El Tule felt that since they had obtained the ejido lands, which were much better quality, it was not worth continued bloodshed to hold onto the mountain associated with their origin as a community. Since the 1950s, relationships between the communities have been strained at events such as local dances, but the continued violence and legal confrontations have ceased.

THE LEGACY OF CÁRDENAS AND
ZAPATA IN THE EJIDO OF EL TULE

The historical narratives offered by the ejidatarios of El Tule have shown that, by the time the community members took full possession of their ejido lands, they had waged long and bitter battles with their Zapotec neighbors from Tlalixtac and with the hacendados they had worked for. From the perspective of many, agrarian officials had been instrumental in achieving the long-delayed victory. Under the administration of Cárdenas, the promises of the revolution that they had first read of in a local circular in 1917 were finally realized.

Analysis of further conversations with the ejidatarios of El Tule, in the following section, shows how local ejido history is connected to national narratives of the Mexican Revolution, the figure of Emiliano Zapata, and the legacy of the revolution claimed by the administration of Lázaro Cárdenas.

In oral histories told to me by the original ejidatarios of El Tule, or by their relatives, Cárdenas and Zapata are linked, as heroes, to the story of the founding of the ejido. In a narrative told to me in summer 1993 by 92-year-old Mario González, as in those of others, Cárdenas assumes the role of standard bearer for the ideology of Zapata.

As previously noted, Cárdenas made two visits to El Tule, one in April 1934, while campaigning for the presidency, another in March 1937, while promoting programs for agrarian reform and socialist education. Both visits are well documented in the Oaxacan newspapers *El Oaxaqueño* and *Oaxaca Nuevo,* and both were framed by large meals and public presentations under the famous "Tule tree," billed as the largest tree in the world. Mario González, after discussing the formative period of the ejido, recalled Cárdenas's visits. We were talking in the shade of his front yard, behind a corrugated aluminum fence made of flattened soft drink and beer cans:

> We were content with our ejido. The government suffered and Emiliano Zapata suffered. He gave his life, he gave his blood, so that all of the poor could improve their lives with their land. . . . When he [Zapata] won the war, they say he spoke with his soldiers and said, "Let's go to work. Go to your fields, those that [they had] received. Work. We have already suffered. And now we have won."
>
> We [in Santa María del Tule] had nothing to maintain ourselves with, because the Carrancistas killed off a lot of us.[6] We were dying of hunger. These Carrancistas were on the side of the hacendados, of the rich. They were against the poor. Because of this, when we went to accompany Cárdenas to Oaxaca,

we came first to the city hall. We asked him what he thought of our city hall. I was eighteen years old and was a local volunteer policeman. We also went to leave a banner there. Then he shouted, "Que se mueran los ricos, arriba los pobres" [roughly, "Death to the rich and up with the poor"].

At the beginning of Mario's narration, Zapata assumed a Christlike image in which his blood was sacrificed for the good of poor campesinos. The government was linked to Zapata, in its mutual suffering for the cause of the poor. Zapata had meaning as a local martyr—reminiscent of the photograph of Zapata Marcos said was carried around by el viejo Antonio in Chiapas and presented to Subcomandante Marcos (see chapter 6). His memory tightened the tie between the suffering of Zapata and the suffering of the government; both sacrificed for the community. After explaining what happened after Zapata won "the war"—that is, that people in El Tule and elsewhere who received ejido land could finally survive—Mario moved seamlessly to Cárdenas's visit to El Tule and Oaxaca. Because Mario remembered Cárdenas shouting "Death to the rich and up with the poor," in his mind Cárdenas was clearly linked with Zapata.

In earlier conversation, Mario had provided a long explanation of who Zapata was and what his ideas were. This exchange occurred in the context of a larger conversation with a group of four older ejidatario men and women. We were waiting for an ejido assembly to begin, on a Sunday afternoon. While I had meant to ask about the founding of the specific ejido of Santa María del Tule, Mario responded in an interesting way, first talking about Zapata and then skipping to Cárdenas's visit. Indeed, every time he discussed the founding, he talked about Zapata and Cárdenas, as did many other ejidatarios. Zapata and Cárdenas were clearly assimilated as key characters in the formation of the ejido—something I had to learn.

LYNN: Whose idea was it to organize the ejido here?
MARIO: It was Emiliano Zapata (echoed by several others). Don't you know how it was? The Carrancistas were in favor of the rich. They were against the poor.
LYNN: So Carranza was against the poor. . . .
MARIO: Zapata got together his people. Because, first—well, what they say is that when Zapata was a little boy, he was working on an hacienda with his father when he saw that the Carrancistas . . . no, I mean, what do they call them? . . . the overseers of the hacienda, the mayordomos, beat the workers. Emiliano saw this. When he was a little boy he saw that this overseer was beating his father. So he spoke and

said, "Ay, Papa . . . the day is going to come when we will take this
land away [from the hacendado]." . . . Then there was a war.

Here, Mario initially substituted Carrancistas for hacienda overseers.
Carrancista soldiers had occupied the region of Mario's community in
1915–20 and had intermittent battles with Zapotec soldiers from the
Sierra Juárez, politically aligned with Francisco Villa and Emiliano Zapata. It seems that, for Mario, the overseers on the haciendas and the
Carrancistas had become interchangeable, because both were in opposition to Zapata and to poor landless (primarily indigenous) laborers.

Earlier in this discussion, Mario and others identified the people of
Santa María del Tule as "pure Indians" who lived in extreme poverty.
Cárdenas and, by implication, Zapata, and probably also the government, were seen as having lifted the community out of poverty. Mario
stated:

> When Cárdenas came here, he fed us. His servants brought us food, there be-
> low the Tule tree, as he spoke to us. We were *puros indios* then. We didn't
> speak Spanish, only Zapotec. We were all really poor. We wore white cotton
> pants and didn't have any shoes. All we had were little cane houses that could
> just blow over in the wind.

Other historical narratives I listened to in Santa María del Tule had a
similar tone. All of the original ejidatarios I spoke with in El Tule repeated that "Zapata was on the side of the poor and the hacendados
were with the rich." Ejidatarios associated Zapata with Cárdenas, since
it was under Cárdenas's presidency that Zapata's ideas were carried out
and that people finally took full possession the full ejido land awarded
in 1917. Local men and women often worked Cárdenas and Zapata into
their histories and memories of their ejido's formation. The relationship between the two heroes was clearly articulated in a conversation I
had with Carlos Gómez during the summer of 1999. He was eighty-five
years old at the time, and had assumed the role of a distinguished community historian. We had agreed to talk about Cárdenas and Zapata, as
they had been themes in previous conversations and in his telling of the
story of the ejido. Carlos, a longtime ejidatario, had been a young man
when Cárdenas first visited the ejido.

LYNN: What do you remember about the first time that Lázaro Cárdenas
           visited El Tule?
CARLOS: I remember how proud we were that he presented himself to El Tule
           as a presidential candidate. He came walking into town from the
           camino real, what later became the Pan American Highway.[7] He

Figure 11.   Ejidatario from Santa María del Tule. Photo by
Lynn Stephen.

came walking down the road toward the big tree to where the municipal offices were. He arrived greeting each and every person who
was present, reaching out to hug them. No other presidential candidate had ever come to El Tule. In talks that he had with the municipal authorities and with the people from this town, they asked
him to help us finish the primary school and to help us get back the
ejido lands that had been taken from us in 1924 by Tlalixtac de Cabrera. These requests were later granted. El Tule was very grateful,
and we still remain appreciative of the attitudes and actions of Gen-

eral Cárdenas. As a sign of our appreciation, when we built a secondary school here, we called it the General Lázaro Cárdenas del Río school. What else would you like to know?

LYNN: Could we return to our discussion of what you think about the relationship between Cárdenas and Zapata?

CARLOS: Well, they are very closely linked, because, when Cárdenas became president of the Republic of Mexico, he followed the ideas of General Zapata and kept on expropriating land from what they call latifundias. He expropriated lands from the latifundias for the indigenous and poor people.

LYNN: And how did you first hear about Emiliano Zapata?

CARLOS: I first heard about him during the ceremonies they have on the day of his death, which was 10 April 1919. These ceremonies were first carried out by what we called the Campesina [Confederación Campesina Mexicana, or Mexican Peasant Confederation] and then later by the CNC.

LYNN: How many people used to go to these ceremonies from El Tule?

CARLOS: About forty or fifty people.

LYNN: What did they talk about at these ceremonies?

CARLOS: They would tell us how the struggle of Zapata started, how he achieved his objective with the support of the people who followed him—because they thought he had good intentions and worked for the good of the poor. Things like this. That's where I learned a lot about Zapata.

Carlos had also talked about what people in Santa María del Tule thought of Zapata in an earlier conversation, saying: "They think that everything that Zapata did is good, because he said that the land belongs to whomever works it. Zapata defended poor people with his deeds. More than anything, he gave his life for his cause. In Oaxaca, we celebrate his holiday. We pay homage to him." Carlos's assessment is probably linked to memories of annual ceremonies on the anniversary of Zapata's death, which featured speakers paying homage to the guerrilla fighter of the south. For example, on 10 April 1937, the Confederación Campesina Mexicana organized a commemoration in the Macedonio Alcala Theater that Carlos and other ejidatarios attended. On the same day, Governor Coronel Constantino Chapital gave provisional ejidal land grants to ten communities (Oaxaca Nuevo 1937a). Beginning in the 1930s, especially under Cárdenas, it became a tradition for the government to announce ejido land grants on the anniversary of Zapata's death, reinforcing the government's claim to his legacy. President Carlos Salinas de Gortari built on this tradition, giving out thousands of

PROCEDE certificates to ejidatarios on 10 April 1994 as part of his government's campaign to redefine Zapata's message to suit neoliberal restructuring and NAFTA (see chapter 2).

Programs from such celebrations have themes resonating with the kinds of ideology and stories laid out in the Secretaría de Educación Pública's curriculum for socialist education (see chapter 3). In 1935, the Oaxacan celebration included items such as the Corrida Agrarista (Agrarian Anthem), a revolutionary poem, a speech on "Emiliano Zapata and Agrarianism in Mexico" and the installment of the first stone for the monument dedicated to Zapata by the governor (*El Oaxaqueño* 1935). These celebrations provided ejidatarios such as Carlos with historical material on Zapata that they later reworked in their own versions of local and national events.

Cerbando Hernández, who was eighty-nine when we spoke, also recollected Cárdenas and his connection to the legacy of Zapata, while we were discussing the history of the ejido:

LYNN: So, what do you remember about Zapata?

CERBANDO: Well, Carranza was against him. . . . It was Zapata who asked that they take the land away from the hacendados. Those from Villa Alta attacked here.[8] The people from El Tule supported Zapata.

LYNN: So the town was with Zapata?

CERBANDO: Well, yes. The town was allied with Zapata.

LYNN: So what do you think about when you hear the name of Emiliano Zapata now?

CERBANDO: We give thanks to him because he gave us the ejido and it was Lázaro Cárdenas who gave us possession of our ejido.

The association between the government, Zapata, Cárdenas, and the granting of ejido land in El Tule seems to be shared by the elder women ejidatarios as well.

It should be noted that the ejido of El Tule has a total of 413 ejidatarios, of whom 126, or 30 percent, are women. Like their male counterparts, the women ejidatarios are elderly. In El Tule, the average age, of 61 male and female ejidatarios randomly surveyed in 1994, was 57.8 years. Seven, or 22 percent, of the 31 female ejidatarias surveyed were under the age of 45, the remaining 24 (78 percent) were over 45. Fourteen, or 45 percent of those surveyed, were over 60. Nine of these women were widows. Some women were granted ejido rights as single mothers or from their fathers, but the demographics of the women surveyed suggest that almost 30 percent of the ejidatarias were elderly widows who had inherited their ejido rights after their husbands died.[9]

One of these elderly widows was Elvira Bautista Méndez, born in 1923. Her memories reflect several conversations I had with elderly ejidatarias. One morning in 1997, we had a long conversation about her life and the ejido. The name of Cárdenas came up in relation to the history of the ejido and his visit. Her memory focused on two important events—the celebration on the day in 1935 when Santa María del Tule finally took possession of all its ejido land, and Cárdenas's visit in March 1937. The gendered aspect of her memory was evident in her focus on food. She first concentrated on the work she and other girls and women had to do for the celebration, then on the fact that she personally was fed by Cárdenas's entourage during his visit. We also briefly discussed Zapata:

LYNN: Did your grandfather receive ejido land?

ELVIRA: Yes, I remember when they distributed the ejido land. We had a fight with Tlalixtac. . . .

LYNN: With Isaac Ibarra?

ELVIRA: Yes. Tlalixtac was in charge of our ejidos. So we got into a fight. So an engineer came here to El Tule and they decided in favor of El Tule. Then the engineers came, they measured, and they killed goats to eat. . . . I helped to make the food. There weren't any stoves then, we just cooked with firewood. All of the pots were made of clay. We had a fiesta for the land that was distributed. We made a lot of food. I was little then. I even got worn out from patting tortillas. I had to make them on the metate because there weren't these things like there are now—*planadores* (wooden presses) to flatten the tortillas. . . . No, before we just had the things of poor people. . . . We had to work really hard. . . .

LYNN: So there was this fight with Tlalixtac. Then the interim governor gave half of the ejido land to Tlalixtac. They had the land for eleven years, but then a favorable decision granted the land to El Tule. . . .

ELVIRA: The land was returned to El Tule. I remember when Lázaro Cárdenas was president of the republic. He came to visit here in El Tule. . . . They made a huge meal. It was all full here of soldiers from the military. You should have seen the food.

LYNN: Oh yes?

ELVIRA: Yes. It was a huge meal. . . .

LYNN: When you were little, did they talk about Emiliano Zapata here?

ELVIRA: Well, not so much. . . . That was before my time.

LYNN: Have you heard of him?

ELVIRA: Yes, I have heard of him. They said that he was in favor of us, the campesinos. . . .

LYNN: Why?

ELVIRA: Because he gave us our land. I am an ejidataria. My husband was an ejidatario, and when he died, they recognized me as an ejidataria. . . .

LYNN: So they say here that Emiliano Zapata gave the ejido.

ELVIRA: Yes. That is why . . . the teachers make a holiday honoring Emiliano Zapata here in town.

LYNN: And when you remember Lázaro Cárdenas? How do you remember him?

ELVIRA: He came here to visit the big tree here in El Tule. He came here and they made a big meal, a huge meal for him, but he paid for it. He even brought his own cooks.

LYNN: Did he feed people here in the community?

ELVIRA: Yes. He gave everyone something to eat. Even I got something to eat. I was a little girl the size of my granddaughter. "Niña, niña, come here," they said. They gave me my taco of barbecued goat. They even gave food to me. . . .

My conversation with Elvira reveals some elements consistent with the connections made by other ejidatarios among Zapata, Cárdenas, and the ejido. She did not directly invoke the government, but seemed to feel a strong personal connection with Cárdenas's visit, recalling that, even though a little girl, she too had been given a goat taco when he visited. Cárdenas cared enough even to have little children fed.

Elvira's description in some ways resonates with a story in a Oaxacan newspaper that also focused on the meal below the large Tule tree. The first lines read, in bold print: "The meal that local authorities and residents offered in honor of General Lázaro Cárdenas, president of the Republic, and other important persons who accompanied him on the occasion of his visit, took place yesterday at midday in the nearby town of Santa María del Tule" (*El Oaxaqueño* 1937). This newspaper had also reported enthusiastically on Cárdenas's 1934 visit, under the headline "Major Banquet Offered to General Cárdenas Yesterday in El Tule." A smaller headline added: "Under the magnificent tree, more than one thousand peasants congregated, who shared a few hours with the popular candidate" (*El Oaxaqueño* 1934). It seems that eating with Lázaro Cárdenas under the big tree, whether in 1934 or in 1937, is etched in the memories of many people.

The enthusiasm with which Elvira told the story of the 1937 visit can be seen in the continuation of the newspaper story about this visit:

With delirious enthusiasm, the inhabitants who were lined up all the way to the entrance of the town broke out in joyful exclamations the instant that General Lázaro Cárdenas entered the town. . . . Accompanied by Governor Chapital, General Cárdenas went to the municipal offices in the midst of the demonstrations of enthusiasm shown by the people paying tribute to him." (*El Oaxaqueño* 1937)

People like Elvira and Carlos (quoted above) remember the 1937 visit with passion, warmth, and a deep respect for the person of Cárdenas.

Another interesting element of Elvira's discussion is her statement that the teachers have an annual holiday honoring Emiliano Zapata. El Tule was the site of a SEP rural federal school established in the 1930s under Cárdenas. The community applied for federalization of their community primary school and were initially turned down, but their petition was granted after Cárdenas's 1937 visit. It is likely that the teachers then began public commemorations of Zapata, which everyone in town was aware of and often attended.

Only three weeks after Cárdenas shared a meal with Elvira and others from Santa María del Tule in 1937, the community was designated as the site of a "model ejido." This status was supposed to result in a new residential zone with "houses for peasants with potable water, bathrooms, public washing bins, sports fields, and other types of services that have not yet been built in any other ejido in the state," according to an article in *Oaxaca Nuevo* (1937b). The community did gain some of the services requested.

Thus, for Mario, Carlos, Cerbano, Elvira, and dozens of other ejidatarios I spoke with in Santa María del Tule, the story of the formation of the ejido is directly linked to the legacy of Zapata and, through his visit and actions, to Cárdenas. Many older ejidatarios who came of age in the 1930s are today looked to as authorities on ejido history. Their memories still carry significant weight in the public oral record. Most people I interviewed, including ejidatarios under the age of thirty, would direct me to elderly ejidatarios for the most legitimate version of history.

Their narratives suggest somewhat paternalistic linkages between the symbolic mediators of Cárdenas and Zapata and the community. While most praise government efforts in the past to help them secure their ejido land, and continued to vote for the PRI until 2001, detailed discussions emphasizing feelings about current government policies reveal varying levels of dissatisfaction. This will be further discussed in chapter 11.

CHANGING ECONOMICS AND ATTITUDES
IN SANTA MARÍA DEL TULE

As time has gone on, Santa María del Tule has grown; the ejido has become less important in the local economy as other paths of economic activity have opened up. After the community received ejido lands, men continued to mine and produce lime and to sell charcoal in Oaxaca, as many did during the colonial period. Women produced tortillas for sale in the Oaxaca markets, washed clothing in Oaxaca, and labored as domestic workers in Oaxaca and for the few well-off families in El Tule. In many cases, wage labor was undertaken to accumulate cash to buy oxen and plows to work ejido land. During the 1940s, men from El Tule went to work as *braceros* in the United States, and some of them continued to migrate after the bracero program ended in 1964.[10]

By the 1970s, the economy of Santa María del Tule was diverse. Women began to work as secretaries and waitresses and continued the traditional work of selling tortillas in Oaxaca. The famous tree in El Tule, often billed as the world's largest in girth, became the hub of tourism for the community. Men worked as gardeners and construction workers, and a few began to work as taxi and truck drivers. Some men eventually purchased vehicles and started transport businesses of their own. In a survey of sixty-four ejidatarios from El Tule (thirty-one men and thirty-three women) in 1994, about one-third of the male respondents indicated that they had held primary occupations other than that of subsistence farmer for most of their lives; most prevalent was work in transportation as truck drivers, office work in Oaxaca, and small-business catering to tourists. One-third of women respondents also indicated that they had spent most of their lives in nonagricultural work.[11] Such work included small-business catering to tourists (selling food or crafts), domestic servant positions, and office jobs in Oaxaca. In sum, today, even among ejidatarios, more "traditional" in their economic activities than others in El Tule, about one-third of both men and women have a history of nonagricultural work.

In the late 1990s, Santa María del Tule looks like a cross between a village and a growing town. It is not only surrounded by ejido lands planted with corn and other crops, but bordered by a PEMEX plant on one side and a gas plant on the other. The main square has been nicely fixed up, and the municipal president's office and the ejido office dominate one side. The famous big tree of El Tule is surrounded by an iron

Figure 12.   An ejidataria with her pig in Santa María del Tule.
Photo by Lynn Stephen.

fence in front of the church. The church has a new paint job, an artisans'
and food market dominates one side of town, and there are businesses
ranging from auto repair shops to shoe stores. A number of the main
streets are paved, with houses built close together. Further from the center there are larger yards with chickens, pigs, occasionally cattle, and
pickup trucks parked in the mud.

The integration of the ejido of Santa María del Tule with the urban economy of the nearby city of Oaxaca has placed the ejidatarios in a border zone of a type characteristic of much of Mexico, simultaneously rural and urban. Given the ejido's historical proximity to Oaxaca, this hybrid rural-urban identity is not a new one for people like Mario, Carlos, Cerbando, and Elvira. They and members of their families have been commuting to Oaxaca for decades for a variety of needs. Historically, their proximity to the state capital also resulted in the relatively easy dissemination of state politics and policy to the community. Community members were among the first in the state to solicit and receive ejido land, and, as demonstrated above, ejidatarios have consistently participated in state-initiated organizations, and have absorbed state policy while refashioning it to their own versions of local history and endowing it with local meaning.

In contrast to that of the ejidos of Guadalupe Tepeyac and La Realidad in Chiapas, the historical experience of ejidatarios in Santa María del Tule has involved considerable conflict with a neighboring indigenous community and the help of the government in winning their struggle with their hostile neighbors. In local histories of the ejido, their Zapotec neighbors in Tlalixtac are the enemy. The good guys in the struggle are Zapata, Cárdenas, and the government agrarian officials who came to their aid. The personal visits of Cárdenas to the community, and his connection to the final resolution of the conflict between El Tule and Tlalixtac for ejido lands, also left a strong imprint on local versions of history. In addition, Cárdenas's claim to the legacy of Zapata has been adopted by some ejidatarios. The national figures of Cárdenas and Zapata have been appropriated by the ejidatarios of El Tule and are part of their local history.

The narratives of these ejidatarios reveal how their personal biographies are embedded in local codes of reception about shared local histories. The stories of these ejidatarios link the national to the local through a deliberate reclaiming of nation-building symbols and the incorporation of these symbols into the history of "their ejido." The geographies of identities (Radcliffe and Westwood 1996) represented in the narratives link the physical place of Santa María del Tule, and its material details—the big Tule tree, the church and the Virgin, the ejido lands, local rivers, the physical boundaries with Tlalixtac, even local food—to the representational space that links local and national history. Thus, in the contemporary telling of local histories, not only are multiple geographies invoked that are tied to a series of layered identities (ejidatarios of Santa María, poor and indigenous, from Oaxaca, from Mexico), but the past is fashioned and refashioned through the lens of the present. The following chapter tells the contrasting story of Unión Zapata, where ejidatarios claim close links to Zapata but have, collectively, a much shorter history than have the ejidatarios of El Tule.

CHAPTER 10

The Formation of the Ejido of Unión Zapata

Cárdenas y Zapata, presente!

UNIÓN ZAPATA, OAX., 27 APRIL 1937
SEÑOR GRAL DE DIV. D. LÁZARO CÁRDENAS
MÉXICO, D.F.

Very Respectable Mr. President,

Please permit us to direct our attention to you in order to offer you our most abundant thanks for the kind assistance that you have sent to us in order to alleviate our precarious existence.

At the same time we are pleased to report to you that señor Ingeniero D. Cliserio Villafuerte was in a meeting with the señor Delegate of the Agrarian Department telling him what he thought was pertinent to the urbanization of our community, which is now being designed to our great satisfaction. Now they are gathering the construction materials to make the house of the campesino with the collaboration of the people of this community.

The commissioned engineer who is working very hard is making plans for the introduction of running water. . . . At the same time, under his direction, the school is almost finished, using the donation you sent, and will probably be inaugurated on the first of May.

The señor Engineer Villafuerte gave us the good news that you have ordered that we be presented with five oxen with their respective plows and a sewing machine for the Feminine League of Social

Struggle [Liga Femenil de Lucha Social], which has already been formed. For all of this we very sincerely thank you.

We will inform you in a timely manner, Mr. President, of the date on which our water pump will be installed, which will bring this liquid to our community, as well as the date for the installation of the corn mill, which will bring so many benefits to our compañeras.

In the name of all of the children of this town we beg you to do us the favor of giving our most abundant thanks to your respectable wife for the presentation of one hundred pesos she made to the children for their sweets. . . . We have also received and thank you for the first-aid kit and the clothing that was sent for the children in the school.

We are deeply grateful to you and to your respectable wife Mr. President and we shall retain eternal gratitude to you and your family members.

Yours with all respect,
Anacleto Olivera
President of the Ejidal Commission
Unión Zapata

Like that of Santa María del Tule, the local history of Unión Zapata is strongly tied to the figure of Lázaro Cárdenas. The letter above was written shortly after a visit the president paid to the community in 1937. Unlike Santa María del Tule, Unión Zapata barely existed as a population site prior to the formation of the ejido. In fact, it was cobbled together in the early 1930s to facilitate such formation. Twenty families were needed to form a group to petition for land. Such a group quickly came together as Loma Larga, which later changed its name to Unión Zapata. The families involved came from local communities as well as from resident populations of several local haciendas.

The community petitioned for land in 1933, prior to the beginning of Cárdenas's presidential term, and after his inauguration, the future ejido authorities of the community developed an intense correspondence with him, culminating in a visit by him and his wife in 1937, part of a larger swing through Oaxaca. The visit occurred one year after the community received a positive presidential resolution, signed by Cárdenas, granting ejido land. The correspondence between ejido authorities and officials from the Agrarian Department in both Oaxaca and Mexico City, as well as a series of letters written directly to President Cárdenas, offer a rich record of an ejido organized at the height of the Cárdenas government's program to organize rural peasants, educate them, and establish national culture and policy in the countryside. The new ejidatarios of Unión Zapata were adept at filling their letters with revolutionary rhetoric and enthusiastic proclamations of commitment to the programs advocated by the Cárdenas government. At the same time, they succeeded in obtaining fairly speedy resolution of their initial ejido petition—three years—and in securing additional land within a year, as well as a school building, an ejido meeting hall, a pump, five oxen, sewing machines, corn mills, clothing, and probably more. The granting of these installations and resources were documented in a Oaxaca City newspaper, which stated that the work was being done "to carry out the will of General Cárdenas" (*Oaxaca Nuevo* 1937c).

The ejidatarios of Unión Zapata carefully deployed revolutionary rhetoric to take advantage of the material and political gains to be made through forming an ejido. Community members' perceptions of their close relationship with President Cárdenas then are captured in local ejido histories and were important in influencing how ejidatarios in the 1990s experienced current politics and agrarian policy. In this chapter, I offer an abbreviated history of the formation of the ejido of Unión Zapata, and examine how this is interpreted by current ejidatarios, who also make connections between Zapata (namesake of their ejido), Cárdenas, and their long-standing relationship to the Mexican government.

The history of the ejido of Unión Zapata is less complex than that of El Tule. Most ejidatarios divide their narration into two key time periods: (1) exploitation and life on the haciendas prior to the ejido, and (2) formation of the ejidos and community ties to Cárdenas. In their story, the main protagonists are: (1) the ejidatarios of Unión Zapata, (2) the owners and managers of the Don Pedrillo, del Fuerte, and Tanibé haciendas, (3) Lázaro Cárdenas and Emiliano Zapata, and (4) to a lesser degree, other agrarian officials.

LIFE BEFORE THE EJIDO UNIÓN ZAPATA

Before the 1930s, the site of Unión Zapata had been known as Loma Larga. It was a small rancho of families that worked on the surrounding haciendas of Don Pedrillo, del Fuerte, Xaaga, and Tanibé. Most of these families do not seem to have been of indigenous origin, and they were historically attached to the haciendas as laborers. Other families who joined the ejido community were recruited directly from among the peons living on haciendas; a few more families were recruited from surrounding Zapotec communities such as Mitla, Díaz Ordaz, and Santa Catarina Albarradas. The first two communities were pre-Hispanic population sites, while the third had come into existence early in the colonial period.

The ejido lands of Unión Zapata came from three surrounding haciendas. Lands awarded in the original presidential resolution (1 July 1936) came from the properties known as del Fuerte and Don Pedrillo. Both were created in the 1600s and bordered on the communal lands of Mitla and Tlacolula. Don Pedrillo was created in the 1590s by Cristóbal Ramírez de Aguilar, heir to the first entailed estate in Oaxaca (Taylor 1972, 154). In 1727, the Don Pedrillo estate was mortgaged to the Dominicans, who took possession of it in the 1730s, along with the estate of del Fuerte. In 1740, the del Fuerte estate was absorbed by the large hacienda of Xaaga (ibid., 137); the Xaaga hacienda was bought by Dominicans in 1758. These properties were owned by the Dominicans until the reform period of the 1850s, when they were sold (ibid., 219).

In addition to lands received from del Fuerte and Don Pedrillo, twenty-eight hectares were received by the ejido of Unión Zapata as an addition (*ampliación*) in 1937. These came from the bordering hacienda of Tanibé (also written as "Tanivet"). The Tanibé hacienda was part of the entailed estate of Cristóbal Ramírez de Aguilar (Taylor 1972, 154). Tanibé continued to be owned privately until it was awarded as ejido lands to Unión Zapata and to the ejido of Tanibé. Taylor (ibid., 131) indicates that the Tanibé hacienda had unbonded sharecroppers who worked the land in 1712. The hacienda drew on local populations of peons as well.[1]

All of those who came together to form the ejido of Unión Zapata shared the experience of being landless; most were extremely poor people who worked as peons or sharecroppers on several haciendas. Most recall a difficult life, characterized by hard physical labor, harsh treatment by overseers, and uncomfortable living conditions. Angela López Martínez of Unión Zapata worked with her husband as a sharecropper. Before they had their own oxen, they worked a parcel of land for the hacienda owner of Tanibé and would turn over half their harvest to him after paying off the owner of the oxen. In some years, harvests were very small and they retained nothing.

Angela was eighty years old when we first talked in 1993, and her

Figure 13. Angela with her granddaughters in Unión Zapata.
Photo by Lynn Stephen.

husband was still alive, but sick. We spoke on her front porch, where she gave me the seat of honor, a kind of bucket-seat office chair planted in front of her old adobe house as chickens scurried by. Her husband, Juan, sat in a low wooden chair and listened, often correcting her or helping to recall details—when he could hear; his hearing was failing and he was blind. Angela took constant care of him, watching him as one would a small child, brushing flies off him, feeding him, and bringing water when he was thirsty and blankets if he grew cold. Juan basically lived on the front porch until he was eased into bed at night.

My 1993 conversation with Angela was the first of many. She became a good friend, as I continued to visit the community in later years. Her husband Juan died in 1995.

We began discussing what happened during bad harvest years to those who worked as sharecroppers before the ejido was formed:

LYNN: So what did you do when the harvests were small?

ANGELA: Well, there were years in which we had no corn. We had to turn over half of our harvest to the hacienda. So when the harvest was small, there was hardly anything left over for us. So we would borrow corn from the hacienda.

LYNN: How much would you borrow?

ANGELA: We would borrow about fifty *almudes*[2] or so and we would have to work it off. When there was work, they would tell us to come and shuck the corn. We would go and I would get one-half almud of corn and my husband would get two almudes. That is how we would pay off our debt, or else we would work for corn to eat that day.

Our conversation then switched to the experience of being a worker on the hacienda:

LYNN: How were you treated as workers by the hacendados?

ANGELA: Well, those who were overseers in the haciendas were very bad. . . .

LYNN: Why were they bad?

ANGELA: Well, they were bad because. . . . One time I saw that the *mozos* were harvesting, and a woman arrived from Mitla. I saw this because I was going to leave my husband his lunch. He was working there harvesting, too. The overseer saw that this woman wanted to pick the scraps of corn that were left after the harvest, what we call *el repisco,* do you understand what this means?

LYNN: Yes. The leftover corn.

ANGELA: Uh-huh. The woman wanted to get in there. And this man, the overseer, rode over on his horse and said, "Hey, you? Who gave you permission to do that?" And he hit her with his horsewhip. I saw this happen that time and that is why I am telling you about it.

LYNN: Did they hit the peons, as well?

ANGELA: Yes, they beat them. This overseer was really bad. . . .

LYNN: Were there some overseers who were better, or not as bad?

ANGELA: They say that all of them were really bad. . . . If the peon arrived at the hacienda when the sun was already high in sky, late in the day, then the overseer would tell [him], "It's too late. Come back tomorrow. Go home and go sleep some more. Come back to work to-morrow." And they wouldn't let them work that day.

The mistreatment of workers by overseers was a common theme emphasized by many ejidatarios in Unión Zapata. The physical beating of workers was seen by some as placing them in the same position as animals. As one person commented, "One of the overseers grabbed me and started beating me with a horsewhip, like an animal." Many examples given also covered small indignities, such as not letting people work if they arrived a few minutes late, or not letting them stop for lunch if it arrived at the wrong time. A general lack of respect for the workers is what many described.

Francisco (Paco) García Gonzales and Emilia Aragón discussed similar details in recalling their youth working for the hacendados. The first time I spoke with them about life on the hacienda, Paco mentioned being beaten with a horsewhip by an overseer. He also focused on other details mirroring those cited by Angela. In 1993, when we first met at an ejido meeting, Paco was sixty-eight. He had served in community *cargo* positions, having been both president of the community and commissioner of the ejido. During our first conversation, I asked him to share memories of the hacendados:

LYNN: What do you remember about the hacendados?

PACO: The hacendados were really fucked up. . . . They would beat the workers. A lot of times we would go there, a group of nine or ten people, to work. We would take our oxen to work for the hacendados. We would eat our lunch from one o'clock until two o'clock. If the wife of one of the workers got there after two o'clock, when the lunch hour was over, then the overseers wouldn't let him eat his lunch. He had to work until nighttime. People would work again from two o'clock of three o'clock until eight o'clock at night . . . and then, at night, they would make people wait for their pay for their days' work. Sometimes the workers would have to wait until nine o'clock at night to get paid for the work they did that day. Then they would bring home the corn so that the women could prepare it for the next day. If they had not worked the day before, then there was no corn. Sometimes they wouldn't even pay people until the next day. . . . And if a worker didn't arrive at work until 6:15 or 6:30 in the morning, they would say, "Go home and sleep some more. You can't work today. Go on and get out of here."

Those interviewed cited the creation of the ejido in 1936 as a historical turning point that pulled some out of devastating poverty. There were apparently no surpluses, and people were not sure where their next meal would come from. Periodic draughts and infestations of locusts also diminished food.

A report written in 1935 to the Oaxacan Delegate of the Agrarian Department by the Auxiliary Engineer José L. Gallegos emphasized the poverty of Loma Larga (Gallegos 1935). The report was written after the community formed to petition for ejido land, and was part of the paperwork required in deciding petitions for land; it was part of the folder sent to Cárdenas to consider in determining whether to grant land to the community. The report begins by noting that the landless laborers of Loma Larga are in an even more difficult situation since having formally petitioned for land. Their former employers, the hacienda owners, will no longer employ them, because they have filed a petition that may result in a redistribution of land from the haciendas to the laborers of Loma Larga. The report also notes that the hacienda owners have been supported in their boycott of Loma Larga laborers by the municipal authorities of Mitla, the county seat, which had, and continues to have, legal jurisdiction over Loma Larga/Unión Zapata.

In one section, "Economic conditions in the hamlet" the report provides great detail:

> The poverty of the people of Loma Large is immediately seen when entering the community. The houses are completely rustic and made of branches and cane. There is not one house in the entire settlement made of adobe or any other permanent construction material. And even the construction of these huts made of branches is difficult because there is no nearby wooded area. Nutrition is very poor, as is people's clothing. We could practically say that the only thing that people eat is tortillas and beans. In the majority of cases, the only clothing that people have is a simple pair of pants and a shirt made of white cotton. It also seems that many of the people here don't have blankets to keep themselves warm, despite the fact that during the winter the temperature can get quite cold and the huts don't keep the cold out. All of this is due to the bad economic conditions that intervene here. (Gallegos 1935)

Following this section, Gallegos then goes through calculations to demonstrate that most inhabitants of Loma Larga do not make enough money in one year to survive, and that the only way that they will be able to survive in the future is through a land grant. He recommends six to eight hectares of land per person, and indicates which surrounding haciendas could provide the land. He is obviously quite sympathetic to the people of Loma Larga, appalled at their poverty, and supportive of their petition for land. He is one of the "good guys" from the government who come to form part of local history.

THE FORMATION OF THE EJIDO

Unlike Santa María del Tule, where local officials apparently decided to solicit ejido land after reading a presidential circular in 1916, Unión Zapata formed as an ejido at the impetus of an outsider, a politician from nearby Tlacolula named Preciliano Pais. He came to the rancho of Loma Larga from the neighboring larger town of Tlacolula, and recruited the Aragón brothers, who were local leaders, to work with him on organizing an ejido. Apparently, the discussions began while the men were drinking with local politicians in Tlacolula. The two brothers were known as agrarian activists; they went from Loma Larga to speak to peons working on the Don Pedrillo and El Fuerte haciendas. The owners of both haciendas tried to stop the formation of the ejido, offering bribes to leaders from Loma Larga and threatening people from the community. Paco García commented on this:

LYNN: Did anything happen to those people who began organizing the ejido?

PACO: Yes, Victor Olivera, the owner of the hacienda del Fuerte, tried to buy off Lauro Aragón. The hacendados from Tanibé and Don Pedrillo also offered people money not to organize the ejido. But people didn't accept it. They said, "Why should we take money just to end up in the same miserable situation?"

LYNN: Did people from Loma Larga have to be careful when they were organizing the ejido?

PACO: Of course we did. I remember one time when I was in Tlacolula in a store. There in the same store was the owner of the Don Pedrillo hacienda. He had a house in Tlacolula. When he saw that I was one of the people from Loma Larga who was from a family organizing the ejido, he took out his pistol and told me that he was going to shoot me. He was threatening me when the storekeeper intervened and I ran out the door. Yes, we had to watch out for ourselves, everyone from our town.

Angela López Martínez remembered being frightened about the formation of the ejido, and she pointed out that there were people who resisted forming it, those who worked most closely with the hacienda owners. "These people said, 'Why should we get involved with the government? It will just cause trouble.' They would also comment about how the hacendados, the rich, were a big help to everyone because they gave them work. They said that we shouldn't do anything against them." She continued:

It frightened me. I was worried about what was going to happen. My father was against it and so was my husband Juan's father. Juan was fighting with both of our parents. I was against it, but because it's as they say—the men are in charge—what was I going to do? I was eventually convinced and went along with the idea.

While some people refused to join the effort to organize the ejido, others left their communities and came to live in Loma Larga so that the required number of families could petition. Twenty families were the minimum needed, and several ejidatarios recalled how people literally dismantled their huts and then reassembled them in Loma Larga.

This patched-together community sent a formal petition for ejido land to the governor of Oaxaca in 1933. It named the owners of the three haciendas surrounding the community, and stated, "Because we don't have our own land to fulfill our necessities, we are obligated to sell our labor at a low price and to not educate our children" (Grijalva, Bautista, Aragón et al. 1933). The original petition was signed by twenty-four men and used the rhetoric of a "class without resources" to back the request for land. It was formally published in September of that year in the *Periódico Oficial,* or official newspaper, of the state of Oaxaca.

The following year, 1934, saw the beginnings of a steady stream of correspondence from Unión Zapata to agrarian officials at the state and national levels, as well as a series of letters written to President Abelardo Rodrígues and, later, to President Lázaro Cárdenas. The motive of the correspondence, written in 1934–36, seems to have been both to remind the presidents and agrarian officials of the continuing hardships faced by people in Unión Zapata (particularly after local hacendados threatened, and refused to give work to, those who had signed the petition for ejido lands), and to continually push the government to move quickly on Unión Zapata's petition for land. Although it took three years for the petition to be approved by the president, this was, compared to the experiences of many, a short turnaround. The request for additional lands (as an *ampliación*) only took one year to be granted—in great contrast to the experience of Guadalupe Tepeyac in the 1970s and 1980s. There, ejidatarios waited seventeen years for an extension to their ejido and were only allowed to occupy a part of what they were promised.

The series of letters written to Rodrígues and Cárdenas in 1934–36 provides a close record of the harassment that the petitioners received from local hacendados, and of the continued deployment of revolutionary rhetoric to describe the community's difficult situation. On 23 March 1934, two men from the local agrarian committee of Loma Larga, Anacleto Grijalva and Guadalupe Bautista, wrote Rodrígues describing how local hacendados Julian Díaz Ordaz and Isauro Ruiz "flatly refuse to let us sharecrop on lands we have worked for years and years" and are "denying us a livelihood." They signed the letter with "Land, Justice, and Liberty," invoking the memory of Zapata (Grijalva and Bautista 1934a). A follow-up letter was written three days later, explaining the situation in greater detail and urging that the president, given his "revolutionary" sentiments, speedily complete the process so that the rural laborers of Loma Larga could legally occupy the lands they had been working (Grijalva 1934). Copies of each letter were sent to the Oaxacan Peasant Confederation (COC). Each letter also received a reply within a few weeks from a staffperson at the National Palace.

The following month, a telegram was sent to the president informing him that one of the local hacienda representatives had kicked the laborers from Loma Larga off hacienda lands that they had already planted for sharecropping (Bautista 1934). Soon afterward, a Oaxaca state official intervened and held a meeting with the offending hacienda representative, and according to a memo written on 30 April 1934, the laborers were permitted to keep working on the hacienda land already planted (Velasco 1934). In May and July of 1934, two other letters were sent Rodríguez, urging him to sign a presidential resolution for the land the community was occupying as ejido land, before the rainy season started (Grijalva and Bautista 1934b and 1934c). The July letter also informs the president of lands on a bordering hacienda, Tanibé, which should be made available for appropriation.

In 1935, the community of Loma Larga—still waiting for its ejido petition to be granted—voted in public assembly to officially change its name to Unión Zapata, cementing its connection to the right to land and, obviously, to the revolutionary hero whose name it took. That same year, community officials began to correspond with President Cárdenas, repeating many requests they had made the previous year but adding new rhetorical flourishes, which seem to mirror the language the Cárdenas government was promoting in Oaxaca and elsewhere. In a letter dated 19 June 1935, eight ejido petitioners reiterated their requests for specific lands from three area haciendas, framing their request within the concept of a need to "resolve the distinct problems which interrupt our cultural, economic, physical, and social development as proletarian peasants" (Grijalva, Bautista, Aragón et al. 1935); they talk about needing land to "elevate our class." The use of terms such as "class" and "development" that emerged in these letters to Cárdenas did not appear in the letters of 1934 to Rodrígues. Rather than assume that the petitioners of Unión Zapata suddenly developed a class consciousness between 1934 and 1935, it makes more sense to give them credit for quickly adapting their writing style to the new president and for using the language of his administration to push forward their appeals. Other letters written in 1935, addressed to the head of the Agrarian Department in Mexico City, with copies sent to Cárdenas, made specific requests for developing a school, a cooperative society, a band, and other local projects—all cast in terms of organized peasants working for the "passion of the class struggle, which can transform our lives" (see chapter 2; Ramírez, Aragón, and Bautista 1935). The letters to Cárdenas continued in 1936, when the community finally took possession of its ejido land (on 26 July).

Forty-eight single, married, and widowed men had rights to the land granted in the original presidential resolution for the Unión Zapata ejido, but only eighteen actually received land. About thirty persons deemed eligible for ejido land received none, because the resolution did not provide sufficient acreage. Thus, in November 1936, only four months after coming into formal possession of their ejido land, the people of Unión Zapata solicited more land.

At this time, a group of laborers who had not received ejido land, and who had worked as sharecroppers on the Tanibé ranch, continued to work their land but informed the Tanibé managers that they would only provide 10 percent of their harvest, instead of the customary 50 percent. In a formal complaint to the governor of Oaxaca, Gustavo Ruiz, who said he rented land from the hacienda, complained about the nonpaying sharecroppers and stated that they had threatened to burn the houses of sharecroppers who did not join those organizing the ejido, and had also threatened to set fire to buildings on the hacienda. Ruiz asked that the governor "provide the necessary guarantees so that [he] would receive the percentage of the harvest" he was due (Ruiz 1936). He reported that the nonpaying sharecroppers were supported by an armed group in Loma Larga.

It seems clear that in 1936, when some from Unión Zapata received ejido land, this did not stop the community's agrarian activism. Many still needed land and were willing to act as if the lands they sharecropped were theirs, even though the land had not been formally awarded to them. They were militant in their occupation of further land and continued to pressure the government to grant more land on the Tanibé hacienda, and to do so quickly. Their correspondence to Cárdenas continued.

The year after the initial ejido grant was received by Unión Zapata, Cárdenas visited the ejido in his March 1937 swing through Oaxaca to talk directly with rural citizens and to promote his national programs.

The historian José Luz Ornelas López describes the climate during and preceding Cárdenas's visit to Oaxaca as filled with radical slogans and leftist ideology promoted by the PNR, student groups, and the local press (Ornelas López 1988, 141). Cárdenas spent long hours—as he was to throughout his presidency (see Craig 1983)—meeting with local ejido committees like the one from Unión Zapata, listening to grievances, seeing the local poverty, and hearing time and again that people needed more than land to survive; they needed houses, oxen and plows to work their land with, and schools and other public buildings. As a result of his visit, the newly formed ejido of Unión Zapata received some of the basic infrastructure requested; it also used the occasion to continue to press for more land.

In 1937, the community's request for additional lands was granted, but only a small amount of additional land, totaling twenty-eight hectares, was provided. In November 1937, this additional land was formally taken into possession; it resulted in parcels for only another six people, five of whom received prime irrigated land. According to the document authorizing the measuring and endowment of the additional land, many who qualified did not receive parcels (Secretaría de Reforma Agraria, Delegación de Oaxaca 1937). As previously mentioned, the eighteen ejidatarios who received land from the original piece endowed to the community had received parcels of eight to ten hectares of rainfed land.

The net result was that many had still not received land; at nearly the moment the ejido was created, a division was opened between those with land and those without. This would later lead to high levels of tension in the community.

One original ejidatario and his extended family, who came from the hacienda Don Pedrillo, were held responsible for several murders in Unión Zapata in the 1940s. In 1947, five families related to the murderer from the Don Pedrillo hacienda left, fearing retaliation, and their ejido land was redistributed. In comparison with ejidatarios from Santa María del Tule, those who came to make up Unión Zapata did not have a common sense of community history. Their bonds, if any, came more from a shared experience of exploitation at the hands of the hacendados they worked for, of extreme poverty, and of a much newer sense of community, one that came out of the creation of the ejido in the time of Cárdenas. Descriptions of what the rancho of Loma Larga was like before the formation of the ejido and before the endowment of infrastructure, leave little doubt that the creation of the ejido was a transforming experience for those community members who received land. Those who didn't remained bitter.

Once community members were convinced of the importance of forming an ejido, they were unrelenting in their pressure on officials from the CNC, the Agrarian Department, and the president to come through on their promises. What stands out in the story of Unión Zapata is that the president of the country and other officials did make good on many of their promises in the 1930s and created a well of good faith in the community that still endured in the 1990s, although not among all ejidatarios.

UNIÓN ZAPATA IN THE 1990S

Oral histories from Unión Zapata suggest that some in the community who did not receive ejido land in 1936 and 1937 dedicated themselves to raising domestic animals (primarily sheep and goats), which were sold in local markets. Others simply continued as day laborers, working for private property holders in Mitla.[3] The historical economic profile suggested above for men and women from Unión Zapata is confirmed by survey data from 1994, when people were asked to talk about their economic history. A majority of male ejidatarios in the 1994 survey, 88 percent, indicated that subsistence farming had been their primary employment during most of their lives. The other 13 percent made a living as wage laborers in construction or as truck drivers. Ninety-three percent of the women surveyed, ejidatarias and ejidatarios' spouses, indicated that they had worked in subsistence agriculture and in related tasks for most of their lives. Seven percent indicated that they had worked in commercial activity, selling cheese to neighboring communities. In comparison with Santa María del Tule, ejidatarios in Unión Zapata in the 1990s had a fairly homogeneous economic profile and remained more closely tied to subsistence farming. In the 1990s, the economic lifestyle of most of the community remained closely linked to the land and thus to the inheritance of Zapata.

The name of Zapata in fact became part of the furniture of the community, so to speak, being mentioned each time anyone spoke of being from Unión Zapata. Most people in this community did not think twice about what it meant to utter Zapata's name, on a daily basis, as part of identifying where one was from. Most also walked by the large mural of Zapata painted on the front of the Casa Ejidal several times a day without thinking or talking about it.

Figure 14. Image of Zapata painted on the outside of the ejido meeting hall of Unión Zapata. Photo by Lynn Stephen.

But when specifically asked about the meaning of Zapata, many would respond, especially those active in the politics of the ejido and whose families had been involved in the original struggle for ejido land. The group of founding families who received original ejido land and continued to work it were in the strongest economic positions in the community, as well as being important in structuring local political opinion through men who served as hamlet mayor and commissioner of the ejido. I interviewed five of the founding extended families and found a common discourse among them in terms of the meaning of Zapata. Since only two women were active ejidatarias in Unión Zapata, and women did not attend the meetings in the numbers seen in El Tule, they tended to have less to say, although those few women who were active in ejido community politics had strong opinions, as seen in the person of Angela (cited above and in the next chapter). The following conversation with Pedro García Sánchez and his wife Refugio Ruiz is representative of my conversations with members of the original ejidatario families. If the women were not active in the ejido, they tended to hold back in the discussions and said little about Zapata, even in private conversation.

LYNN: What comes to your mind when you hear the name of Emiliano Zapata?

PEDRO: When we hear the names of Emiliano Zapata and Francisco Villa, we feel a lot of pride. We are benefiting from what they did. They fought so that there was no more slavery, so that we have a free Mexico.

REFUGIO: I don't have a lot of thoughts about Zapata. He was a revolutionary.

PEDRO: Emiliano Zapata took away the land from the rich. That is why we remember this man. Villa and the other one? What is his name?

REFUGIO: And Porfirio Díaz was with them?

PEDRO: No, he was a friend of the hacendados. . . . Well, for me, the fact that this town is called Unión Zapata fills me with pride. I feel proud just at hearing his name. This place is named for Zapata because we took the land away from the hacendados and we redistributed it here. It is our pride in this legacy here that allows his name to continue.

LYNN: Where did you learn about Zapata?

PEDRO: I learned about Zapata in the school here and we also have his photograph here [in the Casa Ejidal]. Several people have come and tried to take that photo. This is an original photo of Zapata. We don't want any one to take it away. We are not going to give our photograph to anyone. It belongs here.

While initially it seemed difficult to determine whether Pedro truly felt proud of living in a place named after Zapata, or whether he thought that this was what an outsider would like to hear, later in the conversation he made it clear that he and the community indeed had a claim on Zapata—specifically, through the photograph of him in the Casa Ejidal. An important connection that Pedro made, which came up in conversation with others about feelings toward the contemporary Zapatistas, is that Pedro identifies the origin of the community as directly linked to the legacy of Zapata. "We took the land away from the hacendados and we redistributed it here." In other words, this is what Zapata did and we did the same thing, thus we acted in the spirit of Zapata. This sense of actively participating in the redistributing of land from local haciendas fits with the archival record for the community, which contains plenty of evidence that the former sharecroppers and peons occupied hacienda land before it was theirs, fought with the former hacendados to force them off the land, and refused to pay the hacienda owners 50 percent of the harvest after petitioning for more land. The personal connection that people like Pedro felt to Zapata is important in understanding sympathy with the contemporary Zapatistas, as seen in the next chapter.

Refugio, who never participated directly in community politics or the ejido, clearly felt much less connection with Zapata than did her husband. She attempted to help him remember history, but was corrected by him when she tried to lump Porfirio Díaz together with Villa and Zapata. This may reflect the fact that her husband was present and women often talked less when their husbands were also involved. But a discussion I had alone with Refugio suggested that she had little more to say on the subject.

The missing third figure from Pedro's trio of Zapata and Villa was probably Lázaro Cárdenas. For others in the community, as in Santa María del Tule, Cárdenas was closely tied to the figure of Zapata through the president's association with the creation of the community's ejido and through his visit to the community. In the process of participating in the government's land measuring, mapping, and titling program (PROCEDE), the ejidatarios of Unión Zapata ran into a major obstacle. A long-standing question regarding the boundaries between Unión Zapata and Mitla arose from there being two maps with differing boundaries. The map drawn by engineers outlining the original ejido land for Unión Zapata, drawn in 1936, showed a section of a mountain within the community's ejido land. A different map, drawn to show the boundaries of the communal lands of Mitla, placed the same strip of land within the jurisdiction of Mitla. In arguments about which map was correct, ejido authorities from Unión Zapata often cited theirs as more legitimate *because* it was a part of the presidential resolution signed by Cárdenas. One official told me, for example: "We have a map signed by Lázaro Cárdenas that they don't want to respect. This is the map that matters. There in Mitla they have a map from 1948. That is much later and it isn't right. The one that matters is the one signed by President Cárdenas." This sort of comment was typically made in assemblies when the difference between the two maps was discussed. As of

the writing of this book, the boundary dispute has still not been resolved, and Unión Zapata is stalled in the mapping and measuring process of the PROCEDE.

Besides feeling connected to Cárdenas through his signing of this map
and the land grant to the community, the people of Unión Zapata still
remembered his visit and the gifts he and his wife made to the community in 1937 (see the letter to Cárdenas reproduced at the opening of this
chapter). Cárdenas's presidency was often described as the best and most
responsible—as the government that cared the most about peasants.
Many told me specifically of the five oxen he had "personally" given the
community. Luis García's comments were typical. Like some of those in
El Tule, his comments about Cárdenas were prefaced by discussion of
the Mexican Revolution:

LUIS: Here in the valley, the people in the mountains, the Serranos, were
         aligned with Villa and Zapata against the Carransistas. We had a lot
         of important things happen here. . . . Did you know that Lázaro Cár-
         denas came here? He went to Mitla, to here, to El Tule, and to Oaxaca.
         He had already signed the papers for our ejido when he came. The
         ejido already existed for about one year. When he came here, he asked
         us what we needed, and we said, "We need resources to work the land.
         We need oxen." We asked him for oxen, and he came through. He sent
         us five oxen and five steel plows for our ejido so that it could function.
         He was a good president who cared about the campesinos.

Later, Luis reinforced his comment about Cárdenas's concern. In response to a question about whether the government was currently helping (in 1993), he answered, "Sure—well, they offer help, but you have
to pay. Cárdenas did more. When the people asked for something, he
came through, not like now." Discussing Cárdenas not only reminded
Luis and others of their personal connection to him through his visit, but
also permitted them to compare what many saw as the mediocre "help"
offered by the present government with what is remembered as a better
time, when the government truly did care.

CONCLUSIONS

The stories of the formation of the ejidos of Santa María del Tule and
Unión Zapata are quite distinct from those of the two ejidos in eastern
Chiapas, and also from each other. In the case of Santa María del Tule,
one primary obstacle to successfully occupying and working all of the
land granted the community came from a neighboring Zapotec com-

munity; local hacendados also resisted, but not to the extent the Zapotec neighbors did. In the case of Unión Zapata, opposition came in part from hacendados and in part from other rural laborers who remained loyal to the hacendados and resisted joining the agraristas forming the ejido.

In both cases, there remains in the 1990s close personal identification on the part of some ejidatarios with Lázaro Cárdenas, who visited and was significant in granting land to both communities. Cárdenas also serves as a mediator for the figure of Emiliano Zapata, claimed as a character in local histories of both ejidos. Finally, in both communities, agrarian officials affiliated with the Agrarian Department (in Oaxaca and in Mexico City) are favorably viewed in the community histories told by ejidatarios. Some can even recall the names of specific officials—particularly that of Engineer Calderón, the Oaxaca delegate to the Agrarian Department during the Cárdenas administration. Remembering the names of, and interactions with, government officials from almost sixty years earlier demonstrates their permanent importance in these ejidatarios' minds.

The close, almost familial, status that Zapata and Cárdenas occupy in the discussions and narratives of many ejidatarios in Santa Maria del Tule and Unión Zapata contrasts with the ways these figures are symbolized in eastern Chiapas, in ejidos like Guadalupe Tepeyac. Many of my discussions with ejidatarios in Oaxaca have left a sense that they viewed their relationship with Cárdenas and Zapata as personal, but unequal; Zapata and Cárdenas were on their side, on the side of the poor, but had superior power and possibilities. Some conversations have also suggested the obligation people felt, and still feel, to the government, as well as a sense of obedience—at least on the surface. This sense of obligation drove people to vote for the PRI at least until 2000. As we shall see in the next chapter, while ejidatarios feel that their faith in and obedience to the government have been rewarded, their loyalty is tenuous and open to sympathies with antigovernment ideologies, such as contemporary Zapatismo. Another way of thinking about this is to note that the ejidatarios' formal political behavior—for example, voting—is quite different from their political thinking and ideology.

While I would be the last to argue that the sentiments about Zapata and Cárdenas espoused by the persons I interviewed are representative of all ejidatarios in Unión Zapata and Santa María del Tule—there are of course individual, gendered, class, and other differences—the fact that a significantly unified rhetoric around Zapata and Cárdenas seems to exist among these ejidatarios, particularly among the older citizens, is not to be ignored. Because older ejidatarios are often regarded as the most legitimate spokespersons and historians of a community—I was, for instance, often sent to them and constantly referred to them—their ideas occupy significant space in local political discourse. The public and private narratives and conversations of experienced ejidatarios, both male and female, provide the outlines for preferred versions of local histories, and, because they are articulated with national projects and history, they also serve as guideposts for what we might call local nationalisms (imagined communities in the plural)—for, that is, differential views of nationalism based on local history and experience, or what Prasenjit Duara (1996) calls multiple "nation views" informed by local identities and histories.

As suggested by Mary Kay Vaughn (1997), JoAnne Martin (1993), and others, local nationalisms produce different interpretations of the larger nation. These different interpretations are part and parcel of the construction of local nation views—what Florencia Mallon (1995) has called "community hegemonies." In the cases of Unión Zapata and Santa María del Tule, the communal dialogue about current government programs and policies, and feelings about social movements such as the contemporary Zapatistas, are influenced by the experiences and interpretations of local intellectuals. In a community of ejidatarios, the local intellectuals are most likely to be elderly ejidatarios—often male, although some are women.

In Chiapas, local intellectuals in the ejidos of Guadalupe Tepeyac and La Realidad were, in some cases, elderly ejidatarios, but also included those who worked with the Catholic Church espousing liberation theology as deacons, those who worked with peasant organizers, and those who joined the EZLN. The local ideologies they created invoked some of the same symbols used in Oaxaca—particularly that of Zapata—but with significantly different meanings for contemporary politics. Before moving on to compare the nation views found in the ejidos in Oaxaca and Chiapas, and to reflect on their implications for the future path of Mexico as a whole, we shall in the next chapter explore the local nationalism of some ejidatarios of Unión Zapata and Santa María del Tule in greater depth, to see how these persons can be sympathetic to the government (at least, on the surface, until 2000) yet often closely identify with the indigenous families in Chiapas who support or have joined the EZLN and have an explicit antigovernment stance.

CHAPTER 11

The Contradictions of Zapatismo in Rural Oaxaca

This chapter seeks to clarify what I have come to call the "pro-Zapatista *and* pro-PRI" stance found among some ejidatarios in Unión Zapata and Santa María del Tule in the mid 1990s, and to explain how this contradiction contributed to a vote for the Partido Acción Nacional (PAN) in El Tule in the presidential elections of July 2000. The contradictory stance involved is all the more interesting given important differences between the two communities in ethnicity, economic activities, landholdings, and education. Some of these differences were discussed in the previous chapter; others are elaborated in what follows.

The common pro-Zapatista and pro-PRI stance articulated by a significant number of ejidatarios in both communities suggests that despite the diversity of experience and living conditions in the two, they share a perspective about their historical relationships to the state, as well as sympathies for the EZLN in Chiapas. In terms of how different local nation views are produced, analysis of the views of ejidatarios from El Tule and Unión Zapata suggests that different ethnic identities, class positions, and educational levels can underlie local convergences in what nationalism means. The similar stances in El Tule and Unión Zapata with respect to their relations, as communities, with the government over time, and on what their place in the nation means, are strongly linked to physical location (proximity to the state capital and officials, official visits), the historical period in which they consolidated their ejidos (i.e., the 1930s under Cárdenas), and the ideological content of nationalism when they received the ejido land with which they consolidated as communities (socialist education, promotion of class-based and rural identities by the state, links to Zapata and the Mexican Revolution).

I focus on these "pro-Zapatista and pro-PRI" ejidatarios because they represent what at first appears a contradictory position but is in fact consistent with their history and experience. While people's superficial participation in government programs linked to economic restructuring might be read as approval of such policy and of the government, a more nuanced exploration suggests the complex and contradictory interpretations that these rural Oaxacans have of contemporary economics and politics. Once below the surface, we can see significant identification with the plight of those indigenous poor in Chiapas who have joined, or who support, the EZLN and have opposed the Mexican government.

By July 2000, this opposition was more openly expressed in elections as well in Oaxaca. In Chiapas, although the PRI (the government party) won the state in the presidential elections, with 45 percent of the vote, many from Zapatista communities did not vote. And in the gubernatorial election in Chiapas in August 2000, the PRI lost. The opposition candidate Pablo Salazar Mendiguchia, representing a coalition of eight opposition parties, including the PAN and the Partido de la Revolución Democrática (PRD), defeated the PRI candidate, with 51.50 percent of the vote; the PRI gubernatorial candidate, Sami David, received 45.68 percent of the vote; but, most important to note, 50.25 percent of the electorate abstained (Castro Soto 2000b).

The identification felt by Oaxacan ejidatarios with the plight of the Zapatistas is not clearly seen if one focuses only on formal political behavior such as voting. Rather, it is revealed through lengthy discussions about community history and the use of such histories to interpret contemporary events, including the Zapatista rebellion. Unpacking the pro-Zapatista and pro-PRI stance also suggests that the loyalty articulated by people in these two communities for the government is tenuous and unpredictable—as seen in a switch in voting patterns in El Tule between 1994 and 2000. There, in 1994, the PRI took more votes than either the PAN or the PRD; in the 2000 elections, the PAN received a majority. More often than not, both in 1994 and in 2000, a vote for the PRI was tied to a desire to continue participating in government antipoverty programs rather than to any ideological identification with PRI policies. This seemed the case in Unión Zapata, where the PRI continued to win in the 2000 elections but people articulated their vote as a desire to continue receiving farm subsidies through the PROCAMPO program and antipoverty subsidies through PROGRESA (Programa de Educación, Salud y Alimentación).

The apparent support for the government expressed by some in the overall 1994 voting was unpredictable, as shown by the national election returns in 2000, which gave the presidency to the PAN, with 43 percent of the vote. The PRI received 36 percent, while the PRD-based coalition received 17 percent (Dillon 2000, 1). While the PRI's major bastion of support had always been the rural vote, in the 2000 elections, it won this vote by only 10 percent. This means that, at the national level, the apparent support for the PRI in rural Mexico, often assumed from past voting patterns (through 1994), was insecure and unpredictable. The 2000 elections brought this fact clearly into focus.

Since July 2000, many more researchers have come to question the act of voting as indicative of support for a particular candidate or specific campaign platform. The PAN presidential victory in 2000 is best understood as a rejection of the PRI and a desire for change, rather than as a massive show of support for the specific policies of Vicente Fox Quesada. In reality, many of Fox Quesada's economic policies have been very similar to those of Ernesto Zedillo from 1994 to 2000.

Before discussing the evolution of these communities' pro-Zapatista and pro-PRI stance, I shall more clearly explicate the differences between El Tule and Unión Zapata in ethnic, racial, regional, and national identities, in economic activities and landholdings, and in education.

ETHNIC, RACIAL, REGIONAL, AND NATIONAL IDENTITIES

Contemporary Oaxaca is characterized by local identities reflecting "the asymmetrical incorporation of structurally dissimilar groupings into a single political economy" (Comaroff and Comaroff 1992, 50–51). Before the arrival of the Spaniards, political identities tied to language and region created hierarchical ethnic relations, through trade, tribute, and conquest, among indigenous peoples in the Oaxaca valleys. With the arrival of the Spaniards and the homogenization of all Oaxaca ethnic groups into "Indians," another layer was added to local ethnic constructions. And racial categories were created for a wide range of so-called "mixtures." Authors such as John Chance (1978) demonstrate how the racial categories of the Oaxaca caste system were constructed (with more than ten regularly used categories); terms such as *indio, mes-*

tizo (of mixed Spanish and Indian descent), and *castizo* (of mixed Spanish and *mestizo* descent) came to be viewed by Oaxacan society as categories found in nature. With the emergence of the Oaxacan sovereignty movement in 1915–20 (Ruiz Cervantes 1985), the regional identity of *Oaxaqueño* was added to local repertoires; after the Mexican Revolution, great importance was given to creating a national identity. Thus, by the 1930s, Oaxacans could claim not only a regional identity, but also national citizenship as *Mexicanos*. Since the early 1990s, all of these layers of identity have come to coexist in local social life. Which ethnic and racial identities people choose to use, and when, and how often, reflect how they view themselves and their communities historically. In turn, identities also influence how specific policies and programs are perceived and integrated into the meaning of everyday life.

In Unión Zapata and El Tule, ejidatarios use five primary categories to specify their origins.[1] These terms include specifications of race, ethnicity, regionality, and nationality and are often used in combinations that suggest how national and regional identities are laden with racial significance. The five terms are *mestizo, Zapoteco, Oaxaqueño, Mexicano,* and *revuelto.* There are also contextual combination terms usually combining *Zapoteco* with another designation.

The national identity category of *Mexicano* clearly has strong resonance. About one-third of respondents from El Tule (31 percent) and Unión Zapata (35.5 percent) responded to an open-ended survey question by stating that they were *Mexicanos.* Public education and public policy have sought to inspire a national identity that would transcend local identity constructions, as discussed in previous chapters. As for El Tule and Unión Zapata, the primary difference is in relation to the presence or absence of a specific local ethnic identity.

In response to an open-ended question about origins, almost half (45 percent) of ejidatarios surveyed in El Tule identified themselves as Zapotec—either alone or in combination with another racial, ethnic, or identity label.[2] Many in El Tule whose first answer was *revuelto,* or mixed, referred to mixtures of Zapotec, Indian, Oaxacan, and other labels when pushed to elaborate. In Unión Zapata, only 8 percent of the respondents specifically responded "Zapotec." Thus, Zapotec identity, expressed primarily in terms of language, has a higher profile among ejidatarios from El Tule than among those from Unión Zapata. More than half of the ejidatarios surveyed in El Tule stated that they were bilingual in Zapotec, and 60 percent surveyed stated that they understood Zapotec. Only

11 percent of ejidatarios and their spouses interviewed in Unión Zapata indicated that they were bilingual or understood Zapotec.

Of course, linguistic use of Zapotec does not automatically imply a sense of Zapotec ethnicity in the way that self-labeling does. In Santa María del Tule, ethnic identity is also woven into historical memories of the ejido. Most ejidatarios recall their community as *puro Zapoteco* (pure Zapotec) and *puro indio* (pure Indian) at the time (1917) their ejido was founded by presidential resolution. The land itself is one of the strongest historical symbols of Zapotec identity in the community. Local constructions of history emphasize the community's claim on land given by Tlalixtac and their struggle to maintain it for hundreds of years; the creation of the ejido merely returned land perceived as theirs by right.

The ethnic meaning of ejido land was also brought home in 1993 and 1994 during the measuring and mapping that the ejidatarios of El Tule conducted with the officials from the PROCEDE program and engineers from INEGI. As they traversed the ejido and measured the land, the ejidatarios talked about local myths, spirits, witches, and mythic creatures associated with particular geographic landmarks. One spot was marked with Zapotec idols, which ejidatarios have also incorporated into their homes. Another site had a spring said to house small creatures (*duendes*), who play mischievous pranks on passersby. In the process of touching and measuring the land, the ritual and mythic landscape came alive with Zapotec terms and tales.

After we returned from the measuring, I chatted with Marina Mendoza, an ejidataria, in her shaded courtyard. She pointed to the head of a stone idol embedded in a tree near us:

MARINA: Do you see this? I found it out there where we were measuring the land. It has a lot of value for us. Not for the money, but for what it is. It tells us who our ancestors are on that land.

LYNN: Who are the ancestors?

MARINA: We are not ashamed. We have to say that they are Zapotecs. We are Zapotecs.

When the ejidatarios of El Tule map and measure their land and debate its future status, the meaning of their debate at some level includes the land's historical significance. In Unión Zapata, this historic significance is not strongly tied to a long-term sense of ethnically based territory but rather to memories of exploitation by local hacendados. These memories are also part of local identity discourses in El Tule, although crosscut with references to ethnic claims to the land. Current economic relations of power in the two communities build on these differences.

ECONOMIC ACTIVITIES AND LANDHOLDING

As discussed in the previous chapter, a primary difference between Unión Zapata and El Tule is the degree to which ejidatarios in each make a living based on subsistence agriculture. While a majority of ejidatarios (88 percent of the men and 93 percent of the women) surveyed in Unión Zapata reported that subsistence farming had been their primary source of employment during most of their lives, more than one-third of men and women ejidatarios surveyed in El Tule indicated having held primary occupations other than subsistence farming during most of their lives. Simply put, in Unión Zapata, there are few alternatives to subsistence agriculture; there are more economic options in El Tule. This stems in part from the latter's location close to Oaxaca, but also partly from the tourist industry—including food stands, restaurants, crafts booths, and stores—built around the giant tree that has made El Tule an essential tourist stop. Land, and making a living from the land, are much more important in Unión Zapata.

While we did not systematically survey income and expenditures in ejidatario households in the two communities, the ejidatarios of El Tule, as a group, are—if consumption reflects income—significantly better off economically than those in Unión Zapata. Evidence can be seen in the brick-and-concrete house construction, cars, and beds, televisions, telephones, tape players, and stereos in ejidatario homes in El Tule. With some notable exceptions, such items were rare among the ejidatarios of Unión Zapata in the 1990s, although higher levels of outmigration to the United States since 1999 have resulted in more consumer goods.

In 1994, a much higher percentage of ejidatarios had irrigated land in Unión Zapata than in El Tule. In Unión Zapata, 27 percent (17 of 62) of the ejidatarios and spouses surveyed had at least one irrigated parcel: 9 had irrigated parcels totaling one hectare, 5 had irrigated parcels totaling two hectares, and 3 had irrigated parcels totaling more than two hectares. One ejidatario had irrigated parcels totaling 7.5 hectares. In Santa María del Tule, only 6 percent (4 out of 64) of the ejidatarios surveyed had access to at least one irrigated parcel.

When the sizes of ejidatarios' rain-fed holdings in both communities are compared, about 13 percent more ejidatarios surveyed in Santa María del Tule hold parcels of two or more hectares than do so in Unión

Zapata. While this difference is not particularly significant, it gains importance when viewed in relation to the economic profiles of each community. For at least 30 percent of El Tule's ejidatarios, farming is not the primary economic activity. In Unión Zapata, supplying small amounts of fresh produce and cheese to the market is the primary source of income for the great majority of subsistence farmers. Differences in parcel sizes and quality are thus more important for understanding economic stratification among ejidatarios in Unión Zapata than for explaining economic differences in El Tule. In Unión Zapata, differences in landholdings translate into other tangible differences—such as ability to build a larger home, own more animals, and consume more meat, liquor, and cigarettes.

GENDER AND EDUCATION IN UNIÓN ZAPATA AND EL TULE

A final set of factors, in addition to economic activities and land, that differentiates populations within and between the two ejidos includes gender and education. In Santa María del Tule, 126 of 413 ejidatarios, or about 30 percent, are women—a proportion typical of many ejidos (see Botey Estapé 1993). The ejido of Unión Zapata is unusual in that only 3 of 74 ejidatarios (with certificates of agrarian rights) and *posesionarios* (in possession of ejido land but without certificates of agrarian rights) are women.

Educational differences between ejidatarios from the two communities are most interesting when viewed in relation to gender. In El Tule, 13 percent more women than men have no more than one year of education. In Unión Zapata, ejidatarias, and female spouses of ejidatarios, surveyed have slightly more education than male ejidatarios. Among male ejidatarios, those from El Tule have more education than have those from Unión Zapata; 48 percent of males surveyed in El Tule have three years or more of education, while only 28 percent of those in Unión Zapata reach this level.

These educational differences within and between ejidos can be important in individuals' levels of comfort and trust when dealing with the engineers and agrarian officials linked to the PROCEDE program and other government institutions. The higher levels of education attained by men in El Tule may have given them more confidence in dealing with the stream of PROCEDE visitors sent by the Procuraduría Agraria. These ejidatarios often checked and double-checked the math, measurements, and legal codes used in the mapping and certification process. At ejido assemblies in El Tule, local authorities seemed firmly in charge. Women in El Tule had less contact with agrarian officials but would caucus with men and with one another, in both Zapotec and Spanish, to ensure that they understood and agreed with the proceedings. Ejidatarios in Unión Zapata seemed more timid in dealing with officials from the Procuraduría Agraria, and to feel rather helpless when their certification process was held up by a protest lodged against them by Mitla. They were not as active in the process as were ejidatarios from El Tule.

A METHODOLOGICAL NOTE

During the summer of 1994, a major focus of my fieldwork in Oaxaca was to try to determine the underlying feelings and perceptions of ejidatarios about the North American Free Trade Agreement, the Mexican government, and the Zapatista rebellion that had emerged earlier that year. In particular, I wanted to unravel how the local nation views I was uncovering in Unión Zapata and in El Tule were used by ejidatarios to interpret contemporary economic policy and political events, and to see what these people thought about the contemporary Zapatistas in Chiapas. I specifically wanted to see if, under their apparent agreement with government policy, there was also a critique. How deep was their apparent loyalty? To get at these questions, I focused my conversations about the impact of NAFTA on people's concrete experiences in the land mapping, measuring, and titling program, PROCEDE (described in chapter 2), and on their feelings about the government crop subsidy (PROCAMPO) program launched shortly before the 1994 elections. These two programs were direct manifestations of the Mexican accommodation to NAFTA designed to end land redistribution, encourage privatization of what had been inalienable, collectively held land, and—on the other hand—to provide some help to desperate farmers who were receiving rock-bottom prices for their corn in the Mexican market as a result of cheap U.S. imports. I sounded out people's feelings about the Mexican government primarily through discussion of the 1994 elections, of whom they might be voting for and why. Conversations about the Zapatistas focused on how ejidatarios had heard about the EZLN; what, if anything, they thought of it; and how they related the Zapatistas to their own community histories. I hoped to develop, through wide-ranging discussions of these topics, a better understanding of how people perceived government policy and current political events (such as the Zapatista uprising) and how they used the tools of local histories to interpret and re-

act. The result—what I have called a pro-Zapatista and pro-PRI stance—
is all the more interesting, given the significant differences between Unión
Zapata and El Tule highlighted above.

PROCEDE AND PROCAMPO

The mid 1990s in Oaxaca were characterized by high levels of interaction between agrarian officials and ejidatarios. PROCEDE was heavily
promoted in the central valleys of Oaxaca, as was the crop subsidy program known as PROCAMPO. Not only were ejidatarios encouraged to
sign up for both programs, but they were informed by publications, an-
nouncements, and bulletin boards about ejidatarios elsewhere in the
country joining.

In the summer of 1994 in Oaxaca, news of the growing number of land
certificates handed out in other parts of the country was viewed with
interest by ejidatarios in Santa María del Tule and Unión Zapata. Some
wondered if they themselves would ever be featured on the bulletin board
of the Agrarian Attorney General's Office or in a brochure when their
community completed the land certification program. Some communities
were more likely candidates for the bulletin board than others—those
that entered the program early, finished quickly, and were willing to express public gratitude for what had been done for them.

Ejidatarios from Santa María del Tule completed the certification process during the summer of 1994 and received their certificates in the fall.
At that point, they decided not to proceed with obtaining individual titles
to their land, and continued to meet regularly as an ejido, publicly stating
in assemblies their commitment to remaining a functioning ejido. Unión
Zapata remained locked in a disagreement with the neighboring community of Mitla over boundaries between the two ejidos. Santa María
del Tule and Unión Zapata both continued to be actively engaged, on a
weekly and sometimes almost daily basis, with officials from the Agrarian Attorney's Office.

Ejidatarios in El Tule reacted favorably to the staff of the Agrarian
Attorney's Office when they completed the certification process in 1994.
However, by 1999, some were having second thoughts about the PRO-
CEDE program. More than fifteen ejidatarios had quietly sold their parcels of land to outsiders without the approval of the ejido assembly. "They
disobeyed the content of Article 27, which says that the parcel should
be passed along to the wife, the concubine, the sons, the daughters, or
to another person in the ejido," Carlos Gómez said. "An error is being

Figure 15.   Measuring ejido plots for PROCEDE with officials from INEGI in
Santa María del Tule. Photo by Lynn Stephen.

committed by ejidatarios here. They are selling their ejido parcels to outside people without consulting the ejidal community." Plans for a new
superhighway to connect the city of Oaxaca to the Isthmus in just over
two hours were also raising concerns. The plans for the new road called
for two on/off ramps that would run through the ejido lands of Santa
María del Tule. Not only would the ejido lose ejido land to the road and
its ramps, but more individuals would be tempted to sell their parcels to
outsiders. Worries expressed in ejido assemblies while the community
was completing PROCEDE in 1993 — such as concerns over outsiders
buying up ejido land, over the government expropriating land for development projects, and the ultimate breakdown of the ejido — were now
coming home to roost.

Ejidatarios in Unión Zapata remained suspicious of the Agrarian Attorney's Office and PROCEDE, a result of the problems with Mitla. They
continued with the process and placed a modicum of trust in the Procuraduría's staff, but consistently expressed doubts about the ability or willingness of government officials to resolve their case. Their conflict with
Mitla remained in the Agrarian Tribunal, unresolved, as of late 2000.

In addition to intense contact with officials from the Agrarian Attorney's Office in 1994, ejidatarios received numerous visits from Ministry of Agriculture staff, who were promoting another new government program. As a result of protests by producer organizations during the process of negotiating NAFTA, the Mexican government had initiated a program for peasants in 1993 called the Programa de Apoyo Directo al Campo (Direct Rural Support Program), or PROCAMPO. The program offered Mexican farmers of corn, beans, wheat, rice, soybeans, sorghum, and cotton a subsidy of between U.S.$70 and $100 per hectare over fifteen years.[3] Guaranteed price supports for these crops were phased out in the autumn and winter seasons of 1994–95, as called for by NAFTA, pitting Mexican producers against cheaper U.S. imports and aligning Mexican crop prices with international prices.

PROCAMPO was introduced to ejidatarios with the words *libertad* and *justicia* prominently displayed in the summaries of goals, in an effort that seemed to mirror the rhetoric of PROCEDE (see chapter 2). A detailed publication passed out to ejidatarios by the Ministry of Agriculture in 1993 emphasized that "PROCAMPO is based on the principle that producers direct their own transformation with liberty, and that their progress occurs with justice and equality." It added that "PROCAMPO forms part of the Federal Government's strategy of modernization of the countryside to achieve more justice, equality, and liberty among Mexican peasants" (Secretaría de Agricultura y Recursos Hidráulicos 1993, preface, 5).

The government's announcement of this program evidenced a certain amount of backpedaling in the structural adjustments carried out to facilitate NAFTA. PROCAMPO may have slightly softened the blow of being "eased" out of the rural sector for the three million ejidatarios (and their families) whom the Mexican government was predicting would benefit from PROCAMPO (Moguel 1993, 8). Once price supports would be phased out, however, the small subsidy offered by PROCAMPO would clearly not offset the loss of higher crop prices for small farmers. During the summer of 1994, corn prices fell by 30 percent, and, in communities in Oaxaca with low yields, the benefits of PROCAMPO did not come close to offsetting the costs of planting and harvesting. In 1995, the lower subsidy was even less successful in offsetting farming costs. This was the case in subsequent years as well.

PROCAMPO subsidies are available to farmers who signed up during 1993–94. Those who did not were no longer eligible for the program, even though it was supposed to run for fifteen years. There was only one opportunity to register for the program; those who missed the deadline in 1994 were unable to register later. Many complained, but the policy was not changed. The deadline of course also limited the support the government had to pay out.

PROCAMPO has two cycles of subsidies. The fall-winter cycle is geared toward those with irrigation and who harvest winter crops. The spring-summer cycle is for those with irrigation as well as those with rain-fed crops. The majority of participants receive checks from the spring-summer cycle.

PROCAMPO became a very high-profile program a few weeks before the 1994 presidential elections, when hundreds of thousands received their first PROCAMPO checks. Ejidatarios from the two ejidos described in this chapter who registered for PROCAMPO spent long afternoons in lines that snaked for blocks as the people waited for checks. The spring-summer planting cycle checks were paid out between 15 July and 18 August in Oaxaca, just days before the national elections. (The planting cycle began for most in May or June.) Oaxaca PROCAMPO officials estimated in an interview that about 95 percent of Mexico's peasants (about 27 percent of the population) signed up for the program. A review of the PROCAMPO registrations from the ejidos studied, however, revealed that less than 50 percent of those eligible signed up. Some people stated that they did not sign up for fear of having to pay back the subsidy checks later. Others, however, felt that they needed the assistance and could not do without it.

PRI = PROCAMPO

I conducted interviews with about fifty male and female ejidatarios regarding their feelings about PROCAMPO and about how they related the program to the elections. In addition to continued connections made among the PRI, the ejido, and the Mexican Revolution, the most common reason given for voting for the PRI was the disbursement of PROCAMPO checks. Many were quite bold in their statements about the links between PROCAMPO and votes for the PRI. "They set up this program to give us checks in order to buy our vote for the PRI," stated a middle-aged ejidatario from Unión Zapata. A young ejidataria from Santa María del Tule answered my question about which party she was going to vote for by simply stating, "I am going to vote for the PROCAMPO party."

Maximina Pérez Martínez of Santa María del Tule was quite clear about the link between voting for the PRI and receiving a PROCAMPO check. She felt that if she did not vote for the PRI, the party would know and prevent her receiving future PROCAMPO checks. Our conversation began with my asking whether she had received a check:

MAXIMINA: Yes, our checks arrived. Because of PROCAMPO, we have to vote for the PRI. If we don't vote for the PRI, they won't help us out. Next year they are going to look at the names of who voted for the PRI and, if we didn't vote for them, then they won't help us out. If you go and vote for the PAN, for example, then they might take away your check. Because of this, you have to vote for the PRI. . . .

LYNN: So it is important to vote?

MAXIMINA: Yes. I vote for PROCAMPO. To vote for the PRI is to vote for PROCAMPO.

One ejidataria I interviewed, Herminia Hipolito, aged sixty-one, talked about the government in familial terms. Her description also nakedly declares her PRI vote as premised on receipt of her PROCAMPO check:

LYNN: Did you get your PROCAMPO payment yet?

HERMINIA: Sure. I got it.

LYNN: Do you think that the check is related to the upcoming elections in any way?

HERMINIA: This is what *Papa gobierno* [government] gave to help us out. It's clear that this Papa has a lot of children and he is taking care of them. This PROCAMPO check is helping me out a lot. I wouldn't have planted if it weren't for the PROCAMPO program. If they hadn't sent the money, I wouldn't have thought about voting. I am going to vote for "Papa gobierno." Yes. I have to vote for Papa, because he sent us the money.

LYNN: Do you think you would have voted without PROCAMPO?

HERMINIA: No. If the money hadn't arrived, I wouldn't have voted.

Herminia expresses her relationship to the government as a daughter to a father. She clearly feels the need to obey the government and to "help out" with her vote. When her "Papa"'s help disappears, however, her vote will as well. In unequal relations of power with the government, she sees her vote as the only leverage she has to continue receiving a small amount of assistance. Her vote is not an endorsement of PRI party ideology, of any specific election platform, or of a particular candidate. It is a minimal tool for helping her economic survival. While no one may actually keep track of her PRI vote or the fact that she receives a PROCAMPO check, in her mind the two are linked. What certainly happened, right before the elections, was that local PRI politicians used PROCAMPO to promote their campaigns, assuring voters that the checks they received were a result of the PRI government. If the opposition were voted in, they implied, PROCAMPO could end and no more checks would be paid out.

While both PROCAMPO and PROCEDE are promoted as decreasing the paternalism of the government, in the minds of some, like Herminia, one's personal relationship to the government remains that of an inferior subject obeying orders from a superior authority. Some elderly ejidatarios compared the government's role in "helping out" with PROCAMPO to its role in establishing the ejidos over sixty years ago, with remarks such as, "How can we not sign up for the PROCAMPO? It's like when the president told us all to organize ejidos. We have to obey."

The above conversation and comments, which are representative of those I had with many more people, clearly reflect the importance of programs like PROCAMPO in ensuring some ejidatarios' continued loyalty to the PRI. In many cases, the check is looked at as people's rightful due, since the government has ignored them for so long. Some also felt that PROCAMPO was welcome evidence of the state's continued support of campesinos, a legacy they associate with the Mexican Revolution.

LOYALTY TO THE GOVERNMENT?
ELECTIONS AND ZAPATISMO

The state's deployment of Zapata's image in the marketing of PROCEDE and PROCAMPO influenced some ejidatarios in their support of the PRI in the 1994 elections—ejidatarios who simultaneously expressed sympathy for the Zapatistas. Many ejidatarios in the communities I studied voted for the PRI in 1994; however, many did not—particularly in Santa María del Tule. Voting patterns in El Tule in 1994 and the significant number of ejidatarios expressing sympathy for the EZLN suggested that loyalty to the government and to the PRI was volatile and likely to be unpredictable. Voting returns from the 2000 elections bore this out.

In 1994, in the polling places representing the Santa María del Tule ejido, the PRI received 413 votes (52 percent) for its presidential candidate, the PAN 219 votes (28 percent), and the PRD 160 votes (20 percent). The PAN and PRD votes together came to 48 percent. Thus, while in El Tule, the PRI received a majority among the three parties, the antigovernment vote of the two opposition parties was almost as strong. This suggests that, even in formal voting terms, support for the government was eroding in El Tule in 1994. This trend was further suggested by the sympathy expressed for the EZLN by those who said that they voted for the PRI; the pattern was even more clearly seen in Unión Zapata. There, the PRI got 175 votes (87 percent), the PRD 13 (6.5 percent), and the PAN 13 (6.5 percent) in the presidential election. But while a majority in Unión Zapata voted for the PRI, many expressed sympathy for the EZLN at the same time.

The remainder of this chapter seeks to understand how a pro-Zapatista and pro-PRI position was constructed by ejidatarios, and what this position means in terms of the kind of nation view ejidatarios use to read and interpret contemporary politics. I shall suggest that local nationalisms result in significantly different interpretations of economic policy and political events than does the nationalism projected from the center. I end with a brief discussion of the 2000 elections and of the meaning of an opposition response clearly reflected in the vote in El Tule but not in Unión Zapata.

Most Mexicans experienced the Zapatista rebellion through the radio, the spotty television coverage, and the mainstream press. Because some state-controlled news media, such as Televisa, tried to downplay the importance of the event, radio coverage was very important. In the Oaxaca countryside, radio reports were spread by word-of-mouth in remote areas, and rumors quickly spread that the rebellion had reached Oaxaca. Such notions were also fueled by the sight of intense mobilization by the hundreds of troops stationed in army garrisons in and around the city of Oaxaca.

Given six months of low-level exposure to the Zapatistas, to their objectives, and to the constant invocation of the figure of Zapata by the EZLN, how did rural men and women in Oaxaca see the Zapatistas? Had they indeed heard of the Zapatistas? How did they interpret what the rebels were doing? Did they connect the struggle of the Zapatistas with their own fight for land after the Mexican Revolution?

In a random-sample survey carried out during the summer of 1994 with 126 ejidatarios from Unión Zapata and Santa María del Tule (64 women and 62 men), people were asked an open-ended question, "What do you know about the EZLN?"[4] If the person answering was inclined to make a statement beyond whether he or she had heard of the EZLN, the person was encouraged to express an opinion about the Zapatistas. About 9 percent (11 people out of 126) simply declined to answer this question; most stated they felt it concerned too dangerous a topic. This was not an unreasonable response given the stepped-up presence of the army and federal police on the main roads of Oaxaca that July and August.

Of those who did respond to the question, 62 percent (71 of 115) said they had heard of the EZLN. The quick response of some in stating "I don't know anything about it" suggests that more probably had heard of the EZLN but did not want to discuss the topic. Most who responded positively indicated that they had become aware of the Zapatista uprising through radio news or by being told by others in their community. Some, particularly those in El Tule, stated that they had seen the EZLN rebellion on television news, although with very little information about what was going on and why. Some stated that it was a frequent topic of conversation during the first two weeks of January and during the peace negotiations in the San Cristóbal Cathedral in 1994. As government media had downplayed the rebellion, its profile had dropped in Oaxaca as well.

Of those giving specific opinions about the EZLN (49 of 115 who responded to the question), 47 percent (23 people) offered clearly positive statements. These remarks focused on the just struggle for land engaged in by the EZLN, on false promises made by the government, which drove people to rebellion, on the persistent mistreatment of indigenous people in Mexico, and on the extreme poverty in Chiapas. Most offered reasons serving to justify the Zapatistas' armed uprising. Of those who responded, about 24 percent (12 people) offered negative comments about the EZLN, with all but two simply stating, "I don't agree with their use of arms." About 29 percent (14 people) of the specific comments were neutral; they focused on how far away Chiapas was and how both the EZLN and the government seemed right, and they often repeated the reasons given by the EZLN for its struggle while simultaneously stating that the army was present in the community to provide safety.

Perhaps most interesting were the comments of those 21 people (18 percent of the 115 who responded the question) who spoke of the general lack of information, in particular from the media. Statements such as "We don't know anything because they never give us any news on TV" or "They never gave us any information about the people in Chiapas or why the rebellion took place" were typical. "We only know what was on the TV and the radio, and they didn't tell us much," many said. Thus, about one-third of those who responded said lack of information made it difficult for them to have an informed opinion.

More men (14) than women (9) provided specific positive comments on the EZLN. Almost equal numbers of men and women had negative comments (7 men and 5 women), and more women (10) than men (4) had neutral comments. I am not sure that these differences reflect significant variation between male and female opinions. Instead, they may be more indicative of women's reluctance to speak frankly with strange interviewers, particularly male interviewers; two of the five people who worked with me on the questionnaire were men.

It is important to note that, while surveys can provide some information, they are not the preferred method for getting people to discuss their positions on an armed rebellion that is still active. In many cases, those responding had not had previous contact with me or with those working with me to administer the questionnaire. It could be dangerous to answer questions of such a political nature. In addition, a survey does not provide space to articulate how an event such as the Zapatista rebellion resonates with one's own identity and experience—a basic area of interest that summer. To obtain a better idea of what each person really thought, and how he or she related this to the self and to community identities and histories, I decided to discuss the Zapatistas with forty-eight ejidatarios (half of them men, half women) through in-depth interviews—interviews more accurately characterized as conversations. These "interviews" were not done as a random sample, but were, deliberately, with people I had established previous relationships with. I tried to talk to people providing a range of political opinions regarding the state and its programs. When I conducted the interviews, I found much more openly stated sympathy for the Zapatistas than I found in responses to the EZLN question in the survey.

Of those I interviewed, many commented that they were initially convinced that the EZLN would arrive in Oaxaca during January 1994. When they recalled hearing about the Zapatista rebellion in Chiapas, they immediately cited the fighting during the Mexican Revolution as proof that the war could come to Oaxaca. The words of Angela López Martínez of Unión Zapata demonstrated an identification with the Zapatistas and a sympathy for their cause that was expressed by many I interviewed:

ANGELA: We first heard of them on the radio. The party of the Zapatistas is named after Zapata. Because he was the first one to redistribute land, and fought for this, they are fighting for this same thing in his name. They are fighting for land now in Chiapas. It seems as if the rich are getting rich again. . . . It is like before, when Zapata saw the suffering of the poor peasants at the hands of the rich. That is what is going on in Chiapas. This is why Zapata died.

LYNN: Do you think there could be an uprising in Oaxaca?

ANGELA: It's quite possible that there could be a war here. It's possible that
            there could be a war, because if the government doesn't help the
            peasants and takes the help away, people will fight. . . . It's good
            that the Zapatistas are there in Chiapas. They keep on giving hope
            to the peasants for their fight. There are a lot of people who want
            to take the peasants' land away. They are getting rich down there,
            like they did all over the country before the revolution. They say
            that there are people so rich in Chiapas that they give each other
            cars for Christmas. All people want is to be equal.

Angela's responses to the plight of the poor of Chiapas contained
important echoes of the injustices suffered by her and others who became ejidatarios in Oaxaca during the 1920s and 1930s. She cited extreme wealth differences between rich and poor in Chiapas as compa-
rable to conditions before the Mexican Revolution. Angela had worked
as a peon on a nearby hacienda, and could still recall bitterly the hard
times and labor conditions she and her husband suffered as early as age
fourteen. She clearly identified with Zapata as the figurehead of the Zapatista movement. While she had never met Marío González of El Tule,
who spoke of Zapata as a Christ-like figure giving his blood for the campesinos, she invoked a related image in stating "Zapata saw the suffering of the peasants . . . that is why he died." For ejidatarios like Angela,
whose personal experience was close to the time of the Mexican Revolution, the struggle of the EZLN made perfect sense.

While it might be expected that older ejidatarios would be more sympathetic to the EZLN than younger ones, I found this not to be the case.
Some who expressed the most sympathy were younger and did not have
their elders' personal links to the founding of the ejido and thus the elders' more direct connection to the figures of Zapata and Cárdenas. Silvia López from Santa María del Tule, who was twenty-seven when we
talked in 1994, was a recent ejidataria who had received ejido rights from
her paternal great-uncle. She responded to my question about whether
she had heard of the Zapatistas by commenting first on media coverage.

SILVIA: We heard about what was going on from the television. We found
            out more afterward. The problem in Mexico is that the news is
            manipulated. There were a lot of things that we didn't know about
            Chiapas. . . .

LYNN: What do you think about the Zapatistas and their issues?

SILVIA: Indigenous people are oppressed in this country. We are indigenous
            here, too. The problem is that the middle class doesn't really know

what is going on. They don't want to see how the majority live. The
Zapatistas are acting within their rights.

While Silvia did not respond to the Zapatistas by recalling her own
historical links to Zapata, as many elderly ejidatarios did, she made a
connection to the Zapatistas through her indigenous identity. Through
this device, she placed herself on an equal and empathetic level with the
Zapatistas, and stated that they were within their rights.

Ramón Grilhalva, a middle-aged ejidatario from Unión Zapata, had
a lot to say about the Zapatistas. He was definitely sympathetic, and one
of the few who indicated that he would not be voting for the PRI—or any
party. Ramón was a seasoned community authority who had watched
many political struggles and kept his distance from formal politics. In
past conversations, he had expressed pride in living in an ejido named
for Zapata and had sometimes cited Zapata's struggle as still important.
He did not make this link, however, in the following conversation, focusing instead on what he thought about the EZLN, and on his lack of
confidence in all political parties.

LYNN: Where did you first hear of the Zapatistas?

RAMÓN: We saw them on the television and then heard about it on the radio.
The uprising grabbed us by surprise. We thought that they would
advance to Oaxaca, but the government stopped them.

LYNN: What do you think of the EZLN and their issues and demands?

RAMÓN: Their demands are just. The indigenous race has suffered a lot. That
could happen here too.

LYNN: What do you think of Subcomandante Marcos:

RAMÓN: It's true what he says, "Ya basta." Because the government has already deceived us a lot.

LYNN: What do you think will happen now in Chiapas?

RAMÓN: I don't know if the government is going to accept their proposals.
They are asking for things for the whole country. If the government
accepts their proposals, it could affect us as well. The government
is going to have to respond to the demands of more people to get
them to be quiet.

LYNN: What do people in Unión Zapata think about the Zapatistas? Do
they talk about them?

RAMÓN: Well, we talk about them in our private conversations. A lot of
people think that what they did is good. We'll see if it helps us to
get out of our poverty. We don't have the support of the government
either.

LYNN: Do you think that there could be another uprising?

RAMÓN: If the system doesn't change, then it will get to the point where
            people will take up arms. It could happen here in Oaxaca. . . .

LYNN: Will a lot of people here vote for the PRI?

RAMÓN: Yes, they will, but there are also some people who will vote for the
            PRD too, a few. . . . I am going to abstain. I am not voting for the
            PRI, the PAN, the PRD . . . they are all the same. It doesn't matter
            who wins. When they get into office, they forget all about us. They
            totally forget whatever they promised in their campaigns.

Ramón's sympathies for the Zapatistas made sense in an antigovernment paradigm. He identified with their demands, their sense of injustice,
and their statements that the Mexican government did not come through
on its promises. In fact, his position on voting was similar to that of many
in the EZLN: "Why bother voting, since it doesn't matter who wins? Indigenous people and the poor are always ignored once a politician takes
office."

While Ramón's position on the government and the EZLN made
sense, I listened to many more men and women who, while expressing
identification with the plight of the poor of Chiapas and the justice of the
Zapatistas' struggle, simultaneously indicated their passive support for
government programs like PROCEDE and PROCAMPO. In many cases,
these men and women were voting for the PRI. One interchange stood
out, in explaining how the men and women I was working with could
be both pro-Zapatista and pro-PRI in 1994.

Pedro García Sánchez and Refugio Ruiz from Unión Zapata discussed
their support for the PRI and the Zapatistas in the same seamless conversation. When I had talked at length with Pedro in 1993, he had been
quite critical of PROCEDE and other government development programs. In the summer of 1994, he not only had a different perspective
on these programs but told me outright that he was voting for the PRI.
It was when he and Refugio tied their support for the PRI to the fact that
they had received their ejido land from the government that I finally understood how the mediating figure of Zapata, claimed by both the state
and the Zapatistas, was working to integrate seemingly contradictory
discourses for some ejidatarios in Oaxaca. Here is a partial transcript of
our interchange:

LYNN: Who did you vote for?

REFUGIO: We voted for the PRI because they gave us our land. We keep on
            supporting the government party because they gave us the ejido
            land we are living from now.

LYNN: Well, last year when we talked, you were very critical of past government problems and of their perpetual failure to fulfill their promises.

PEDRO: We realize that the government is helping now. Before, they used to always promise and never deliver. Now they are helping more. Before, when we asked for help, they would forget us. Now you ask for help for your piece of land [referring to PROCAMPO], and they give it. We look more favorably upon the PROCEDE as well.

LYNN: How did you first hear about the Zapatistas and what did you think about them?

PEDRO: We thought that the fire had started and that it was going to arrive here. . . . The Zapatistas want land to be redistributed. They want to get rid of the big landholders in Chiapas. If they don't take care of that problem, the fighting will continue. The Zapatistas didn't have any other road open to them. . . . We sympathize with them. We realize on the one hand that the government doesn't like them and on the other hand those fucking *terratenientes* [large land-holders] want to take all of their money.

I'm going to tell you why I understand them, through making a comparison. When I was a young man, about thirteen years old, my parents were peons for the hacendados. My parents worked their land, but they had to turn over most of the harvest to them. My parents couldn't produce enough to eat.

Whoever disobeyed the hacendados got beaten with a horse-whip. One day when I was watching some cows, one of them went onto the land of the hacendados and began eating. After that, one of the hacendados' bosses grabbed me and started beating me with a horsewhip, like an animal. That's why we took their land away from them. That is what they are fighting for now in Chiapas. They are going to do the same thing to the large landowners there. . . . When we woke up here and saw what was going on, we took the land away from the large landowners. The government helped us to do that here, in our struggle for the ejido. The ejido law never reached Chiapas. Nobody helped them there. Now the PRI has to help them get their land there or the blood will keep flowing.

Pedro interpreted the alarm sounded by the Zapatistas as an indication that what happened in his community in Oaxaca—where the government helped Unión Zapata secure land expropriated from the hacenda-dos—had not happened in Chiapas. From the role that Zapata assumed in the local history of Pedro's own ejido, and his interpretation of Mexican nationalism, Pedro felt that those without land in Chiapas certainly had a right to it; it was their right as Mexicans. If the government did not assist them in getting land, then the violence would continue.

The historical connection that some ejidatarios made to Zapata was also linked to the government. As reflected in my discussion with Refugio and Pedro, the ejido was tied not only historically to Zapata but also to the government—specifically, to the PRI—as the bearer of original agrarian reform. As we have seen, in the ejido histories of Unión Zapata and Santa María del Tule, government officials played a strong positive role in securing land for the community. For most middle-aged and older ejidatarios, the ejido land they currently lived off was a daily reminder of what the state had done for them and their families sixty or seventy years earlier. Comparisons of what happened in Oaxaca during the revolution to the current situation in Chiapas suggested an evolutionary analysis. For many I interviewed in Oaxaca, what was going on in Chiapas was a logical outcome of a revolution that they believed never reached the southernmost part of the country. They identified with the struggle of the Zapatistas and expected the government to facilitate land redistribution in Chiapas, taking it from large landholders and providing it to those without land, as in Oaxaca.

THE PRESIDENTIAL ELECTIONS IN 2000

In Santa María del Tule and, to a much smaller degree, in Unión Zapata, some ejidatarios whose vote had demonstrated tenuous support for the PRI and the government in 1994 switched to an antigovernment vote in the year 2000. Voting patterns in Santa María del Tule strongly favored the PAN in the 2000 presidential vote. In the polling places representing the bulk of the ejido population, the PAN received 363 votes (54 percent), the PRI received 193 votes (29 percent), the PRD received 99 votes (15 percent), other parties received 1 percent of the vote, and 1 percent of the presidential votes were declared void. The PAN almost doubled its portion of the presidential vote from 1994 to 2000 in El Tule (from 28 percent to 54 percent). Of the ejidatarios with whom I spoke, a few talked about voting for the PAN so as to vote "for a change." Most felt the PAN candidate was the mostly likely opposition candidate to defeat the PRI and participated in what became known as the *voto útil*—the "useful vote." They were cautious about the actual outcome, making comments like, "Let's hope it isn't worse than the PRI."

Even Carlos Gómez, who had confessed to me in many conversations that he was a diehard PRI supporter, almost had an epiphany in the voting booth. He came close to defecting from the PRI. He spoke of this as we talked about the outcome of the elections and what the challenges for the new president would be after December 2000:

LYNN: So, you voted for the PRI?

CARLOS: Yes, I continued to vote for the PRI.

LYNN: Why did you keep supporting them?

CARLOS: Because I have always been in the PRI, for many, many years. . . .
          I didn't change parties, but the main point of the opposition was
          something that Mr. Cuauhtémoc Cárdenas said that I really liked.
          He said he wants to revise this reform that they made to Article 27.
          I was undecided. At the final moment I said . . . okay.

LYNN: So you were thinking about voting for Cárdenas.

CARLOS: Yes, really I was. I almost did right there in the voting both. But
          then. . . . [He threw up his hands.]

He laughed after that admission. We continued to discuss what the
government of Vicente Fox could bring. Carlos's feelings of uncertainty
reflected those of many I spoke with after the elections, regardless of who
they had voted for.

LYNN: So why do you think that people voted for change, for the PAN?

CARLOS: I think that a lot of people felt that a change was necessary. But we
          still can't see the reality of what will happen when Sr. Fox is actu-
          ally the president. Unfortunately, the tactics of the government of
          General Cárdenas have been lost. I hope that Fox will engage in
          some of these tactics to benefit the nation.

LYNN: What were these tactics?

CARLOS: The idea of him [General Cárdenas] was to help the poor. . . . Be-
          cause ultimately the governments always say they will help out the
          poor, but in fact they don't. They are more inclined toward the
          people in Mexico City, the big businessmen, and all these people
          with money. I hope that Licenciado Fox is genuinely concerned
          about the poor, especially the peasant sector that is really poor.

LYNN: What do you think will happen if it turns out that Mr. Fox isn't
          concerned about the poor?

CARLOS: Well, there would be a contradiction there. There would be those
          who would oppose him for acting this way. Right now the elections
          were peaceful, nothing happened. But in spite of everything, some-
          thing [more violent] could happen, don't you think? . . . There are
          people waiting and watching to see what happens. This señor [Fox]
          has offered us a change, but let's see concretely what kind of change
          it is. He made a lot of promises, but we still haven't seen concretely
          what will happen in reality.

Carlos's remarks offer a good synthesis of the complex feelings that
many experienced at the outcome of the elections. While the elections
were peaceful and people have great expectations of positive changes—

particularly concerning the poor—everyone will be watching carefully to see what happens.

In Unión Zapata, where the PRI won by a large majority, voting patterns in the 2000 presidential elections were more consistent with those in 1994. The two opposition parties picked up a significant number of votes, however; the PRI won with 105 votes (59 percent), followed by the PRD with 39 votes (22 percent), and the PAN with 26 votes (15 percent), and 4 percent of the votes were declared void. The combined opposition vote climbed from a mere 13 percent of the total in 1994 to 37 percent in 2000.

In Unión Zapata, too, a number of people had become more open about their oppositional leanings. There were a variety of signs posted for all three political parties, which had not been the case in 1994. Those who voted for the PRI talked about elections more as a "ritual," and cited "fear of change" as a reason for remaining with the PRI, rather than citing any positive affirmation of the party's ideals or concrete plans. María, (daughter of Angela López Martínez, quoted above and in the previous chapter), talked with me about the elections while she eased her mother into a chair. I had not visited with the family for almost three years. Angela had lost her sight and part of her hearing and had been seriously ill in the hospital; she cried as we held hands and talked, recalling how well she had felt the last time we had been together, in 1997. Upon hearing that the PAN had won, she snapped to attention and shouted, "The PAN won—well, then, I lost too. I am with the PRI." Her daughter María smiled at seeing her mother perk up, and explained her own perspective on the voting. Another sister, Ana, stood by and listened.

MARÍA: You know, we already are used to voting for the PRI. The people from the other parties came here and they said, no, you shouldn't vote for the PRI. All they do is deceive you. Look at what Salinas de Gortari did, all the money he stole. But, you know, here we are used to voting for the PRI, so we did.

ANA: Let's see if the PAN is able to fulfill the promises it made. Will we keep getting PROGRESA (a government antipoverty program)? I worry about that.

María and Ana agreed that the antipoverty programs of the PRI were important, but pointed out that not everyone received their benefits. Ana's question, however, reflected the campaign strategy of the PRI in many parts of rural Mexico, which was to suggest that, if the PRI did not win, all antipoverty programs would end. Thus, some people like Ana voted for the PRI hoping to continue to get monthly checks to subsidize the costs of education, health, and nutrition for their families. Unión Zapata is a significantly poorer community than Santa María del Tule, where economic options beyond subsistence agriculture and migration exist and where the small business sector of roadside restaurants, crafts vendors, and others was no doubt attracted to the promises of Vicente Fox to aid that sector. In Unión Zapata, where a significant number of people depend on government antipoverty programs and have few options, the threats of the PRI were taken seriously.

Conversations in both communities after the election suggest high hopes and expectations for positive change but also lingering suspicions that, in the end, the poor will be forgotten by whoever is in power. Some suggest that, if the PAN fails, the PRI will make a comeback, because at least it delivered some basics needed by the people. At the bottom line, mixed loyalties in both communities remain. People continue to identify with many demands of the Zapatistas, recognize both what the PRI governments have done for them and where those governments have fallen short, and hope that change will bring positive benefits to their communities rather than result in a worsened situation.

As suggested by the discussions and comments of rural men and women that I have highlighted, participation in government programs and rural voting patterns in Mexico is not a referendum on the population's endorsement of particular political parties, political ideologies, or overall party platforms. The political ideology of the men and women from Unión Zapata and Santa María del Tule analyzed here is a complex mix of competing discourses oriented by the selective traditions of local history and nation views and by the changing elements of the dominant and grassroots messages projected through the national media, the alternative media, and the state and its communication apparatus.[5]

LOCAL HISTORIES RE-ENVISION THE NATION

The interesting question in relation to the 1994 pro-Zapatista and pro-PRI stances of these ejidatarios, as well as to the decidedly antigovernment stance of ejidatarios in Zapatista communities in Chiapas, is how did the symbols that the state had appropriated for the purposes of rule —Emiliano Zapata as a patriot-hero, for example—become grounds to contest or question the state once these symbols were given local meaning and integrated with community histories? Mary Kay Vaughn, following William Roseberry (1994), maintains that what emerged from the state's national culture-producing project of the 1930s was the forging of a common language for consent and protest in Mexico (Vaughn 1997, 20). This argument does not mean that everyone in Mexico absorbed the official version of nationalism promoted by the government beginning in the 1930s. What it does suggest is that a great many absorbed the symbols of that culture-producing project and appropriated them for their own purposes. The Mexican state continued to claim a direct connection to Emiliano Zapata and to the Mexican Revolution and used this claim to market a wide range of agrarian policies, including PROCEDE, and the end of its obligation to redistribute land. Ejidatarios claimed Emiliano Zapata as their own and made him part of their local ejido histories. Grassroots organizers working in peasant and other regional movements used the same symbols to develop organizations and promote demands. Thus, the same symbols unleashed by the state through a campaign of postrevolutionary nationalism were available for all to claim as their own. These symbols were deployed through what Antonio Gramsci (1971) has called a hegemonic process. But hegemony can also be thought of as a tool for understanding contested processes, as proposed by Roseberry:

> This is the way hegemony works. I propose that we use the concept not to understand consent but to understand struggle: the ways in which the words, images, symbols, forms, organizations, institutions, and movements used by subordinate populations to talk about, understand, confront, accommodate themselves to, or resist their domination are shaped by the process of domination itself. What hegemony constructs, then, is not a shared ideology but a common material and meaningful framework for living through, talking about, and acting upon social orders characterized by domination. (Roseberry 1994, 360–51)

Roseberry further suggests that we think of hegemony as the current that connects ruling and subaltern groups into a "field of force of organic relations between State or political society and 'civil society'" (Roseberry 1994, 360). Thus, the specific current of the force field of connecting relations in this story is the ensemble of symbols, images, concepts, visions, and memories of the past that are bound to the postrevolutionary process of state formation *and* made meaningful through integration with specific local histories and experiences. The flexibility inherent in the government's discourse of the 1930s, which laid the basis for the next six decades of common language, had to allow for regional diversity and multiple views of the nation. As Vaughn points out, "[B]ecause the postrevolutionary process of state formation in Mexico engaged local communities so intensely, the very construction of state principles and ideals depended upon how they were understood, reshaped, and discarded at the local level" (Vaughn 1997, 22–23).

One chief tool of interpretation used by local men and women (both in the case-study ejidos here and more generally) in their engagement with the government is local history. Such history is contained in the individual and collective memories of community members. In her discussions of the Zapatista past in a community in Morelos, JoAnne Martin found that "the coherence that characterizes contemporary representations . . . reflects the complex interaction between local and official history" (Martin 1993, 45). This interaction is similar to the mixing of national history and figures such as Zapata and Cárdenas into the local histories of Unión Zapata and El Tule. Martin writes that local memories in Morelos, even visual memories, drew heavily on locally based oral histories "as well as images of Zapata borrowed selectively from government propaganda and history books" (ibid., 457). Thus, the local histories of the Mexican Revolution and its actors that Martin discussed in the 1980s with members of a community interacting with Zapatistas codified the dialogue between state and society about the Mexican Revolution.

Discourses on the past such as local histories are usually mobilized in particular moments in relation to the present. In fact, they are given life and meaning when constituted in the present. Part of their in-the-moment constitution is the mobilization of selective versions of the past to serve the present. One of the chief ways that ejidatarios have responded to state policy changes such as NAFTA or the ending of land redistribution through the rewriting of Article 27 of the Mexican Constitution has come about through deployment of their own local histories. In selective traditions such as that of El Tule, which lines up both Zapata and state agrarian officials as "the good guys" in the struggle for ejido lands, the Zapatistas and their goals could be integrated by some ejidatarios with a partial endorsement of the government and its programs, because the latter back their demands for land. The invocation of Zapata resonates with the struggles many went through in Oaxaca to obtain their own land.

The ability of ejidatarios to empathize with the Zapatistas also tells us that words of support for the government, even votes of support, are tenuous and unstable. This was demonstrated in the electoral results of 2000. While the local histories and experiences of ejidatarios in Unión Zapata and El Tule are significantly different from those of Zapatista ejidatarios in Guadalupe Tepeyac and La Realidad, there is a convergence in their association of Zapata at the local level with the land rights that

Figure 16. Image of Zapata used in march in support of the EZLN in Oaxaca City. Photo by Lynn Stephen.

Figure 17. Images of Subcomandante Marcos, Che Guevara, and Emiliano Zapata on a wall in Juchitán, Mexico. Photo by Anya Peterson Royce.

the legacy of Zapata confers on all rural Mexicans. In fact, what binds together the ejidatarios from these four communities are commonalities in local interpretations of nationalism and parallel yet very different assimilations of Emiliano Zapata into local stories. While there are clearly contrasting nation views found in the ejidos in Oaxaca and Chiapas—particularly regarding the quality of past engagements with the government—the ways each community connected the legacy of Zapata to its own histories of struggle provide a point of commonality. In both contexts, the government's statement that it is "honoring the memory of Emiliano Zapata" (in the words of Salinas de Gortari in 1994) rings hollow. The common interpretation of nationalist discourse centered around Zapata in all four ejidos includes the right of all rural Mexicans to land, the responsibility of the government to respond to the needs of the people, and the moral authority of struggles for freedom from exploitation and poverty; these are the common threads linking the four ejidos. And, by the year 2000, these had resulted in more formally articulated opposition to the PRI as well, at least in Santa María del Tule.

The previous discussion of how a pro-Zapatista and pro-PRI position emerged among some ejidatarios in Oaxaca suggests that one will not find unified strategies of resistance to state programs or to the PRI among Mexico's rural population. Regional variation within Mexico on whether or how agrarian reform has been carried out since the Mexican Revolution; the importance of local selective tradition in the reconstruction of community history; differences within local populations; and thus the variation and creativity used to interpret and reinterpret dominant discourses of the state and grassroots discourses, such as that of the Zapatistas, all discourage analysis of the countryside as a homogeneous sector. Specific historical and ethnographic case studies allow us to perceive the process by which a specific group comes up with a particular political position, but can also alert us to regional convergences that come out of very different experiences. Political analysts seeking to understand Mexico's political future should not underestimate regional and local diversity in exploring how political positions are formed. The Conclusion of this book takes the specific historical interpretations of Zapata and the Mexican Revolution woven into the local histories and nation views of Unión Zapata, El Tule, Guadalupe Tepeyac, and La Realidad and discusses their implications for understanding nationalism, citizenship, and alternative ways for constructing and claiming the Mexican nation in the twenty-first century.

Conclusion

Reclaiming the Mexican Nation for the Poor and the Indigenous South

CHALLENGES AND HOPES FOR THE FUTURE

The local histories of Unión Zapata, Santa María del Tule, Guadalupe Tepeyac, and La Realidad show that people appropriate aspects of national identity for their own purposes. An "experiential knowledge of the past transmitted through personal recollection can be harnessed in the context of political action," Joanne Rappaport observes (1994, 19). Government-claimed nationalist icons are reprogrammed with local meaning and then mobilized in response to particular local and national conflicts and policies. Ejidatarios in Oaxaca and Chiapas have fashioned their own responses to the neoliberal economic policy that ended land reform, encouraged privatization, and has resulted in increasing socioeconomic stratification in Mexico. The role of culture has been key in how these men and women have been talking back to capital, to the government and its agencies, and indirectly to the institutions and actors, such as the World Bank and the International Monetary Fund, that design global financial policy. While local identities and the ideas of local intellectuals found in this process of "talking back" cannot be called autonomous, because they have incorporated past nationalist ideas and discourses, they do offer hope for new ways of envisioning the nation on more equitable and democratic terms.

The outcome of the July 2000 presidential elections in Mexico confirms the idea of "talking back" to the status quo. Toppling the Partido

Revolucionario Institutional (PRI) after its seventy-one years in power was the work of a deep current of anti-PRI sentiment rather than an affirmation of the political and economic policies of Vicente Fox as candidate of the Partido Acción Nacional (PAN). As summarized by the political analyst Wayne Cornelius: "Exit-poll data show that for two-thirds of those who voted for Fox, the main reason was a generalized desire for 'change.' Only one out of four voted for Fox because of the candidate's personal qualities. Only 8 percent supported him because of his party affiliation" (Cornelius 2000). Other significant factors in the PRI's defeat included changing demographics (many more younger voters were credentialed than previously and most of these voted for Fox), a more level electoral playing field, the establishment of an autonomous Federal Electoral Institute to run the elections, and the grassroots organization of thousands of electoral poll watchers and participants (Cornelius 2000).

The gubernatorial elections in Chiapas in August 2000 also sent a clear message of change when voters elected Pablo Salazar Mendiguchia on an opposition alliance ticket. While the federal elections were no doubt some of the cleanest in the nation's history, their outcome—and some of their little-publicized problematic aspects—suggest some future challenges faced by Mexico, as well as the complex factors underlying the ouster of the PRI in July 2000 and Salazar's victory in Chiapas.

In this chapter, I highlight two aspects of the continued reality of rural Mexico: high levels of militarization and intimidation, on the one hand, and a strong national movement for indigenous rights and autonomy, on the other. The two are related, and are indicative of the contradictory factors that continue to coexist in Mexico despite the mandate for change spelled out by the 2000 elections. At the local level, particularly in the south, there are major problems to be resolved, yet also waves of hope generated by local and national movements, such as that for indigenous rights, that persistently plod ahead pushing for change.

THE SURVEILLANCE AND MILITARIZATION OF MEXICAN SOCIETY

The political opening in Mexico solidified by the outcome of the July 2000 elections has been accompanied by a history of intimidation and harassment of opponents to the government, including opposition political parties such as the PRD, nongovernmental organizations (NGOs) working with peasants, indigenous peoples, human rights organizations, and a wide range of social organizations. The long-present culture of political intimidation permeating many parts of Mexico operates in many realms outside the electoral process and involves parts of the military as well as multiple state and federal police forces. This strategy of intimidation involves three key pieces:

1. A war of covert intelligence and the development of a sophisticated intelligence apparatus

2. A civilian-targeted low-intensity war that involves intimidation, harassment, and a constant military presence in selected parts of Mexico—particularly in parts of the states of Oaxaca, Guerrero, and Chiapas

3. The militarization of police forces and the central role of the military in all public security and intelligence-gathering operations (Canal 6 de Julio 1998)

The integration of the U.S. and Mexican economies through NAFTA is reflected by the role of the United States as the supplier of weapons, technology, and training for Mexican police and military personnel, upgrading their capacity for surveillance, intimidation, and the militarization of public space. The training Mexican military personnel and police receive has come in large part from the School of the Americas (SOA), renamed the Western Institute for Security Cooperation in November 2000. This combat training school for Latin American soldiers, located at Fort Benning, Georgia, has offered instruction in, among other things, "counter-guerrilla manuals, extortion, physical and psychological torture and military intelligence, courses in commando and sniper operations, interrogation techniques, terrorism, urban guerrilla warfare, counterinsurgency, low intensity warfare, irregular warfare, jungle warfare, counterintelligence training, and anti-drug operations" (Castro Soto 1999).

The Mexican Department of National Defense has stated that over a twenty-year period (1978–98), 4,172 military personnel received training abroad, of whom 61 percent have taken courses since 1994 (Castro Soto 1999). In the first year following the Zapatista rebellion, 766 military personnel were trained at the SOA. Between 1996 and 1999, around 3,200 members of the Special Forces Air Transportation Group graduated from a counterinsurgency course with the Seventh Group of the U.S. Special Forces, or Green Berets (ibid.).

According to *Proceso* magazine, a Pentagon document confirmed that in early 1997 the Mexican government sent 1,500 military personnel for training in the United States. The document adds that military technology transfer from the United States to Mexico increased by 400 percent in 1997. That same year, the Mexican Department of Defense budget increased by 800 percent its allocations for the training of Mexican military personnel (*Proceso* 1106 [11 January 1998], as cited in Castro Soto 1999). In 1995, the Mexican Army became formally involved in the work of public security, "substituting civil police forces or placing middle and high ranking Army officers in positions of authority within the state police forces" (López y Ménendez 2000, 55). By 1999, the military was participating in public security operations in twenty-nine of the thirty-two Mexican states. In 1999, a new police force called the Federal Preventative Police (PFP) also involved the incorporation of army soldiers and officers. Since its inception, the PFP has been involved in intelligence activities, counterinsurgency, and civilian-targeted operations (ibid., 58–60; see Ledesma Arronte et al. 2000 for more details on the development of the Mexican armed forces).

The training that Mexican police and military forces have received has been used to target and intimidate human rights organizations and international observers, as well as opposition political parties and independent organizations. During a visit to Mexico in late November 1999, Mary Robinson, the U.N. High Commissioner for Human Rights, stated that the heavy presence of Mexican troops in Chiapas was causing human rights abuses at the grassroots level, including disappearances, detentions, torture, and violence against women. Robinson said that she was "overwhelmed" by the documentation of abuses she had received, and had had to buy two new suitcases to carry all the testimonies and evidence (Kraul 1999).

Other victims of human rights abuses are those very organizations formed to defend human rights. Most human rights organization staff in Mexico regularly face death threats by phone, office break-ins, and theft of computers and their electronic information, as well as, in some cases, detention, kidnapping, and torture. For example, staff of the Centro de Derechos Humanos Miguel Agustín Pro Juárez, A.C. (Miguel Agustín Pro Juárez Human Rights Center), or PRODH, which produced critical reports and documentation of militarization and human rights abuses throughout Mexico, have received severe threats for their work. During the summer and fall of 1999, and in the winter of 2000, the threats escalated. Death threats were sent by mail, and more threats were found at the center in locked offices and locked desks.

In August 1999, the attorney Digna Ochoa was kidnapped and held in a car for several hours, during which she was subjected to threats and interrogation. On the night of 28–29 October 1999, she was the victim of an attempted homicide (as well as verbal aggression, interrogation, and intimidation) by unknown individuals who entered her house. For a period of more than nine hours, she was interrogated and tied up.

> That same morning, October 29, 1999, the door to the main entrance to the PRODH office was found open, and the Legal Defense Department offices, located on the second floor of the building, had been broken into. The window was left open and the desks were in disarray, with papers thrown around. On one desk a folder was placed in an obvious position with the words "PODER SUICIDA" (SUICIDE POWER) printed on it in red. In addition, the surveillance video camera/recorder on the first floor had been turned off. (Servicio Internacional para la Paz 1999)

Human rights organizations such as the Centro Pro have clearly known that they were being watched. They asked for international accompaniment in an effort to deter their tormentors. In February 2000, the threats against the Centro Pro escalated to include foreigners working with the center.

In order to combat this kind of occurrence, as well as to discourage the systematic use of torture by the police to extract confessions, President Vicente Fox has appointed a special ambassador for human rights, Mariclaire Acosta, a pioneer in the struggle for human rights in Mexico. This development signals a changes in the political climate for those doing human rights work but cannot guarantee that the armed forces, police, and those in the judicial system will reform their behavior.

The economic integration of U.S. and Mexican capital supported through NAFTA apparently did not include parallel integration of civil-society organizing for human rights. Beginning in 1994, the Zedillo government developed a policy of deporting foreigners engaged in human rights monitoring. From 1994 to June 2000, the Mexican immigration authorities expelled over 300 international visitors, accusing them of violating the terms of their tourist visas. In 1998 alone, the government expelled 144 foreigners (Global Exchange 1999). In 1999, 79 foreign tourists were ordered out of Mexico after they had visited Chiapas (Dillon 2000). After Fox took office in December 2000, foreigners were allowed more freedom in human rights observation.

Thus, the political package accompanying NAFTA and the political opening at the top of the formal political power structure have been accompanied by a high level of political control, surveillance of opposition, and closure of public spaces for civil participation. The increasing militarization of Mexican society over the past decade has come to be seen by some as normal. As long as it does not involve extensive violence, some may even see such militarization as a positive indication of democratic transition, as indicated by some press reports of the storming of the Universidad Nacional Autónoma de México by the Federal Preventative Police in February 2000.[1]

The political culture of surveillance and intimidation that has become entrenched in Mexico is a key challenge to further redefining the Mexican nation. While the 2000 elections were a major improvement over previous ones, militarization and surveillance remained an important part of the election context for those in the conflict zones in Chiapas and other parts of Mexico, where daily life continued to be fraught with violence, fear, and high psychological stress.

MILITARIZATION, INTIMIDATION, AND RECENT FEDERAL ELECTIONS IN CHIAPAS

During May and July of 2000, I participated as a pre-electoral and electoral observer with two delegations. Both groups were sponsored by Global Exchange, a San Francisco–based NGO that focuses on processes of human rights and democratization in the United States and Latin America, and by Alianza Cívica (Civic Alliance), a national coalition of grassroots groups in Mexico that carries out civic and voter education and that promotes democratic practices. On both trips, I was part of groups deliberately sent to parts of Mexico where tensions were high and voters might encounter difficulties in voting freely and gaining easy, safe access to polling places. I share some of my experiences in Chiapas in May 2000 as a way of highlighting some of the tensions and unmediated contradictions that continue in Mexico despite the outcomes of the 2000 federal elections.

As part of a pre-electoral delegation in May 2000, I went to several areas of Chiapas, particularly where there was concern about military and paramilitary activity and how these might impede electoral participation. We observed a high level of military and police presence in places we visited, including Acteal, Polhó, and the municipal seats of San Pedro Chenalhó and Ocosingo. In addition to the Mexican Army, we saw insignia designating Municipal Police, State Security Police, State Transit Police, and Federal Judicial Police. We were stopped both by the army and by representatives of the Federal Institute of Immigration at roadblocks that were also manned by the army. We also observed the detention and searching of local vehicles. The presence of the Federal Preventative Police is officially recognized in the state of Chiapas. Even the opposition gubernatorial candidate Pablo Salazar Mendiguchia (who became governor of Chiapas in August 2000) was stopped by the army while on the campaign trail, and spikes were placed in front of his car when he refused to have it searched. Everyone was routinely stopped, asked for documents, and searched at police and military checkpoints. As of fall 2000, there were sixty fixed checkpoints and ninety-three movable checkpoints in the state of Chiapas (Castro Soto 2000b, 103). Between December 2000 and March 2001, however, a dozen or so of the permanent checkpoints were removed.

We were told by the municipal president of Chenalhó that there were thirteen different army bases in the region, including Chenalhó, Yabteklum, Colonia la Libertad, Takiukum, X'oyep, Majomut, Colonia Miguel Utrilla (Los Choros), Acteal Alto, Chimix, Tz'anembolom, Tz'anemchon, and Las Limas. He could give us no figures for the total number of soldiers. Outside the Chenalhó area, estimates given us of the number of soldiers in Chiapas ranged from 39,000 to 70,000. What was striking was that nobody could give an exact number; "only the Mexican Army knows the exact number," everyone said. This seemed to be a closely guarded secret, which kept everyone guessing. "[T]here are more than seven hundred different military installations, which include bases, mixed operations bases, living quarters, commercial centers, campamentos, and roadblocks, which are concentrated in the Tzotzil region of Los Altos and in the Selva Lacandona," the newspaper *La Jornada* said before the elections in Chiapas in May 2000 (Bellinghausen 2000).

On one day, we had three striking experiences that threw into sharp relief the tensions experienced on a day-to-day basis by many in the highland region of Chiapas, and probably elsewhere in the state. These three experiences suggest the continuing contradictions and provide some context for understanding Mexico's political future.

On 25 May 2000, we began our day by interviewing the municipal president of Chenalhó, Julio López Jíménez,[2] who had been municipal secretary at the time of the massacre at Acteal of forty-six Tzotzil women, children, and men by paramilitaries (see chapter 6). As several local people pointed out, he had held the latter office when carloads of guns were smuggled into the municipality that ended up in the hands of those who carried out the massacre. His parents are Zapatistas who live in the nearby community of Polhó, one of thirty-three self-declared autonomous government seats in Chiapas; his brothers and sons, however, have been associated with local paramilitary groups, both directly and indirectly. He began by addressing us with a ten-minute speech in which he explained his version of local history—particularly the Acteal massacre—and assured us that the area had calmed down and everyone was safe now. He readily granted me permission to tape-record the conversation:

JULIO: Our intention is to work with the people without distinguishing [among] political parties, religious sects. While, here in Chenalhó, the majority of us are from the Institutional Revolutionary Party, we also have people from the Bees Civil Society, members of the EZLN. The strongest religion in the municipality is the Catholic one, [but] we also have evangelical believers. Over the religious question, we don't have any questions. We are fine. We respect political and religious differences. Each person has complete liberty.

When the problem of 22 December occurred [the Acteal massacre], I was the municipal secretary, and before that I was also municipal secretary, beginning in July of 1996. So I was municipal secretary when forty-six indigenous brothers and sisters died on 22 December. I was also here earlier [prior to December 1997] when eighteen Cardenistas [members of a small party aligned with the PRI] and PRIistas were assassinated and twenty-two were wounded. The last death was that of the respected Señor Agustín Vásquez Ceju. He was killed on 17 December 1997. We notified the governor of the state and the State Justice Department, but they didn't pay any attention to us. I think that what happened on 22 December was revenge for the eighteen deaths and twenty-two wounded that were Cardenistas and PRIistas. . . . Because of what has happened, we don't want to see any more violence.

At this point, he stopped and several in the group asked him, "How do you feel about the presence of paramilitary groups and the Mexican Army here?" His response reflected his references (see the excerpt above) to the deaths of people from the PRI and the Cardenista party prior to December 1997. In suggesting that Acteal was "revenge" for these other deaths, he indirectly suggested that the EZLN or Zapatista sympathizers had been the perpetrators of these earlier deaths:

JULIO: First, in terms of the presence of supposed paramilitary groups, I am unaware of them. . . . You see, I am here to support my people. My intention is to work with them. That is why, when the people from the EZLN accused me of being a part of that thing [the Acteal massacre], I completely denied the existence of these kinds of paramilitary groups. . . . In terms of the second question, about the presence of the Mexican Army, as the municipal president of Chenalhó, as municipal authorities, we have a close relationship with them. That is be-

cause, before the presence of the Mexican Army and the Public Security Police, when there were eighteen deaths of people who were
PRI-istas and Cardenistas, the State Public Security Police weren't
here and the Mexican Army wasn't here. . . . Now, with their presence, the community is controlled, and we don't have as many threats,
there isn't so much death. For this reason, I have total confidence in the
Mexican Army and the State Public Security Police. In addition, the
inhabitants of the municipio of Chenalhó are happy with the presence of the army and of the State Public Security Police.

Julio painted a picture of stability after several years of violence and
credited it both to the presence of the Mexican Army and the State Public Security Police and to the efforts of his administration to create a climate of peace. He did not mention that during the Acteal massacre in
1997, State Public Security Police officers stood by a few hundred yards
away and completely ignored what was going on. In our conversation, he
projected complete confidence in the liberty felt by everyone in the municipality, echoing Chiapas state officials, who continually downplayed
the tensions.

Later in the day, we traveled a few miles down the road to the community of Acteal, the site of the 1997 massacre. Once a community of
only 20 families, Acteal now has about 110 families and houses refugees from many neighboring populations, driven out by paramilitary
violence. Some were already in Acteal at the time of the massacre; others came afterward, fearing to remain in their homes and to farm their
fields. The forty-six women, children, and men who were victims in the
Acteal massacre were members of the Bees Civil Society, which began in
1992 and had been initiated through pastoral work in the parish of San
Pedro de Chenalhó in the 1980s and 1990s. Acteal also has active Zapatistas, as well as some people who sympathize with the PRI.

Our discussion with representatives of the Bees Civil Society began by
focusing on how they came to be organized, on the massacre, and on
current conditions in the region. Their perspective offers a very different
picture from that presented by the municipal president of Chenalhó. We
spoke with three men who were part of the leadership of the Bees. One,
Andrés Martínez Perez,[3] who witnessed the massacre, told us how the
State Public Security Police paid no attention when he went to plead
with them to intervene to stop the killing:

ANDRÉS: We were praying there on 22 December when the shooting started.
           It was 11:30 in the morning when we heard shots there [pointing]
           . . . Textic. That was the place where everyone was concentrated,

where they made an agreement to come and massacre us. They all arrived there. People from Los Chorros, Esperanza, Chimix, Canolal, Arroyo Chico, Bajoveltic. They all gathered there and decided at what time, what day, they would shoot us. They already knew that we were concentrated here. So at 11:30 the shooting began. We didn't know that we were already surrounded here. We had just heard the shots in Textic when they began shooting here. I heard everything because I was here with my family. I heard the shots, but there were waves and waves of shots that didn't stop. They just sprayed the shots everywhere and people had nowhere to go because they were here praying—men and women.

I ran away behind the school over there after about an hour and a half of lying completely still. I saw five big eight-ton trucks parked over there by the school that belonged to the State Public Security Police. I said, "Please, señores, please come and see who is doing the shooting."

They said to me, "You, what are you doing here? You are a Zapatista." "No, I am not, sir," I said. "I don't even know how to shoot a gun." "No," they said, "You are a Zapatista." "No," I said. "Please listen to me. A lot of people have already died—men and women. Just listen to the screaming." "So what, what does it matter to me," the guy from the State Public Security Police said. The shooting just went on and on. It began at 11:30 in the morning and ended at 5 in the afternoon. . . . The whole time, the Public Security Police were here.

LYNN: Where did the guns come from? Were they purchased, did they come from the army?

ANDRÉS: The soldiers in the army who were here knew about the transport of the guns. The municipal president [of Chenalhó] made an agreement with the government and the government sent the guns with the army. The guns were those used by the army. . . . These were the guns people used. They were high-powered weapons. We know perfectly well that the people around here are poor. Who could afford to just buy a gun like that? They were machine guns and other kinds. . . .

Later in the conversation, we were told that the municipal president of Chenalhó was the one who wrote a request for the arms used in the massacre. "We know that he was the one who solicited the arms," the Bees representatives, speaking almost in unison, told us. From their perspective, the relationship between the Bees and the current municipal president of Chenalhó continued to be extremely strained. Being complete pacifists, the Bees we spoke with said they had no desire for revenge. They stated that they knew most of the killers, because they were "our cousins, our aunts and uncles, and even our children." When asked why relatives would kill one another, Andrés replied, "We can only guess that it had to do with money. That they were paid."

We then moved on to the topic of the elections and the strong continued presence of the army and the State Public Security Police in Acteal. In contrast to the municipal president, the members of the Bees were clearly still quite frightened, not only by the presence of official police and army units, but also by the continuing presence of paramilitaries in many surrounding communities. The strong military and police presence was no source of comfort and security for them. Instead, when the army would fire guns within its camps, many in Acteal would begin to relive the massacre, frightened and confused. Andrés responded to the municipal president's comments, relayed by us, that there were no paramilitary groups; Pedro joined in:

ANDRÉS: We know that there still are paramilitaries here in the communities. And the problem was the theft of our things, of our lands. This part has gotten better. But the paramilitaries are still there. They still are armed. We know they are there, and that is why we can't return. We haven't heard as many threats during the year 2000, but we still can't go back to our communities.

LYNN (and others in group):   Do you feel that the presence of the Federal Preventative Police, the Mexican Army, and the State Public Security Police provides security for people to vote? Does it make you feel secure?

PEDRO: No. The presence of the Public Security Police, the presence of the army, doesn't feel good to us because we have already been really frightened by shootings, deaths, guns, and all of this. The army fires their guns in their encampments next to the communities and it frightens us. It has happened several times in the past few months. When we hear that, we run and hide. Because of this, they don't make us feel safe. We don't feel like they protect us. . . .

LYNN: Do think there are people who would not go to vote if they had to go and vote in certain places?

PEDRO: Yes, like us. Like me, I really don't want to walk very far. For example, I am from Canolal. That is where I am supposed to go and vote, but I can't go there. I know that the army is there in the road and they could do something to me. And I am afraid to go. . . .

ANDRÉS: The same is true for me. I know that I can't go to vote in the community where I am from, because there are still a lot of paramilitaries there. I can't go to vote there. Where

> I can vote is here [in Acteal] in the refugee camp. . . . I will
> vote in an extraordinary polling station set up here.

Thus the Bees in Acteal voted in a special polling place (*casilla extraordinaria*) installed in their refugee camp, because it was clearly unsafe to return home to vote (most of the Bees qualified to vote at the special polling place ended up not voting, following an EZLN decision to abstain as a sign of continued protest). The need for these special polling places in Acteal and other locations was a sign of the tension and state of continuing civilian-targeted warfare in parts of Mexico. The psychological scar of the massacre seemed constantly visible in everyone in Acteal, and the high level of militarization of daily life through roadblocks, military and police patrols passing slowly by, circling military helicopters, and ongoing violence continued to produce a climate of uncertainly and tension. Indeed, just a few weeks prior to our visit, three men were ambushed and assassinated while riding in a pickup truck on a road that connects the town of Chenalhó with Acteal, Polhó, and other communities. One was a member of the Bees. The murders were still unsolved at the time of our visit.

On 25 May, we were also scheduled to speak with authorities from the Autonomous Municipal Council of Polhó, governed by the EZLN and home to about nine thousand refugees, distributed in a number of camps. We were unable to speak with the authorities there, however, because they were meeting with others in the command structure of the EZLN. It turned out that, just before we met with the PRI municipal president of Chenalhó, two trucks full of Judicial Police, an army truck, and another truck full of what the Zapatistas in a written communiqué called "authorities from Chenalhó dressed up in the uniforms of Public Security Police" entered the hamlet of Ic'alteil (within the autonomous municipality of Polhó), where they found a group from the EZLN. One in the group was detained and accused of stealing an AK-47 from a local paramilitary. Present with the authorities from Chenalhó were relatives of the municipal president we had spoken with. The EZLN accused the invading group of containing "those directly responsible for the massacre in Acteal." According to an EZLN communiqué we received, "[A]fter the EZLN person was tied up and beaten with a rifle butt, a group of women laid down in the road [and] closed it with tree trunks, allowing others to rescue the accused man." The communiqué added that the paramilitaries issued threats.

Thus, within one day in a very small geographic area, we saw ample evidence of the ways in which militarization and paramilitarization not only terrify people and inhibit their movements on a daily basis, hardly providing an open climate for voting. While the situation in Chenalhó, Acteal, and Polhó no doubt appeared less tense on election day, because of the decrease in patrols and orders to the army to stay in its barracks, by the next day, matters returned to the reality we had observed.

In order to understand the contradictory nature of postelection Mexico, detailed pictures of places such as Chenalhó in Chiapas are necessary. For even while a political culture of intimidation and militarization prevailed in parts of Mexico like Chiapas in the 1990s, this period also saw the emergence of a nationally articulated movement for indigenous rights throughout Mexico. Such movements illustrate the importance of grassroots sources of change, as well as shifts in the national political system. Much of what will continue to be significant for change in Mexico now exists outside the formal political system.

THE NATIONAL MOVEMENT FOR
INDIGENOUS RIGHTS AND AUTONOMY

The alternative nationalist discourse of Zapatismo since 1994 has provided an important political and ideological opening for movements seeking to redefine Mexico as a multi-ethnic nation and challenging the state to engage in a new relationship with indigenous peoples. This post-1994 challenge has involved local cultural forms that rework top-down nationalism and create an alternative to the marginalized position of many indigenous communities in national and regional politics and economic development schemes. The movement also provides a future vision of the Mexican nation alternative to that invoked by NAFTA. Since 1994 (and even earlier), indigenous movements in Mexico have been calling for two key changes in the relationship between indigenous peoples and the state: the redefinition of the Mexican nation as multi-ethnic—legally, socially, and politically—and guarantees for indigenous self-determination.

Indigenous autonomy, or self-determination, as defined by Mexico's indigenous movements, is understood as respect for the internal practices and decision-making modes of indigenous pueblos (the term has multiple uses in Mexico, including "towns," "communities," and "peoples," and it can mean small numbers of people in a few hamlets, a municipio, or a region who share an ethnic identity and history). Autonomy also means the participation of indigenous communities in the levels of economic, political, cultural, and legal decision-making associated with the government. This resembles the call of the Pan-Mayan movement in Guatemala for collective cultural, linguistic, and political rights for Maya citizens and "cultural and political space in the country's educational, judicial, and administrative systems" (Warren 1998, 13). Generally, calls for indigenous autonomy in Mexico seek to allow local and regional forms of ethnic and cultural identities to function both within the larger indigenous movement and within the nation.

The struggle for indigenous rights and self-determination in Mexico has involved four key areas: (1) actual experiences of autonomy, both historic and current; (2) the signing in 1996 of the San Andrés Peace Accords on Indigenous Rights and Culture, and the obstacles to their implementation; (3) the creation and maintenance of a national movement for indigenous autonomy in Mexico, evolving out of diverse experiences and interpretations of self-determination; and (4) a redefinition of the relationship between Indian peoples and the Mexican state, away from the historical focus on indigenism, which had assimilation as its goal.

The Zapatista rebellion provided an important political opening for the negotiation of indigenous autonomy in Mexico at the national level. Movements for indigenous autonomy at the regional and local level, however, have had a long history. For example, in 1974, the multi-ethnic First Indigenous Congress was held in San Cristóbal de las Casas (see chapter 5). Impressive regional indigenous gatherings were held elsewhere in Mexico as well in the 1970s and 1980s. At the community and regional levels, in many areas throughout Mexico, indigenous peoples have historically acted autonomously. Among the Mixe of Oaxaca, for example, community autonomy has existed for centuries; an ethnically and linguistically homogeneous Mixe district was created in 1938, which remains intact to this day. In Chiapas, thirty-eight self-declared autonomous municipalities and pluri-ethnic regions have established governing structures since 1994. The Wixaritari (Huicholes) of Jalisco have since 1989 reaffirmed their self-determination by organizing their communities into a regional organization, which has regained traditional territory through petitions to government land tribunals. And in a transnational political space that spans the U.S.–Mexican border, Zapotecos, Mixtecos, and Triquis have created organizations and coalitions that defend indigenous rights and self-determination across the boundaries of nation-states.

The second area key to understanding the struggle for indigenous rights and self-determination in Mexico in the 1990s was the crafting and signing of the San Andrés Peace Accords by the Zapatista Army of National Liberation and the Mexican Federal Government in 1996, as well as the obstacles to their implementation. The Accords on Indigenous Rights and Culture lay the groundwork for significant changes in the areas of indigenous rights, political participation, and cultural autonomy. Most important, they recognize the existence of political subjects called *pueblos indios* (indigenous peoples/towns/communities) and give conceptual validation to the terms "self-determination" and "autonomy" by using them in the signed accords. These accords emphasized that the government took responsibility, not only for reinforcing the political representation of indigenous peoples and their participation in legislatures, but also for guaranteeing the validity of internal forms of indigenous government. They further noted that the government promised to create national legislation guaranteeing indigenous communities the rights (1) to freely associate themselves with municipalities that are primarily indigenous in population, (2) to form associations among communities, and (3) to coordinate their actions as indigenous peoples.

In addition, the accords stated that it was the legislatures of individual states that could determine the best criteria for self-determination and autonomy. These criteria should accurately represent the diverse aspirations and distinctions of indigenous peoples. It is important to note that the accords *did not* deal with the key issues of land redistribution and agrarian policy—notably, the revision of Article 27 of the Mexican Constitution in 1992 ending land reform and encouraging privatization of communally held land. Under the rubric of the San Andrés Peace Accords, these issues were to be dealt with in subsequent discussions on political reform, economic development, and land reform. The original response of Zapatista base communities to the Accords on Indigenous Rights and Culture accepted them but also noted the absence of resolutions regarding land and indigenous control of resources.

In October 1996, the EZLN and the Comisión de Concordia y Pacificación (National Commission of Concord and Pacification), or CO-COPA, announced that a joint commission had been formed to verify and follow up on the accords signed in February 1996. The commission included representatives from the EZLN, from the Mexican government, from COCOPA, and from the Comisión Nacional de Intermediación (National Intermediation Commission), or CONAI. Following the formation of the follow-up commission, a proposal for legislation elaborated by the COCOPA and endorsed by the EZLN was rejected by President Ernesto Zedillo in December 1996. Zedillo stated that the

COCOPA legislative proposal for the San Andrés Accords could result in the creation of a system of reservations and the "balkanization" of the country. In addition, he argued that Mexico's Indians should not be granted "special rights," but should be given the same rights as all other Mexicans. The Zedillo government did not move from this position. In the fall of 1998, Bishop Samuel Ruiz disbanded CONAI, noting a complete lack of conditions for further peace negotiations. One of these missing conditions was the government's failure to implement its own treaty on indigenous rights.

The results of the presidential elections of 2000 opened a new window of opportunity for the implementation of the San Andrés Accords. President-elect Vicente Fox Quesada made a campaign promise to honor these accords and to reopen the government's peace dialogue with the EZLN. In July 2000, Fox said in an interview: "[T]he principal way to a solution is to return to dialogue. We have to arrive at agreements which include all parties. It can't be something personal between Marcos and me. If the San Andrés accords come up again in the negotiations, they would have to go to Congress as an initiative, with the suggestions of the COCOPA" (Gallegos and Venegas 2000). In April of 2001, a watered-down version of the accords was approved by the Mexican Congress and the Senate, but rejected by the EZLN as an insult to the intent of the original document signed by the EZLN and the government of Ernesto Zedillo.

Although the Zedillo government made no progress in implementing the accords on indigenous rights, it did take the movement for indigenous autonomy extremely seriously, not only embarking on a sustained campaign to disable the legislative process for implementing the peace accords it had signed in 1996, but also engaging in a brutal and highly visible campaign to "take out" autonomous municipalities in Chiapas that ran parallel, self-declared autonomous governments in opposition to counties and town councils run by those affiliated with the PRI. This campaign to dismantle autonomous communities through the combined force of the State Public Security Police and the army was waged in the spring and summer of 1998. In addition, local paramilitary groups collaborated with local PRI members to harass, intimidate, and murder local activists involved in autonomous parallel governments sympathetic to the Zapatista Army of National Liberation; such a paramilitary group was responsible for the 1997 massacre in Acteal.

A third key element in understanding the struggle for indigenous rights and self-determination in Mexico has been the creation and maintenance of a national movement for indigenous autonomy in Mexico. One reason there is currently the potential to build a strong national movement can be found in the historical strength of regional indigenous movements throughout Mexico, particularly since the 1970s. When indigenous militancy grew in the 1970s, Mexican government policy switched from top-down indigenism to "participatory indigenism" in an effort to co-opt and incorporate some indigenous leaders and organizations into government-aligned and government-funded indigenous organizations and support institutions. While in some cases such efforts succeeded, in others, such as that of the government-created Coordinadora Nacional de Pueblos Indios (National Council of Indian Peoples), or CNPI, the "official" organization split, generating an autonomous branch, which still is active in the autonomy movement. In the late 1980s, when Mexico was the first country in Latin America to ratify Convention 169 of the International Labor Organization (ILO), which focuses on indigenous rights, an additional political opening was created for indigenous organizing. The government opened up further room for political debate and opposition when, after changing Article 4 of the Mexican Constitution in 1990 to recognize Mexico as a pluri-cultural nation and acknowledge the cultural rights of indigenous peoples, it conducted several fly-by-night "consultations" with indigenous peoples that left out most organizations and communities. Such tactics led to autonomous regional meetings protesting the lack of input by indigenous peoples into the legislation implementing Article 4 of the constitution, and providing a platform for furthering indigenous discussions on the meaning of autonomy at a national level. For example, in Oaxaca, on 6 September 1993, a National Forum on Civil Society, titled "The Poor Construct Their Own Social Policy," brought together indigenous representatives from Guerrero, Oaxaca, Chiapas, and Hidalgo, who jointly developed a critique of the government's plan for implementing Article 4. Similar meetings took place throughout Mexico. Many indigenous organizations also participated in the 1992 activities protesting five hundred years of colonialism. These activities are examples of significant precedents for a struggle for indigenous autonomy before the launching of the Zapatista rebellion in 1994. The signing of the 1996 accords was the most significant event after the rebellion to mobilize the struggle for autonomy.

In October 1996, after six months with no government action to implement the signed accords, a new national constellation emerged in Mexico, the Congreso Nacional Indígena (National Indigenous Congress), or CNI, which included people who had participated in previous national efforts to organize and network, as well as new actors incorporated for the first time into a national grouping. The first meeting of the CNI was held in Mexico City. Prominent in this new constellation was a proposal for the adoption of "customs and traditions," which derived from the experience of Oaxaca. The notion of Oaxacan communal autonomy was based in collective institutions such as *tequio* (communal work obligations), methods of selecting local authorities, and the preservation of language and ritual. In 1995, in recognition of the indigenous autonomy movement, the Oaxaca state legislature had approved a change in the state constitution to allow election of municipal authorities by *usos y costumbres* ("traditions and customs"). In 1998, the Oaxaca legislature implemented these 1995 changes by approving a legislative plan giving indigenous communities the right to name their municipal authorities without the intervention of political parties, in accordance with local traditions. The example of Oaxaca, and the fact that the state government legitimized local forms of government there, were important in fueling the national autonomy movement. A question often raised was, "Why is it legal to elect local officials according to customs and traditions in Oaxaca, but the government has refused to implement such a proposal at the national level?"

Even before the signing of the San Andrés Accords in February 1996, at the Zapatista-organized National Indigenous Forum (3–8 January 1996) in San Cristóbal de las Casas, the notions of autonomous regions (to constitute a fourth level of government, between the county/municipal level and the state level) and of "customs and tradition" were the basis of discussion. Out of this forum came a set of proposals that the EZLN took to negotiations with the government, and that were influential in the February 1996 accords. What is particularly significant is that indigenous groups, organizations, and communities from throughout Mexico participated in the forum and provided input into the range of specific regional realities that accords on indigenous rights would have to represent.

Thus, a key force in the creation of the accords and the demand for their implementation was an emergent national movement for indigenous autonomy, which pulled together local and regional indigenous movements, as well as previously unorganized indigenous community authorities. The goal of the movement in pushing for the implementation of the accords was, and is, not secession from Mexico but inclusion as part of a multicultural nation embracing many pueblos and granting them regional autonomy.

This vision of indigenous autonomy projected from Mexico provides a hopeful vision for ethnic conflict, conflict that so often results in either ongoing war or secession.[4] If the original accords are implemented, they will serve as an important example of how an alternative nation view— formed and projected from the margins of the state—can come to formally reshape the nation.

RECONSIDERING CITIZENSHIP IN THE NATION

One of the ideas contained within the alternative Zapatista view of the nation and partially reflected in the San Andrés accords has to do with the relationships among individuals, community, and nation. The struggle over implementing the original accords is also a battle to redefine the meaning of citizenship. The idea of citizenship often contains a principle of universality that implies an abstract subject with no identity other than that produced by the law—"The citizen should be understood in the first instance not as a type of person . . . but as a position in the set of formal relations defined by democratic sovereignty" (Donald 1996, 174). In such a perspective, citizens are substanceless, living outside of hierarchies of power, outside of culture, outside of local history, outside of multiple identities, and outside of daily life. They are uniform empty spaces to be understood only in relation to the dominant imagined community, usually known as "the nation." The stories I have related of four ejidos in Oaxaca and Chiapas suggest otherwise. For if there are different views of the nation constructed in relation to local history and experiences, then there are also different views of what it means to be a citizen in the nation.

The movement for indigenous autonomy provides an alternative vision of who citizens are, of what kinds of rights they have, and of how individuals, communities, and regions should relate to the nation and be integrated into the political, social, and economic concentration of power administered by it. Advocates of indigenous autonomy are suggesting a type of internal flexible citizenship, defined by Aiwa Ong (1999), that requires a reconfiguring of the relationship between the Mexican government and indigenous peoples and suggests the possibility of multiple levels of sovereignty: of the community, of the region, and finally of the multi-ethnic nation that respects plurality.

The heart of the national proposal for recognizing indigenous autonomy in Mexico is a tripartite cultural-political model that brings together multiple indigenous pueblos, the Mexican nation as multi-ethnic and diverse, and the state as a political and legal framework that defends and supports the multi-ethnic nation (see Regino Montes 1996). The glue holding the national movements for indigenous autonomy together is a type of indigenous Mexican nationalism. In this model, the national political boundaries of Mexico should defend an internal plurality of cultural boundaries, not through assimilation, but through the granting to self-defined cultural entities of autonomy in regional and local economic, political, and social decision-making. Thus the *pueblos indígenas* would be autonomous within the Mexican nation, but with a shared sense of participation and inclusion in the functioning of the state, including political and economic aspects in particular. In their analysis, indigenous leaders sever the "nation" from the state and liberate the concept of "nation" for reappropriation from below in relation to particular regional and historical circumstances. Such a "model of the nation" allows for the simultaneous existence of a larger nation tied both to a state political structure and to indigenous pueblos with unique historical constructions.

The realization of such indigenous autonomy as discussed above would require major political, economic, and cultural realignments, extending far beyond a change in presidential political party. And today the on-the-ground reality in many indigenous communities, particularly in the south, is one of intense militarization by both the police and the army and of frequent harassment, imprisonment, or worse for any effective indigenous leaders. Nevertheless, for the first time, indigenous movements and communities from throughout Mexico are talking together over a sustained period at the national level. This unique development can be tied to the political opening created through the Zapatista rebellion, as well as to pressure both within and outside Mexico to improve that country's record on indigenous rights and the human rights of indigenous communities.

INDIGENOUS STRATEGIES IN
OTHER LATIN AMERICAN NATIONS

What indigenous movements suggest, in Mexico as well as in other countries, such as Colombia (Field 1994; Rappaport 1996) and Guatemala (Warren 1998), is the importance of multiple levels of struggle to transform Latin American nations from elite constructions based on a homogeneous national identity that often prioritizes *mestizaje* into multi-ethnic nations. Strong local and regional movements are important in mobilizing personal and community geographies of identity and local senses of history as people engage with the concept of nation. Local and regional movements also often produce the most concrete and visible changes in daily lives, such as the transformation of a municipal council from one dominated by *mestizos* or indigenous political bosses to one with representation by local indigenous leaders. Efforts at articulating strong local and regional movements, such as the National Indigenous Congress in Mexico and the pan-Mayan intellectual movement in Guatemala are also key to reimagining a multicultural nation. National articulation around specific issues, campaigns, or even legislation is crucial in pressuring reluctant states.

Usually, self-determination does not imply secession from the nation-state but, rather, the broadening of rights within the structure of the nation-state. Engaging in a movement for "autonomy" entails, that is, both an assertion of a specific ethnic identity or identities and the reformulation from below of what is meant by "the nation" and how the rights of citizens are understood.

In 1991, the nation of Colombia ratified a new constitution recognizing "its indigenous population as an integral component of the nation and granting [this population] full citizenship for the first time" (Dover and Rappaport 1996, 2). In Colombia, the notion of a pluri-ethnic nation was promoted with a model granting indigenous people a degree of autonomy to administer finances, development programs, and systems of justice within their own territories. The creation of administrative units called Indigenous Territorial Entities created a "new form of citizenship that would recognize native peoples as holding a different type of citizenship from other Colombians, and bequeathed the right to govern according to cultural criteria different from those used by the rest of the population" (ibid.). Paraguay has also changed its constitution in favor of indigenous rights and included indigenous representatives in the constitutional reform process (Van Cott 1995, 12). In Nicaragua, a Miskito autonomy proposal signed in 1987 called for multi-ethnic assemblies; the autonomy proposal written into the constitution "granted political autonomy for the entire coastal population, divided into two autonomous regions. In each autonomous region there would be an election to pick a regional assembly that would legislate regional matters" (Diskin

1991, 164–65). Initial Miskito ethnic militancy in the 1980s, which involved a "strategic essentialism," has given way to what Charles Hale has called "strategic multiplicity" (1996, 52). Hale found that there was no "unified discourse of identity and common values that orients collective action," but instead a hybrid politics reflecting both a state that had downplayed cultural differences and undermined Miskitu autonomy and, perhaps, a new path responding to unscrupulous actions and poor decisions by leaders after 1980 (ibid., 49, 51). On the optimistic side of his analysis, Hale saw a multiple political subjectivity as possibly helping to resolve the greatest problem of autonomy: "to forge a multiethnic consciousness, which unifies members of six distinct ethnic groups behind the goals of regional self-government, and creates a space for the egalitarian participation of each in the resulting benefits" (ibid., 53). Hale's insightful analysis points to key issues inherent in any long-term autonomy struggle, which must always forge temporary unity out of diversity, cope with historical power differentials among ethnic groups, and consider the ever-shifting position of states.

A MEXICAN INDIGENOUS STRATEGY

Indigenous peoples such as those discussed in Oaxaca and Chiapas have developed local cultural identities that emphasize both their particular historical and regional location (mono-ethnic, multi-ethnic, or membership in a particular community) and their specific claims to rights as Mexican citizens. As demonstrated in the previous chapters, in the process of articulating their local identities and histories, they also appropriated major national symbols. The Zapatistas have crafted a regional identity built around both identification with the national hero, Emiliano Zapata, and the specific regional circumstances of struggle for land, political participation, and self-determination. The Zapatista model—claiming a Mexican (national) identity as part of each person's cultural packaging—is important in unifying indigenous peoples from disparate regions and experiences, and has been a key part of the political strategy of the national indigenous movement for autonomy, a strategy that builds on the multilayered identities of most indigenous Mexicans. For example (as seen in the discussion of ejidatarios in El Tule), national identity forms part of many people's cultural packaging of the self; when asked about their origins, most ejidatarios responded with combinations that included national (Mexicano), regional (Oaxaqueño), and ethnic/racial (Zapoteco, mestizo, or revuelto) designations. That there are these multiple dimensions in identities in Oaxaca suggests there may be elsewhere as well.

Connecting local ethnic identities with regional and national identities is critical for unifying Mexico's disparate indigenous pueblos into one movement. Two further examples indicate how this can work.

The first occurred on October 12, 1996, before six hundred indigenous delegates gathered for the National Indigenous Congress in Mexico City. There, Zapatista Comandante Ramona, weak from a long journey and a battle with kidney disease, turned over a Mexican flag that she had brought from the depths of Chiapas to Felix Serdán, one of the original guerrillas who fought under Ruben Jaramillo in the state of Morelos to continue Zapata's tradition of agrarian struggle—seen by many as the core of the Mexican Revolution. "This [flag] is so that they never forget that Mexico is our patria [native land] and so that everyone recognizes that there will never be a Mexico without us," Ramona said, (Pérez and Rojas 1996).[5] Ramona then greeted the crowd in Tzotzil and read a communiqué sent by the Clandestine Indigenous Revolutionary Committee of the Zapatistas. After this, Ramona was presented with red roses by twenty-two Purepechas, Nahuas, Tontonacas, Huicholes, and Mixtecos chosen by the Congress. They lit copal (hardened tree resin burned as ritual incense) and blew the smoke in the four cardinal directions and at Ramona. Then they paid honor to the Mexican flag and sang the national anthem. Except for Ramona's Tzotzil introduction, all exchanges were carried out in Spanish (Pérez y Rojas 1996).

What does this scenario suggest? Comandante Ramona emerges as a unifying symbol in the National Indigenous Congress by blending local Tzotzil culture with redefined Mexican nationalism projected from below. She is dressed in a *huipil* (indigenous women's blouse) from San Andrés Larráinzar (site of the negotiations that led to the San Andrés accords), and presents a Mexican flag—the ultimate symbol of the nation-state—to Felix Serdán, a living connection to the revolutionary figure of Zapata and the struggle for land. The entire exchange is framed by the presence of indigenous delegates from throughout the country, engaged in a common ritual with copal, in paying homage to the flag, and in singing the national anthem.

On a gendered note, the choice of Ramona as the EZLN's representative evoked contradictory nationalist symbols: both the "suffering woman," most often projected through the Virgen of Guadalupe and the revolutionary *soldaderas* (female soldiers) of the Mexican Revolution, often depicted holding guns. This moment captures the imaginative way the model of nationalism projected from below and infused with local indigenous traditions has worked for the EZLN in gaining recognition throughout Mexico and has further permitted a conjunctural articulation of Mexico's diverse indigenous populations in a movement for self-determination and autonomy. The indigenous delegates who came together that 12 October 1996 continued to work together in regional meetings, and mounted further national indigenous congresses in 1997, 1998, 1999, 2000, and 2001.

The second scene took place almost a year later, in September 1997, when a delegation of 1,111 masked but unarmed civilian Zapatista representatives from hundreds of communities journeyed in buses from San Cristóbal de las Casas to Mexico City, fulfilling their promise of 1 January 1994 to go to Mexico City. They partially retraced the route of Emiliano Zapata when he took control of the capital in 1914 during the Mexican Revolution. Their first stop was in the city of Juchitán, where they were received by the Coalition of Workers, Peasants, and Students of the Isthmus (COCEI). There, thousands of Huaves, Chontales, Popolucas, Mixes, Nahuas, Zapotecos, Zoques, Chinantecos, and Mixtecos greeted them, and some joined the Zapatistas on their journey to the capital. The Zapatistas proudly displayed Mexican flags along with their regional costumes. They demanded the end of militarization in Chiapas and other indigenous regions, the implementation of the San Andrés Accords, and to be heard as citizens of Mexico. Here again, reconstructed nationalism served to bind indigenous peoples from disparate experiences into a cohesive unit converging on the capital, where they continued their work.

A SITE FOR CHANGING THE NATION

At the beginning of the twenty-first century, Mexico remains full of contradictions: at the presidential level, a change of political regime after seventy-one years of one-party rule; ongoing militarization and paramilitarization in parts of the country; a new national movement for indigenous rights and autonomy; and many differing visions of what Mexico is and can be, each tied to local history and experience. Given this complex reality, one might ask what, if any, is the most important strategy and level at which change toward a more equitable and inclusive nation might successfully be instituted? The cases of Oaxaca and Chiapas suggest that there are multiple sites for the struggle to redefine Mexico. As pointed out succinctly by Marc Edelman in connection with small farmers' responses to a free market onslaught in Costa Rica, such transitions—particularly those related to structural adjustment—operate on at least three distinct levels: (1) the demands made by international financial institutions upon countries; (2) the specific policies implemented by governments in their efforts to meet those demands; and (3) the "varied political practices of non-elite groups, which. ... draw heavily on long historical experiences of struggle and highly specific sorts of assumptions about political possibilities" (Edelman 1999, 208). To broaden Edelman's list to accommodate cultural arenas as well, we must enlarge upon each of his levels. With regard to the international level, we must not only consider the role of international monetary institutions, but also look at the influence of international political bodies and coalitions. In terms of government policies, we need to consider not only policies deployed to meet the demands of lending institutions, but also the kind of ideology and symbols used to try to market such policies. Finally, in terms of the political practices of nonelite groups at the local and regional level, we must consider the particular local historical experiences of people and how political, cultural, and material aspects of these histories become resources for political action (and sometimes for inaction).

In terms of redefining Mexico as a multicultural nation, the international political arena has become a crucial political space as more and more indigenous movements use international forums such as the International Labor Organization and the Working Group on Indigenous Populations of the United Nations to pressure their governments to undertake constitutional and legislative reforms that can bring the rhetoric of a multicultural nation respecting indigenous rights closer to a reality. To counter the assimilationist policies characteristic of most Latin American countries in the twentieth century toward indigenous peoples, movements since the early 1990s have focused on the concept of "self-determination," drawing on the precedent in international law following World War I. The extensive participation of nonwhites and non-Westerners in World War I was key to the development of visions of human rights and self-determination. The Paris Peace Conference of 1919 generated an international legal foundation for the protection of the rights of minorities within nations requiring signatory "states 'to assure full and complete protection of life and liberty' of all their inhabitants 'without distinctions of birth, nationality, language, race or religion.' In addition they provided that all nationals would be equal before the law and able to enjoy the same civil and political rights" (Lauren 1998, 95). The United Nations has been the chief body to which indigenous peoples have appealed for the right of self-determination, more recently appealing to ILO Convention 169, which sets forth a broad range of economic, political, land-related, social, and cultural rights for indigenous peoples. Indeed, multilateral and transnational political strategies have become key avenues for pushing states to change (see Stavenhagen 1996; Van Cott 1995).

While some activist researchers, such as Les Field, have pessimistic assessments of the capabilities of states to become the grounds for forging new definitions of the nation (Field 1999a, 216), others have drawn different conclusions. "[E]ven after more than a decade of neo-liberalism, state agencies remain absolutely central points of reference, foci of demands, and sites of struggle, despite the undermining of traditional power centers that accompanies economic globalization and the by-now-old assertions of 'new social movements' theorists that emancipatory politics takes place primarily in spaces outside or at the margins of the state," Edelman writes, for example (1999, 187). Rejecting the state as a potential source, Field looks instead to loosely bound, nonessentialized local identities shaped by "the experience of daily work and connected to place without the mediation of either national or minority ethnicity" as sites for reimagining the nation (Field 1999a, 235). For this to happen, however, Field notes, there must be a "hypothetical neutralized state." Such a prospect seems unlikely in Mexico or any other country in Latin America at the moment. While Mexico can be said to be undergoing a political transition that includes the emergence of viable political opposition parties, this transition is still very much in process and incomplete. In the meantime, many state actors, regardless of what party they belong to, still want to consolidate power at the political center. As a result of tensions within not only the PRI but all political parties, there are some individuals committed to horizontal collective action who may help facilitate not only a political transition but also a cultural one. As pointed out by Jonathan Fox (1996), competing factions within the same state, working at cross-purposes, can provide important political openings for the strengthening of civil society and the possibility of at least some change.

The state is not the most likely site for reimagining the nation, but the possibility cannot be discounted. While contemporary states are surely being transformed by global capitalism, and may function in many ways to facilitate the hypermobility of capital, as through sponsoring multilateral legislation such as NAFTA, the state still remains, in the words of Saskia Sassen, "the ultimate guarantor of the 'rights' of global capital through the protection of contracts and property rights" (Sassen 1998, 197). In this role, states are unlikely to occupy passive positions with regard to economic transactions within the realm of what can be construed as their sovereignty. In guaranteeing the rights of capital, states must constantly defend their sovereignty. In part, the current political, cultural, and economic struggles in Mexico (including that for indigenous autonomy) are about the state's ongoing crises of representation at the margins, particularly in places like Chiapas and Oaxaca. The fact that these crises of representation have been regional is another indication of the importance of regional and local activity for change. And this is one of my primary points in this book: local and regional history, experience, and political activity not only form a lens for the reinterpretation of government-driven policy but can in turn impact what is done at the center.

The current militarization of indigenous regions of southern Mexico reflects this importance of regional cultural and political processes challenging the legitimacy of the Mexican state (see Stephen 2000). Oaxaca and Chiapas have become the centers of strong regional indigenous and peasant organizations that, in the wake of the Zapatista rebellion of 1994, have indeed begun to articulate at a national level. The heart of these movements takes place outside the formal political arena of electoral politics. As a result—because, that is, these movements offer new political forms that move the contest for political power outside of the electoral arena—they have attracted and sustained the attention of the Mexican government. They are key to understanding the complex dynamics of politics in the future of Mexico.

The responses by the Mexican government to movements for indigenous autonomy suggests that there are many state actors who are not willing participants in reimagining the nation in alliance with indigenous movements. The political juncture at which this book closes—Spring 2001—finds the Mexican Congress and the legislatures of seventeen states approving a proposed constitutional amendment for "Indigenous Rights and Culture" that is a watered-down version of the San Andrés Accords. Indigenous groups are protesting the amendment as a sham that undermines indigenous self-determination; recognition of collective

rights to land, territory, and natural resources; and the right of indigenous communities to regional affiliation. It continues as a subject of intense debate.

THE ROLE OF U.S. ANTHROPOLOGISTS
IN MEXICO'S FUTURES

Ever since I can remember, I have heard Mexican friends correcting visiting Americans with the reminder that "America" includes Mexico.
Now, in the United States, Latino and Latina scholars and others write
of "the Americas," referring to the large block more conventionally
called North, Central, and South America. The term "Americas" attempts to put everyone on neutral footing and to recognize all historical
inhabitants and cultural contributions to the continents. If we are to operate from a worldview that places us in "the Americas," then we must
carefully consider the future role of U.S. anthropologists in Mexico.

Throughout this book, I have made a case for what might be called
an engaged, activist anthropology. This includes recognizing that as anthropologists, we are always "in the field," setting research agendas and
strategies collaboratively with those we work with, recognizing that our
work is inherently political and cannot be thought of as "objective" or
"neutral," using the tools and insights of anthropology to document difficult and even violent circumstances, acknowledging the difficulties of
maintaining a sustained dialogue with activists in the arenas we work in,
serving as witnesses and observers, and using the tools of ethnography
to bring out the human experiences of social suffering as well as of joy.
The final steps to this engaged, activist agenda have to do with how we
conceive of the exchange of information with those with whom we work.

While working *collaboratively* in Mexico as U.S. anthropologists may
be an improvement over past models of anthropological imperialism,
where information was efficiently collected and removed, true collaboration and exchange must also involve two-way relationships, where
those we study also have the chance to come to the United States to learn
and study and receive access to tools, knowledge, and resources in the
United States. One of the most interesting aspects of U.S.–Mexican binational activism since the early 1990s have been the ongoing attempts
to build long-term ties between political sectors such as labor, environ-
mental groups, women's groups, and indigenous organizations (see Fox
1999; Keck and Sikkink 1998; Stephen forthcoming). While few of these
attempts have resulted in balanced relationships, the transnational link-

ages forged offer fodder for anthropology. If everyone from immigrant families to national policy makers to grassroots organizers is engaging in binational relationships and transnational advocacy and support, why not anthropologists and those they work with?

In fact, some anthropologists and social scientists have been key actors in cross-border organizations, such as the Oaxacan Indigenous Binational Front described in chapter 8. Several U.S.-based academics, as well as some in Mexico, have worked with this organization to carry out studies and supply information and consultation. A further step for all U.S. anthropologists working in Mexico is to ask themselves how they can begin to build lasting binational partnerships with the organizations, communities, people, and entities they work with. If this process becomes the basis for an engaged anthropology, than we can truly describe ourselves as living and working as part of the Americas.

In the course of carrying out the work to write this book over the past eight years, I have made many new and lasting friendships and partnerships with Americans—people from both the United States and Mexico. It is my sincere hope that we can continue to strengthen these relationships and continue to work together for more just, more inclusive, and more equitable nations on both sides of the border, so that one day we may all be truly equal citizens of the Americas.

Notes

PREFACE

1. In his discussion, Field builds on Claudio Lomnitz-Adler's (1992) term "internal articulatory intellectuals" in describing individuals who "elaborate identities internally to their communities and articulate their communities' political demands to the elite-dominated state" (Field 1999a, 9).

CHAPTER 1. INTRODUCTION

1. I thank Kay Warren for pointing this out and for encouraging me to include a discussion of this history in Latin American anthropology.
2. This is a definition of violence taken from Carole Nagengast's discussion of Raymond Williams's "key word" (Nagengast 1994, 11).

CHAPTER 2. GOVERNMENT CONSTRUCTION AND REAPPROPRIATION OF EMILIANO ZAPATA

1. A wide range of schools, not only in rural areas but in urban areas as well, had textbooks that codified the Mexican Revolution and Zapata as a hero. In 1935, the Secretaría de Educación Pública published a book, *Zapata: Exaltación,* by Germán List Arzubide, which does precisely what its title suggests—it is an exaltation, a passionate offering of the history of Zapata and the Mexican Revolution. Written for the series The Library of the Worker and the Peasant, the book is accompanied by others with such titles as *Marx, What Marx Wanted to Say,* and *How to Organize and Run a Union.* In his volume on Zapata, List

Arzubide concludes, "Emiliano Zapata is now a symbol: the man passed on but his work has been transmitted in an idea." The symbol and idea of Zapata were indeed passed on and skillfully woven by the SEP into publications and programs.

In the *Libro de lectura para uso de las escuelas nocturnas para trabajadores* (Lecture Book for Use in Night Schools for Workers), published in 1938, a page on the army discusses the downfall of "the dictator" (Díaz), the rise of other armies, and finally the new revolutionary army composed of peasants and workers. Zapata's name enters the pantheon of heroes here as well. This book provided continuity with the *Simiente* series in linking peasants and workers as the defenders of the Mexican revolution.

> THE ARMY
> I. First was the army of the dictator. He who was obligated by the command of mercenary officials bloodied his bayonet with the blood of martyred workers. . . .
> II. Later: Madero, Aquiles Serdán, Zapata. Deserted factories and abandoned fields because people filled the ranks of the new battalions.
> III. And Today: Workers and peasants ready to abandon once again the factory and the plow to take up the gun. An army of workers that is formed by a sole front of uniformed brothers to defend their rights. Soldiers, workers, and peasants: the new Army of the Revolution.
>
> Secretaría de Educación Pública 1938, 81

This text disseminated in urban areas helped to cement a new image of the revolution in urban culture. It also bound together as "the Army of the Revolution" the three sectors that Cárdenas sought to control by creating mass organizations: peasants through the National Peasants' Confederation (CNC), workers through the Confederation of Mexican Workers (CTM), and the army. Published in 1938, the same year that Cárdenas created these mass sectoral organizations, the book is an example of how the state's rewriting of history was disseminated through a variety of channels.

2. The average rural household consists of about 5.5 persons.

3. Chiapas has between 1,873 and 2,015 ejidos, depending on how they are counted (Instituto Nacional de Estadística, Geografía e Informática 1995, 16). INEGI records two different categories of ejidos. The figure of 2,015 includes those designated "new ejido population centers."

4. I thank Jennie Purnell for clarifying the legal history of the category *comunidad agraria* in the twentieth century.

5. Book 4 of the *Simiente* series focuses even more on the evils of individualism and the possibilities of collectivism. See "Los intereses individuales deben subordinarse a los intereses colectivos" (Individual Interests Should be Subordinated to Collective Interests) and "Sirvamos dignamente a la colectividad" (We Serve the Collectivity with Dignity), in Lucio 1935d, 23–24, 32–33.

6. The subsequent two quotations are taken from a 1994 video production by Dan Hallin, "Dan Hallin Unmasks Jacobo Zabludovsky on Televisa in Chiapas" (Hallin 1994).

CHAPTER 4. THE HISTORICAL ROOTS
OF INDIGENOUS STRUGGLE IN CHIAPAS

1. See Thomas and Brody (1988, 1–2) for another description of the settlement process of Tojolabal communities. Leyva Solano and Ascencio Franco 1996 also provide an excellent description of the settlement and organization of the Lacandon jungle, with emphasis on the Tzeltal population.

CHAPTER 5. THE NEW ZAPATISMO
IN THE LACANDON JUNGLE

1. A real is a monetary unit that was, at this time, equal to one-eighth of a peso.

2. I thank Shannan Mattiace for articulating this point for me.

3. Fray Bartolomé de las Casas, who lived from 1484 to 1566, was a Dominican friar who became an advocate for Indian rights. Las Casas became bishop of Chiapas in 1544 and promoted the implementation of the New Laws of the Indies, which were supposed to provide for the welfare, care, and survival of the Indians. Chiefly, these permitted Indian communities to change from *encomiendas* to free Indian towns where labor could not be bound as under the encomienda system. In addition, slavery was abolished. Las Casas left San Cristóbal in 1547 and returned to Spain, where he died. He is primarily remembered for his *History of the Indies,* which tells the story of thirty years of conquest, beginning in the Caribbean. Las Casas's ideas were quite influential in the formulation of liberation theology. "The 'preferential option for the poor' articulated at the 1968 conference of Latin American Bishops in Medallín, Colombia, draws heavily on many of de Las Casas' more important ideas" (Rand Parish 1997, 733).

4. A document from the fifth CIOAC congress, held in 1983, states:

> We conceive of the problems of this large population (indigenous) from the point of view of the class struggle, from the contradictions of class that can be found within the indigenous population and in the exploitation they experience.
>
> We try to incorporate the indigenous who work as salaried laborers, who sell their labor as rural workers, who are many hundreds of thousands, into the labor struggle through the creation of the Sindicato Regional de los Obreros Agrícolas [Regional Union of Agricultural Workers].
>
> We catalogue the indigenous population that possesses a piece of land in indigenous communities through buying it or having a title in Bienes Comunales, or through ejidos or as small property owners as peasants, and because they are peasants, we try to organize them into Uniones Regionales de Comuneros [Regional Unions of Communal Landholders], and we already have formed many.
>
> There are hundreds of thousands of indigenous people who have solicited land and, in spite of many years of struggle, for generations, have not received confirmation of or restitution for their lands through the secretary of agrarian reform. To address this problem we try to create . . . groups of indigenous peoples constituted like the National Council of Indigenous Peoples. . . .
>
> Our organization, CIOAC, needs to devote a great deal of attention to the grave, complex, and specific problems of Indian peoples. In the defense of their customs, of

their traditions, their language, their forms of government and religion. We need to consider them as national characteristics of each group because that is what they are. We have to engage in a great struggle for their territories, for those lands from which they have been displaced, lands that are used and exploited primarily for the benefit of the population that is not indigenous.

We need to incite and support the struggles of Indian peoples and communities for the restitution of lands that have been taken away by large agricultural landowners and forestry interests.

We need to try to guarantee education for the indigenous population, but also make sure that it is in their own language so that it is conserved.

We need to fight against the propositions of the bourgeois government to incorporate them into so-called civilization.

Mejía Piñero and Sarmiento Silva 1987, 214–15

5. One indigenous organization that also grew in Chiapas during the 1980s is the Coordinadora Nacional de Pueblos Indígenas (National Coordinator of Indian Peoples), or CNPI. Outside Chiapas, its influence is limited. It grew out of a previous organization with the same acronym created by the government in the 1970s to diffuse growing indigenous militancy, particularly over land rights. In 1981, some members of this first CNPI left to join the CNPA, where they were already heavily invested, some remained with the official CNPI, and others formed the new CNPI (Mejía Piñero and Sarmiento Silva 1987). This CNPI is closely identified with its primary promoter and leader, Genaro Domínguez, who also participated in the first CNPI, formed in Patzcuaro.

6. This interview was recorded on the site of Aguascalientes, built on the ejido lands of Guadalupe Tepeyac in 1994 to be the host site for the National Democratic Convention, which brought together 6,000 delegates and observers from a wide range of organizations and sectors of Mexican society. The spot was named for the 1914 site of the first constitutional convention, attended by Emiliano Zapata, which resulted in Mexico's 1917 constitution.

7. Interview and discussion with Amado Avendaño, June 12, 1995.

8. John Womack contests Marcos's version of the consultation process, saying that of the 385 communities that had ejidos in the cañadas, only 30 were asked by the EZLN to adopt the final accord and go to war. "Their assemblies groaned for consensus for the armed way, but it would not come. Maybe 25 voted for it. The most Zapatista community in the canyons [La Sultana, according to Womack] could finally do no better than a vote of 67 for war, 21 against" (Womack 1999, 43). It should be noted that Womack cites no sources at all in his book. His account often, but not always, parallels that of Tello Díaz 1995, and I find it questionable for that reason.

CHAPTER 6. ZAPATA LIVES

1. I thank Peter Guardino for this simple but elegant observation, which was lacking from this chapter.

2. This is in reference to the 1992 reforms to Article 27 ending the government's mandate to redistribute land and allowing ejidatarios to gain title to their land and hold it in private tenancy.

3. Ramón Ordoñez y Aguiar, an eighteenth-century Mexican antiquarian, allegedly discovered a colonial-era Tzental Maya document known as the Provanza de Votan, said to have been written by one Votan III, discussing the rise and fall of the Maya city of Palenque. Although many Chiapas scholars doubt whether any such codex ever existed and suspect that Ordoñez y Aguiar fabricated the story, Subcomandante Marcos's Votán Zapata may conceivably bear some relation to Ordoñez y Aguiar's Votan III. See Ramón Ordoñez y Aguiar, "Historia de la creación del cielo y la tierra conforme al sistema de la gentilidad americana: Theología de los Culebras figurada en ingeniosos gerolíphicos, symbolos, emblemas y metáphoras" (1794), in *Biblioteca mexicana del siglo XVIII*, ed. Nicolás León, sec. 1, pt. 4,1–265, Boletín del Instituto Bibliográfico Mexícana, 8 (Mexico, D.F.: Viuda de Francisco Díaz León, 1907).

4. Votán Zapata may also have filled an important religious vacuum, if there is any truth in the rumor of Marcos's antipathy to the Church. Enrique Krauze reports that toward the end of the 1980s, the EZLN and the diocese of Samuel Ruiz came into conflict, and observes: "The confrontation had much to do with the 'unmasking' of Subcomandante Marcos's hostility to religion. Marcos was known to have officiated at 'revolutionary marriages' and to have commented frequently that 'God and his word are worth zilch'" (Krauze 1999, 71).

CHAPTER 7. CONVERSATIONS WITH ZAPATISTAS

1. While under Mexican law, women can have landholding rights while married and as single mothers, in many communities women only receive land rights when they are widowed.

2. The dialogue" refers to the peace dialogues that were supposed to begin again between the EZLN and the Mexican government. The peace dialogue did in fact begin shortly after our conversation, in May 1995. This was the peace dialogue that led to the signing of the San Andrés Accords on Indigenous Rights and Culture, which the Mexican government signed but refused to implement. In April 2001, the Mexican Congress approved a watered-down version of the accords, which the Zapatistas refused to endorse because they departed from the original version they had signed on several significant points. The new version of the accords do not include broad autonomy for Indians to control local politics, justice, land rights, and natural resources based on traditional practices, outside the jurisdiction of federal law.

CHAPTER 8. THE HISTORICAL ROOTS OF LAND CONFLICT AND ORGANIZING IN OAXACA

1. I thank Jennie Purnell for clarifying ideas in this paragraph and for pointing out that most land privatized in the central valleys during this period probably went to community members, not outsiders.

CHAPTER 9. THE STORY OF SANTA MARÍA DEL TULE

1. This detail was repeated by everyone I interviewed about work conditions on the hacienda. Getting up and going to work, and then not being allowed to work because of arriving late, seemed to be a particularly cruel rule that stuck in people's minds. In such cases, they had to face an idle day with no source of income or food.

2. *Mayordomo* refers to those men and women named as sponsors for the cult celebrations of local saints, such as the Virgen de Asunción in the case of Santa María del Tule. Mayordomos spent large amounts of money on food, drink, music, and masses for the saints during their tenure. Until the 1930s, in the Tlacolula Valley, people were named without having given consent, in what locals called *mayordomía a la fuerza*, or forced mayordomía sponsorship. In many cases, those named would have to borrow large sums of money to pay expenses, and they often lost communal or private land they had put up as collateral. Elsewhere, I have written about this process in the nearby Zapotec community of Teotitlán del Valle and about its role in stratifying the community long before its incorporation into circuits of international capital (Stephen 1991, 105–7).

3. According to Taylor, the specific conditions of entailment in New Spain usually included primogeniture or, in the absence of a legitimate son, succession by the nearest blood relation, with preference given to males; the exclusion of clerics and mentally deranged heirs from the line of succession; and the retention of the founder's family name (Taylor 1972, 153). While entailment contracts explicitly forbid the taking out of liens on entailed estates, many land-poor *mayorazgos* took out mortgages on their property to raise cash. José de Guendulain was allowed to secure a lien of 36,400 pesos from the Cathedral of Oaxaca on his haciendas near Santa María del Tule and Cuicatlán in 1727 (ibid., 154, 253, n. 132).

4. Another possible explanation is that when ownership of land was disputed between two communities (as between Santa María del Tule and Tlalixtac), one town might rent the land to an individual as a way of bolstering its claim against the other town. Thus, Tlalixtac might have rented the land (even though it might not have belonged to Tlalixtac) to the Guendulain family. Under the Lerdo law, tenants (in this case, the Guendulain family) had the right to purchase land rented from communities; it seems that quite a few claims were made by landowner tenants, or landowners claiming to be tenants, in 1856 and 1857, immediately after the promulgation of the Lerdo law. The Guendulain family thus might have tried this, disputing Tlalixtac's ownership and attempting to gain the land as private property. I thank Jennie Purnell for this interpretation.

5. Eugenio does not specify the specific date of this agrarian congress, but it may well have been in 1932.

6. The Carrancistas were fighting against the neighboring Zapotec Sierra troops, who were aligned with Zapata and Villa. Marío and other ejidatarios from Santa María del Tule remember the town as having been loyal to Zapata. A few people told me that the community had remained neutral. Here, Mario merges several decades, approximately 1910–40.

7. This is a reference to one of the roads established by the Spanish, which in many cases simply followed already constructed indigenous roads. The portion of the road he is referring to later became part of the Pan-American Highway, built in the 1930s under Lázaro Cárdenas.

8. This is a reference to the Zapotec soldiers from the Sierra Juárez who supported Villa and Zapata and fought against the soldiers of Carranza.

9. The demographic picture for men is quite similar. Of thirty male ejidatarios surveyed in 1994, eight, or about 27 percent, were under 45; twenty-two, or 73 percent, were over 45; and sixteen, or 53 percent, were over 60.

10. In the random sample questionnaire carried out in 1994 with 64 male and female ejidatarios from Santa María del Tule, 30 percent of the men indicated that they had migrated to the United States. Of these, 72 percent had left temporarily and 28 percent had migrated permanently. Thirteen percent of the women indicated that they had migrated.

11. In Santa María del Tule, as in other communities in the Tlacolula Valley, women engage in a wide variety of agricultural tasks, including planting, weeding, harvesting, and the grazing of animals (Stephen 1991, 76–80). Some women have also plowed fields when necessary. Ejidatarias would most likely be involved in this range of agricultural tasks should their primary economic activity be agricultural.

CHAPTER 10. THE FORMATION OF THE EJIDO OF UNIÓN ZAPATA

1. Peons were usually landless people paid a daily wage to work the land of the hacienda. Sharecroppers who worked on hacienda lands contributed 50 percent of their harvest to the hacienda owners. If they needed food, sharecroppers would work as daily peons as well, often receiving their pay in corn.

2. An *almud* is a dry measure that, when filled with corn, is equivalent to two kilograms.

3. People from Unión Zapata did not participate in the 1942–64 U.S. bracero program in any significant numbers. No one recalled migrating before the 1970s. In a random-sample survey carried out with sixty-two ejidatarios and their spouses in Unión Zapata in 1994, no women had migrated and only 8 percent of the men had; all had done so within the past fifteen years. During the summer of 1995, however, an additional twenty men were estimated by locals to have emigrated, in response to the devaluation of the peso and rising local unemployment.

CHAPTER 11. THE CONTRADICTIONS OF ZAPATISMO IN RURAL OAXACA

1. The categories were identified through an open-ended survey question, and in everyday conversations and open meetings. As part of a random-sample survey administered to ejidatarios in the two communities, respondents were asked to clarify their origins, the answers coming in response to the question,

"De qué origen es Usted?" We tested several kinds of questions and decided on an open-ended one that most people seemed to understood. On more than one occasion, we had long and interesting discussions about what "origin" meant to those responding to the questionnaire. As demonstrated by the results, many people could not choose a single "origin." Their multiple responses reflect in part the many layers of ethnic, racial, and national identities that people in the central valleys have inherited.

2. Of sixty-four respondents, 17.2 percent (eleven) stated that they were *Zapoteco*, 9.4 percent (six) stated that they were *revuelto* with *Zapoteco* and another category, and another 18.8 percent (twelve) stated that they were *Zapoteco* in combination with another category, such as *Oaxaqueno* or *Mexicano*.

3. During the summer of 1994, the subsidy was about U.S.$100.00 per hectare. After the severe devaluation of the Mexican peso in December 1994, the subsidy retained about half of its original value. In the summer of 1995, the subsidy was $440 new Mexican pesos per hectare, or between U.S.$65.00 and U.S.$70.00 per hectare, depending on the exchange rate.

4. The survey covered a wide range of issues, including basic demographic data, production, migration, political participation, and ethnic identity. In Santa María del Tule, a complete list of the names and addresses of ejidatarios was obtained and the random sample of men and women was chosen by assigning each name a number and using a random number table to select survey participants. In Unión Zapata, all ejidatarios or their spouses were interviewed.

5. The age composition of ejidos is also important to consider in how some ejidatarios arrived at their pro-Zapatista and pro-PRI positions in 1994. Given that the average age of many ejidatarios is the late fifties, most are still close to the legacy of Zapata and the revolution, either personally or through stories told them by parents and other relatives. The moral appeal of the Zapatistas and their passion for their cause can stir up emotional testimonials among elderly ejidatarios about the violence they faced, their ill treatment at the hands of hacendados, and their lives of never-ending toil. The fact that elderly ejidatarios are often granted the role of local intellectuals—at least in terms of interpreting ejido history—means that their interpretations of occurrences like the Zapatista rebellion will be given weight in local political discussions by people of all ages.

CONCLUSION. RECLAIMING THE MEXICAN NATION FOR THE POOR AND THE INDIGENOUS SOUTH

1. Mexico is making progress in becoming more democratic, according to Julia Preston of the *New York Times*. After hundreds of Federal Preventative Police took over the campus of the Universidad Nacional Autónoma de México and arrested more than six hundred students, Preston reported: "The operation, carried out without bloodshed, was the most important intervention by government forces at the National Autonomous University of Mexico since the student movement of 1968, which ended in a massacre that traumatized a generation of Mexicans and left them more determined to make the country more democratic.

The end of the long strike showed how far Mexico has moved toward that goal" (Preston 2000, 1a).

2. I have given him a pseudonym since I was not able to ask his permission to publish parts of the conversation he agreed to let me tape.

3. This pseudonym is chosen to protect the speaker.

4. Partha Chatterjee is pessimistic about such options, however, "because the modern state, embedded as it is within the universal narrative of capital, cannot recognize within its jurisdiction any form of community, except the single, determinate, demographically enumerable form of the nation," and believes that other forms of collectivity and visions of community can only be validated by "claiming an alternative nationhood with rights to an alternative state"—in other words, secession (Chatterjee 1993, 238).

5. Earlier, upon her arrival at the airport in Mexico City, Ramona had raised the flag and declared: "We want democracy, liberty, and justice for all Mexicans. This is a gift from our general command—the Mexican colors. This is so we never forget that our fatherland is Mexico" (Kleist 1996).

References

Acta de conformidad con los trabajos de ante-proyecto de segunda ampliación de ejido al poblado "Guadalupe Tepeyac," del municipio de las Margaritas, Chiapas. 1992. Expediente 3024.2A. 12 October 1992. Poblado Guadalupe Tepeyac. Acción Segunda Ampliación. Tuxtla Gutiérrez: Registro Agrario Nacional.

Acta que se levanta en el poblado "Realidad Trinidad" municipio de las Margaritas, estado de Chiapas, con respecto a la conformidad en recibir los terrenos localizados para amplicación de ejido del poblado que se cita. 1985. Expediente 2773. 25 September 1985. Población La Realidad. Acción Primera Ampliación. Tuxtla Gutiérrez: Registro Agrario Nacional.

Aguirre Beltrán, Gonzalo. 1992. *Teoría y práctica de la educación indígena*. México, D.F.: Fondo de Cultura Económica.

Alonso, Ana María. 1995. *Threads of Blood: Colonialism, Revolution, and Gender on Mexico's Northern Frontier*. Tucson: University of Arizona Press.

Amnesty International. 1986. *Mexico: Human Rights in Rural Areas. Exchange of Documents with the Mexican Government on Human Rights Violations in Oaxaca and Chiapas*. London: Amnesty International.

Anderson, Benedict. 1983. *Imagined Communities: Reflections on the Origin and Spread of Nationalism*. New York: Verso.

Appadurai, Arjun. 1996. *Modernity at Large: Cultural Dimensions of Globalization*. Minneapolis: University of Minnesota Press.

Archer, Christon L. 1997. Wars of Independence. In *Encyclopedia of Mexico: History, Society, and Culture*, Michael S. Werner, 2: 1595–1601. Chicago: Fitzroy Dearborn.

Arellanes Meixuero, Anselmo. 1988. Del camarazo al cardenismo (1925–1933). In *Historia de la cuestión agraria mexicana: Estado de Oaxaca*, ed. Leticia

Reina, vol. 2: *1925–1986*, 23–126. México, D.F.: Juan Pablos Editor / Gobierno de Estado de Oaxaca, Universidad Autónoma Benito Juárez de Oaxaca, and Centro de Estudios Históricos del Agrarismo en México.

———. 1999. *Oaxaca: Reparto de la tierra, acenes, limitaciones, y respuestas.* 2d ed. Oaxaca: Universidad Autónoma "Benito Júarez" de Oaxaca, PROOAX.

Arnove, Robert. 1993. *Education as Contested Terrain: Nicaragua, 1979–1993.* Boulder, Colo.: Westview Press.

———. 1999. *Comparative Education: The Dialectic of the Global and the Local.* Boulder, Colo.: Rowman & Littlefield.

Aviso de posesión. 1957. No. 1460. Acción Dotación, Poblado Guadalupe Tepeyac. Expediente 1725. 26 June 1957. Tuxtla Gutiérrez: Registro Agrario Nacional.

Baitenmann, Helga. 1994a. Las irregularidades en el programa de certificación ejidal. *Jornada del Campo,* 6 September 1994.

———. 1994b. La procuraduría agraria: Juez y parte del procede. *Jornada del Campo,* 31 October 1994.

———. 1997. Rural Agency and State Formation in Postrevolutionary Mexico: The Agrarian Reform in Central Veracruz (1915–1992). Ph.D. diss., Department of Anthropology, New School for Social Research, New York.

———. 1998. The Reforms to Article 27 and the Promise of Local Democratization in Central Veracruz. In *The Transformation of Rural Mexico: Reforming the Ejido Sector,* ed. Wayne Cornelius and David Myhre, 105–24. La Jolla: Center for U.S.–Mexican Studies, University of California, San Diego.

———. 2000. Gender and Agrarian Rights in Twentieth-Century Mexico. Paper delivered at the 2000 meeting of the Latin American Studies Association, Miami, 16–18 March 2000.

Balleza Jr., Carlos R. 1933. Memo to the governor of Oaxaca, "Asunto: Loma Larga, Mitla, Tlacolula remite solicitud de dotación de ejidos." Legado 1151, Expediente 3. 19 July 1933. Loma Larga / Unión Zapata. Archivo General del Estado de Oaxaca.

Barry, Tom. 1995. *Zapata's Revenge: Free Trade and the Farm Crisis in Mexico.* Boston: South End Press.

Bautista, Guadalupe. 1934. Telegram to Presidente de la Republica. Loma Larga / Unión Zapta, Expediente 23: 13385: (723.7). 20 April 1934. Registro Agrario Nacional, Oaxaca.

———. 1936. Letter to Lázaro Cárdenas. Asuntos: Los Campesinos esperan la resolución final del expediente agraria sea favorable de acuerdo con los propositos e intereses. Expediente 23: 13385 (723: 7). 4 June 1936. Loma Larga / Unión Zapata. Registro Agrario Nacional, Oaxaca.

Bellinghausen, Herman. 2000. Hostilidad y prepotencia, signos de la PFP en Chiapas. *La Jornada,* 21 May 2000, 5.

Benjamin, Thomas. 1996. *A Rich Land, a Poor People: Politics and Society in Modern Chiapas.* Albuquerque: University of New Mexico Press.

Berry, Charles R. 1981. *The Reform in Oaxaca, 1856–76.* Lincoln: University of Nebraska Press.

Binford, Leigh. 1996. *The El Mozote Massacre: Anthropology and Human Rights.* Tucson: University of Arizona Press.

Botey Estapé, Carlota. 1991. La parcela ejidal es un patrimonio familiar. *Uno Más Uno* supplement, 18 November 1991.

————.1993. La proletarización de la mujer en la última década del siglo XX. Paper presented at the Thirteenth International Congress of Anthropological and Ethnological Sciences, México, D.F., 29 July–4 August 1993.

Borofsky, Robert. 2000. Public Anthropology: Where To? What Next? *Anthropology News* 41, 5 (May 2000): 9–10.

Bourdieu, Pierre. 1967. Systems of Education and Systems of Thought. *International Social Science Journal* 19: 338–58.

————. 1977. *Reproduction in Education, Society and Culture.* Translated by Richard Nice. Beverly Hills, Calif.: Sage Publications.

Bourgois, Philippe. 1991. Confronting the Ethics of Ethnography: Lessons from Fieldwork in Central America. In *Decolonizing Anthropology: Moving Further toward an Anthropology for Liberation,* ed. Faye V. Harrison, 111–26. Washington, D.C.: Association of Black Anthropologists and the American Anthropological Association.

Brachet-Márquez, Viviane. 1997. Politics and Government, 1910–1946. In *Encyclopedia of Mexico: History, Society, and Culture,* ed. Michael S. Werner, 2: 1118–21. Chicago: Fitzroy Dearborn.

Britton, John A. 1997. Liberalism. In *Encyclopedia of Mexico: History, Society, and Culture,* ed. Michael S. Werner, 1: 738–42. Chicago: Fitzroy Dearborn.

Brunk, Samuel. 1997. Emiliano Zapata. In *Encyclopedia of Mexico: History, Society, and Culture,* ed. Michael Werner, 2: 1633–35. Chicago: Fitzroy Dearborn.

Brysk, Alison. 2000. *From Tribal Village to Global Village: Indian Rights and International Relations in Latin America.* Stanford, Calif.: Stanford University Press.

Campbell, Howard. 1990. Zapotec Ethnic Politics and the Politics of Culture in Juchitán, Oaxaca (1350–1990). Ph.D. diss., University of Wisconsin, Madison.

————. 1993. Class Struggle, Ethnopolitics, and Cultural Revivalism in Juchitán. In *Zapotec Struggles: Histories, Politics, and Representations from Juchitán, Oaxaca,* ed. Howard Campbell, Leigh Binford et al., 213–44. Washington, D.C.: Smithsonian Institute.

Canal 6 de Julio. 1998. *La Guerra Oculta.* México, D.F.: Canal 6 de Julio. Film [www.laneta.apc.org./canal6/].

Carmack, Robert. 1988. *Harvest of Violence: The Maya Indians and the Guatemalan Crisis.* Norman: University of Oklahoma Press.

Carroll, Patrick J. 1991. *Blacks in Colonial Veracruz: Race, Ethnicity, and Regional Development.* Austin: University of Texas Press.

Castellanos, Laura. 1994. Las mujeres de Chiapas, protagonistas invisibles. *Doble Jornada,* 7 February 1994, 4.

Castellanos, Manuel. 1935. Inspector de la Zona Manuel Castellanos to C. Director Federal de Educación Prof. Elpidio López in Tuxtla Gutiérrez, dated from Ciudad Las Casas, 6 April 1935. Caja 1332 (191). Expediente 8. Folio 11. Archivo Histórico de la Secretaría de Educación Pública, Departamento de Escuelas Rurales, México, D.F.

Castro Soto, Gustavo. 1999. S.O.A.: The School of the Americas. *Chiapas al Día Bulletin*, no. 181 (English version), 5 November 1999. Center for Economic and Political Investigations of Community Action (CIEPAC), San Cristóbal de las Casas, Chiapas [www.ciepac.org].

————. 2000a. The Armed Forces in Chiapas. In *Always Near, Always Far: The Armed Forces in México*, ed. Ernesto Ledesma Arronte, Gustavo E. Castro Soto, and Tedford P. Lewis, 83–103. San Francisco: Global Exchange.

————. 2000b. Resultados electorales en Chiapas. *Boletin "Chiapas al Día,"* no. 212, 15 September 2000. CIEPAC, San Cristóbal de las Casas, Chiapas [www.ciepac.org].

Ce-Acatl. 1995. Grupo de trabajo 4: Situación, derechos, y cultura de la mujer indígena [Situation, rights, and culture of indigenous women]. Declaración de asesores e invitadas del EZLN. *Ce-Acatl* 73: 21–27, 7 November 1995.

————. 1996. Acciones y medidas para Chiapas [Actions and measures for Chiapas]. Compromisos y Propuestas conjuntas de los Gobiernos del Estado y Federal y el EZLN. Documento 3.2. *Ce-Acatl* 78–79: 55–61, 11 March–19 April 1996.

Centro de Derechos Humanos Fray Bartolomé de las Casas. 1998. *La legalidad y la injusticia*. San Cristóbal de las Casas: Centro de Derechos Humanos Fray Bartolomé de las Casas.

Centro de Información y Análisis de Chiapas and Coordinación de Organismos No Gubernamentales por la Paz en Chiapas. 1997. *Para Entender Chiapas: Chiapas en Cifras*. México, D.F.: Servicios Informativos Procesados, A.C.

Cevallos, Diego. 1998. Business Moving Ahead for Some. Interpress Services, 26 April 1998. Reprinted in *Mexico News Pak* 6, 137 (20 April–4 May 1998): 1.

Chassen-López, Francie R. 1994. "Cheaper than machines": Women and Agriculture in Porfirian Oaxaca, 1880–1911. In *Women of the Mexican Countryside, 1850–1990: Creating Spaces, Shaping Transitions*, ed. Heather Fowler-Salamini and Mary Kay Vaughan, 27–50. Tucson: University of Arizona Press.

Chance, John. 1978. *Race and Class in Colonial Oaxaca*. Stanford, Calif.: Stanford University Press.

Chatterjee, Partha. 1993. *The Nation and Its Fragments: Colonial and Postcolonial Histories*. Princeton, N.J.: Princeton University Press.

Cockcroft, James D. 1998. *Mexico's Hope: An Encounter with Politics and History*. New York: Monthly Review Press.

Collier, George A. With Elizabeth Lowery Quaratiello. 1994. *Basta! Land and the Zapatista Rebellion in Chiapas*. Oakland, Calif.: Institute for Food and Development Policy.

Comaroff, John, and Jean Comaroff. 1992. *Ethnography and the Historical Imagination*. Boulder, Colo.: Westview Press.

Comisión Agraria Mixta. 1955. Dictamen de la Comisión Agraria Mixta del Estado de Chiapas [Report to the Mixed Agrarian Commission of the State of Chiapas]: Acción dotación, Poblado Guadalupe Tepeyac. Expediente 1725. Registro Agrario Nacional, Tuxtla Gutiérrez.

———. 1965a. Acción Primera Ampliación [First Expansion Act], Guadalupe Tepeyac. Expediente 1725. 21 June 1965. Registro Agrario Nacional, Tuxtla Gutiérrez.

———. 1965b. Acción Dotación [Endowment (Land) Act], Poblado La Realidad, Municipio de Las Margaritas. Expediente 2132. 17 August 1965. Registro Agrario Nacional, Tuxtla Gutiérrez.

———. 1978. Dictámen que se formula sobre el expediente numero 2773-A formado con motivo de la solicitud de ampliación de ejidos presentados por los vecinos del poblado La Realidad Trinidad [Report in response to record no. 2773-A written in response to request for an extension of *ejido* lands by the population of La Realidad Trinidad]. Expediente 2773-A. 16 May 1978. Acción Primera Ampliación. Registro Agrario Nacional, Tuxtla Gutiérrez.

———. 1980. Dictámen formado con motivo de solicitude de segunda ampliación de ejidos, presentada por los vecinos del poblado Guadalupe el Tepeyac [Report written in response to request for a second extension of *ejido* lands presented by the people of Guadalupe Tepeyac]. Expediente 3024.2/A. 5 March 1980. Acción Segunda Ampliación. Registro Agrario Nacional, Tuxtla Gutiérrez.

Consejo Estatal de Población de Oaxaca. 1994. *Población indígena de Oaxaca, 1895–1990*. Oaxaca: Consejo Estatal de Población.

Cornelius, Wayne A. 2000. Fox's Victory Will Lead to Change—and a Disintegrating PRI. *San Diego Union Tribune*, July 16, 2000, G4.

Cornelius, Wayne A., and David Myhre. 1998a. Introduction. In *The Transformation of Rural Mexico: Reforming the Ejido Sector*, ed. Wayne A. Cornelius and David Myhre, 1–24. La Jolla: Center for U.S.–Mexican Studies at the University of California, San Diego.

———, eds. 1998b. *The Transformation of Rural Mexico: Reforming the Ejido Sector*. La Jolla: Center for U.S.–Mexican Studies at the University of California, San Diego.

Correa, Guillermo, Salvador Corro, and Julio César López. 1994. Campesinos e Indígenas de todo el país apoyan las demandas del EZLN y marchan hacía la capital. *Proceso*, no. 910 (11 April): 36–40.

Cortés, Hernán. 1983. *Cartas y documentos [de] Hernán Cortés*. México, D.F.: Porrúa.

Countiño Farrera, Mario Arturo. 1991. Letter to C. Lic. Francisco Javier Molina Oveido, Presidente de la Sala Estatal del Cuerpo Consultivo Agrario. Expediente 1725. 4 June 1991. Ación Primera Ampliación, Población Guadalupe Tepeyac. Registro Agrario Nacional, Tuxtla Gutiérrez.

Craig, Ann L. 1983. *The First Agraristas: An Oral History of a Mexican Agrarian Reform Movement*. Berkeley and Los Angeles: University of California Press.

Cuadro comparativo de la iniciativa de COCOPA y las observaciones del ejecutivo. 1997. *La Jornada*, 13 January 1997.

De Vos, Jan. 1995. El Lacandón: Una introducción histórica. In *Chiapas: Los rumbos de otra historia*, ed. Juan Pedro Viqueria and Mario Humberto Ruz, 331–62. México, D.F.: Universidad Nacional Autónoma de México.

Díaz Ordaz, Gustavo. 1968. Visto para resolver en definitiva el expediente relativo a la ampliación de ejido solicitada por vecinos del poblado denominado "Guadalupe el Tepeyac." Presidential resolution. Expediente 1725.
16 February 1968. Primera Ampliación, Poblado Guadalupe Tepeyac. Registro Agrario Nacional, Tuxtla Gutiérrez.

Dillon, Sam. 2000. Mexico Voting in New Leader Begins a Political Sea Change.
New York Times, 4 July 2000, A1, A6.

Diócesis de San Cristóbal. 1986 Plan Diocesano. San Cristóbal de Las Casas:
Diócesis de San Cristóbal.

Diskin, Martin. 1991. Ethnic Discourse and the Challenge to Anthropology: The
Nicaraguan Case. In *Nation-States and Indians in Latin America,* ed. Greg
Urban and Joel Sherzer, 156–80. Austin: University of Texas Press.

Donald, James. 1996. The Citizen and the Man about Town. In *Questions of
Cultural Identity,* ed. Stuart Hall and Paul du Gay, 170–96. Thousand
Oaks, Calif.: Sage.

Dover, Robert, and Joanne Rappaport. 1996. Introduction. *Journal of Latin
American Anthropology* 1, 2: 2–17.

Duara, Prasenjit. 1995. *Rescuing History From the Nation: Questioning Narratives of Modern China.* Chicago: University of Chicago Press.

———. 1996. Historicizing National Identity, or Who Imagines What and When.
In *Becoming National: A Reader,* ed. Geoff Eley and Ronald Grigor Suny,
151–78. Oxford: Oxford University Press.

Eber, Christine. 1999. "Seeking our own food": Indigenous Women's Power and
Autonomy in San Pedro Chenalhó, Chiapas, 1980–1998. *Latin American
Perspectives* 26, 3: 6–36.

———. 2000. *Women and Alcohol in a Highland Maya Town: Water of Hope,
Water of Sorrow.* Austin: University of Texas Press.

———. 2001. Buscando una nueva vida: Liberation through Autonomy in San
Pedro Chenalhó, 1970–1998. *Latin American Perspectives* 28, 2: 45–72.

Edelman, Marc. 1999. *Peasants against Globalization: Rural Social Movements
in Costa Rica.* Stanford, Calif.: Stanford University Press.

Ejército Zapatista de Liberación Nacional. 1994. *EZLN documentos y comunicados 1: 1 de enero/8 de agosto de 1994.* México, D.F.: Ediciones Era.

———. 1995. *EZLN documentos y comunicados 2: 15 de agosto de 1994/29 de
septiembre de 1995.* México, D.F.: Ediciones Era.

El Oaxaqueño. 1934. Significativo banquete se ofrecio ayer en El Tule al Sr.
Gral. Cárdenas. No. 5,679 (17 April 1934): 1.

———. 1935. Emiliano Zapata es glorificado hoy. No. 5,974 (10 April 1935): 1.

———. 1937. Los pueblos del centro con el Gral. Cárdenas: Transcendental dis-
curso al conglomerado campesino de alta significación fue el ágape en Santa
María del Tule. No. 6,681 (22 March 1937): 1.

El Socialista [fortnightly publication, Putla, Oaxaca]. 1935. Vol. 1, no. 1 (1 July
1935). Fondo de Educación, Archivo General del Estado, Oaxaca.

Escobar, Arturo. 1995. *Encountering Development: The Making and Unmak-
ing of the Third World.* Princeton, N.J.: Princeton University Press.

Esparza, Manuel. 1988. Los proyectos liberales en Oaxaca (1856–1910). In *His-*

toria de la Cuestión Agraria Mexicana: Estado de Oaxaca, ed. Leticia Reina, vol. 1: *Prehispanico–1924*, 269–330. México, D.F.: Juan Pablos Editor/ Gobierno de Estado de Oaxaca, Universidad Autónoma Benito Juárez de Oaxaca, and Centro de Estudios Históricos del Agrarismo en México.

Falla, Ricardo. 1994. *Massacres in the Jungle: Ixcan, Guatemala, 1975–1982.* Boulder, Colo.: Westview Press.

Favre, Henri. 1984. *Cambio y continuidad entre los Mayas de México.* 2d ed. México, D.F.: Institution Nacional Indigenista.

Fazio, Carlos. 1994. *Samuel Ruiz: El Caminante.* México, D.F.: Esapa Calpe.

Félix Zárate, Inocencio. 1935. "Asunto.–Remite adjunto un ejemplar del periódico que indica" [enclosing copy of *El Socialista*]. Al Ciudadano, Gobernador Constitucional del Estado Oaxaca, Oaxaca, del Sub-Inspector Escolar, Villa Guerrero, Putla, Oaxaca, 10 July 1935, Inocencio Félix Zárate. Fondo de Educación, 1935. Archivo General del Estado, Oaxaca.

Fernández, Claudia. 1994. Mexican Billionaires Booming. *Financiero Internacional*, 11 July 1994.

Field, Les W. 1994. Harvesting the Bitter Juice: Contradictions of Páez Resistance in the Changing Colombian Nation-State. *Identities* 1, 1: 89–108.

———. 1999a. *The Grimace of Macho Ratón: Artisans, Identity, and Nation in Late Twentieth-Century Western Nicaragua.* Durham, N.C.: Duke University Press.

———. 1999b. Complicities and Collaborations: Anthropologists and the "Unacknowledged Tribes" of California. *Current Anthropology* 40, 2: 193–210.

Fox, Jonathan. 1996. How Does Civil Society Thicken? The Political Construction of Social Capital in Rural Mexico. *World Development* 24, 6: 1089–1104.

———. 1999. Assessing Binational Civil Society Coalitions. Paper presented at Dilemmas of Change in Mexican Politics conference, Center for U.S.–Mexican Studies, University of California, San Diego, 8–9 October 1999.

Fox, Jonathan, Gaspar Rivera, and Lynn Stephen, eds. 1999. *Indigenous Rights and Self-Determination in Mexico. Cultural Survival Quarterly* 23, 1 (Spring 1999).

Fuerzas de Liberación Nacional. 1980. Estatutos de las Fuerzas de Liberación Nacional. México, D.F.: FLN.

Gallegos, Elena, and Juan Manuel Venegas. 2000. Fox: El PAN ya me formó, ahora me tiene que dejar ir. *La Jornada*, 6 July 2000, 6–7

Gallegos, José L. 1935. Rinde informe de los trabajos ejecutados en la Ranchería de Loma Larga, Mitla [Report presented on work carried out in Loma Larga, Mitla], Tlac. Oax. To C. Delegado del Departamento Agraria, Oaxaca. Loma Larga/Unión Zapata. Expediente 23: 13385 (723.7). 19 May 1935. Registro Agrario Nacional, Oaxaca.

Gamio, Manuel. 1916. *Forjando Patria.* México, D.F.: Porrúa.

García, Martha. 1997. Reclaman mujeres indígenas su derecho a palabra y a ser libres. *La Jornada*, 5 December 1997, 8.

García de León, Antonio. 1994. La vuelta del Katun (Chiapas a 20 años del Primer Congreso Indígena). *Perfil de la Jornada*, 12 October 1994.

Geertz, Clifford. 1973. *The Interpretation of Cultures.* New York: Basic Books.

Gilly, Adolfo, Subcomandante Marcos, and Carlo Ginzburg. 1995. *Discusión sobre la historia.* México, D.F.: Taurus.

Global Exchange. 1999. *Foreigners of Conscience: The Mexican Government's Campaign against International Human Rights Observers in Chiapas.* San Francisco: Global Exchange. http//www.globalexchange.org.

Gómez Hernández, Antonio, and Mario Humberto Ruz, eds. 1992. *Memoria baldía: Los tojolabales y las fincas. Testimonios.* Tuxtla Gutiérrez: Universidad Nacional Autónoma de México / Universidad Autónoma de Chiapas.

González, Pablo. 1999. Minimum Wage Loses between 22 and 24 Percent of Its Purchasing Power. *Excelsior,* 8 April 1999.

González Navarro, Moisés. 1958. Indio y propiedad en Oaxaca. *Historia Mexicana* 8, 2: 653–76.

Gramsci, Antonio. 1971. *Selections from the Prison Notebooks of Antonio Gramsci.* Edited and translated by Quintin Hoare and Geoffrey Nowell Smith. New York: International Publishers.

Green, Linda. 1995. Living in a State of Fear. In *Fieldwork under Fire: Contemporary Studies of Violence and Survival,* ed. Carolyn Nordstrom and Antonius C. G. M. Robben, 105–28. Berkeley and Los Angeles: University of California Press.

Grijalva, Anacleto. 1934. Letter to the presidente constitutional de los Estados Unidos Mexicanos. Loma Larga / Unión Zapata. Expediente 23: 13385 (723.7). 27 March 1934. Registro Agrario Nacional, Oaxaca.

Grijalva, Anacleto, and Guadalupe Bautista. 1934a. Letter to the presidente de la Republica. Loma Larga / Unión Zapata, Expediente 23: 13385 (723.7). 23 March 1934. Registro Agrario Nacional, Oaxaca.

———. 1934b. Letter to Abelardo Rodriguez, presidente constitucional de los Estados Unidos de México. Loma Larga / Unión Zapata. Expediente 23: 13385 (723.7). 6 May 1934. Registro Agrario Nacional, Oaxaca.

———. 1934c. Letter to Abelardo Rodriguez, presidente constitucional de los Estados Unidos de México. Loma Larga / Unión Zapata, Expediente 23: 13385 (723.7). 11 July 1934. Registro Agrario Nacional, Oaxaca.

Grijalva, Anacleto, Guadalupe Bautista, Lauro Aragón et al. 1933. Copy of petition for ejido lands sent 14 June 1933 to the govenor of the state of Oaxaca and to the Confederación Oaxaqueña de Campesinos. Loma Larga / Unión Zapata, Expediente 23: 13385 (723.7). Registro Agrario Nacional, Oaxaca.

———. 1935. Asunto: Peticiones de los campesinos solicitando la inmediata dotación de ejidos, montes y aguas para cambiar de situaciones. Letter to Lázaro Cárdenas, presidente de la República. Loma Larga / Unión Zapata. Expediente 23: 13385 (723.7). 19 June 1935. Registro Agrario Nacional, Oaxaca.

Gudeman, Stephen. 1986. *Economics as Culture: Models and Metaphors of Livelihood.* London: Routledge & Kegan Paul.

Gudeman, Stephen, and Alberto Rivera. 1990. *Conversations in Colombia: The Domestic Economy in Life and Text.* Cambridge: Cambridge University Press.

Gunson, Phil. 1998. Bleak Future for Mexico's Rural Poor. *San Francisco Chronicle,* 29 June 1998, 8A.

Gupta, Akhil, and James Ferguson. 1997. Discipline and Practice: "The Field" as Site, Method, and Location in Anthropology. In *Anthropological Locations: Boundaries and Grounds of a Field Science,* ed. Gupta and Ferguson, 1–47. Berkeley and Los Angeles: University of California Press.

Guzmán López, Salvador, and Jan Rus, eds. and trs. 1990. *Kipaltik: La Historia de cómo compramos nuestra finca.* San Cristóbal de las Casas: Instituto de Asesoría Antropológica para la Región Maya, A.C.

Hale, Charles R. 1994. *Resistance and Contradiction: Miskitu Indians and the Nicaraguan State, 1894–1987.* Stanford, Calif.: Stanford University Press.

———. 1996. Mestizaje, Hybridity and the Cultural Politics of Difference in Post-revolutionary Central America. *Journal of Latin American Anthropology* 2, 1: 34-61.

Hall, Stuart. 1981. Notes on Deconstructing the Popular. In *People's History and Socialist Theory,* ed. Raphael Samuel. London: Routledge & Kegan Paul.

Hallin, Dan. 1994. Dan Hallin Unmasks Jacobo Zabludovsky on Televisa in Chiapas. La Jolla: Department of Communications at the University of California, San Diego. Videotape.

Hamilton, Nora. 1982. *The Limits of State Autonomy.* Princeton, N.J.: Princeton University Press.

Haraway, Donna. 1991. *Simians, Cyborgs, and Women: The Reinvention of Nature.* New York: Routledge

Harvey, Neil, ed. 1994. *Rebellion in Chiapas: Rural Reforms, Campesino Radicalism, and the Limits to Salinismo.* Transformation of Rural Mexico, no. 5. La Jolla: Center for U.S.–Mexican Studies, University of California, San Diego.

———. 1996. Rural Reforms and the Zapatista Rebellion: Chiapas, 1988–1995. In *Neoliberalism Revisited: Economic Restructuring and Mexico's Political Future,* ed. Gerardo Otero, 187–208. Boulder, Colo.: Westview Press.

———. 1998. *The Chiapas Rebellion: The Struggle for Land and Democracy.* Durham, N.C.: Duke University Press.

Heredia, Carlos. 1996. Downward Mobility: Mexican Workers after NAFTA. *NACLA Report on the Americas* 30, 3: 34–40.

Hernández, Jorge. 1996. Las organizaciones indígenas Oaxaqueños en el contexto de la globalización. Paper presented at the Second Biannual Research Conference on Oaxaca, Welte Institute, Oaxaca, Mexico, August 1996.

Hernández-Castillo, Rosalva Aída. 1997. Between Hope and Adversity: The Struggle of Organized Women in Chiapas since the Zaptista Rebellion. *Journal of Latin American Anthropology* 3, 1: 102–20.

Hernández Chavez, Alicia. 1979. *La mecánica cardenista.* México, D.F.: El Colegio de México.

Hernández-Navarro, Luis. 1992. Cafetaleros: Del adelgazamiento estatal a la guerra del mercado. In *Autonomía y nuevos sujectos sociales en el desarrollo rural,* ed. Julio Moguel, Carlota Botey, and Luis Hernández, 78–97. México, D.F.: Siglo Veintiuno Editores.

———. 1994. The Chiapas Uprising. In *Rebellion in Chiapas,* ed. Neil Harvey, 51–64. Transformation of Rural Mexico, no. 5. La Jolla: Center for U.S.–Mexican Studies, University of California, San Diego.

————. 1999. The San Andrés Accords: Indians and the Soul. *Cultural Survival Quarterly* 23, 1: 30–32.

Hernández Pérez, Caralampio, and Jorge Jímenez Pérez. 1989a. Letter to C. Lic. Jorge Obrador Capillino, delegado agrario en el estado. Expediente 3024-2/A. 10 January 1989. Poblado Guadalupe Tepeyac, Acción Segundo Ampliación. Registro Agrario Nacional, Tuxtla Gutiérrez.

————. 1989b. Letter to C. Lic. Jorge Obrador Capillino, delegado agrario en el estado. Expediente 3024-2/A. 23 February 1989. Poblado Guadalupe Tepeyac, Acción segundo ampliación. Registro Agrario Nacional, Tuxtla Gutiérrez.

Herzfeld, Michael. 1992. *The Social Production of Indifference: Exploring the Symbolic Roots of Western Bureaucracy.* Chicago: University of Chicago Press.

Howard, Rhoda. 1992. Dignity, Community, and Human Rights. In *Human Rights in Cross-Cultural Perspectives,* ed. Abdullah A. Anna'im, 81–102. Philadelphia: University of Pennsylvania Press.

Human Rights Watch/Americas.1994. *Waiting for Justice in Chiapas.* New York: Human Rights Watch/Americas.

————.1995. *Mexico: Torture and Other Abuses during the 1995 crackdown on alleged Zapatistas.* New York: Human Rights Watch/Americas.

————. 1997. *Implausible Deniability: State Responsibility for Rural Violence in Mexico.* New York: Human Rights Watch/Americas.

Instituto Nacional de Estadística, Geografía e Informática. 1995. *Chiapas: Datos por ejido y comunidad agraria. XI censo general de población y vivienda, 1990, VII Censo Agropecuario, 1991.* México, D.F.: INEGI.

————. 1996. *Estados Unidos Mexicanos. Conteo 95 de población y vivienda: Resultados definitivos, tabulados básicos.* Aguascalientes: INEGI.

Jackson, Jean. 1989. Is There a Way to Talk about Making Culture without Making Enemies? *Dialectical Anthropology* 14: 127–43.

————. 1991. Being and Becoming an Indian in the Vaupés. In *Nation-States and Indians in Latin America,* ed. Greg Urban and Joel Sherzer, 131–55. Austin: University of Texas Press.

Jelin, Elizabeth. 1997. Engendering Human Rights. In *Gender Politics in Latin America: Debates in Theory and Practice,* ed. Elizabeth Dore, 65–83. New York: Monthly Review Press.

Jimenez Pérez, Jorge C. 1988. Letter to Lic. Rodolfo el Cancino Cortes, secretario de la Comisión Agraria Mixta. Expediente 1725. 15 December 1988. Poblado Guadalupe Tepeyac, Acción Primera Ampliación. Registro Agrario Nacional, Tuxtla Gutiérrez.

Joseph, Gilbert M., and Daniel Nugent, eds. 1994. *Everyday Forms of State Formation: Revolution and the Negotiation of Rule in Modern Mexico.* Durham, N.C.: Duke University Press.

Kearney, Michael. 1996. *Reconceptualizing the Peasantry: Anthropology in Global Perspective.* Boulder, Colo.: Westview Press.

Keck, Margaret, and Kathryn Sikkink. 1998. *Activists without Borders: Trans-

national Advocacy Networks in International Politics. Ithaca, N.Y.: Cornell University Press.

Kleinman, Arthur, Veena Das, and Margaret Lock. 1997. *Social Suffering.* Berkeley and Los Angeles: University of California Press.

Kleist, Trina. 1996. Ailing Rebel Commander Urges Mexican Indians to Demand Rights. Associated Press, 12 October 1996 [wire.ap.org/apnews].

Knight, Alan. 1986. *The Mexican Revolution,* vol. 1: *Porfirians, Liberals, and Peasants.* Cambridge: Cambridge University Press.

———. 1994. Popular Culture and the Revolutionary State in Mexico, 1910–1940. *Hispanic American Historical Review* 74, 3: 393–443.

Kraul, Chris. 1999. Mexico Urged to Cut Chiapas Force. *Los Angeles Times,* 28 November 1999, 13A.

Krauze, Enrique. 1999. Chiapas: The Indians' Prophet. *New York Review of Books* 46, 2 (6 December 1999): 65–73.

Lauren, Paul Gordon. 1998. *The Evolution of International Human Rights: Visions Seen.* Philadelphia: University of Pennsylvania Press.

Le Bot, Yvon. 1997. *Subcomandante Marcos: El sueño zapatista.* Barcelona: Plaza & Janés Editores.

Ledesma Arronte, Ernesto, Gustavo E. Castro Soto, and Tedford P. Lewis, eds. 2000, *Always Near, Always Far: The Armed Forces in México.* San Francisco: Global Exchange.

Lenkersdorf, Carlos. 1996. *Los hombres verdaderos, voces y testimonios tojolabales: Lengua y sociedad, naturaleza y cultura, artes y comunidad cósmica.* México, D.F.: Siglo Veintiuno Editores.

Lenkersdorf, Carlos, and Gemma van der Haar, eds. 1998. *San Miguel Chiptik, testimonios de una comunidad tojolabal = San Migel Ch'ib'tik, ja'jastal 'aytiki.* México, D.F.: Siglo Veintiuno Editores.

Lewis, Stephen. 1997a. Revolution and the Rural Schoolhouse: Forging State and Nation in Chiapas, Mexico, 1913–1948. Ph.D. diss., Department of History, University of California, San Diego.

———. 1997b. Mestizaje. In *Encyclopedia of Mexico: History, Society, and Culture,* ed. Michael S. Werner, 2: 838–42. Chicago: Fitzroy Dearborn.

Leyva Solano, Xóchitl, and Gabriel Ascencio Franco. 1996. *Lacandona al filo del agua.* México, D.F.: Centro de Investigaciones y Estudios Superiores en Antropología Socials San Cristóbal de Las Casa: Centro de Investigaciones Humanísticas de Mesoamérica y el Estado de Chiapas / Tuxtla Gutiérrez: Universidad de Ciencias y Artes del Estado de Chiapas / México, D.F.: Fondo de Cultura Económica.

Leyva Solano, Xóchitl. 1995. Catequistas, misioneros, y tradiciones en Las Cañadas. In *Chiapas: Los rumbos de otra historia,* ed. Juan Pedro Viqueria and Mario Humberto Ruz, 375–406. México, D.F.: Universidad Nacional Autónoma de México.

List Arzubide, Germán. 1935. *Zapata: Exaltación.* México, D.F.: Secretaría de Educación Pública.

Lomas, Emilio. 1994. Salinas: No habrá retrocesos en las reformas a favor a campo. *La Jornada,* 11 April 1994, 3.

Lomelí González, Arturo. 1988. *Algunos costumbres y tradiciones del mundo tojolabal*. Publicación bilingüe de la Dirección de Fortalecimiento y Fomentos a las Culturas de la Sub-Secretaría de Asuntos Indígenas de Chiapas. Tuxtla Gutiérrez: Gobierno del Estado.

Lomnitz-Adler, Claudio. 1992. *Exits from the Labyrinth: Culture and Ideology in the Mexican National Space*. Berkeley and Los Angeles: University of California Press.

López y Menéndez, Marisol. 2000. The Army and the Public Security. In *Always Near, Always Far: The Armed Forces México*, ed. Ernesto Ledesma Arronte, Gustavo E. Castro Soto, and Tedford P. Lewis, 55–61. San Francisco: Global Exchange.

López y Velaquez, Jorge. 1985. Acuerdo. To Consultoria Regional del Cuerpo Consultivo Agrario from Lic. Jorge López y Velasquez, el Consejero Agrario, presidente de la Sala. Expediente 1725. 31 July 1985. Poblado Guadalupe Tepeyac. Acción Primera Ampliación. Registro Agrario Nacional, Tuxtla Gutiérrez.

Lucio, Gabriel. 1935a. *Simiente, Libro 1*. Libro primero para escuelas rurales. México, D.F.: Secretaría de Educación Pública.

———. 1935b. *Simiente, Libro 2*. Libro primero para escuelas rurales. México, D.F.: Secretaría de Educación Pública.

———. 1935c. *Simiente, Libro 3*. Libro primero para escuelas rurales. México, D.F.: Secretaría de Educación Pública.

———. 1935d. *Simiente, Libro 4*. Libro primero para escuelas rurales. México, D.F.: Secretaría de Educación Pública.

Malkki, Liisa H. 1995. *Purity and Exile: Violence, Memory, and National Cosmology among Hutu Refugees in Tanzania*. Chicago: University of Chicago Press.

———. 1997. News and Culture: Transitory Phenomena and the Fieldwork Tradition. In *Anthropological Locations: Boundaries and Grounds of a Field Science*, ed. Akhil Gupta and James Ferguson, 86–101. Berkeley and Los Angeles: University of California Press.

Mallon, Florencia. 1995. *Peasant and Nation: The Making of Postcolonial Mexico and Peru*. Berkeley and Los Angeles: University of California Press.

Manz, Beatriz. 1988. *Refugees of a Hidden War: The Aftermath of Counterinsurgency in Guatemala*. Albany: State University of New York Press.

Martin, JoAnne. 1993. Contesting Authenticity: Battles over the Representation of History in Morelos, Mexico. *Ethnohistory* 40, 3: 438–65.

Martínez, María Elena. 1997. Limpieza de Sangre. In *Encyclopedia of Mexico: History, Society and Culture*, ed. Michael Werner, 1: 749–52. Chicago: Fitzroy Dearborn.

Martínez Vásquez, Victor Raul. 1985. El régimen de García Vigil. In *La Revolución en Oaxaca, 1900–1930*, ed. Victor Raul Martínez Vásquez, 309–73. Oaxaca: Instituto de Administración Pública de Oaxaca.

———. 1994. *Historia de la educación en Oaxaca, 1825–1940*. Oaxaca: Instituto de Investigaciones Sociológicas, Universidad Autónoma Benito Juárez de Oaxaca.

Mattiace, Shannan. 1997. Zapata Vive! The EZLN, Indian Politics, and the Autonomy Movement in Mexico. *Journal of Latin American Anthropology* 3, 1: 32–71.

———. 1998. Peasant and Indian: Political Identity and Indian Autonomy in Chiapas, Mexico, 1970–1990. Ph.D. diss., Department of Political Science, University of Texas, Austin.

———. 2001. Regional Renegotiations of Spaces: Tojolabal Ethnic Identity in Las Margaritas, Chiapas. *Latin American Perspectives* 28, 2: 73–97.

Mejía Piñero, María Conseulo, and Sergio Sarmiento Silva. 1987. *La lucha indígena: Un reto a la ortodoxia*. México, D.F.: Siglo Veintiuno Editores.

Meneses, Juan Anzaldo. 1996. Nunca mas un México sin nosotros: Resolutivos del Congreso Nacional Indigena. Mimeographed.

Merry, Sally Engle. 1997. Legal Pluralism and Transnational Culture: The *Ka Ho'okolokolonui Kanaka Maoli* Tribunal, Hawai'i, 1993. In *Human Rights, Culture, and Context: Anthropological Perspectives,* ed. Richard A. Wilson, 28–48. London: Pluto Press.

Messer, Ellen. 1993. Anthropology and Human Rights. *Annual Review of Anthropology* 22: 221–49.

———. 1995. Anthropology and Human Rights in Latin America. *Journal of Latin American Anthropology* 1, 1: 48–97.

Mestries, Francis. 1990. Testimonio del congeso indígena de San Cristóbal de las Casas, October 1974. In *Historia de la cuestión agraria Mexicana: Los tiempos de la crisis (segunda parte) 1970–1982,* ed. Julio Moguel, 451–89. México, D.F.: Siglo Veintiuno Editores / Centro de Estudios Históricos del Agrarismo en México.

Meyer, Michael C., and William M. Sherman. 1995. *The Course of Mexican History.* New York: Oxford University Press.

Moguel, Julio, ed. 1990. *Historia de la cuestión agraria Mexicana: Los tiempos de la crisis (segunda parte), 1970–1982.* México, D.F.: Siglo Veintiuno Editores / Centro de Estudios Históricos del Agrarismo en México.

———. 1993. PROCAMPO y la vía campesina de desarrollo. *Jornada del Campo* 2, 20 (March 26–October 1993): 8–9.

Montagu, Roberta. 1969. The Tojolabal. In *Handbook of Middle American Indians,* vols. 7–9: *Ethnology,* ed. Evon Z. Vogt, 1: 226–29. Austin: University of Texas Press.

Morales Bermúdez, Jesús. 1992. El congreso indígena de Chiapas: Un testimonio. In *Anuario de cultura e invastigación, 1991,* 242–370. Tuxtla Gutiérrez, Chiapas: Instituto Chiapaneco de Cultura.

Müller-Hill, Benno. 1988. *Murderous Science: Elimination by Scientific Selection of Jews, Gypsies, and Others, Germany, 1933–1945.* Translated by George R. Fraser. New York: Oxford University Press.

Nagengast, Carole. 1994. Violence, Terror, and the Crisis of the State. *Annual Review of Anthropology* 23: 109–36.

Nash, June. 1997. Press Reports on the Chiapas Uprising: Towards a Transnationalized Communication. *Journal of Latin American Anthropology* 2, 2: 42–75.

Nelson, Diane. 1999. *A Finger in the Wound: Body Politics in Quincentennial Guatemala.* Berkeley and Los Angeles: University of California Press.

Nordstrom, Carolyn. 1997. *A Different Kind of War Story.* Philadelphia: University of Pennsylvania Press.

Nordstrom, Carolyn, and Antonius C. G. M. Robben, eds.. 1995. *Fieldwork under Fire: Contemporary Studies of Violence and Survival.* Berkeley and Los Angeles: University of California Press.

Nugent, Daniel. 1993. *Spent Cartridges of Revolution: An Anthropological History of Namiquipa, Chihuahua.* Chicago: University of Chicago Press.

Nugent, Daniel, and Ana María Alonso. 1994. Multiple Selective Traditions in Agrarian Reform and Agrarian Struggle: Popular Culture and State Formation in the *Ejido* of Namiquipa. In *Everyday Forms of State Formation: Revolution and the Negotiation of Rule in Modern Mexico,* ed. Gilbert Joseph and Daniel Nugent, 209–46. Durham, N.C.: Duke University Press.

Oaxaca Nuevo. 1937a. Solemne conmemoración de la muerte de Zapata, la obra de revoluciónes ya una realidad, numerosos campesinos tomaron posesión de sus tierras. *Oaxaca Nuevo,* 10 April 1937, 1.

———. 1937b. Un ejido modelo será creado en Santa María del Tule. *Oaxaca Nuevo,* 12 April 1937, 1, 6.

———. 1937c. Importantes trabajos en Unión Zapata, Tlacolula: Se realiza la localización y planeación técnica del poblado yotras mejoras. *Oaxaca Nuevo,* 15 April 1937, 1, 5.

———. 1937d. La dotación ejidal se intensifica en Oaxaca. *Oaxaca Nuevo,* 19 April 1937, 1, 2.

Oficina de Derechos Humanos del Arzobispado de Guatemala. 1998. *Nunca más: Informe proyecto interdiocesano de recuperación de la memoria histórica.* 4 vols. Guatemala: Oficina de Derechos Humanos del Arzobispado de Guatemala.

Ong, Aiwa. 1999. *Flexible Citizenship: The Cultural Logics of Transnationality.* Durham, N.C.: Duke University Press.

Ordoñez, José A. 1985. Report from José Adrian Ordoñez to C. Ing. Luis J. Garza Torres, delegado de la Secretaría de la Reforma Agraria. Expediente 3024.2/A. 25 April 1985. Población Guadalupe Tepeyac, Acción Segundo Ampliación. Registro Agrario Nacional, Tuxtla Gutiérrez.

Ornelas López, José Luz. 1988. El periodo cardenista (1934–1940). In *Historía de la cuestión agraria Mexicana: Estado de Oaxaca,* ed. Leticia Reina, vol. 2: *1925–1986,* 127–88. México, D.F.: Juan Pablos Editor/Gobierno de Estado de Oaxaca, Universidad Autónoma Benito Juárez de Oaxaca, and Centro de Estudios Históricos del Agrarismo en México.

Ortega, Miguel Angel. 1994. La guerilla anunciada. *Financiero,* 18 November 1994, 54–55.

Palacios, Guillermo. 1998. Postrevolutionary Intellectuals, Rural Readings, and the Shaping of the "Peasant Problem" in Mexico: El Maestro Rural, 1932–1934. *Journal of Latin American Studies* 30: 309–39.

Paré, Luisa. 1990. The Challenge of Rural Democratization in Mexico. *Journal of Development Studies* 26 (July): 79–96.

Payán Velez, Carlos, Epigemio Ibarra, and Hernán Vera. 1994. *Viaje al Centro de La Selva: Memorial Zapatista, enero–agosto 1994.* México, D.F.: Servicios Informativos S.A. de C.V. Videotape.

Pérez Castro, Anna Bella. 1995. Bajo el símbolo de la ceiba: La lucha de los indígenas cafeticultores de las tierras de Simojovel. In *Chiapas: Los rumbos de otra historia,* ed. Juan Pedro Viqueria and Mario Humberto Ruz, 301–19. México, D.F.: Universidad Nacional Autónoma de México.

Pérez, Matilde. 1994. Nuevo desarollo rural, piden 50 mil personas en el Zócalo. *La Jornada,* 11 April 1994, 5.

Pérez, Matilde, and Rosa Rojas. 1996. La bandera fue el regalo que entregó ayer la comandante Ramona al Congreso Nacional Indígena y allá pidió a los 600 delegados presentes seguir luchando unidos y no quedarse rezgados. *La Jornada,* 12 October 1996.

Periodico Oficial. 1955. Solicitudes de dotación y ampliación de ejidos de la Comisión Agraria Mixta. Publicación No. 74. *Periódico Oficial* 72, 7 (16 February 1955): 5–6. Gobierno Constitucional del Estado Libre y Soberano de Chiapas, Tuxtla Gutiérrez.

——. 1963 Resolución del expediente relativo a la privación de derechos agrarios y reconocimientos de los correspondientes a campesinos del poplado Guadalupe Tepeyac, Municipio de Las Margaritas, Chiapas. Publicación No. 37-B. *Periodico Oficial* 80, 26 (26 June 1963): 5–6. Gobierno Constitucional del Estado Libre y Soberano de Chiapas, Tuxtla Gutiérrez.

Petrich, Blanche, and Elio Henríquez. 1994. Ellos dijeron: "La muerte es nuestra. Ahora decidimos como tomarla." *La Jornada,* 6 February 1994, 6–7.

Pinacho, Juventina. 1938. Inventorio de los muebles e útiles escolares [Inventory of furniture and educational tools] existentes en la Escuela Mixta Federalizada de la Villa Tlalixtac de Cabrera en el año de 1938. Fondo de Educación, Sección Administrativa, Archivo General del Estado, Oaxaca.

Preston, Julia. 2000. Peaceful Raid in Mexico Ends Students' Siege. *New York Times,* 17 February 2000, A1, A3.

Primer Congreso Nacional Pro-Educación Popular. 1937. Memo outlining program of Congress from Professors Luis Chávez Orozco, Ignacio Marquez R., Miguel Huerta, Rafael Méndez Aguirre, Candido Jaramillo, and Moreno García, México D.F., 5 October 1937. Fondo de Educación, 1937, Caja 2, Educación, Educación Federal, Varios Districtos, Archivo General Del Estado, Oaxaca.

Proceso. 1998. No. 1106, 11 January 1998.

Procuraduría Agraria. 1993a. *PROCEDE, Programa de certificación de derechos ejidales y titulación de solares urbanos: Documento guía.* México, D.F.: Procuraduría Agraria.

——. 1993b. *Procuraduría agraria, libertad, y justicia al campo mexicano.* Brochure. México, D.F.: Procuraduría Agraria.

——. 1993c. *Yecapixtla, Morelos: Crónica.* México, D.F.: Procuraduría Agraria.

——. Delegación Oaxaca. 1996. *La situación agraria en Oaxaca.* Oaxaca: Procuraduría Agraria.

——. Delegación Chiapas. 1996a. *Coordinación estatal del procede.* Tuxtla Gutiérrez: Procuraduría Agraria.

——. 1996b. *Procede Chiapas, Corte* [Cut-off date] *15/6/96.* Tuxtla Gutiérrez: Procuraduría Agraria.

Purnell, Jennifer. 1997. Cristero Rebellion. In *Encyclopedia of Mexico: History, Society and Culture*, ed. Michael S. Werner, 1: 374–78. Chicago: Fitzroy Dearborn.

———. 1999. *Popular Movements and State Formation in Revolutionary Mexico: The Agraristas and Cristeros of Michoacán*. Durham, N.C.: Duke University Press.

Radcliffe, Sarah, and Sallie Westwood. 1996. *Remaking the Nation: Place, Identity, and Politics in Latin America*. London: Routledge.

Ramírez Erastro, Ernesto. 1935. A los C.C. Directores y Señoritas Directoras de las Escuelas ubicadas en los lugares que al margen se expresen. Circular 3, Etla, Oaxaca, 19 February 1935, from Ernesto Ramírez. Loose unclassified bundle from 1935. Fondo de Educación, Archivo General Del Estado, Oaxaca.

Ramírez, Isaias, Lauro Aragón, and Guadalupe Bautista. 1935. Letter to jefe del Departamento Agrario, México, D.F. Asunto: Se apoyan gestiones hechas con anterioridad para obtener dotación definitive reproduciendo algunos puntos imporantes del proyecto de la organización agraria del lugar. Expediente 23: 13385 (723.7). 11 October 1935. Loma Larga / Unión Zapata. Registro Agrario Nacional, Oaxaca.

Ramos, Alícida. 1998. *Indigenism: Ethnic Politics in Brazil*. Madison: University of Wisconsin Press.

———. 1999–2000. Anthropologist as Political Actor. *Journal of Latin American Anthropology* 4, 2–5, 1: 172–89.

Rand Parish, Helen. 1997. Bartolomé de Las Casas. In *Encyclopedia of Mexico: History, Society, and Culture*, ed. Michael S. Werner, 1: 730–33. Chicago: Fitzroy Dearborn.

Randall, Laura. 1996. *Reforming Mexico's Agrarian Reform*. Armonk, N.Y.: M. E. Sharpe.

Rappaport, Joanne. 1994. *Cumbe Reborn: An Andean Ethnography of History*. Chicago: University of Chicago Press.

———. 1996. Ethnicity Reconfigured: Indigenous Legislators and the Colombian Constitution of 1991. *Journal of Latin American Anthropology* 1, 2 (Spring 1996).

———. 1998. *The Politics of Memory: Native Historical Interpretation in the Colombian Andes*. 2d ed. Durham, N.C.: Duke University Press.

Regino Montes, Adelfo. 1996. Los derechos indígenas, en serio. *La Jornada*, 22 October 1996.

Registro Agrario Nacional. Delegación Chiapas. 1997. Avances del procede por regiones economicas. 31 May 1997. Registro Agrario Nacional, Tuxtla Gutiérrez.

———. Delegación Oaxaca. 1997. Numero de ejidos certificados por región. 10 April 1997. Registro Agrario Nacional, Oaxaca.

Reina, Leticia. 1988. De las reformas borbonicas a las leyes de la reforma. In *Historía de la cuestion agraria mexicana: Estado de Oaxaca*, ed. id., vol. 1: *Prehispanico–1924*, 181–269. México, D.F.: Juan Pablos Editor / Gobierno de Estado de Oaxaca, Universidad Autónoma Benito Juárez de Oaxaca, and Centro de Estudios Históricos del Agrarismo en México.

Renteln, Alison Dundes. 1990. *International Human Rights: Universalism versus Relativism*. Thousand Oaks, Calif.: Sage.

Reyes Ramos, María Eugenia. 1992. *El reparto de tierras y la política agraria en Chiapas, 1914–1988*. México, D.F.: Universidad Nacional Antónoma de México, Centro de Investigaciones Humanísticas de Mesoamérica y del Estado de Chiapas.

Reyes Ramos, María Eugenia, and Álvaro F. López Lara. 1994. Una década de programas agrarios en Chiapas. *Cuadernos Agrarios*, n.s., 4, 8–9: 10–19.

Reza, Rocio. 1995. *"Paz con justicia y dignidad para los pueblos Indios." Testimonios: Comandante Tacho y Mayor Moisés. Documentos de La Selva Lacandona III*, vol. 1, parts 1 and 2a. México, D.F.: Medios del Sur. Videotapes.

Riley, G. Michael. 1997. Marquesado del Valle. In *Encyclopedia of Mexico: History, Society, and Culture*, ed. Michael S. Werner, 2: 781–82. Chicago: Fitzroy Dearborn.

Rivera Salgado, Gaspar. 1999. Welcome to Oaxacalifornia. *Cultural Survival Quarterly* 23, 1: 59–61.

Rojas, Rosa. 1994. *Chiapas: ¿y las mujeres qué?* México, D.F.: Ediciones la Correa Feminista, Centro de Investigación de la Mujer, A.C.

Romero Frizzi, María de los Angeles. 1988. Epoca colonial (1519–1785). In *Historía de la cuestion agraria mexicana: Estado de Oaxaca*, ed. Leticia Reina, vol. 1: *Prehispanico–1924*, 107–80. México, D.F.: Juan Pablos Editor/Gobierno de Estado de Oaxaca, Universidad Autónoma Benito Juárez de Oaxaca, and Centro de Estudios Históricos del Agrarismo en México.

Roseberry, William. 1989. *Anthropologies and Histories: Essays in Culture, History, and Political Economy*. New Brunswick, N.J.: Rutgers University Press.

———. 1994. Hegemony and the Language of Convention. In *Everyday Forms of State Formation: Revolution and the Negotiation of Rule in Modern Mexico*, ed. Gil Joseph and Daniel Nugent, 355–66. Durham, N.C.: Duke University Press.

Ross, John. 1994. *Rebellion from the Roots: Indian Uprising in Chiapas*. Monroe, Me.: Common Courage Press.

Rovira, Guiomar. 1994. *¡Zapata Vive! La rebelión indígena de Chiapas contada por sus protagonistas*. Barcelona: Virus Editorial.

———. 1997. *Mujeres de Maíz*. México, D.F.: Ediciones Era.

Rubin, Jeffrey W. 1990. Rethinking Post-Revolutionary Mexico: Popular Movements and the Myth of the Corporatist State. In *Popular Movements and Political Change in Mexico*, ed. Joe Foweraker and Ann L. Craig, 247–70. Boulder, Colo.: Lynne Reinner.

———. 1997. *Decentering the Regime: Ethnicity, Radicalism, and Democracy in Juchitán, Mexico*. Durham, N.C.: Duke University Press.

Ruiz, Gustavo. 1936. Suplica que se le den garantías. Letter from Gustavo Ruiz to Ciudadano Gobernador Constitutional del Estado. Loma Larga/Unión Zapata. Legado 999, Expediente 18. 7 November 1936. Asuntos Agrarios, Archivo General del Estado de Oaxaca.

Ruiz Cervantes, Francisco José. 1985. El movimiento de la soberanía en Oaxaca (1915–1920). In *La revolución en Oaxaca, 1900–1930*, ed. Victor Raul

Martínez Vásquez, 225–308. Oaxaca: Instituto de Administración Publica de Oaxaca.

———. 1988. De la bola a los primeros repartos. In *Historía de la cuestion agraria mexicana: Estado de Oaxaca*, ed. Leticia Reina, vol. 1: *Prehispanico-1924*, 333–423. México, D.F.: Juan Pablos Editor / Gobierno de Estado de Oaxaca, Universidad Autónoma Benito Juárez de Oaxaca, and Centro de Estudios Históricos del Agrarismo en México.

———. 1990. Movimientos Zapatistas en Oaxaca: Una primera mirada, 1911–1916. In *Lecturas históricas del estado de Oaxaca*, vol. 4: *1877–1930*, ed. Maria de los Angeles Romero Frizzi, 273–88. México, D.F.: Instituto Nacional de Antropología e Historia.

Runsten, David, and Michael Kearney. 1994. *A Survey of Oaxacan Village Networks in California Agriculture*. Davis: California Institute for Rural Studies.

Rus, Jan. 1983. Whose Caste War? Indians, Ladinos, and the "Caste War" of 1869. In *Spaniards and Indians in Southeastern Mesoamerica: Essays on the History of Ethnic Relations*, ed. Murdo J. Macleod and Robert Wasserstrom, 127–68. Lincoln: University of Nebraska Press.

———. 1989. The "Caste War" of 1869 from the Indian's Perspective: A Challenge for Ethnohistory. In *Memorias del Segundo Coloquio de Mayaistas*, 2: 1033–47. México, D.F.: Universidad Nacional Autónoma de México.

———. 1994. The "Comunidad Revolucionaria Institutional": The Subversion of Native Government in Highland Chiapas, 1936–1968. In *Everyday Forms of State Formation: Revolution and the Negotiation of Rule in Modern Mexico,* ed. Gilbert M. Joseph and Daniel Nugent, 265–300. Durham, N.C.: Duke University Press.

Rus, Jan, Diana Rus, and José Hernández, eds. and trs. 1990. *Abtel ta pinka: Lo'iletik sventa il inyoetik tzotziletik ta pinkaetik sventa kajvel ta Chiapa / Trabajo en las fincas: Pláticas de los Tzotziles sobre las fincas cafetaleras de Chiapas*. San Cristóbal de las Casas: Instituto de Asesoría Antropológica para la Región Maya.

Ruz, Mario Humberto. 1981. *Los legítimos hombres: Aproximación antropológica al grupo tojolabal*. 4 vols. Mexico, D.F.: Centro de Estudios Mayas de la UNAM.

———. 1992. Tributarios y peones, pueblos y estancias, en los llanos de Chiapas (siglos XVIII y XIX). Paper presented at the Second International Congress of Mayanists, 24–28 August 1992, Centro de Estudios Mayas de la Universidad Nacional Autónoma de México e Instituto de Cultura de Yucatán, Gobierno del Estado de Yucatán, Merida,.

———. 1994. *Los Tojolabales*. Instituto Nacional Indigenista [INI] monograph. México, D.F.: INI.

Sáenz, Moisés. 1928. *La educación rural en México*. México, D.F.: Publicaciones de la Secretaría de Educación Pública.

Salinas de Gotari, Carlos. 1993. Palabras del Presidente de la Republica, Lic. Carlos Salinas de Gotari en la reunion efectuada en el salon "Adolfo López Mateo" en la residencia oficial de los pinos. Programa de Apoyos al Campo, 1993. México, D.F. a 24 de Febrero de 1993. Speech. Mimeographed.

Sam Colop, Luis Enrique. 1990. Foreign Scholars and Mayas: What Are the Issues? In *Guatemala Scholars Network News,* coordinated by Marilyn Moores. Washington, D.C.: Guatemalan Scholars Network.

Sassen, Saskia. 1998. *Globalization and Its Discontents: Essays on the New Mobility of People and Money.* New York: Free Press.

Scheper-Hughes, Nancy. *Death without Weeping: The Violence of Everyday Life in Brazil.* Berkeley and Los Angeles: University of California Press, 1992.

Scott, James C. 1998. *Seeing Like a State: How Certain Schemes to Improve the Human Condition Have Failed.* New Haven, Conn.: Yale University Press.

Secretaría de Agricultura y Recursos Hidráulicos. 1993. *PROCAMPO: Vamos al grano para progresar.* Booklet. México, D.F.: SARH.

Secretaría de Educación Pública. 1935. *Plan de accion de la escuela primaria socialista.* México, D.F.: SEP.

———. 1938. *Libro de lectura para uso de las escuelas nocturnas para trabajadores 1er grado.* México, D.F.: Comisión Editor Popular de la Secretaría de Educación Pública.

———. 1982. *Memoría 1976/1982,* vol. 1: *Delegaciones estatales.* México, D.F.: SEP.

Secretaría de Reforma Agraria. 1992. *Ley Agraria 1992.* México, D.F.: SRA.

Secretaría de Reforma Agraria, CORETT. 1996. *Atlas agrario del estado de Oaxaca.* Oaxaca: Registro Agrario Nacional, Procuraduría Agraria.

Secretaría de Reforma Agraria, Delegación de Oaxaca. 1917a. Informe que rinde el Delegado de la Comisión Nacional Agraria en el Estado de Oaxaca, para acompañarlo en complimiento de la misma comisión y de las circulares relativas al expediente sobre restitución de tierras (ejidos) al pueblo denominado Santa María del Tule. File for Santa Maria del Tule. 18 August 1917. Registro Agrario Nacional, Oaxaca; previously in the Archive of the Secretaría de Reforma Agraria, Delegación de Oaxaca.

———. 1917b [1922 copy]. Dictamen relativo al expediente del pueblo de Santa María del Tule, Centro, Oaxaca. File for Santa María del Tule. 14 August 1917. Copy dated 15 September 1922. Written by Juan Olivera, Secretario de la Comisión Local Agraria en el Estado de Oaxaca. Registro Agrario Nacional, Oaxaca; previously in the Archive of the Secretaría de Reforma Agraria, Delegación de Oaxaca.

———. 1926a. Memorandum del Oficio Mayor de la Comisión Nacional Agraria al C. Delegado de la Comisión Nacional Agraria en el Estado de Oaxaca, ordenándole remíta datos é informes con justificación acerca de la situación de hecho o de derecho guarde asuno agrario del pueblo de Santa María del Tule, Oaxaca. File for Santa María del Tule. 25 August 1926. Registro Agrario Nacional, Oaxaca; previously in the Archive of the Secretaría de Reforma Agraria, Delegación de Oaxaca.

———. 1926b. Memorandum del Oficio Mayor de la Comisión Nacional Agraria para el C. Vocal Ing. Ignacio M. Cabañas Flores, relativo al estado de tramitación que guarda el expediente de dotación de ejidos promovidos por los vecinos del pueblo de Santa María del Tule. File for Santa María

del Tule. 20 September 1926. Registro Agrario Nacional, Oaxaca; previously in the Archive of the Secretaría de Reforma Agraria, Delegación de
Oaxaca.

———. 1927. Memorandum del Jefe del Departamento Tecnico de la Comisión
Nacional Agraria, Ing. Bartolomé Vargas Lugo, al Delegado de la Comisión
Nacional Agraria en Oaxaca, que procede hacer la rectificación del ejido del
pueblo de Santa María el Tule. File for Santa María del Tule. 7 March 1927.
Registro Agrario Nacional, Oaxaca; previously in the Archive of the Secre-
taría de Reforma Agraria, Delegación de Oaxaca.

———. 1935. Acta complementaria de posesión y deslinde relativa a dotación
de ejidos al pueblo de Santa Maria del Tule, municipio del mismo nombre,
del ex-dto. del Central del Estado de Oaxaca. File for Santa María del Tule.
28 October 1935. Registro Agrario Nacional, Oaxaca; previously in the Archive of the Secretaría de Reforma Agraria, Delegación de Oaxaca.

———. 1937. Acta de posesión provisional y deslinde por amplificación relativa
al poblado de Unión Zapata, Municipio de Mitla, ex-Distrito de Tlacolula,
Estado de Oaxaca. File for Unión Zapata. 13 November 1937. Registro
Agrario Nacional, Oaxaca; previously in the Archive of the Secretaría de Reforma Agraria, Delegación de Oaxaca.

Servicio Internacional para la Paz [SIPAZ]. 1999. Urgent Action: In Defense of the Protectors of Mexican Human Rights, 15 November 1999
[www.sipaz.org].

Sikkink, Kathryn. 1991. *Ideas and Institutions: Developmentalism in Brazil
and Argentina*. Ithaca, N.Y.: Cornell University Press.

Smith, Carol. 1990. Origins of the National Question in Guatemala: A Hypothesis. In *Guatemalan Indians and the State, 1540–1988*, ed. C. Smith,
72–95. Austin: University of Texas Press.

Snyder, Richard, and Gabriel Torres, eds. 1998. *The Future Role of the Ejido in
Rural Mexico*. La Jolla: Center for U.S.–Mexican Studies, University of California, San Diego.

Solis Ruiz, Julio César. 1988. Informe al C. delegado de la secretaría de la Reforma Agraria, en el Estado de Chiapas. Annexo, Acta de Conformidad. Expediente 3024–2-A. 13 April 1988. Poblado Guadalupe Tepeyac. Acción segunda ampliación. Registro Agrario Nacional, Tuxtla Gutiérrez.

Stavenhagen, Rodolfo. 1996. *Ethnic Conflicts and the Nation-State*. New York:
St. Martin's Press.

Stephen, Lynn. 1991. *Zapotec Women*. Austin: University of Texas Press.

———. 1995. The Zapatista Army of National Liberation and the National
Democratic Convention. *Latin American Perspectives* 22, 4 (Fall 1995):
88–99.

———. 1997a. The Zapatista Opening: The Movement for Indigenous Autonomy and State Discourses on Indigenous Rights in Mexico. *Journal of Latin
American Anthropology* 2, 2: 2–41.

———. 1997b. Redefined Nationalism in Building a Movement for Indigenous
Autonomy in Southern Mexico. *Journal of Latin American Anthropology* 3,
1: 72–101.

———. 1999a. Introduction. *Cultural Survival Quarterly* 23, 1: 23–26.

———. 1999b. The First Anniversary of the Acteal Massacre. *Cultural Survival Quarterly* 23, 1: 27–29.

———. 2000. The Construction of Indigenous Suspects: Militarization and the Gendered and Ethnic Dynamics of Human Rights Abuses in Southern Mexico. *American Ethnologist* 26, 4: 822–42.

———. Forthcoming. In the Wake of the Zapatistas: U.S. Solidarity Work Focused on Militarization, Human Rights, and Democratization in Chiapas. In *Cross-Border Learning: Lessons from U.S.–Mexico Social Movement Dialogues*, ed. Jonathan Fox and David Brocks. La Jolla: Center for U.S.–Mexican Studies, University of California, San Diego.

Stephen, Lynn, and George Collier. 1997. Reconfiguring Ethnicity, Identity, and Citizenship in the Wake of the Zapatista Rebellion. *Journal of Latin American Anthropology* 3, 1: 2–13.

Stoll, David. 1999. *Rigoberta Menchú and the Story of All Poor Guatemalans*. Boulder, Colo.: Westview Press.

Subcomandante Marcos. 1995. *Shadows of Tender Fury: The Letters and Communiqués of Subcomandante Marcos and the Zapatista Army of National Liberation*. New York: Monthly Review Press.

Sullivan, Paul. 1997. Southern Borders. In *Encyclopedia of Mexico: History, Society, and Culture*, ed. Michael S. Werner, 2: 1363–68. Chicago: Fitzroy Dearborn.

Tambiah, Stanley J. 1990. Presidential Address: Reflections on Communal Violence in South Asia. *Journal of Asian Studies* 40, 4: 741–60.

Taussig, Michael. 1984. Culture of Terror, Space of Death: Roger Casement and the Explanation of Torture. *Comparative Studies of Society and History* 26: 467–97.

Taylor, William. 1972. *Landlord and Peasant in Colonial Oaxaca*. Stanford, Calif.: Stanford University Press.

———. 1979. *Drinking, Homicide, and Rebellion in Colonial Mexican Villages*. Stanford, Calif.: Stanford University Press.

Tello Díaz, Carlos. 1995. *La rebelión de las Cañadas*. México, D.F.: Cal y Arena.

Thomas, John S., and M. Jill Brody. 1988. The Tojolabal Maya: Ethnographic and Linguistic Approaches. In *Geoscience and Man* 26: 1–8.

Thompson, Richard H. 1997. Ethnic Minorities and the Case for Collective Rights. *American Anthropologist* 99, 4: 786–98.

Tutino, John. 1986. *From Insurrection to Revolution in Mexico: Social Bases of Agrarian Violence, 1750- 1940*. Princeton, N.J.: Princeton University Press.

———. 1993. Ethnic Resistance: Juchitán in Mexican History. In *Zapotec Struggles: Histories, Politics, and Representations from Juchitán, Oaxaca*, ed. Howard Campbell, Leigh Binford, Miguel Bartolomé and Alicia Barabas, 42–62. Washington, D.C.: Smithsonian Institution Press.

Urbina, Erastro. 1944. El despertar de un pueblo: Memorias relativas a la evolución indígena en el estado de Chiapas. MS. Library of the Centro de Investigaciones Ecológicas del Sureste, San Cristóbal, Chiapas.

Van Cott, Donna. [1994] 1995. Indigenous Peoples and Democracy: Issues for Policymakers. In *Indigenous Peoples and Democracy in Latin America*, ed.

Donna Lee Van Cott, 1–28. New York: St. Martin's Press, in association with Inter-American Dialogue.

Vasconcelos, José. 1958. Raza cósmica. In *Obras Completas*, 2: 903–1068. México, D.F.: Libreros Mexicanos Unidos.

———. 1997. *The Cosmic Race / La raza cósmica*. Translated with an introduction by Didier T. Jaén. Baltimore: Johns Hopkins University Press.

Vaughn, Mary Kay. 1982. *The State, Education, and Social Class in Mexico, 1880–1928*. DeKalb: Northern Illinois University Press.

———. 1997. *Cultural Politics in Revolution: Teachers, Peasants, and Schools in Mexico, 1930–1940*. Tucson: University of Arizona Press.

Velásquez Andrade, Manuel. 1933. *Fermín: Libro de lectura para primer año*. México, D.F.: Secretaría de Educación Pública.

Velasco, Ismael [procurador de pueblos of the Departamento Agrario]. 1934. Informe sobre dificultades del poblado citada. Loma Larga / Unión Zapata, Expediente 23: 13385 (727.7). 30 April 1934. Registro Agrario Nacional, Oaxaca.

Villafuerte Solís, Daniel, Salvador Meza Díaz, Gabriel Ascencio Franco, María del Carmen García Aguilar, Carolina Rivera Farfán, Miguel Lisbona Guillén, and Jesús Morales Mermúdez. 1999. *La tierra en Chiapas: Viejos problemas nuevos*. México, D.F.: Plaza y Valdes Editores.

Viquera, Juan Pedro. 1995. Chiapas y sus regiones. In *Chiapas: Los rumbos de otra historia*, ed. Juan Pedro Viqueira and Mario Humberto Ruz, 19–40. México, D.F.: Universidad Nacional Autónoma de México.

Warman, Arturo. 1993. Primer informe de labores. *Espacios* (Boletín Informativo de la Procuraduría Agraria) 2 (May–June 1993): 2–6.

Warren, Kay. 1992. Transforming Memories and Histories: The Meanings of Ethnic Resurgence for Mayan Indians. In *Americas: New Interpretive Essays*, ed. Alfred Stepan, 189–219. New York: Oxford University Press.

———. 1993. Interpreting *La Violencia* in Guatemala: Shapes of Mayan Silence and Resistance. In *The Violence Within: Cultural and Political Opposition in Divided Nations*, ed. Kay Warren, 25–56. Boulder, Colo.: Westview Press.

———. 1998. *Indigenous Movements and Their Critics: Pan-Maya Activism in Guatemala*. Princeton, N.J.: Princeton University Press.

Wasserstrom, Robert. 1983. *Class and Society in Central Chiapas*. Berkeley and Los Angeles: University of California Press.

Waterbury, Ronald. 1975. Non-revolutionary Peasants: Oaxaca Compared to Morelos in the Mexican Revolution. *Comparative Studies in Society and History* 17, 4: 410–42.

Wilson, Richard A. 1997. Human Rights, Culture, and Context: An Introduction. In *Human Rights, Culture, and Context: Anthropological Perspectives*, ed. Richard A. Wilson, 1–27. London: Pluto Press.

Williams, Raymond. 1994. Selections from Marxism and Literature. In *Culture / Power/History*, ed. Nicholas B. Dirks, Geoff Eley, and Sherry Ortner, 585–609. Princeton, N.J.: Princeton University Press.

Womack, John, Jr. 1968. *Zapata and the Mexican Revolution*. New York: Vintage Books.

————. 1999. *Rebellion in Chiapas: An Historical Reader.* New York: New Press.

Yashar, Deborah. 1999. Democracy, Indigenous Movements, and the Postliberal Challenge in Latin America. *World Politics* 52, 1: 76–104.

Zedillo, Ernesto. 1997. *Tercer informe de gobierno, primero de septiembre, 1997: Annexo.* México, D.F.: Presidencia de la República.

Zúñiga, Juan Antonio, and Herman Bellinghausen. 1997. Me hice zapatista para que mejoren nuestras comunidades: Trinidad. In *Las Alzadas*, ed. Sara Lovera and Nellys Paloma, 339–41 (México, D.F.: Comunicación e Información de la Mujer/Convergencia Socialista, Agrupación Política Nacional, 1997; rev ed. 1999).

.

Index

ACIEZ (Alianza Campesina Independiente "Emiliano Zapata"), 137
Acosta, Mariclaire, 320
Acteal, Chiapas, 15, 321, 322–27; massacre of Tzotziles (1997), 22, 172–73,
199, 322, 323, 324–27, 331
activism, 150; anthropological, 14–15,
25, 343–44; assassinations influencing, 129; Church and, 114–15; U.S.-
Mexican binational, 343–44. See also
agrarismo; demonstrations; EZLN;
grassroots movements; indigenous
rights movements; labor organizations;
peasant organizations; rebellions
adjudiciaciones, 228
African descent, 84–85, 86
age: Oaxaca *ejidatarios,* 259, 351n9,
352n5; voters in 2000 election, 317
Agrarian Agreement Program (1988-92),
Chiapas, 78, 79
Agrarian Attorney General's Office. *See*
Procuraduría Agraria
Agrarian Department, Oaxaca, 55–57,
233, 243, 251–53, 269, 274, 280,
285
agrarian reform: Cárdenas programs
(1930s), xxxv, xxxviii, 42–43, 46–50,
53–60, 68–69, 73, 80, 99, 101, 150;
Chiapas, 60–61, 77–80, 99, 107–9,
132; Cristero Rebellion vs. (1926-29),
39; Federal Law (1971), 4, 119; Mexican Revolution and, xxvi, 3, 4, 6–9,

38, 54–58, 67–74, 338; Oaxaca, 227–
29; Plan de Ayala, xxxiii, 37–38, 42–
43, 69–70, 126; regional variation in
evaluating, 315; Salinas de Gortari
programs (1988-92), xxx, xlii, 65, 67,
70–72, 78; and women's land rights,
3–4, 349n1; Zapatista Revolutionary
Law of, 152–58. *See also agrarismo;*
agricultural land; Article 27 (agrarian
reform), Mexican Constitution (1917);
ejidos; land laws; land redistribution
Agrarian Rehabilitation Plan (1984), 77–
78, 130
agrarian tribunals, 66
agrarismo: as national symbol, xxxv, 44–
50, 53–58, 150. See also *agraristas*
agraristas, 46, 54, 275, 278, 285. *See
also* agrarian reform; *agrarismo*
agricultural labor: Chiapas, 60–61, 91–
108, 110–11, 114; migrant, 60, 97–
98, 107, 237–38; Oaxaca, 237–38,
241, 270–74, 276–77, 280, 285,
351n1; physical beatings, 272–73
agricultural land: backlog of petitions
for, 77, 137–38; Chiapas, 91–102,
108–15, 120–33; collective, 153, 154,
155–56, 157; extensions to, 113, 120–
24, 130–33, 136–37, 140, 276; Oaxaca, 219, 220–29, 241–86, 292–93;
Zapata's early defense of, 36. *See also*
agrarian reform; agricultural markets;
communales; ejidatarios; ejidos; land